W9-CCB-526

PLAYA DEL CARMEN, TULUM & THE RIVIERA MAYA

Courtesy of Riviera Maya Tourism Authority

SECOND EDITION

Playa del Carmen, Tulum & the Riviera Maya

Great Destinations Mexico

Joshua Eden Hinsdale

The Countryman Press
Woodstock, Vermont

This book is dedicated to my ever-supportive parents and my beautiful wife, Andrea.

Copyright © 2006, 2009 by Joshua Eden Hinsdale

Second Edition

All rights reserved. No part of this book may be reproduced in any way by any electronic or mechanical means, including information storage and retrieval systems, without permission in writing from the publisher, except by a reviewer, who may quote brief passages.

ISBN 978-1-58157-094-6

Cover photo © Gary Walten/locogringo.com
Interior photos by the author unless otherwise specified
Book design by Bodenweber Design
Page composition by Susan McClellan
Maps by Mapping Specialists Ltd., Madison, WI © The Countryman Press

Published by The Countryman Press, P.O. Box 748, Woodstock, Vermont 05091

Distributed by W. W. Norton & Company, Inc., 500 Fifth Avenue, New York, NY 10110

Manufactured in the United States of America

10 9 8 7 6 5 4 3 2

GREAT DESTINATIONS TRAVEL GUIDEBOOK SERIES

Recommended by *National Geographic Traveler* and *Travel + Leisure* magazines

[A] crisp and critical approach, for travelers who want to live like locals.
—*USA Today*

Great Destinations™ guidebooks are known for their comprehensive, critical coverage of regions of extraordinary cultural interest and natural beauty. The authors in this series are professional travel writers who have lived for many years in the regions they describe. Each title in this series is continuously updated with each printing to ensure accurate and timely information. All the books contain more than one hundred photographs and maps.

Current titles available:

THE ADIRONDACK BOOK

ATLANTA

AUSTIN, SAN ANTONIO
& THE TEXAS HILL COUNTRY

THE BERKSHIRE BOOK

BERMUDA

BIG SUR, MONTEREY BAY & GOLD COAST WINE
COUNTRY

CAPE CANAVERAL, COCOA BEACH
& FLORIDA'S SPACE COAST

THE CHARLESTON, SAVANNAH
& COASTAL ISLANDS BOOK

THE CHESAPEAKE BAY BOOK

THE COAST OF MAINE BOOK

COLORADO'S CLASSIC MOUNTAIN TOWNS

COSTA RICA: GREAT DESTINATIONS CENTRAL
AMERICA

THE FINGER LAKES BOOK

THE FOUR CORNERS REGION

GALVESTON, SOUTH PADRE ISLAND
& THE TEXAS GULF COAST

THE HAMPTONS BOOK

HAWAII'S BIG ISLAND

HONOLULU & OAHU: GREAT DESTINATIONS
HAWAII

THE JERSEY SHORE: ATLANTIC CITY TO CAPE MAY

KAUAI: GREAT DESTINATIONS HAWAII

LAKE TAHOE & RENO

LOS CABOS & BAJA CALIFORNIA SUR:
GREAT DESTINATIONS MEXICO

MAUI: GREAT DESTINATIONS HAWAII

MICHIGAN'S UPPER PENINSULA

MONTREAL & QUEBEC CITY:
GREAT DESTINATIONS CANADA

THE NANTUCKET BOOK

THE NAPA & SONOMA BOOK

NORTH CAROLINA'S OUTER BANKS
& THE CRYSTAL COAST

PALM BEACH, FORT LAUDERDALE, MIAMI & THE
FLORIDA KEYS

PALM SPRINGS & DESERT RESORTS

PHOENIX, SCOTTSDALE, SEDONA
& CENTRAL ARIZONA

PLAYA DEL CARMEN, TULUM & THE RIVIERA MAYA:
GREAT DESTINATIONS MEXICO

SALT LAKE CITY, PARK CITY, PROVO
& UTAH'S HIGH COUNTRY RESORTS

SAN DIEGO & TIJUANA

SAN JUAN, VIEQUES & CULEBRA:
GREAT DESTINATIONS PUERTO RICO

SAN MIGUEL DE ALLENDE & GUANAJUATO:
GREAT DESTINATIONS MEXICO

THE SANTA FE & TAOS BOOK

THE SARASOTA, SANIBEL ISLAND & NAPLES BOOK

THE SEATTLE & VANCOUVER BOOK

THE SHENANDOAH VALLEY BOOK

TOURING EAST COAST WINE COUNTRY

WASHINGTON, D.C., AND NORTHERN VIRGINIA

YELLOWSTONE & GRAND TETON NATIONAL PARKS AND
JACKSON HOLE

YOSEMITE & THE SOUTHERN SIERRA NEVADA

If you are traveling to, moving to, residing in, or just interested in any (or all!) of these enchanting regions, a Great Destinations guidebook is a superior companion. Honest and painstakingly critical, full of information only a local can provide, Great Destinations guidebooks give you all the practical knowledge you need to enjoy the best of each region. Why not own them all?

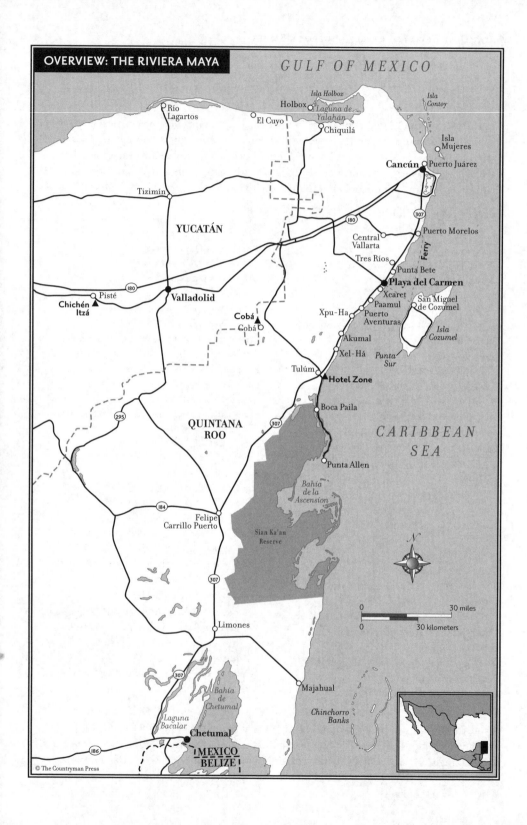

OVERVIEW: THE RIVIERA MAYA

GULF OF MEXICO

Isla Holbox
Holbox
Laguna de Yalahán
Isla Contoy

Río Lagartos
El Cuyo
Chiquilá
Isla Mujeres

Cancún
Puerto Juárez

Tizimín

YUCATÁN

Puerto Morelos

180

307

Ferry

Central Vallarta
Tres Ríos
Punta Bete
Playa del Carmen

180
Pisté
Valladolid
Xcaret
Paamul
San Miguel de Cozumel

Chichén Itzá
Cobá
Cobá
Xpu-Ha
Puerto Aventuras
Isla Cozumel

Akumal
Xel-Há
Punta Sur

Tulúm
Hotel Zone

QUINTANA ROO

307
Boca Paila

CARIBBEAN SEA

Punta Allen

Bahía de la Ascensión

295

Sian Ka'an Reserve

184
Felipe Carrillo Puerto

307

Limones

N

0   30 miles
0   30 kilometers

307
Bahía de Chetumal

Majahual

Chinchorro Banks

Laguna Bacalar
Chetumal

186
MEXICO
BELIZE

© The Countryman Press

Contents

Acknowledgments

I am forever grateful for my friends, family, and total strangers who have directly or indirectly led to or assisted with this project:

My mother, a self-proclaimed Italian urban gypsy, introduced me to Jonathan Livingston Seagull, Willie Nelson, the beach, and a sense of wonder and delight with life. She encouraged me to explore the world, took motorcycle riding lessons with me when I was 15, cried when I left for college, and always made coming home a warm and wonderful experience.

My father taught me to water-ski, play baseball, and understand the stock market. He took me fishing, learned scuba so we could dive together, validated my wanderlust, and always led by example. He taught me that you can have an exciting life and still be responsible.

I met Andrea in Austin, Texas, and took her to Playa del Carmen hoping she'd fall in love with me (lucky for me, it worked). She travels with me when she can and understands that I still need to go when she can't. I carry her in my heart wherever I am. And when I return, she reminds me why there's no place like home. She is the most patient, most supportive, and most beautiful person I could ever know.

Thanks also to my first dive buddies, Eric "Rico" Andrews, Keri Kennerly, Chris Glisan, Ellen Lock, and Amanda Miller; my firefighting friend and dive instructor, Davis Graham; my ninth-grade Spanish teacher, Mrs. Milby; the Villalobos family, my hosts in Costa Rica; my Cancún companion, Michelle Craft; my ranch rebel, Shana McGuyer; my colleague and friend, George Hunter; Lorena B. Mendoza; my accidental Spanish tutor, Sandy Welch; fellow dreamer, Chip Rankin; my personal supporters, Robyn Eden, Leslie Williams, Jeremy Reed, Sean Mitchell, Shawn Moran, Joy Taylor, Sam Shelby; my good-times friends, Marshall York, Mike Leon, Sean Rasberry, and Derek Palisoul; Barry Diller; Jimmy Buffett; Willie Nelson; and everyone I've ever been to Mexico with or met while there.

I am thankful for the kindness, support, and assistance of the hundreds of hoteliers, restaurant owners, tour operators, bartenders, and others who I visited during my research. Thanks to the hotel associations, tourism boards, and other official organizations that offered information and support. Thanks also to my faceless friends on online message boards and e-mail discussion groups who shared their thoughts and feelings about the destination. And thanks to the people of the Riviera Maya, who smiled at me as I walked the beaches and streets of their hometowns.

Finally, thanks to Dr. John E. Anderson, University of Manitoba, for his contributions to chapter 5, Mayan Ruins.

FOREWORD

When I was asked to write a foreword to this guidebook, I thought about how I could spend 10 years traveling through Mexico, with each day bringing a sense of discovery, new faces, and plenty of surprises. I have been visiting Mexico for more than 30 years and love it so much that I make my home in Los Cabos, where I run the Cabo Wabo Cantina, hang out, drink tequila, and jam with friends. Whether I'm down there or across the country in Playa del Carmen and the Riviera Maya, it's always great to be in Mexico.

Many people have discovered the charms of Mexico during the past 30 years, but I find that some things never change. I can still get the thrill of being the only gringo in a backstreet cantina and find adventure and exploration around every corner. Often, a sunrise means my day is ending, not beginning. For me, Mexico is a magical and mystical place. There is a timelessness and sense of a deep-rooted folklore that is personified in the people.

Most of all, I love the white sand beaches, the music, the food, the fiestas, and enjoying time with family and friends. It's a place where the warmth of the sun is equaled by the warmth of the people. My family and I try new food, meet new people, and generally kick back on the world's greatest beaches. Mexico inspires me. It might mean a new song, a new idea, or a renewed outlook on life. Whatever it does to you, Mexico will remind you to enjoy life.

See you on the beach!

Sammy Hagar

There are still miles of deserted beaches in the Riviera Maya.

INTRODUCTION

My parents first traveled to the Riviera Maya in 1980, when it was known only as the not-so-catchy "area south of Cancún." They went to Xcaret when it cost 25 cents and the road was yet to be paved. They went to Xel-Ha and Garrafon, in Isla Mujeres, and marveled at the tropical fish and the deserted beaches. They ate lobster on the beach in Cancún and snorkeled the virgin reefs of Cozumel. When they came home, they showed me their pictures and talked of their adventures, and I knew I'd go there one day.

My first experience with the Caribbean was in Belize, when I was 16. I went diving at Turneffe Island and was blown away by the color of the water, the number of fish, and the relaxing island lifestyle. A year later, I went on a dive trip to Cozumel with a group of friends from school. I loved the food, the freedom, and the excitement. We took the ferry to the then-tiny town of Playa del Carmen and could hardly find a place that was open to eat lunch.

For each of the next 10 years, I went to Mexico every chance I could, eventually leading group trips, selling travel packages, and making friends around the country. In college, I spent a year at the University of Costa Rica, studying Spanish and traveling around. After graduating from the University of Texas, I went to work for a Mexico-based tourism developer and worked on the early stages of the creation of Playacar.

I moved to Cozumel, worked in a hotel, and traveled the region extensively. I later moved to Cancún, worked for the *Cancún News* (the English daily newspaper, now closed), and made frequent trips to Playa del Carmen. In 1993 I visited the construction site of one of the first all-inclusive hotels, in Xpu-Ha, for a photo shoot, but I could never have imagined the development that would follow up and down the coast.

Over the years, I have stayed active in the Riviera Maya community, splitting my frequent trips between Cancún, Cozumel, and Playa. As many others have, I've watched the area boom and grow, amazed with each trip at the new hotels, restaurants, and other attractions.

The region continues to draw me, almost magically, to its sandy beaches, taco bars, secret fishing holes, and buzzing nightspots. It is in my soul and has become a large part of who I am. I love being there, I love talking about it—and I love sharing it with other travelers.

Courtesy of Mike Stone

HISTORY OF THE PLAYA DEL CARMEN REGION

"In the beginning all was invisible. The sky was motionless. There was only water, the quiet ocean, the silence, the nights. Then there came the word."
—FROM THE POPOL VUH, SACRED MAYAN SCRIPTURES

Playa del Carmen owes its growing popularity to the nearby resort town of Cancún, just 40 miles to the north, and Cozumel Island, just 12 miles to the east. The influence of these two towns has helped shape Playa since the days of the Mayans.

Playa del Carmen is named for Our Lady of Mount Carmel, who is the patron saint of Cancún. She was named for a town in Italy, which was the first place where a chapel was built in her honor, in 1263, before her ascension into heaven.

The first recorded visitors to the beaches of what is now Playa del Carmen came during the Early Classic Period (A.D. 300–600) of the Mayan civilization. Then called *Xaman-Ha*, or "waters of the north," Playa was a rest stop of sorts for travelers making their way from the great cities of the Mayan world to the island of Cozumel. These travelers readied their dugout canoes and prepared for the journey across the straits on the same shores that now house the restaurants, hotels, and nightspots of modern-day Playa del Carmen.

Cozumel, called *Ah Cuzamil Petén*, meaning "island of the swallows," by the Mayans, was a sacred site and home to Ix-Chel, the goddess of fertility and wife of Itzámna, the god of the sun. Young women across the Mayan empire, from present-day Yucatán, Honduras, Belize, and beyond, journeyed to Cozumel on a sacred pilgrimage to pay homage to Ix-Chel and pray for fertility and healthy childbirth.

In return for the dozens of shrines and temples that the Mayans constructed, Ix-Chel is said to have gifted the people with the graceful swallow, or *cuzamil*, which led the Mayans to give the island its name. Many of the temples for Ix-Chel have survived, including San Gervasio, which can still be visited today.

Meanwhile, on a sheltered sandbar known to the Mayans as *Kankun*, or "nest of snakes," the temples of El Rey were constructed as a ceremonial site and resting place for the society's nobles. The site is adjacent to a golf course and across the highway from what is now the Hilton Hotel, making it a popular destination for visitors to Cancún who want to experience the Mayan ruins but are not able to get to the more major sites in the region, such as Tulum, Cobá, or Chichén Itzá.

Cancún did not have many other sacred sites because it was so narrow and did not have

Growth

If you think the explosive growth of the Riviera Maya comes as a surprise to the Mexican government, think again. The growth plan was forecast in the mid-1970s by then-governor of Quintana Roo, Rojo Gomez. The following message was sent to President Luis Echeverria:

"We have prepared an integral plan for the development of the coasts of Quintana Roo, whose beauty is unparalleled and which has many attractive sites. It has beautiful beaches, clear ocean water, wild jungles and hidden Mayan ruins, which have yet to be explored because of the lack of access. We have located 100 km of coastline whose features promise a great future for tourism in the area."

good access to the mainland, though the ocean breezes and proximity to various shallow lagoons did make it a nice place to live for the natives who fished along its shores and harvested food from the mangroves.

During the post-Classic period (A.D. 1000–1500), the area around Playa del Carmen, Cancún, and Cozumel served as a major trade route and religious center, and the Mayan culture flourished and prospered. At its height, the walled city of Tulum contained splendors beyond belief, and the nearby town of Cobá was a spiritual center of the entire Mayan empire, with a population of nearly 50,000. Near the end of this period, the populations dwindled as the natives dispersed due to storms and wars and to seek gentler climates.

Juan de Grijalva, a Spanish explorer, passed close to Playa del Carmen in 1518 and then discovered Cozumel while en route to Cuba, several hundred miles to the east. He didn't stay for long, but word of his find traveled fast, and his countryman Hernan Cortez returned the following year, bringing Catholicism and not much of an appreciation for the Mayan way of life. Cortez and his men demolished Mayan temples and built a Catholic church, and he also brought something else with him when he landed on Cozumel—smallpox. The disease spread quickly within the island's close-knit community, and the population was decimated, dropping from 40,000 to less than 200 within 50 years.

The first European settlement in the region was at Xel-Ha, just a few miles south of Playa del Carmen, which had been a Mayan outpost and is now an ecotourism theme park. Over the next 200 years, the Spanish traveled throughout the Playa del Carmen area and the Yucatán, spreading Catholicism and disease as they went. Many Mayans resisted the new religion, and small communities retained their traditional ways and their sacred cultures. During the 1700s and 1800s, pirates set up shop on the nearly deserted shores of Cozumel, using it as a base for their marauding forays across the channel to Playa del Carmen and elsewhere around the region.

Meanwhile, trade continued in and around Playa del Carmen, given its location midway between the port city of Veracruz to the north and Honduras to the south. Local commodities, including salt and honey, were bartered for goods imported from other regions, giving the area a taste of the diversity, commerce, and—yes—tourism that would eventually secure its place in the Mexican economy.

John L. Stephens and Frederick Catherwood passed through the Riviera Maya in 1842 as part of their expedition to the Mayan ruins, which was documented in their excellent book, *Incidents of Travel in Yucatán*. In the book, Stephens writes about what they saw and the people they encountered, while Catherwood presents exacting drawings of the ruins. The book is incredibly precise and detailed, and it's still used by scholars, archaeologists, and Mayan enthusiasts today.

A single taxi awaits arrivals at the Cancún airport in 1970.

In 1848 the Mayans and various Spanish refugees began to resist the Spanish occupation more aggressively, leading to an uprising known as the War of the Castes. During the struggle, a large group of the oppressed set out from the Yucatán town of Valladolid and traveled across the peninsula, settling in Cozumel, which led to a regrowth of the island's population. Other natives took cover in the ruins of Tulum, which made a great fortress given its walled perimeter. The town of San Miguel de Cozumel was officially established in 1840, and several years later, U.S. President Abraham Lincoln pondered using the island as a place to send the freed American slaves and even went so far as talking to the Mexican government about purchasing it.

Due to the remote location and its dense, inhospitable jungle environment, Playa del Carmen and the surrounding area kept a low profile for the rest of the 1800s. In 1902 the region was finally granted status as a territory of the country of Mexico, and it was named after General Andreas Quintana Roo, of the Mexican army. That same year, on November 17, the town of Villa del Carmen was officially founded near the site of what is now Playa del Carmen's Leona Vicario Park. Charles Lindbergh stopped in Cozumel in 1928 in the storied *Spirit of St. Louis* plane. The island was used as a base by the U.S. Navy during World War II, and was then abandoned again until the 1960s, when scuba adventurer and documentary film producer Jacques Cousteau visited the island with an underwater camera crew and began to show the world the beauties of the Great Mayan Reef. Second in size only to Australia's Great Barrier Reef, it runs between Cozumel and Playa del Carmen and stretches for hundreds of miles down the coast.

Tourism visionary Fernando Barbachano purchased much of the land that currently makes up Playacar in 1966 and two years later, the actual term *Playacar* was coined.

Playa was a tiny outpost in the 1970s. The church in the background is still there, at the northwest corner of the town square.

Barbachano's purchase included nearly a mile of barren beachfront, stretching south from where the ferry dock now sits. The price tag was a now-paltry $13,600, but it was a serious risk at the time. He subdivided the land and sold it in small parcels, the first of which sold in 1977 for $15,550, proving just how masterful his idea really was. The single most important factor in the development of the region came in 1967, when the Bank of Mexico and the country's tourism development commission identified Cancún as the location for one of its mega-development projects (along with Ixtapa, Los Cabos, Loreto, and Huatulco). In the original government documents, the area was called "Kan Kun," which quickly morphed into the more Spanish "Can Cun," and then eventually shortened to just "Cancún."

Bridges were built, sewer lines were laid, and electrical poles sprang up. The first Cancún hotels, opened in the early 1970s, were the Palacio Maya, Playa Blanca, Cancún Caribe, Camino Real, and Club Med. In 1970 a wooden boat dock was built on the central beach in Playa del Carmen, and shortly thereafter, ferry service started to Cozumel. In 1974 Quintana Roo was granted Mexican statehood and the Cancún International Airport opened for business, with a bamboo and palm air-traffic control tower and a single taxi waiting for arriving planes. Two years later, the city's Pok-Ta-Pok golf course opened with 18 holes, many with views of the ocean and minor Mayan ruins. Over the next 10 years, Cancún grew from a coconut jungle visited only by traveling fishermen and a few loco gringos to a world-class tourist destination. The local population boomed as workers from across the country poured into Ciudad Cancún to find jobs and establish their families. The Playa del Carmen airstrip was laid in 1979 and the area's first hotel, the Balam Ha (where the Playacar Palace is now), opened the next year, and land along Fifth Avenue was given away to employees of the Calica mining company.

The Riviera Maya *name was coined in the early 1990s.*

Cozumel experienced a growth spurt of its own as recreational scuba diving became more popular and affordable and more and more divers came to witness for themselves what they had been able to see only on the Jacques Cousteau television show.

Despite a few bumps along the way, including lack of airline support, the devaluation of the peso, and a series of hurricanes, Cancún and Cozumel continued to grow and prosper. Somehow, though, Playa del Carmen lagged behind, as the city to its north and the island to its east developed more quickly. As the growth went on around it, Playa del Carmen was still known only as the ferry landing for boats traveling back and forth between Cozumel and the Quintana Roo mainland. A handful of fishermen lived in huts on the beach and a few optimistic entrepreneurs sold tacos and handicrafts to the hurrying travelers, but tourists and locals moved quickly through town on their way to the more established locales.

In its hippie heyday, Playa del Carmen's visitors would while away the day along the beaches south of town. The small cove now occupied by the Gran Purto Real Resort Playa del Carmen hotel was close enough to the town square to be convenient but just out of sight of the ferry dock, making it the preferred place for those who liked to sunbathe au naturel. At night, tourists returned to the beach for the freewheeling and ultracasual nightlife under the stars, a refreshingly unpretentious antidote to the pulsating discotheques that were becoming so popular in nearby Cancún. During a full moon, locals and tourists alike congregated on the beach for a ceremonial "lunata" celebration, complete with bonfires, cold Coronas, and skinny-dipping—a tradition that must have made the Mayan gods smile (especially Ix-Chel, the goddess of fertility!).

But starting in the early 1980s, little by little, street by street, the tiny fishing village

Where Did My Bathing Suit Go?

If you continually misplace something on your trip, don't blame your traveling companion—it may be an alux (pronounced "aloosh") playing pranks.

Aluxes are, according to Mayan superstition, mischievous elfin or childlike creatures who live in the tropical jungle and play tricks on people who do not believe in them or give them the respect they deserve. Some stories claim that the aluxes were originally clay or stone carvings that were placed in the Mayan religious temples and then later came to life.

Many Mayans and other locals claim to have had run-ins with aluxes. They can cause the phone to ring at odd hours of the night, and when it's answered, no one is on the other end. They can move objects around the room and sometimes even steal bits of food. To curry the favor of the aluxes, many people build them little houses or shrines on their property. Once appeased, the aluxes become good luck charms, helping to ensure a good harvest, bring about good fortune, and protect the believers from other dangers.

Many hotels in the Riviera Maya, even some large and well-established ones, have homes for the aluxes on-site, in hopes that appeasing them with a comfy dwelling will encourage them to be friendly, though they rarely talk about it. Ask your waiters and housekeepers, though, and chances are they'll know what you're talking about—and will probably have a story of their own to share.

and ferry town began to grow. New shops, restaurants, and even a couple of hotels opened their doors, luring the passing visitors to stay a while. The first hotels were built of bamboo and palm fronds, with slatted wood doors—not to keep out thieves, but to prevent the wild pigs from entering and looking for food.

Disaster struck in September 1988 when Hurricane Gilbert slammed into Cozumel and the Riviera Maya with 170 mph winds, blowing the roofs off hotels, pulling trees out by their roots, smashing windows, and flooding the streets. Inside the storm, the barometric pressure was 26.23 inches, the lowest sea-level pressure ever recorded in the Western Hemisphere. The hurricane caused more than $80 million in damage in Cozumel alone, and it changed the face of the region for years.

In the early 1990s, Playa del Carmen became a regular stop for the cruise lines, exposing Playa to a new breed of revelers. Soon after, the outdated Cozumel ferryboats were replaced with sleek and modern jet-powered watercraft, which made the trip from the island faster and easier on the stomach and brought in even more visitors.

Guadalajara-based tourism giant Grupo Sidek purchased thousands of acres of land along the shoreline just south of the ferry landing, with designs to develop the area that had been dubbed "Playacar." First came the Continental Plaza (in 1992, now the Playacar Palace). Later that year, the Diamond Resort (now the Occidental Allegro) was inaugurated, marking the first opening of an all-inclusive resort in the Riviera Maya. A golf course opened in September 1994, and then hotel after hotel rose from the jungle, changing the face of the community forever.

On the other side of the ferry dock, development continued as well, but government-imposed density restrictions kept away large-scale hotel projects, and small, family-run inns dominated the landscape. From 1990 to 1997, the local population grew from 2,000 to 20,000, and 100 new families were moving to town each month, establishing Playa del Carmen as Mexico's fastest-growing city, a title it now shares with the booming town of Tulum, just down the coast.

The main road paralleling the beach, Quinta Avenida, or Fifth Avenue, became the town's principal street and was lined with restaurants, shops, hotels, and other businesses catering to the tourist trade. Favored by European backpackers and U.S. and Canadian budget travelers, Playa del Carmen began to make a name for itself on the international travel scene. Known as the place where the hippie lifestyle was not only accepted but celebrated, "Playa," as the in crowd called it, had arrived.

By the late 1990s, Quinta had extended more than a mile north of the ferry dock, and much of it was closed to vehicular traffic, creating a pedestrian-friendly walkway that developed a unique character unknown in other parts of the world. In the early 2000s, Quinta stretched past Constituyentes Boulevard (between 18th and 20th Streets), and the area was dubbed "La Nueva Quinta," sometimes called "Little Italy," "Upper Playa," or simply "The New Playa." Italian-style cafés stood next to taco stands that stood next to gourmet steakhouses, creating a town with a truly eclectic and international flair. The beach north of Constituyentes also saw some changes. A second ferry dock was built, a few

Local Lingo

Cenote: A rare geological feature of the Yucatán, a cenote is a freshwater sinkhole formed when the limestone ground caves in and fills with water from underground rivers.

Colectivo: A sort of taxi-bus combination, a colectivo is a van or similar vehicle used for local transportation. It has semi-fixed routes and is cheaper than a taxi.

Costa Maya: The coastline south of the Riviera Maya (which officially ends at Tulum).

Federal: Used when referring to Highway 307, a federal highway.

Ha: Mayan for "water." You'll see it used everywhere.

Mole: A chocolate-based sauce made with dozens of herbs and spices, used in traditional Mexican cooking.

Muelle: Spanish for "dock," it's commonly used when referring to the ferry landing, which is also called the "embarcadero."

Nopales: Sliced cactus from the nopal plant, it's used locally in breakfast juice and can be served grilled or sautéed with any meal of the day.

Palapa: Thatched palm used to make roofing in the Riviera Maya. The tight weave keeps out rain and has to be replaced every couple of years. The word is also used generically to refer to any structure that has a thatched-palm roof.

Pan dulce: Literally, "sweet bread," it's used to describe a variety of delicious locally made breakfast pastries. For a quick start to your day, order a café con pan dulce.

Parada: Spanish for "bus stop."

Playa: Meaning "beach" in Spanish, this is the short name used locally when referring to Playa del Carmen.

Playacar: A name created in 1992 to refer to the tourist development located just south of 1st Street and the ferry dock.

Propina: Spanish for "tip." Make sure you check your bill to see if a tip has already been added: propina incluida.

Quinta: Spanish for "fifth," it's the name used for Fifth Avenue, the main tourist strip in Playa del Carmen.

Riviera Maya: The name used to refer to the area from just south of Cancún to Tulum. The actual boundaries tend to change a little bit, depending on whom you talk to. The phrase was coined in the early 1990s. The English version, "Mayan Riviera," is sometimes used, also.

Tacos al pastor: Pork tacos cooked on a vertical spit, seared with licking flames and served with pineapple slices.

Tiempo compartido: Spanish for "time share." If a deal is too good to be true, like a Jeep rental for $20 a day, chances are it's part of a tiempo compartido offer.

Hurricane Emily: An Unwelcome Guest

At 5 PM on July 17, 2005, management at the Moon Palace announced an immediate termination of alcohol sales and room service and instructed guests to stay indoors until further notice. Earlier in the day, the staff had lashed down all the outdoor furniture and plucked all the coconuts from their trees. The guests, many from the northern United States, Canada, and Europe, were complete strangers to tropical weather and immediately lost any romantic notions of hurricane parties or the amusing thrill of riding out a storm. It was an ominous sign of what was to come, as the largest Atlantic hurricane ever recorded in the month of July was bearing down on the Riviera Maya.

Just after midnight, Hurricane Emily, a category 4 storm, ripped across the southern tip of Cozumel Island, enveloping the Punta Sur lighthouse in the eerie calm of the eye. The hammocks at the Reggae Shack swung wildly until the wooden poles supporting them collapsed in a heap, followed by the palapa roof of the bar. Up the east side of the island, angry waves licked at the walls of Mezcalito's restaurant as wind-driven rain lashed into the kitchen. A 160 mph gust of wind tore at the roof, pulling it apart bit by bit and spitting it into the ocean. Hundreds of trees along Rafael Melgar Boulevard, the main road along the western beachfront, fell, almost in unison, as the storm continued east. At 1 AM the clock tower in the town square clanged a single time, but the howling wind and distant sirens made it impossible for anyone to hear it.

As the eye moved across the Cozumel channel, the normally ubiquitous ferryboats were nowhere to be seen. The angry storm stirred up massive waves as it traced a path for Puerto Aventuras, hungry for the luxury yachts docked at the marina. Waves crashed over the bulkhead, flooding into shops, restaurants, and hotels. The roof of the Copacabana (now Catalonia Royal Tulum) hotel came crashing down, exposing the lobby to the full force of the storm. Luckily, all the guests were huddled in the relative safety of the hotel's ballroom. A huge metal navigational buoy broke free from its anchor and barreled toward shore, beaching itself in front of the Riu Palace in Playacar. Concrete and wooden utility poles across the region snapped like twigs while billboards along Highway 307 advertising XX Beer and Xcaret Park were crumpled like paper in a fist.

Thousands of people hunkered down in shelters from Cancún to Tulum. Several hundred sought refuge in the convention center at the Mayan Palace, thousands more crowded into the Playa del Carmen municipal gym, and some 600 others waited and prayed from inside the concrete walls of a bordello on the outskirts of town. Locals and visitors in Cancún rode out the storm together in the tiny rooms of an elementary school. When one room flooded, the group had to brave the elements and run to another. Shortly thereafter, the door to that room was torn from its hinges.

The eye passed right by Paamul, rumbling the mobile homes and testing their window seals with driving rain. Palm trees were gouged from the ground, and rain-soaked sand whipped into the trailers, sounding like thousands of BBs being shot into beer cans.

As the night wore on, bloggers tapped away on computer keyboards in sheltered Internet cafés, updating Internet users around the world of the storm's progress. Their missives grew less frequent as

corporate-owned hotels were constructed, and a couple of beach clubs sprang up, offering food and drink service, *palapa* and chair rentals, and towel service for the cruise passengers, day-trippers, and guests from hotels that aren't on the beach.

As the upscale all-inclusive hotels of Playacar introduced the town to more affluent travelers, the tone of the village continued to change. The thatched-roof bus station was rebuilt with electric displays and molded plastic seats. Across the street, McDonald's opened up, then a couple of Starbuck's, and up and down the coast, more and more resorts

power lines fell and connection became impossible. A key Tel-Mex cell phone tower swayed in the wind, then bent and fell, cutting off yet another mode of communication.

It was still drizzling when dawn broke, but the heavy winds were gone and the furious sea had calmed. Locals and visitors alike crept from their shelters and spilled into the streets to survey the damage. Along Quinta Avenida in Playa, many shops suffered from broken glass and ruined merchandise. Water was nearly waist deep along Constituyentes. Many homes in the humble residential area north of the tourist zone had collapsed and laid in ruin, and distraught locals sat on the beach and on the street, numb from shock and unsure of where to go. Swimming pools were filled with sand and debris, street signs littered the streets, the beaches were full of trash, palapas were torn down, and uprooted or stripped trees outnumbered healthy ones.

The National Guard arrived early to begin clearing the streets and cleaning up the heavily touristed areas, including Quinta. There were widespread power outages, but some stores were open, selling food, water, and other supplies. Hotel guests and staff worked side by side to clear broken glass, sweep out flood waters, and repair damages.

It quickly became apparent that things were not nearly as bad as they could have been. Though powerful, the storm was compact and fast moving, so it did not cause as much damage as it could have. Cozumel, Puerto Aventuras, and Akumal were the hardest hit, with thousands of trees downed and many roofs torn off and buildings flooded. The beach in Playa Paraíso was badly eroded, but in Tankah, just down the coast, there seemed to be more sand than before. Two gas stations lost their roofs and were in shambles, but no fires had broken out. Local farms suffered greatly, with the summer's corn, papaya, and citrus crops enduring major losses.

It was clear that the Riviera Maya had learned the hard lessons since being caught severely underprepared for Hurricane Gilbert in 1988. The large-scale evacuation effort had worked. A convoy of 500 buses had moved 60,000 tourists to safety in less than 12 hours. Some hotels in the Riviera Maya sent guests to sister properties in Cancún, while others were sent to shelters in Vallodolid, Mérida, and elsewhere. Hundreds of petrochemical workers were evacuated from rigs and oil platforms in the storm's path.

The storm claimed the lives of four people in Jamaica, and two men working on oil rig evacuations were killed when their helicopter crashed in the Gulf of Mexico. A German dive instructor living in Playacar also died when he was electrocuted as he prepared his home for the storm. Miraculously, no other major injuries or deaths were reported.

The airports in Cancún and Cozumel opened the day after the storm, and hotels and restaurants opened as quickly as they could. Some were back in business in days, while others took weeks or even months before they were ready again. The people of the Riviera Maya kept their faith, helping each other make it through the hard times. New palm trees were planted, palapas were constructed, signs replaced, homes built, and lives repaired. No doubt Hurricane Emily was strong, but she was no match for the determination, the will, and the community spirit of the Riviera Maya.

were carved from the jungle. Renovations began on Quinta as work crews buried the utility lines and paved the gravel road with cobblestones, giving the road a bit of colonial inspiration to go along with its nouveau chic attitude.

Hurricanes Emily and Wilma, both devastating storms with deceivingly demure names, tested the region's will in the summer and fall of 2006 when they sliced similar paths across Cozumel, Cancún, and the Riviera Maya. Emily raged with sustained winds of 135 mph, shearing off rooftops, leveling trees and signs, shattering windows, rearranging

A damaged rooftop, courtesy of Hurricane Emily

beaches, and sending 60,000 tourists scrambling for shelter. Wilma completed the one-two punch by hammering the area three months later with 150 mph winds and a storm surge topping 11 feet in Cancún. Tourists were confined to shelters for days, and it took some nearly two weeks after the storm to finally get a flight back home. Hotels in Cancún were hit the hardest, though all along the Riviera Maya there was extensive flooding and wind damage. Some hotels closed for days, while others took weeks or even months to reopen.

The region bounced back, though, as the communities worked together to rebuild and restore the splendor of the area. In fact, the town's resilience through adversity seemed to prove its staying power, as the condo boom kicked into high gear in early 2007. One of Playa's original hotels, the Corto Maltes, turned to condos. The El Faro Hotel, site of the landmark lighthouse, did the same. Up and down each block, workers could be seen converting hotels to condos and building new structures where there were none. The area north of Constituyentes saw an especially strong push, with new developments going up on nearly every block. Most complexes were small, with no more than 12 or 14 units, but others were much larger, threatening to change the face of the town. Rumors of W Hotels

The End of the World—Or Just the Beginning?
The Mayan calendar ends at 11:11 AM on December 21, 2012 (the winter solstice), which coincides with an extremely close alignment of the path of the sun and the galactic equator (the Milky Way's midpoint). The Mayans did not necessarily foretell the "end of the world," but they did say that on this date, the world as we know it will be complete, and a new "Golden Age" will begin. Mayan scripture reveals that the ancient peoples predicted that our society will have great advances in technology, that time and money will become meaningless, and that human beings will be upgraded from the center of the galaxy. The event is even cryptically captured in images carved into the walls of Mayan sacred temples.

Modern astronomy and archaeology researchers have recognized the amazing accuracy of the Mayan calendar and its ability to calculate and forecast the movement of the stars, and they have confirmed that the alignment will indeed happen as predicted. Whether it will have any great impact on life on Earth is yet to be revealed.

Next time you're in Playa, at least you'll have a good excuse to celebrate life, so wake up early to get the best beach chairs, order the surf and turf at dinner, and savor an extra top-shelf margarita.

building a large hotel and condo complex still linger and maybe by the time you're reading this, it will be a reality. Donald Trump's development company also announced in 2008 that it was considering investing up to $530 million to develop areas near Tulum, tentatively called the Trump Ocean Resort.

By the middle of 2008, the Riviera Maya was celebrating its status as one of the top international tourist destinations in the world, with nearly 35,000 available hotel rooms and 6 million visitors a year—70 percent of whom are European. Expatriates from 46 countries around the globe call Playa del Carmen home, and the town seems to thrive on the notoriety. And through it all, Playa has stayed true to its roots, somehow preserving its almost magical charm and exceptional character. It is still a place where travelers from around the world come together to lounge on the beach, toast the day with a cold beer, sip a hot cappuccino, and celebrate life. And in a town where backpackers from crowded hostels, newlyweds from fancy all-inclusives, and European trendsetters from chic new condos all cozy up to the same bars, it's easy to understand why Playa so easily works its way into your heart.

The ruins of Xaman-Ha can still be seen in modern-day Playa del Carmen. The main temple is along the beach just south of the Playacar Palace hotel and is now a popular spot for wedding ceremonies. Many other shrines dot the Playacar development, including the golf course. And though it may be hard to envision a time when the Mayans carved their dugout canoes from local trees and plied the waters to Cozumel, today's visitors to Playa will undoubtedly feel a sense of the grand history, the sacred importance, and the incredible natural beauty that have lured visitors to its sandy shores for thousands of years.

As one longtime local resident puts it, "No one knows what makes Playa so special, but everyone seems to return."

Courtesy of Philip Gammon

Practical Information

Travel should be easy, it should be carefree, and it should be comfortable. Unfortunately, that's not always the case. Getting around, having the proper paperwork, and making sense of unfamiliar rules and regulations can cause a fair amount of stress during any vacation, and travel to the Riviera Maya is no different.

An old adage that scuba divers use is "plan your dive and dive your plan." This concept should be applied to vacation travel as well. Taking some time before your trip to learn a bit about the region where you are traveling and to create a plan for how you're going to get around is essential to enjoying your vacation to the fullest. After all, wouldn't you rather use your vacation time relaxing on the beach rather than visiting the consulate, searching for maps, or asking everyone you see for help?

A Note about Geographical Terms & Addresses

This book focuses heavily on the town of Playa del Carmen, which is in the geographic center of the Riviera Maya (Mayan Riviera) and is home to the largest concentration of hotels, medical facilities, grocery stores, restaurants, and tourist services south of Cancún. The town's name translates to "Carmen's Beach," though it is always referred to by its Spanish name. The shortened version, favored by locals, is simply *Playa* (pronounced ply-a, with an accent on the first syllable). There is also substantial coverage of the surrounding villages and tourism developments of the Riviera Maya, including the towns of Cancún, Puerto Morelos, Akumal, Puerto Aventuras, and Tulum. Unless otherwise noted, "downtown" refers to the central business and tourism district of Playa del Carmen.

The main pedestrian street through Playa del Carmen is Fifth Avenue, which, in Spanish, is Quinta Avenida, or just *Quinta* (pronounced keen-ta, with an accent on the first syllable), as it's known locally. In this book, all references to this road will be made using the local term, to help travelers get accustomed to using it.

Addresses in Playa del Carmen do not follow the standard that many travelers are accustomed to. Many streets do not have lot numbers, and if they do, they are seldom used. The most common—and easiest way—to identify and find a specific location is to use the nearest intersection or list the nearest cross streets. A restaurant may list an address of 10th Avenue at 6th Street if it is on or very close to that intersection. If it is in the middle of the block, the address would look more like: 15th Avenue between 8th and 10th Streets. Though this system doesn't specify the precise location or on which side of the street a particular business can be found, the blocks are generally fairly short, and it's easy to find what you're looking for once you go to the location given. After all, it's part of the charm of Third World travel.

ARRIVAL BY AIR

Most international visitors get to Playa del Carmen and the Riviera Maya by flying into the Cancún International Airport (CUN), which is 45 miles north of Playa and 10 miles south of the resort city of Cancún.

The Cancún airport was inaugurated in 1974 but has had regular renovations, including the addition of a third terminal in 2007 and another runway in the works, leaving it in excellent condition. There are two commercial terminals, each with several gates, plus a dedicated terminal for charters and cargo. Planes either pull up to the Jetway or stop short and allow passengers to exit down the stairs and onto the tarmac, which provides a delicious first taste of the warm tropical air.

There is a food court in Terminal 3, where most international flights depart, with a Margaritaville Café and Berryhill Tamale House, plus several local eateries and fast-food counters. Terminal 2 handles mostly domestic flights and does not have quite the same level of services, though both terminals have multiple souvenir shops, money exchange counters, ATM machines, public phones, and duty-free centers with jewelry, liquor, tobacco, chocolates, and other goodies.

All Americans must have a valid passport to enter Mexico. Prior to arrival on an international flight, visitors will be required to fill out a tourist card (good for up to 90 days) and customs form. These are usually handed out on the plane, though they are available at the airport as well. After landing you will be funneled through the main airport departure lounge (don't wander off) and then downstairs to the immigration room. Depending on how many flights are arriving, the wait can be a couple of minutes to nearly an hour. Have your proof of citizenship and your forms ready, and then remember to save your copy of the tourist card, which the agent will return to you with your proof of citizenship, as you

Going home with new sombreros

Restrictions on Importing Items Into Mexico
- Gifts of no more than $300 in value
- One video camera and one regular camera per person, plus 12 rolls of film
- Two bottles of liquor or wine
- 400 cigarettes or 50 cigars
- Perfume and cologne limited to personal use only

will need it when you depart. If you lose it, it will cost you $40 to replace it, plus you could be in for a bit of an interrogation at the airport when you leave.

Once through immigration, you will enter the baggage claim area, which can get a bit crowded. Once you claim your bags, if you checked any, you will proceed to the back of the room to the customs checkpoint. Hand your customs form to the agent standing next to the vertical traffic light mounted on a pole about chest high. You will be asked to push the button. Green means "go," and red means your baggage will be opened and inspected.

The customs area leads to the main exit, where the atmosphere transitions from neat and orderly to frenzied and chaotic. Rental car counters and local transport agencies line the walls, and women in colorful dresses pass out coupon books and advertising flyers. There are some good coupons and free maps available, so it may be worth the trouble to take what's offered.

AIRPORT TRANSPORTATION

The Cancun Airport has three terminals. Terminal 1 is primarily used for private aircraft and won't likely be in your travel plans. Terminal 2 is used for many domestic flights and a few international flights. Most visitors will arrive and depart at Terminal 3, which opened in 2007. It is quite modern and efficient, with a Starbuck's and other familiar conveniences. If you're on a package trip or you have hotel transportation prearranged, you can look for your name on a placard or for the representatives holding signs with the names of the tour group. Though there is lots of scurrying to and fro, the reps all seem to know each other and are generally willing to help point you in the right direction.

If you don't have transportation prearranged, you will find several options for getting to your hotel or wherever else you may want to go. The primary options are taxi, shuttle bus, city bus, or car rental.

TAXIS

Taxi service from the airport is heavily regulated. Only specially licensed cabs are allowed to pick up passengers, and as a result, fares from the airport are higher than for the return trips to the airport. Taxi fares, which

Sample Taxi Fares from Playa del Carmen

Destinations to the north:

Cancún Airport	$40
Downtown Cancún	$42
Cancún Hotel Zone	$47
Crococun Zoo	$30
Maroma Beach	$20
Iberostar Resort	$20
Puerto Morelos	$30
Tres Rios	$15

Destinations to the south:

Playacar	$ 5
Calica	$10
Xcaret	$10
Puerto Aventuras	$15
Paamul	$16
Xpu-Ha	$18
Akumal	$25
Xel-Ha	$40
Dos Ojos Cenote	$40
Tulum	$45

you can pay in dollars or pesos, are paid in advance at one of the counters in the exit area. You will then take your receipt out to the curb, and you will be directed to the next available cab. The official fare at press time from the airport to the Cancún hotel zone is $40, and a trip to Playa del Carmen will run you $50 to $60. Fares are good for up to four passengers, so feel free to look for ride-share partners if there aren't enough people in your own group to fill the cab.

A taxi to the area between the airport and Puerto Morelos is $34, and a cab to the Puerto Aventuras area will run you $90. To Tulum and nearby hotels, the fare is $115. Any local taxi can be hired for a return trip to the airport. Fares from Playa del Carmen run around $40, with areas farther south costing more. Negotiating can sometimes get you a better rate. For larger groups, Suburbans and vans can be hired to transport five to eight passengers. The fare to Playa is $85, and a trip to Tulum would be $140.

Private Shuttle
(Accommodates up to 10 passengers)

Location	One-Way	Round-Trip
Cancún hotel zone	$35	$65
Downtown Cancún	$35	$65
Moon Palace	$35	$65
Puerto Juárez	$40	$75
Puerto Morelos	$50	$95
Playa del Secreto	$55	$105
Mayan Palace	$55	$105
Playa del Carmen	$60	$115
Puerto Aventuras	$65	$125
Xpu-Ha Beach	$70	$135
Akumal	$75	$145
Xel-Ha	$85	$165
Tulum	$100	$190

SHUTTLE BUSES

Shuttle buses, called *colectivos*, are available for $24 for each passenger to Playa del Carmen. You will ride with other travelers and stop at other hotels along the way, but it can be a good way to save a few pesos. If your group has kids, you can often bargain for a discount for the younger passengers. For the return trip, you can arrange for pickup through your hotel or at one of the various kiosks located on Quinta, in downtown Playa. It is best to do it the day before your departure, and remember to keep your receipt, as you will need it to board. A shuttle to Cancún is $9 per person; to Puerto Morelos is $16; and to Tulum is $50 per person.

CITY BUSES

There is public bus service between the Cancún airport and the main terminal in Playa del Carmen (Quinta and Juárez), which is a short walk or taxi ride to most Playa hotels. Tickets can be purchased just after you clear customs and immigration and before you leave the airport. Look for the booths advertising ADO, since that's the company that provides the service. Once you have your ticket, you'll be directed to the departure location. If you get lost, any local will point the way, but make sure you are getting on the right bus, and don't be talked into paying an additional fare for a different service. Return trips can be arranged at the same station where you are dropped off, and the rate is the same. The fare is $8, and no advance purchase is required. The service runs from 10 AM to 8:30 PM.

Buses going from the Cancún airport to Playa del Carmen leave at 10:30 AM, 11:45 AM, 12:45 PM, 1:45 PM, 3:00 PM, 4:45 PM, 5:45 PM, 7:00 PM, and 8:30 PM. Buses going from Playa del Carmen to the Cancún airport leave at 8:00 AM, 9:00 AM, 10:30 AM, 11:45 AM, 1:00 PM,

The main Playa bus station at the town square

3:00 PM, 4:00 PM, 5:00 PM, and 6:15 PM.

Buses also run from the Cancún airport to the Cancún bus station in downtown. They leave every 30 minutes from 9 AM to 10 PM, and the fare is $3.50 each way.

CAR RENTAL

If you plan to do much local exploring and you prefer to have a self-guided trip rather than go on planned excursions, renting a car may be your best option. And since the price of car rental for a day is about the same as taking a taxi from the Cancún airport to Playa del Carmen, it usually makes sense to pick up the car at the airport and drop it off on your way back. Alternatively, you can choose to get your car once you're at your hotel or drop it off early at one of your rental agency's offices in the Mayan Riviera.

Most of the American chains have offices at the Cancún airport, and cars can be reserved through the companies' toll-free numbers or Web sites. There are usually plenty of rental cars available, though you may have to check with a couple of companies before finding one. Most do not honor the U.S.-based frequent renter clubs, so brand loyalty may not be as much of an issue, anyway.

When renting a car in Mexico, it is important to investigate your insurance options. You are required to carry at least liability, and it will be clearly marked on your rental contract. Collision and comprehensive add-ons are available and can add 50 to 100 percent to the price of the car rental. Verify in advance whether your existing car insurance or even credit card contract provides for rental car coverage, and double-check to ensure that the coverage extends to vehicles rented in Mexico, as many times it will not. For peace of mind, it

Go Hog Wild in the Riviera Maya

For some travelers, taking a guided trip in a tour bus or even setting out on their own in a rental car is just too tame. For these intrepid travelers, renting a Harley Davidson may be the best way to visit the ruins, discover hidden beaches, and make a style statement, all while getting a tan. **Playa Harley Davidson,** located on Highway 307 at Constituyentes Avenue, offers 883 Sportsters, 1200 Customs, and Softtail Fat Boys for around $125, $175, and $225 per day. **Eaglerider Cancún** (km 13.5 Kukulkan Blvd., 801-783-4274 (U.S.) or 998-885-0626 (Cancún); www.eaglerider cancun.com) rents Electra Glide, Road King, Heritage Springer, and Yamaha Road Star bikes for $185 per day. Customized travel maps and tour suggestions are available at both locations. Riders are encouraged to exercise extreme caution while riding along busy sections of Highway 307 and any unpaved roads they may encounter.

sure is nice to have full coverage, especially if you plan to drive the car in remote areas or leave it unattended/unsecured overnight. Most rental contracts also specify that taking the car off paved surfaces (down dusty beach roads, for example) will void your insurance. I have heard of stories where a car will develop a flat tire while on a rock-strewn back road, and the driver will have the car towed back to the asphalt before calling the rental company.

Renters are also advised to check their rental contract as it relates to whether or not the car must be returned full of gas. Some companies (Hertz, Avis, and maybe others) require the renter to prepurchase a tank of gas, which means that the car need not be refueled prior to returning it. The flip side to this benefit is that any gas left in the tank is essentially a gift from you to the rental agency, with no refund given for the amount of fuel with which the car is returned. Many drivers prefer not to prepay the gas and to fill up the tank on their own just prior to turning in the car. Since almost all rental offices are located in urban areas, finding a nearby gas station is never an issue. If you are returning your car to the Cancún airport, there is a station just south of the exit, so you'll hit it on the way from Playa to the airport.

If you have reserved your car in advance, you should check in at the company's rental desk near the airport exit. The agent will take your information, then point the way to the company's main office, most of which are just across the street from the main airport parking lot. The process will probably take a bit longer than you're used to, but while you wait, you can skim through the available maps and chart your course to your destination. Though popular late-model SUVs, Jeeps, and sedans are available, most of the budget cars will be names that you're probably not familiar with, such as the Dodge Atos, Verna Ikon, or VW Pointer. Cars are available in manual or automatic transmission, and with or without A/C, stereo, and other options. Choose your car based on what you expect your needs to be. The lower-end cars can be substantially cheaper, if you're willing to sacrifice a bit of luxury and space. Economy cars cost about $40 a day, while SUVs, vans, or four-wheel drives can cost up to $120 a day.

Prior to leaving the rental lot, an agency employee will give you a quick checkout on the car, pointing out the spare tire and jack, the gas tank, and the trunk release. The agent will also do a thorough inspection of the exterior and mark any damages on a checkout sheet that you will be asked to sign to verify that all damage has been marked. It's a good idea to ensure that all damage is reported, including minor paint scratches, since you could be held liable for any new damage when you return the car. Of course, if you have purchased the comprehensive insurance, this won't apply since you're covered no matter what happens to the car. It is smart to check the tire pressure and wiper fluid and have the agent make any adjustments you want before leaving the lot.

Parking can be a bit hard to find, particularly near the busy sections of Quinta in Playa del Carmen. A pay lot is available on 10th Avenue at 8th Street and free parking can usually be found along Constituyentes, between the beach and 20th Street, which provides walking access to most of the town's attractions. Parking along the curb is generally allowed, as long as the curb is not painted yellow, and never on Quinta.

RETURN TRIP TO CANCÚN AIRPORT

Getting back to the airport is slightly less expensive than inbound transfer. Taxis cost $40 from Playa del Carmen to the Cancún airport, and you can also take the city bus from the bus station across from the town plaza for $4. In addition, many companies offer airport transportation in vans and Suburbans that will pick you up at your hotel, with a couple of stops along the way at other hotels. Most hotels can arrange this service, or it can be purchased through one of the many travel agencies around town. One convenient agency, **Cenote Azul** (984-803-2880), is located on 12th Street between Quinta and 10th. The rate is $15, though some hotels charge an additional commission. Make certain your ride lets you off at the proper terminal, as the complex is somewhat sprawling, and walking in the hot sun with all your bags for five minutes may not fit well into your itinerary. A free shuttle bus is available for intra-terminal transfers and departs regularly from the front of the terminal.

HIT THE ROAD

Thankfully, finding your way around Playa del Carmen and the Riviera Maya is relatively simple. The main federal thoroughfare, Highway 307, provides a direct route all the way from Puerto Juárez, north of Cancún, through Puerto Morelos, Playa del Carmen, Tulum, and on down to the Costa Maya and toward the border with Belize. The road is four lanes from Cancún to Xcaret and then narrows to two lanes all the way to the Belizean border. The speed limit averages about 50 mph, with up to 65 mph in more rural areas. Most of the hotels in the Riviera Maya have well-marked entrances from the highway (some are quite elaborate), and the ones that don't are generally easy to find, with at least a few directional signs to help guide you. Signage is best heading away from the airport and some turnoffs can be easy to miss if you are heading north, back toward the airport, so watch for landmarks as much as signs.

When turning left from the highway into some resort entries, drivers first veer to the right, where the road curves and intersects the main road, so you can wait out of the moving lane of traffic for cars to clear before crossing the road. In other spots, an open center lane is available for making turns. To reach the hotels in downtown Playa del Carmen, you will enter into town on either Avenue Constituyentes or Avenue Juárez, depending on whether your hotel is on the north or south side of town. Access to Playacar is through Avenida Juárez or one of the direct-access gated roads on the east side of Highway 307, marked by the ornate flowers and stone carvings.

Playa Commuter Flights

There is a small airfield in downtown Playa del Carmen, just a few blocks behind the Playacar Palace hotel. It is used mostly by private aircraft, but public flights are available to Cancún (25 minutes), Cozumel (10 minutes), and occasionally Cobá (40 minutes), Chichén Itzá (45 minutes), or other nearby destinations. The planes are turboprops with limited seating. The Cozumel plane seats only four passengers and can be a real adventure, but it is worth it just for the sightseeing. The main airline, **AeroCaribe** (987-872-0877), has an office on the street in front of the landing strip.

The Cozumel Ferry

If you hit the ferry schedule just right, getting to Playa del Carmen from Cozumel can take even less time than arriving through Cancún. The Cozumel International Airport is smaller than the Cancún airport and has only two runways and a small terminal. As your plane slows to a stop on the runway, you will think the wingtips are about to snip the treetops off the palm trees that line the strip, but it is a safe and modern facility, even if it lacks the pretensions of the newer and more recently renovated Cancún airport.

Just as in Cancún, taxi service at the Cozumel airport is regulated, and taxi fare or shuttle service must be paid for at a kiosk in the airport. Visitors with little luggage who are looking to save a few bucks can walk off the airport grounds and hail a taxi on the street. An official taxi will cost you $12 to the ferry landing, while a taxi hailed on the street will set you back only $5 or so. Either way, the ride is only 10 minutes and will take you through a quick tour of the town of San Miguel before letting you out at the base of the ferry landing, or *muelle*, as it's called in Spanish.

Catch the Cozumel ferry from the municipal dock.

Buying ferry tickets to Playa del Carmen

Ferry schedules are clearly posted, and you will have your option from a couple of different boats. Each boasts to be the newest and fastest, though any differences in the times are almost negligible. The boats seat more than 200 passengers and have air-conditioning, snack bars, rest rooms, and both indoor and outdoor seating, plus a lower deck with TVs showing funny videos, cartoons, and promotional tourism ads. The ride takes from 30 to 45 minutes, depending on the boat and the water conditions. On windy days the ride can be a little rough, so it's recommended that you use the rest room prior to boarding or before departure, in case it's too rocky to safely move around. Fares can range from $10 to $12 each way, depending on how many boats are available. Round-trip tickets are available and can save the hassle of standing in line again, though it's generally not much of an issue.

To verify ferry schedules, you can contact the ferry office directly at 987-872-1588 or visit their Web site, www.crucerosmaritimos.com.mx.

Upon arrival in Playa del Carmen, you will walk down a metal ramp and onto the

Cozumel Ferry Schedule

COZUMEL TO PLAYA DEL CARMEN	PLAYA DEL CARMEN TO COZUMEL
5:00 AM	6:00 AM
7:00 AM	8:00 AM
8:00 AM	9:00 AM
9:00 AM	10:00 AM
10:00 AM	11:00 AM
noon	1:00 PM
2:00 PM	3:00 PM
4:00 PM	5:00 PM
5:00 PM	6:00 PM
6:00 PM	7:00 PM
8:00 PM	9:00 PM
10:00 PM	11:00 PM

Pedicab, Playa style

wide concrete pier. If you've checked bags, they will be delivered to you on the dock, near the bow of the ferryboat. Tricycle taxis are available to help carry you and/or your bags to the street to catch a proper taxi or all the way to your hotel, if you're staying in the immediate downtown area. A taxi to a downtown hotel should cost $2 to $3; to Playacar hotels, $5 to $6; and to Puerto Morelos, $30. To get to hotels in the southern Riviera Maya, you will pay $20 to $40.

A new ferry dock was constructed in 2005 in front of the Real Resort at Constituyentes Avenue, about a mile north of the old one. It is embroiled in a legal debate since not all of the permits were correctly acquired. It is, however, sometimes used by one or more of the ferry operators.

Sample Taxi Fares around the Riviera Maya

From Playa del Carmen to:

- Punta Bete: 4 miles, $6
- Xcaret: 4 miles, $6
- Paamul: 11 miles, $10
- Puerto Aventuras: 11 miles, $11
- Akumal: 20 miles, $17
- Puerto Morelos: 20 miles, $17
- Xel-Ha: 30 miles, $21
- Cobá: 35 miles, $50
- Tulum: 39 miles, $27
- Cancún: 42 miles, $45

GETTING AROUND IN PLAYA

The hotels in Playa del Carmen proper are nearly all within walking distance of Quinta, the town square, the ferry dock, and most major in-town attractions. Taxis are readily available and charge only a couple of dollars for in-town treks.

Another option for getting around Playa is the communal taxis, or *colectivos*, which crisscross the downtown area and will get you to your destination for a cheap price, if not always as quickly as you like. They are

Exploring is fun, but so is knowing where you are. CancunMap.com sells exhaustively researched and individually produced maps covering Cancún, Cozumel, Isla Mujeres, Playa del Carmen, and the Riviera Maya. The foldout maps highlight hotels, restaurants, nightspots, activities, and other attractions and include personal comments and recommendations from the creators, an American couple who has been traveling around the region for years. One of the owners, known as Map Chick on Internet message boards, is happy to answer specific questions that buyers may have. The maps, especially the Riviera Maya one, are highly recommended for travelers who are planning on renting a car and doing their own adventuring. They sell for $10 each and can be ordered online.

white vans with red lettering, and they regularly pass by the basketball court on 2nd Street and 20th Avenue.

Bike Rental
Renting a bike is a great way to get around Playa del Carmen. **Todo Yellow,** located on 6th Street between Quinta and 10th Street in front of Hotel Casa, offers bikes by the hour ($1.50), morning to evening ($7), 24 hours ($9), or week ($35). **Bike & Scooter Rental** (984-803-2880), located on 12th Street between Quinta and 10th Avenue, offers mountain bikes and Cripton scooters for rent.

Regional Bus Travel
There are two bus stations in Playa del Carmen. The original terminal is on Quinta and Avenue Juárez and offers frequent service to Cancún and Tulum, usually departing every 15 to 30 minutes. Fares are $3 to $4 each way, in an air-conditioned bus with rest room and TVs. It also offers trips to Campeche, Chetumal, Chichén Itzá, and other regional destinations.

A regional and long-distance terminal is *located .5 mile away* (20th Avenue between 12th and 14th Streets) and offers service to other destinations around Quintana Roo and other Mexican states. The buses are generally in good condition, with air-conditioning, rest rooms, uniformed drivers, and TVs, though the audio is in Spanish.

Bus Fare Samples
From Playa del Carmen to:
Cancún: 1 hour, $4
Tulum: 1 hour, $3
Cobá: 2 1/2 hours, $4.50
Felipe Carillo Puerto: 3 hours, $8
Valladolid: 3 hours, $18
Chetumal: 4 hours, $15
Chichén Itzá: 4 1/2 hours, $14
Mérida: 4 1/2 hours, $21
Campeche: 7 1/2 hours, $30
San Cristóbal: 18 hours, $60
Mexico City: 24 hours, $90

Car Rental in Playa del Carmen
Even if you didn't choose to pick up a car at the airport, you can still rent one in town. They can be rented by the day or week and can usually be dropped off at a different location (such as at the airport or in Cancún) for no additional fee.

The following are some local car-rental offices:
Alamo: Plaza Antigua, 984-873-1118
Avis: downtown, 984-873-3842
Budget: downtown, 984-873-2772

Executive: Playacar Palace, 984-873-2354
Hertz: downtown, 984-873-1130
National: Porto Real, 984-873-0360
Payless: downtown, 984-873-1072
Thrifty: downtown, 984-873-0119

A *colectivo* shuttle van departs downtown Playa from 2nd Street between 15th and 20th Avenues and drops passengers off anywhere along the way between Playa and Tulum for $2, even if your destination is off the main road. The van fits eight people and departs as soon as it is full, from 7 AM–8 PM.

City Orientation & In-Town Driving

Playa del Carmen is laid out on a grid system. Cancún is due north, Cozumel is due east, Tulum is due south, and the Quintana Roo interior is due west. Avenue Juárez is the main road into town, cutting through 15 blocks of dumpy hotels, convenience stores, car repair shops, clothing stores, and fruit stands as it carves its way west to east from the highway to the beach. The road is closed to normal traffic a block from the beach, forcing all cars to turn north, except for taxis and buses, which can continue on down to the beachfront.

The streets to the north of Juárez are numbered evenly and go up as you move away from the center of town. For example, 2nd Street is 1 block north of Juárez, 4th Street is 2 blocks north of Juárez, and 10th Street is 5 blocks north of Juárez. The streets to the south of Juárez are numbered with odd numbers and also go up as you move farther from town: 1st Street is 1 block south of Juárez, 3rd Street is 2 blocks south of Juárez, and Ninth Street is 5 blocks south of Juárez.

The beach is the zero point for the roads traveling north–south. The first block from the beach is 1st Avenue, though it starts only at 10th Street and heads north. The next road inland from 1st (and the first road inland when you're south of 10th Street) is Fifth Avenue, or Quinta Avenida (Quinta), which is the main pedestrian walkway through town. The 20-block portion of Quinta (from the town plaza to 40th Street, where it ends—for now) that is closed to vehicular traffic is by far the busiest tourist zone of Playa. Moving westward and farther from the beach, the roads go up in increments of five, so 10th Avenue is just west of Fifth, 15th Avenue is just west of 10th, and so on.

Most streets in Playa del Carmen are one-way, and not all of them are clearly marked. If you do head down the road the wrong way, expect to hear jeers and friendly hollers from

Stay Out of Trouble

One good way to avoid run-ins with the local police is not to give them any good reasons to pull you over in the first place.

Never drink and drive—Nothing is more tempting to a local officer than a rental jeep full of tourists with a cooler in the back seat and everyone holding Corona bottles as they drive down the road.

Wear your seatbelt—Just like in the United States, there is a mandatory seatbelt law in Mexico. The best cops in Playa del Carmen sometimes stand on the street corner where it's easy to peer inside your car, so buckle up every time you get in the front seat of a car.

Pull over to use your mobile phone—Using a mobile phone or other similar gadget while driving is illegal in Mexico. It's also extremely dangerous when driving on unfamiliar roads, especially along Highway 307 and around downtown areas in Cancún, Playa del Carmen, or Tulum.

Drive slowly, even on back roads.

the locals, who make a pastime of watching the tourists do silly things. Most of the traffic around town continues on at a fairly slow pace. The town is relatively small, and no one is in that much of a hurry. Local police direct traffic at the busiest intersections and are known to be quite polite to tourists. Though most do not speak English, they will try to help you if you need assistance or directions.

DRIVING BEYOND PLAYA DEL CARMEN

As mentioned before, Highway 307 will take you almost anywhere in the Riviera Maya you want to go, from Cancún, through Playa del Carmen, and on down to Tulum. What used to be a narrow two-lane road encroached by jungle and seldom driven is now two lanes each way and, in some places, even three. The speed bump marking the Puerto Morelos turnoff is now a traffic light, and turning lanes have been added at the major intersections. At Xcaret and other key attractions, left turns are made by exiting to the right and then curving around perpendicular to the highway, allowing drivers to wait for a clear path while safely off the roadway. Of course this also means you have to cross all lanes of traffic to turn, rather than just waiting for a pause in the oncoming traffic, but it does serve to keep cars out of the center of the road, which can help keep things safe for passing traffic.

Construction seems to be ongoing, and in many parts there is a soft shoulder. Attempts are being made to grade the median and plant palm trees and flowering plants, which has been done close to Cancún but is lagging behind in other areas. The highway is notorious for the many large trucks heading from Cancún to Chetumal and back. Drivers are encouraged to use extreme caution during heavy traffic, as some others on the road do not drive as defensively as American drivers are typically taught. Though fender benders are a daily occurrence and urban legends of honeymooners crashing in their Jeeps can sound horrific, the road is usually traversed without incident. Seatbelts are required by law, and drinking and driving is just as illegal and ill-advised while on vacation as it is back home.

Federal police, infamously known as the *Federales*, patrol the highway and occasionally pull drivers over for speeding or other infractions. Fines can usually be paid at once and range from $10 to $100, depending on how good of a negotiator you are and whether you did anything to deserve being pulled over in the first place. Stories of police torture and abuse are way overexaggerated, and the vast majority of the time, drivers pulled over will be back on their way in a matter of minutes, with only a small fine assessed. Any hints of alcohol or drug use, though, may very well lead to seizure of your vehicle and a ride to the main police station downtown, where the fines and the hassle go up considerably, especially if any drugs (including marijuana) are found. Remember, the Mexican constitution declares that if accused of a crime, you will be considered guilty until proven innocent, which puts detainees in a very different position than those in the States. If you get into serious trouble, a U.S. consulate should be notified, but they will not necessarily be able to help, especially if you are legitimately accused of committing a crime.

Traveling through the Riviera Maya is supposed to be fun, and driving yourself can be a rewarding way to discover the area on your own timetable. So don't be afraid to pack up a cooler, bring some snacks, turn up the radio, and get exploring. Driving your own car lets you see and do many things that you just can't experience on public transportation. In remote stretches, you'll see iguanas, snakes, and even tarantulas (some so large you'll swear you can see their fur) crossing the street. Look closely and you will spot homemade signs placed to mark the trail leading to someone's home. Some use an old shirt tied to a tree, while others paint a family name on a tire and hang it from a branch or cut the bottom from a plastic jug and fit it over the top of a plant. You will see people walking or on horseback in the most remote areas where you would think that nothing is around, but the jungle just beyond the roadside treeline holds many secrets, and you're never as alone as you think you might be.

There are so many things to see that you could spend an entire day driving around, never traveling more than 50 miles away from downtown Playa, and see Mayan ruins, freshwater lagoons, deserted beaches, caves, hidden snorkeling spots, traditional cantinas, fresh seafood restaurants, and many other attractions.

Stopping for Gas

The federal government's oil refinery and gasoline distribution company, Petroleos Mexicanos, operates all of the country's gas stations under the name Pemex. Prices are heavily regulated, and the stations are dispersed throughout the country. The only areas where you really need to make sure you fill up before heading out are south of Tulum, where there is a long stretch without gas before you arrive at a gas station near the Mayan ruins of Kohunlich—if you take the highway or, in Punta Allen, if you take the beach road. It's best to fill up here if you're heading farther south, to the interior of Sian Ka'an or the towns near the Belizean border. Also, if you're heading west across the peninsula, past Chichén Itzá and toward the Uxmal ruins, it's best to fill up whenever you come across a gas station since service stations in that part of the Yucatán are few and far between.

All stations are full service. It's a good idea to check which side your tank is on before pulling in, especially if the station is busy, or you're likely to lose your spot if you're forced to turn around so the hose can reach. You can usually pay with cash or credit card, though cash

Shops in Playa offer local and long-distance calling stations, as well as Internet access.

is recommended, especially if you're in a rush. Gas is priced by the liter and is generally a bit more expensive than it is in the States. Tips are not mandatory, but they are definitely appreciated. Just like in the States, most gas stations also have convenience stores. Unlike the States, though, you will need to repark your car away from the pumps after filling up, since there are fewer pumps at each station and yours will soon be needed by another driver.

Be careful when paying, as the attendants are known for sometimes trying a bill-swap scam, where they claim that you haven't given them enough money, quickly swapping your $20 for a $1 to prove their case.

CALLING HOME

Don't dial direct from your hotel room! That's the first lesson for any visitor to the Riviera Maya, as even a quick call home from your hotel can carry a charge of $25 or more, due to high connection fees and even higher per-minute tolls. Most hotels offer local calls for around $1 each, about the same as in the States, but long-distance calls—especially international—are a completely different story. Your best option is to buy a prepaid phone card and make all calls with it. Even then, it's best to make the calls from a public phone to ensure you won't be billed a connection fee, which is common even for "toll-free" calls. The cards, called LADA cards, or *tarjetas LADA*, are available at nearly every pharmacy, grocery store, and convenience store in town and can be purchased in denominations ranging from $2 to $20. A call to the United States or Canada is charged at 50 cents per minute. Since many U.S.-based phone services offer inexpensive calling to Mexico, it can work out great to call home and then schedule a time for your party to call you back at the hotel, since you won't be charged to receive a call in your room.

Many shops in Playa offer inexpensive local and long-distance calling stations, where the attendant will dial your number and then assign you to a semiprivate booth to take your call. Calls are charged by the minute, and you will pay the attendant at the completion of the call. Rates are comparable to using the LADA card. One such place is **Phone Home** (Quinta between 10th and 12th Streets, Playa del Carmen), which offers private booths for long-distance phone calls. They charge 40 cents per minute to the United States or Canada.

If you have some extra pesos jingling in your pockets, you can also use a public phone on the street or in the hotel lobby to place a direct call home. Rates vary depending on the phone owner, but they are generally substantially less expensive than direct-dialed calls from your hotel room. Don't be fooled by the stickers placed on many public phones or printed on flyers advertising discounted credit card calls to the United States. Though they do have English-speaking operators and will effectively place your calls, they often charge exorbitant rates. The same goes for services offering to assist in placing collect or third-party calls.

Mobile phones are booming in popularity in Mexico, and most U.S.-based carriers offer service in the Riviera Maya through roaming contracts with the local providers. Rates vary according to your calling plan and aren't always cheap (around $1/minute or so), but the convenience factor of making and receiving calls with your own phone can count for a lot. Callers from back home will simply call your number like they normally do, and it will ring wherever you are. Call your provider before starting your trip to make sure your international calling is turned on and ask about the rate plans available. Though service is not available throughout the region, it is more and more common to have a sufficient signal. You'll know you're in a coverage area when the name of the local provider shows up on the display of your phone.

If you're making an in-country call to a Mexico-based mobile phone, you will need to add 044 before the area code. This is because in Mexico, the caller—not the one receiving the call—pays for the cost of the call. This is the deft strategy that the Mexican cellular companies have used to help keep costs down for local users.

Numbers Game

Country code for the United States: 01

Country code for Mexico: 52

Area code for Cancún: 998

Area code for Playa del Carmen: 987

Prefix for dialing Mexican mobile phones: 044

Gadget lovers should look into purchasing a Wi-Fi phone, available at electronics stores for around $100. With these phones, which resemble a standard mobile phone, you can place telephone calls over the Internet, thus bypassing the stiff mobile charges. Calls require a wireless Internet connection (by the pool, in a restaurant, in your hotel room) and registration with Skype or a similar VoIP provider and can be made for about a penny a minute. If you're taking your laptop computer, these programs can also run directly over the computer, turning your laptop into a nearly free telephone.

If you really need to stay in touch, another route, albeit the most expensive, is to rent or purchase a satellite phone, which will work in almost any spot on the globe and ensure that you're never out of reach.

INTERNET ACCESS

Finding Internet access in downtown Playa del Carmen is as easy as looking down the road. Nearly every block has at least one Internet café, or "cyber" as they're called here. Most are small affairs, with four to six computers, a couple of phone booths, and a young attendant playing PC games in between customers. Prices range from $1 to $5 per hour, depending on location and the number of tourists who frequent it. Some of the cybers along Quinta are located in full-service restaurants and allow the user to sip a beer or even enjoy an entire meal while checking the Web or sending e-mail. Farther from the beach, the prices drop and the number of locals increases. It's not uncommon to find most stations occupied by friends of the attendant surfing for free, though they willingly relinquish their seats to paying customers.

Most locations have acceptably fast access, though there are a few with slow or sporadic connections. You may have to try a couple of shops before settling on one that works for you. Most cybers also have an extra line available for customers who bring their laptops and just need a connection. Sometimes, a bit of configuration is required on your computer to adapt the network settings. If you'd rather not mess with that, try the next spot. The fee is the same, whether you use their computer or your own. Some locations use an installed program to record your usage times and fees, while others have numbers taped to the sides of the computer and the attendant keeps track with a watch and a pad of paper. Either way, it's best to monitor your own time to ensure you are not overcharged.

The vast majority of Internet cafés you come across will have the software you need pre-installed, including popular word processing and spreadsheet programs. You will also find AIM, MSN Messenger, and Yahoo Messenger already there. If you need a freeware program that's not installed, most computers have administrative access, so you can usually download it and install it without missing a beat.

Always remember to log out of any instant messenger programs and to erase any passwords that may have been saved. It's best to clear your Internet cache and also the cookies in case the computer is set to store your information for the next user. It's not a bad idea to change your passwords when you return home, just to make sure any data you have unintentionally left behind doesn't come back to haunt you.

The following are a few Internet cafés in downtown Playa del Carmen, though new ones open up all the time:

The Point (10th Avenue between 2nd and 4th Streets). This is an Internet café with an attitude—but a good one. It's more like a reggae lounge, with 10 computer stations, carpeted floor (the only one around), cold air-conditioning, free coffee, scanning/printing

Surf Before You Snorkel

Try these free online resources for more information about the Riviera Maya:

InTheRoo.com. Favored by many locals, this site offers hotel info, tour info, reservations, and a thriving message board community.

LocoGringo.com. This superb source for detailed aerial photos, virtual tours, and high-quality photos and descriptions of hotels, attractions, and beaches covers Playa del Carmen, the Riviera Maya, and surrounding areas. You can make reservations for hotels, condos, and villas as well as participate in its active message boards.

MayanHoliday.com. The author's blog, regularly updated with news, travel tips, and features related to travel in Playa del Carmen and the Riviera Maya.

RivieraMaya.com. The Riviera Maya tourism board's site has hotel and restaurant lists, plus attractions, travel stats, and tour info. Hotel reservations can be made online or by phone in the United States at 1-877-7-GO-MAYA (877-746-6292).

Playa.info or PlayadelCarmenInfo.com. This site offers active message boards, detailed hotel reviews from recent travelers, a live Webcam, and real estate information.

PlayaMayaNews.com. A community site for people living in or visiting Playa del Carmen, it provides local movie schedules, classified listings, human-interest stories, health advice, culture, and community action. It makes an entertaining and interesting read whether you're actively planning a trip or just learning more about the area.

PlayaManiac.com. Its message boards cover a wide variety of topics, including living in Playa, all-inclusive hotels, traveler meet-ups, real estate, classifieds, and destinations in and around the Riviera Maya. Browse through the information, or post your question and get responses from recent travelers and Playa regulars.

PlayadelCarmen.com. A commercial site devoted to area hotels, condos, photos, destination guides, and message boards.

SeePlaya.com. Fun site with insider information ranging from how to pick the right hotel to how to spot a fake Cuban cigar.

TripAdvisor.com. This site has user reviews, candid photos, price comparisons, message boards, and reservations information for hotels throughout the Riviera Maya. The site is not specific to the region, so you will need to search to find your specific hotel.

Travel.State.Gov. The U.S. State Department provides a wealth of travel information covering documentation requirements, health, safety, and overseas services.

service, and long-distance phone booths. Music posters decorate the walls, and each computer and phone has its own name and theme—from Bono to Lenny, from Jimi to Frank, and from Bob to Jim. If you don't know who all these people are, you're still welcome to hire their service, but you'll appreciate it more if you do.

The Point (Quinta at 24th Street). This travel-themed Internet café has fast connections, a pleasant atmosphere, good air-conditioning, a scanner and a copier, private booths for long-distance calls, and free coffee.

24 Hour Internet (24th Street between Quinta and 1st Avenue). This aptly named Internet café offers all-day and all-night Internet access, color printing, scanning, copying, and long-distance phone calls. Free coffee and water are available, and there are also sodas and candy bars for sale.

ELECTRICITY

Electrical power is the same as it is in the States: 110 volts AC. The outlets are the same size, and most U.S. plugs will work without any problem. Some hotels do not offer polarized plugs (where one prong is slightly larger than the other), so if your important electronic gadget has a polarized plug, you may want to pick up an adapter at your local hardware or discount store. Adapters are very inexpensive and could save the day if you have the misfortune of having an uncooperative outlet at your hotel.

OFFICIAL TOURISM OFFICE

The state-run tourism office can provide free area maps, promotional information, tour recommendations, safety tips, and lists of approved vendors; it's in downtown Playa del Carmen on Avenue Juárez at 15th Avenue.

POST OFFICE

The main post office (984-873-0300), on Avenue Juárez between 15th and 20th Avenues, is open 8–5 Monday through Friday and 9–noon Saturday. Postcards are cheap and always appreciated by the folks you left back home. It can take weeks for mail to arrive, however, so don't mail home instructions on how you're to be picked up at the airport in a few days, or you will end up waiting on the curb for a ride that never shows. Stamps can be purchased at many convenience stores or hotel gift shops.

To send anything quickly or of any value, it is recommended that you use a private courier, as the Mexican postal service is not generally recognized as being efficient or reliable. **Estafeta** is Mexico's largest document and package delivery company. A FedEx-sized package sent two-day air express to anywhere in Mexico is only $10. Overnight service within the country is $18. Deliveries to the U.S. start at $30. Estafeta is located on 4th Street between 30th and 35th Avenues, across from the Social Security Hospital. It is open Monday through Friday from 8–5. There's also a shipping agent located on 12th Street between 10th and 15th Avenues that can handle orders for FedEx, DHL, and UPS, with guaranteed international delivery.

NEWSPAPERS

The *Miami Herald* prints a Cancún edition, which features local news, weather, and tourism features in English. It is distributed free of charge and is available in the lobby of the major hotels and at some coffee shops downtown. The *New York Times* and *USA Today* are available

---

A Note on the Meal Prices Used in This Book:

Meal prices for most restaurants are expressed using such relative terms as budget, moderate, expensive, and very expensive. Generally speaking, budget means that you can get enough food to fill you up, plus a drink, for less than $7 per person. Moderate meal prices are from $7 to $20 per person. Expensive meals are $20 to $40 per person. And very expensive meals start at $40 and go up to $100 or more per person, though the high end of this range is very rare.

at the larger convenience stores and hotel tobacco shops. Many smaller hotels have subscriptions to the TimesFax news service, which allows them to print mini-versions of the *New York Times* on a computer printer and distribute them to their guests.

MEDICAL CARE

The vast majority of visitors to Playa del Carmen and the Riviera Maya never need to think about medical care during their visit, but accidents do happen—even while on vacation—so it's good to know a little about the area's medical services before heading out on your trip.

Medical facilities in Cancún, Cozumel, Isla Mujeres, and Playa del Carmen are modern and more than sufficient for most moderate emergencies and standard medical care. Most are operated by the Red Cross, or *La Cruz Roja*, and truly are first-class facilities, by any standard. Many of the doctors are U.S. trained and can provide care equivalent to what can be received at an average facility of a similar size in the United States or other First World countries. A fairly large modern hospital called Hospiten opened in 2007, just south of Playacar on Highway 307 in Playa del Carmen. The emergency medical first responders in the region are especially well trained and equipped, and they are well versed on procedures related to scuba-diving accidents, falls, car wrecks, animal bites, broken bones, and other common incidents. There are also many private clinics with English-speaking doctors who can treat nonemergency cases and make house calls to hotels or other locations.

The major facilities have 24-hour pharmacies supplying all necessary medications. There are also numerous pharmacies in town where all manner of medicines can be purchased, with—and frequently without—a prescription. Cancún, Cozumel, and Playa del Carmen each have a hyperbaric chamber, used to treat decompression sickness, or "the bends," which can happen while scuba diving. Most dive operators charge a mandatory $1 chamber insurance fee for each dive trip, which helps keep the chambers operating and provides for free care for affected divers. Divers who want to be extra cautious should investigate the Divers Alert Network (DAN) (www.diversalertnetwork.com) before their visit. For a reasonable yearly fee, DAN provides information about diving safety and also offers air-evacuation insurance should a diver need to be airlifted back home for treatment of a diving-related injury.

The farther you travel from the

Helpful local pharmacies provide lists of available medications.

DRUGSTORE

BRAND NAME	MEXICAN NAME	GENERIC NAME
ZIRTEC	CETRIZINA	VISERTRAL
ALBUTEROC	VENTOLIN	SALBUTANOL
BIAXIN	CLARITOMICIN	MAXITRAL
CELEXA	SEROPRAM	CITALOPRAM
AMOXICILLIN	GILMAXINA	AMOXILINA
PREVACID	LANZOPRAZOLE	RORIFRAN
PRI-LOSEC	OMEPRAZOLE	ALBOZ
FLONASE	FLIXONASE	FLTICASONE
VALTREX	RAPIVIR	VALACYCLOVIR
LEVOQUIN	LEVOFLAXACINA	FLEVOX
Z-PAC	AZITROCIN	ZERTALIN
AZANTAC	RANITIDINA	ULSAVEN
MERIDIA	SIBUTRAMIA	YEDUC 15MG C/30
ZOLOF	SERTALINA	ALUPREX
PESTOPRIM-D	TESTOSTERONE	TESTOPRIM-D C/3
VIAGRA	SILDENAFIL	VIAGRA
PROTONIX	PANTROPRAZOLE	CIPROTON
FLEXERIL	CYCLOBENZAPRINE	BENCOPRIM
SOMA	CARISOPRODOL	BLOCACID
PREMARIN	ESTROGENOS	DNA-EC
SEPTRA	TRIMETOPRIMA	SUXPRIM
LUSTARA	HIDROQUINONE	ELDOPAQUE
CIPRO	CIPROFLOXACIN	GENOFLEX
TORADOL	KETOROLAC	VEROLAX
XENICAL	ORLISTAT	XENICAL
BENICAL	TERBINAFINA	BINAFEX
AMISIL	FLUEXETINE	FLOCET
PROZAC	NANDROLONE	DECA
DECADURABULIN	TESTOSTERONE	SOSTENON
SOSTENON	TEDALAFIL	CIALIS
CIALIS	CLEBUTEROL	OXI FLU
SPIROPENT	TRETINOINE	RETIN-A
RETIN-A	TRETINOINE	RETACNYL
RENOVA	FEXOFENADINE	ALLEGRA
ALLEGRA	TESTOSTERONE	ANDRIOL
ANDRIOL	AMLODIPINO	AKEN
NORVAS	TREMADOL	VELDROL
ULTRAM	TAMOXIFENO	FEMOXTAL
NOLVADEX	FINASTERIDA	LUXFIL
PROPESHIA	FLUCONAZOL	ALFUMET
DIFLUCAN	IDUPROFENO	DOLPROFENO
MOTRIN	SILDENAFIL	MAXIFORT
MAXIFORT(VIAGRA)	SUMATRIPTAN	NOGRAINE
MITREX		NOSIPREN
METICORTEN		

main cities, the fewer medical facilities you will find available. In Akumal, Puerto Aventuras, and Tulum there are small clinics, though emergency services lag behind those of the larger cities in terms of quality and reliability. If heading way south, toward Kohunlich or Sian Ka'an, travelers should not expect to depend on the availability of nearby medical assistance and may need to go to the nearest city, such as Chetumal, for medical care.

Common sense and common precautions will prevent most accidents, and taking good care of yourself, including drinking plenty of water and moderating your alcohol intake, will reduce your chances of getting sick. After all, even though the medical facilities are generally quite good, they're not as nice as the beach.

LAUNDRY

There are laundry facilities in Playa every few blocks anywhere other than Quinta, since the rent is too high. Many offer fluff-and-fold services, button sewing, and related services. **Chic Lavandaria** on Avenue Constituyentes between 10th and 15th Streets even offers free delivery. Others offer free Internet access while you wait.

MONEY

The Riviera Maya plays prominently in the history of money in our civilization. One of the first forms of payment in the New World was the cocoa bean, which the Mayans crafted into a sweet drinkable beverage they called *xocoatl*, which is the origin of the word *chocolate*. They would harvest the cocoa from trees and then transport it by canoe to other villages, trading it for goods not native to the Yucatán. They also bartered for supplies and trinkets with each other and with members of neighboring tribes, using shells, baskets, cotton, and corn as items of trade.

One of the key times that money and trade were important was prior to a wedding ceremony, when tradition called for the family of the groom to bestow gifts upon the parents of the bride. A common form of payment, and a highly prized one, was a live chicken. Depending on the status of the couple, the amount could be as high as a dozen birds. The Mayan word for "chicken" is one that Americans use on a daily basis, probably without ever even knowing it. These feathered fowl were known to the Mayans as *k'aash*, and the word has stuck with us in its current American form: cash. Apparently, in the days of the Mayans, credit was not an option.

Society has changed dramatically since then, and the official currency of Mexico, even for the remaining Mayan population,

Banks & ATMs in Playa del Carmen:
Banamex (984-873-2947), 10th Avenue at 12th Street
Bancomer (984-873-0402), Avenue Juárez at 25th Street
HSBC (984-873-0404), Avenue Juárez at 10th Street
Banco Serfin (984-873-2900), Plaza Playacar
Cajero Automatico, Quinta at 16th Street
Money Exchange Locations in Playa del Carmen:
Quinta between 2nd and 4th Streets
Quinta between 12th and 14th Streets
Quinta between 22nd and 24th Streets
8th Street between Quinta and 10th Avenue
10th Street between Quinta and the beach
Plaza Marina, at the ferry dock, behind Señor Frog's

is now the peso. The value fluctuates daily against the U.S. dollar, though it is much more stable than it used to be. Visitors will rarely notice any official change in the value during their trip. The symbol for pesos is the dollar sign ($)—the same as the U.S. dollar—which can cause a bit of confusion since some businesses list prices in dollars and others list prices in pesos. This book will use the dollar sign ($) to signify U.S. dollars and the word *pesos* to refer to the Mexican peso. American dollars are almost universally accepted in the Riviera Maya, though change will almost always be given in pesos. American coins are not accepted.

There are many banks in downtown Playa del Carmen, which are noticeable by the presence of an armed guard, dressed in Army green and casually holding an automatic rifle at his side. Banks are open 9–4 daily, and it's perfectly acceptable to enter wearing short pants, a T-shirt, and beach sandals. Banks offer money exchange at the official bank rate and without commission, though lines can be long since you sometimes have to wait in the same line as the locals doing their everyday banking or paying bills.

Many hotels offer money exchange at the front desk, and while the exchange rates are not always the best, the convenience can frequently make up for it. Most visitors opt to change money at one of the many public exchange houses, or *casas de cambio*, which can be found every few blocks in the tourist-laden downtown area. These tiny offices are usually painted white and feature the exchange rate on red or black letters hanging from the wall. Different exchange houses offer slightly different exchange rates (up to 5 percent variations are common), so it may help to shop around if you're changing large quantities. Restaurants, bars, and shops can also set their own exchange rate for purchases made in dollars, and some even lure customers in with the promise of a favorable exchange. When in doubt, if you're paying in dollars, always ask in advance to ensure a reasonable exchange rate. Some out-of-the-way locations have been known to offer an exchange rate of up to 15 percent less than the official bank rate, though this is not common.

At any money exchange location, the "buy" price is the rate that they will pay in pesos for your dollars. The "sell" price is the rate they will exchange your pesos back in, should you change too much money. As you'll notice, there is about a 10 percent difference, which should encourage you to exchange only as much money as you will need so you don't have many pesos left over when your visit ends. You can change as little as $5 at a time, so it's always best to exchange too little than too much, since you can always go back for more. Just slide your dollars in the little window and the cashier will slide your pesos back out, along with a printed receipt showing the exchange rate and the number of pesos you should have. Always check the numbers and count your pesos in front of the clerk, and do not be shy about asking for your due if the amounts don't add up.

Fun for Kids

You don't have to leave the kids at home to have a fun vacation in the Riviera Maya. Many resorts have special facilities for kids, including playgrounds, kid-friendly meals, activities programs, and complimentary child care. In-room babysitting can be arranged through hotel concierges, who maintain a list of recommended caretakers. Smaller hotels can often arrange for a housekeeper to look after the kids while the parents enjoy a tour or day trip. At the beach, kids enjoy collecting shells, watching the pelicans dive for fish, and building sand castles. In most areas there is little wave action, so introducing kids to the ocean is a breeze. In 2005 a playground was added to the town square in Playa del Carmen, complete with a sandy play area, jungle gym, monkey bars, slides, and a great ocean view.

Penny Atkinson's Favorite Things about the Riviera Maya:

1. Babe's Noodle Bar. They have the best Thai chicken I've ever had, plus awesome frozen margaritas.

2. Akumal beach; it's the most beautiful beach in the world.

3. Bad Boyz on the beach is a great place for live music and dancing in the sunshine.

4. Shopping on Fifth Avenue (Quinta Avenida) is something I do every trip. I never get tired of it.

5. Pizza Pazza. I dream of this pizza when I'm not in Playa.

6. Ice-cold Sol beer on a hot day at the beach … it just doesn't get any better than that.

7. Hanging out at Kool Beach Club and meeting people from all over the world.

8. Taking a long walk down the beach and stopping at all the friendly little bars along the way.

9. Snorkeling with the turtles is the chance of a lifetime.

10. The best part of Playa is the people. The locals are wonderful, the ex-pats are a great bunch, and I have met the best people in the world.

Riviera Maya regular Penny Atkinson poses with the Federales on the beach.

The *casas de cambio* at the airport, whether at your originating airport or at your arrival airport, will always charge a commission on money exchange transactions. What may look like a good exchange rate often is negated when the commission is factored in. Don't be lured by offers to change pesos at an airport exchange house on a credit card, since the transaction is treated not as a purchase but as a cash advance, which will carry steep finance charges from your credit card company.

Traveler's checks are generally treated like cash, though smaller businesses do not like to accept them since it requires a trip to the bank to get their cash. Some exchange houses will give a slightly lower exchange rate for traveler's checks than cash, but banks will always give full value. If you are traveling with traveler's checks, remember to always keep the check numbers recorded somewhere separate from the checks themselves since you will need the numbers to make a claim if the checks are stolen or lost. Also remember to bring along a photo ID, which is required when countersigning your check to validate it.

Credit cards can be a great solution for making purchases since the charge will post in pesos and then will be converted to dollars at the official exchange rate, which is frequently higher than the shop or restaurant normally gives on cash purchases. Most tourist-oriented businesses will accept credit cards, though it is not safe to assume that they will. For the establishments listed in this book, we mention credit cards only if they're not accepted. Otherwise, you can assume that they are. Note that most credit card companies will tack on a 1 percent fee to international purchases, though many will reverse the charge if it is disputed. If you do not have the cash to cover a purchase, always ask to make sure your credit card will be accepted, or you could end up *lavando los platos* (washing the dishes).

ATM machines (*cajeros automáticos*) can be found at the entrance to nearly every bank and also in some stand-alone locations in Playa del Carmen. After hours, some machines are secured within locking glass entrances and can be accessed only by swiping your card through the locking mechanism. Amazingly, most working ATM cards will open the lock, allowing access to the machine. Most ATMs allow the user to select dollars or pesos, which will be exchanged at the official bank rate. Keep in mind, your home bank will most likely charge you a service fee for using your card at a nonaffiliated bank, so you may consider taking out as much as you need all at once rather than making multiple small withdrawals.

Outside of Cancún or Playa, ATM access is somewhat scarce. Some of the larger hotels have machines available, though it's advisable to get as much cash as you need before leaving town, because the nearest machine may be miles away.

If you're short on cash and don't have an ATM card, there's still hope. A Western Union office is located at Avenue Juárez and 15th Avenue in downtown Playa del Carmen. A passport or government-issued ID is required to collect any wired funds.

It is considered rude in Mexico for a waiter to bring your bill before you request it. This is definitely true in Playa, where lingering over meals is the norm and it's not rare to pass two to three hours savoring dinner, drinks, dessert, and post-meal conversation with friends. To get the bill, ask for *la cuenta* or just gesture to your waiter with a scribbling motion in the air. Tax is frequently factored in to the cost of meals, but gratuity is extra, unless your tab specifically lists *servicio* after the tax.

Tipping is expected for waiters and is appreciated by just about everyone else. At restaurants 10 to 15 percent is sufficient, and $1 for each round of drinks is a nice gesture at a bar. Massage therapists, tour guides, dive guides, and others providing extended service should be tipped around $10, depending on the nature of their service, as gratuities often make up a large percentage of their compensation. Bellhops get 50 cents to $1 per bag, room attendants get $1 a day, and grocery baggers, rest room attendants, and other personal-service providers should be tipped at your discretion. Taxis do not require tips for standard service, particularly local fares. Extraordinary service, though, such as assisting with bags, making multiple stops, providing valuable recommendations, singing mariachi songs, or teaching you naughty phrases in Spanish, does warrant a bit of a gratuity.

WHAT TO BRING

The Mayan Riviera is not considered a remote location. You're never more than 30 to 45 minutes from a grocery store, pharmacy, clothing boutique, electronics store, hair salon, or even hardware store. Contrary to what you may have heard or read before, all standard batteries are easy to find, film is not exorbitantly priced, and mosquito repellent can be purchased almost anywhere.

Packing for a trip to Playa and environs is all about comfort and bringing what you want to have with you to make you more content and your trip more enjoyable. Unless you're planning on a serious camping trip to Sian Ka'an or a long-distance jungle hike, preparing for your trip should be thought of not as survival packing but more in the way of luxury packing. What you need to bring is largely determined by where you are staying and what you plan on doing.

For instance, if you're staying at a five-star all-inclusive hotel, you will need to bring resort wear for your evening meals. If you're going to be horseback riding, you should bring jeans and closed-toe shoes. If you're going to play tennis or golf, make sure to bring the proper attire and footwear. If you plan on scuba diving, you'll want to bring whatever gear you don't want to rent.

All visitors will want to bring a pair of beach sandals, walking shoes, walking shorts, lightweight breathable clothing, plenty of underwear and socks, a bathing suit, toiletries, medicines, hat or sun visor, sunglasses, electronic gadgets, and proof of citizenship. Almost all hotels offer soap, and most come standard with shampoo, conditioner, and even body lotion. If you have sensitive skin or prefer to use your usual brand, bring it along. Most beachfront hotels have beach towels available, so there is usually no need to bring your own unless you are staying at a budget hotel, and even then you can usually sneak your bath towel from your room and use it at the beach, unless you're really looking to spread out on the beach and not get sandy. If you plan on sending postcards, don't forget to bring your addresses.

STAYING SAFE

Playa del Carmen is no longer a sleepy fishing village where everybody knows each other and nobody locks their doors. It is still a happy little town, though, where a lot of people know each other and not everyone locks their doors. Petty theft is the main problem, and tourists are advised to watch their belongings, lock their hotel rooms, and not leave valuables unattended on the beach or elsewhere.

For the most part, Playa is quite safe. It is best not to be on remote parts of the beach late at night, as incidents have been reported. Leave your jewels at home and, like anywhere else, don't flash large amounts of cash or be too showy with expensive equipment or electronic gadgets. Use the hotel safe whenever possible and do not leave valuables in plain

Sample Packing List for a Five-Night Trip (Male):

- 5 pairs of underwear
- 5 pairs of socks
- 3 pairs of shorts
- I bathing suit
- 4 T-shirts
- 4 nice shirts for nightlife
- I pair of light slacks
- I pair of jeans
- Toothpaste and toothbrush
- Shaving supplies
- Antiperspirant/deodorant
- Baseball hat
- Sandals/water shoes
- Walking shoes/evening shoes
- Medicines, sunscreen
- Camera, film, batteries (or digital camera and charger)
- Book, magazines
- MP3 player and travel speakers
- Dive mask and snorkel
- Passport, driver's license, credit card, cash
- Backpack

Sample Packing List for a Five-Night Trip (Female):

- 5 pairs of underwear
- 5 pairs of socks
- I pair of shorts
- 2 pairs of capri pants
- I pair of jeans
- 3 tank tops
- 2 bathing suits
- I swimsuit cover-up
- I pair of sandals
- I pair of walking shoes
- I pair of evening shoes
- I resort-wear outfit
- Toothpaste and toothbrush
- Shaving supplies
- Antiperspirant/deodorant
- Shampoo, conditioner, facial soap
- Body lotion sunscreen
- Sun hat
- Cosmetics, medicine
- Camera, film, batteries (or digital camera and charger)
- MP3 player and headphones
- Book, magazines
- Travel journal
- Dive mask and snorkel
- Passport, driver's license, credit card, cash
- Beach bag

view in your hotel room or rental car. Report suspicious activity at your hotel to the front desk and be alert of your surroundings. Men should carry their wallets in their front pockets on crowded streets, and women should ensure their bags are fully closed and not swinging freely.

There have been reports of drug running, gang activity, and associated crime and violence in the area. If you go looking for trouble, you'll have a better chance of finding it. Visitors are strongly advised to keep their noses clean and to stay well away from any obvious trouble or precarious situations. Do not travel into the destitute neighborhoods, especially at night. Do not associate with questionable individuals, and stay away from problem areas.

The Tourist Police hut, at Quinta at 10th Street, is manned nearly 24 hours a day and is the base for Playa's tourist police force. Most officers are bilingual and can help with any problems you have. They patrol the beach and the main roads in town and are well respected by the locals.

The tourist police are happy to help.

WEATHER

Month	High Temp.	Low Temp.	Ocean Temp.	Rainfall
January	80°F	66°F	75°F	3.75 inches
February	81°F	67°F	76°F	2.25 inches
March	83°F	70°F	77°F	1.75 inches
April	84°F	72°F	78°F	1.75 inches
May	87°F	76°F	80°F	4.75 inches
June	88°F	77°F	83°F	7.75 inches
July	89°F	77°F	85°F	4.25 inches
August	89°F	76°F	85°F	4.25 inches
September	88°F	75°F	84°F	9.00 inches
October	86°F	73°F	82°F	8.50 inches
November	83°F	71°F	81°F	3.75 inches
December	81°F	68°F	79°F	4.25 inches

Playa del Carmen lies just north of the tropics, which start at 20 degrees north latitude. Its actual coordinates are 20°36'30" N, 87°04'30" W, making its official designation subtropical. Don't let that fool you, though—the weather is definitely what most would consider to be tropical. Hot sunny days, sporadic rain showers, high humidity, balmy evenings, and warm ocean breezes are the norm. Summertime highs sometimes reach 100 degrees Fahrenheit with 90 percent humidity, while evenings in the low 60s are common during the winter months, especially when the north winds bring down the remnants of cold fronts across the Gulf of Mexico.

A storm brews over Playa.

June, September, and October are the rainiest months, when it seems to shower almost every day. The monsoonlike rains can come down quite hard, though the showers usually come and go, rarely washing out a whole day of fun in the sun. On the contrary, the rains are welcomed, since they tend to drop the sometimes-stifling temperature a few degrees. Hurricane season is June through November and usually passes without incident, though it's always best to watch the forecast and change your plans accordingly, because being stuck in a foreign land during a serious storm is a scary thing. Most hotels track the weather and will advise guests several days in advance of an approaching storm.

The Cancún airport has had to shut down on several occasions due to high winds and driving rains, leaving tourists to settle in and batten down the hatches with the locals. As long as the storm isn't too serious, though, tourists and locals alike turn the storm-motivated camaraderie into a genuine hurricane party.

Travel to the Riviera Maya is not as seasonal as in some resort destinations, since it attracts such a varied base of travelers. That said, hotel occupancy rates and prices do tend to fluctuate during the year. The year starts off in high season, which lasts from January through April, as Americans get tired of the cold weather back home and head south for a tropical vacation. Low season is May and June, when European travel is at a minimum and most Americans are enjoying comfortable warm weather at home. This is the least expensive time to travel and there are the most singles and student travelers at this time.

Hurricanes of the Riviera Maya

1951, Hurricane Charlie: Made landfall in the Riviera Maya with 125 mph winds.

1955, Hurricane Janet: Walloped the tiny town of Xcalak and Chetumal.

1967, Hurricane Beulah: Came ashore as a category 2, causing widespread damage.

1980, Hurricane Allen: Weakened as it approached the region, sparing it from harm.

1988, Hurricane Gilbert: Smashed into Cozumel with 170 mph winds and a 15-foot storm surge, caused more than $80 million in damage on the island alone, stranded a 125-foot Cuban freighter (the Portachernera) on the beach in Cancún, and killed more than 300 people after it crossed the Yucatán and hit northern Mexico.

1995, Hurricane Roxanne: Slammed into the Riviera Maya with 115 mph winds.

1998, Hurricane Mitch: This massive storm was expected to hit the area but curved away. An American tourist was killed in a boating accident near Cancún related to the rough water.

2003, Hurricane Claudette: Skirted the area with tropical storm-speed winds before continuing on to Texas.

2004, Hurricane Ivan: Made a beeline for the Yucatán, causing heavy rains and high waves along the coast, before curving north and slamming Florida.

2005, Hurricane Emily: Struck Cozumel as a category 4 storm, then crossed the Riviera Maya near Puerto Aventuras, causing widespread damage, some severe, though the area quickly cleaned up and recovered.

2005, Hurricane Wilma: Just three months after Emily, Wilma became the most intense hurricane ever in the Atlantic Basin. The eye lingered over Cozumel and Cancún for nearly a day, causing severe damage to waterfront areas and flooding much of the region.

2007, Hurricane Dean: Made landfall in the middle of the night just north of Chetumal and Mahahual, south of the Riviera Maya, as a Category 5 storm, making it the most intense Atlantic hurricane to make landfall in 20 years. Nearly 150,000 residents evacuated to shelters. Some small towns were cut off for days and about a third of the hotels in Tulum received at least moderate damage.

Hurricane Gilbert damaged many homes and businesses, such as this restaurant, which was abandoned.

CancunValet: Helping You Use Your Vacation Time Wisely

If you're staying at a condo and would rather spend your time on the beach than in the grocery store, consider using CancunValet to do your shopping for you. Through an online ordering process, select your groceries (including beer, liquor, and other miscellaneous goods) and have them delivered to you for a fee.

Visitors can also rent strollers, boogie boards, coolers, VCRs, DVD players, wheelchairs, highchairs, and cribs. In addition, the company rents mobile phones. Numbers can be assigned before your trip, so you can give your number to your contacts back home before you leave.

Log on to www.cancunvalet.com for more information and online transactions. Daily minimums and delivery fees apply.

July and August are the months when many Americans take their summer vacations, diminishing room availability and driving up prices. A second low season starts in September and lasts through the middle of December. The most expensive time of year is the winter holiday season, starting in mid-December and lasting through the New Year holiday. Prices at hotels can fluctuate 50 percent or more, as high demand elevates prices during high season. In general, though, prices for meals, tours, and transportation do not fluctuate.

Whenever you go, you'll notice that temperatures on the beachfront are a few degrees cooler than they are a couple of miles inland. If you have a trip planned to the interior for horseback riding, hiking, jungle exploring, or visiting the ruins, you'll feel noticeably hotter than you do at your beachside hotel.

TIME ZONE

The Mayan Riviera and the entire state of Quintana Roo are on Mexico Central Time, which is GMT-6 hours. This is also the same as U.S. Central Time. The country of Mexico honors Daylight Savings Time beginning on the first Sunday in April and ending on the last Sunday in October, which is shifted a couple weeks from the way it is done in the United States.

EMERGENCY NUMBERS

Police, fire, or ambulance: 066 (free call from any phone)
Red Cross: 984-873-1233 or 065
Cancún Hyperbaric Chamber: 998-884-1202
Hospiten Hospital: 984-803-1002
Playa del Carmen Hyperbaric Chamber: 984-873-1365

Medical problems require immediate attention, whether you're on vacation or not. If trouble strikes when you're in Playa del Carmen, visitors can call on **Emergencias Medicas del Caribe** for 24-hour emergency medical care, ambulance service, outcalls, and clinic care. The company provides free care in most situations, though there are fees for seeing a specialist. The hotline number is 984-879-4745. The clinic is located next to Highway 307 on Constituyentes Avenue at 45th Street.

Another ambulance service, **Akumal Medical Service,** promises 24-hour emergency response to hotels, villas, and condos throughout the Riviera Maya, along with care provided by English-speaking Dr. Nestor Mendoza Gutierrez. The urgent care number is 044-984-806-4616. The clinic is located in Akumal.

Distance Chart
(NOTE: All distances are expressed in miles.)

	Cancún	Puerto Juárez	Punta Sam	Puerto Morelos	Playa del Carmen	Xcaret	Paamul	Puerto Aventuras	Kantenah	Yalku	Akumal	Chemuyil	Xcacel	Xel-Ha	Tulum	Cobá	Chichén Itzá	Mérida	Uxmal	Isla Mujeres	Contoy	Holbox	Cozumel
Cancún	0	3	7	22	42	46	51	54	60	61	66	68	74	76	82	108	111	196	246	3	22	41	45
Puerto Juárez	3	0	4	26	46	49	54	58	63	64	69	71	78	79	85	111	114	199	249	3	20	39	48
Punta Sam	7	4	0	30	50	54	59	62	68	69	73	76	82	84	89	116	119	203	253	3	15	34	53
Puerto Morelos	22	26	30	0	20	24	29	32	38	39	43	46	52	54	59	86	114	205	254	26	44	63	19
Playa del Carmen	42	46	50	20	0	4	9	12	18	19	23	26	32	34	39	66	134	218	268	46	64	83	11
Xcaret	46	49	54	24	4	0	6	9	14	16	20	23	29	31	36	63	138	222	272	49	68	86	14
Puerto Aventuras	54	58	62	32	12	9	6	0	6	7	11	14	20	22	28	54	165	232	282	58	76	95	23
Akumal	66	69	73	43	23	19	14	11	6	4	0	3	9	11	16	43	176	243	293	69	88	106	34
Xel-Ha	76	79	84	54	34	30	25	22	16	15	11	8	2	0	6	32	187	254	304	79	98	117	45
Tulum	82	85	89	59	39	36	31	28	22	21	16	14	8	6	0	26	193	259	309	85	104	123	51
Cobá	108	111	116	86	66	62	58	55	49	48	44	41	35	33	28	0	219	286	336	138	156	175	77
Chetumal	239	242	246	216	196	193	188	184	179	178	173	171	164	163	157	129	353	419	469	242	261	279	145
Chichén Itzá	111	114	119	114	134	138	143	146	151	153	157	159	166	168	173	199	0	67	117	114	133	152	156
Mérida	178	181	186	181	201	204	209	213	218	219	224	226	233	234	240	266	67	0	50	181	200	219	223
Uxmal	28	231	236	231	251	267	259	263	268	269	274	276	283	284	290	316	117	50	0	234	250	269	273
Isla Mujeres	3	3	3	26	46	49	54	58	61	66	68	72	74	81	83	88	114	181	234	0	19	38	51
Cozumel	45	48	53	19	11	14	20	23	29	30	34	37	43	45	51	77	156	223	273	51	55	74	0

Playa del Carmen Fire Department: 984-879-3670
Medica de Carmen Hospital: 984-873-0885
American Hospital in Playa del Carmen: 984-884-6133
Ameri-Med Ambulance Service: 984-881-3400
Playa del Carmen Police: 984-873-4000
Highway Police: 998-884-1107

Other Helpful Numbers:

Directory Assistance: 020
Cancún Airport: 984-873-0804
Bus station: 984-873-0109
Cozumel Ferry Office (Ultramar): 984-803-5581
Cozumel Ferry Office (Mexico Water Jet): 984-879-3112
Taxi office, Playa del Carmen: 984-873-0032

U.S. Consulates

Cancún (998-883-0272), Plaza Caracol Two, second level, No. 320–323, Boulevard
    Kukulkán, km 8.5, Zona Hotelera.
Cozumel (987-872-4574), Plaza Villa Mar en El Centro, Plaza Principal (Parque Juárez
    between Rafael Melgar and Fifth Avenue), second floor, Locales 8 and 9.

LANGUAGE

Spanish is the official language of Mexico and is the primary language spoken in the
Riviera Maya. Playa del Carmen has developed into a very international city, though, and
it's quite common to hear French, Italian, German, and other languages spoken on the
street, in the restaurants, and on the beach. People from all over the world have fallen in
love with Playa and have chosen to make it their home. Many of the best restaurants are
owned and operated by foreigners who have brought their cuisine with them. During your
visit, you'll have the opportunity to meet and make friends with people from all over,
which is one of the things that makes Playa so great.

Many natives, particularly those originally from the Yucatán or Quintana Roo, still speak
the ancient language of the Mayans, though most locals in the area are recent transplants
from elsewhere in the republic, with many coming from Mexico City, Veracruz,
Guadalajara, and other cities where Mayan is not spoken. English is taught in schools, and
most tourism employees have at least a rudimentary ability to speak it. The larger hotels
offer English classes to all employees, who at least learn the basics. Don't expect your average cab driver, hotel maid, or police officer to be fluent, though, so if you have something
important to convey and you are not proficient in Spanish, you may need to enlist the help
of a translator. Remember that you're in their country, so the onus is really on you to find a
way to effectively communicate.

If you're in town for a week or more, you may want to take some Spanish lessons. **International House** (984-803-3388; www.ihrivieramaya.com; 14th Street between Quinta and
10th Avenue, Playa del Carmen) is primarily an English school for locals, but Spanish
classes are also offered. **Playalingua** (984-873-3876; www.playalingua.com; 20th Street
between Quinta and 10th Avenue, Playa del Carmen) is a well-respected local school offer-

Words and Phrases

English	Spanish	English	Spanish
Another one	Otra	Lobster	Langosta
ATM	Cajero automático	Luggage	Equipaje
Bathroom	Baño	Lunch	Comida
Beach	Playa	Money	Dinero
Beef	Carne de rés	Money exchange	Cámbio de dinero
Beer	Cerveza	More	Más
Big	Grande	My name is	Me llamo
Boat	Lancha	Nice to meet you	Mucho gusto
Bottled water	Agua en botella	Orange juice	Jugo de naranja
Breakfast	Desayuno	Please	Por favór
Bus	Autobús	Post office	El correo
Car rental	Renta de autos	Rain	Llúvia
Check/bill	La cuenta	Scuba diving	Buceo
Chicken	Pollo	Shrimp	Camarón
Coffee with milk	Café con leche	Shuttle bus	Colectivo
Dinner	Cena	Sick	Enfermo
Downtown	El centro	Silly tourist	Turista loca
Drunk	Borracho	Small	Pequeña
Eat	Comer	Sunscreen	Bronceadora
Fishing	La pesca	Swim	Nadar
Goodbye	Adiós, hasta luego	Swimsuit	Traje de baño
Good morning	Buenos días	Tax	Impuestos
Good night	Buenas noches	Thank you	Graciás
Happy	Felíz	Tip	Propina
Hello	Hola	Towel	Toalla
How much	Cuánto	Waiter	Mesero
Ice	Hielo	Walk	Caminar
I want	Yo deseo	Why	Porqué
Lime	Limón	You're welcome	De nada

Try a Little Mayan

Hello, what's up?	Ba'ax ka wa'alik?	Hot pepper	Lik
What's going on?	Bix a bel?	Juice	K'aab
I'm fine.	Ma'alob.	Where	Tu'ux
See you later.	Taak tu lakin.	Plaza	K'íiwik
I'm just looking.	Chen tin wilik.	Thank you	Dios bo'otik
How much is it?	Bahúux leti'?	You're welcome	Mixba'al
Tastes good.	Ki'.		

ing crash courses in Spanish, cultural immersion opportunities, customized learning programs, scuba certification, home stays, and comfortable and affordable lodging on-site at its well-maintained inn with pool, courtyard, hammocks, art room, library, cafeteria, and Internet station. Weeklong courses run about $250. At **Solexico Spanish School** (984-873-0755 or 1-877-266-8988 (U.S.); www.solexico.com; 6th Street between 35th and 40th Avenues, Playa del Carmen), as its slogan states, you have the chance to "learn Spanish in paradise." Founded in 1997, this language school offers all levels of instruction, with a maximum of five students per instructor.

As a sign on the wall of the Señor Frog's bar says, we don't speak English, but we promise not to laugh at your Spanish. Not only is learning a bit of the local language a good way to win the favor of the locals you meet, but it can also be a lot of fun. You'll be amazed at how friendly the locals are, especially if you're trying to speak to them in their own language.

In Playa, as throughout Mexico, Americans are usually referred to as "gringos." Though it may sound a bit harsh to some Americans' ears, and in some Latin American countries it does have a negative connotation, it is not at all meant as a derogatory term in Mexico, so don't take offense. To the Mexicans, using the word *Americanos* is confusing and a bit offensive, since all residents of North, Central, and South America could be considered "Americans." Also, since the full name of the republic of Mexico is Los Estados Unidos de Mexico, or the United States of Mexico, it's also not quite adequate to use the textbook translation of *estadounidiense*, which is essentially "United Statesian," for citizens of the United States of America. Americans are sometimes referred to as *norteamericanos*, which means "North Americans," but that's not quite accurate either since it fails to distinguish between the United States and Canada, and the latter's citizens are known simply as *Canadienses*. So, embrace your inner "gringo" and don't consider it a negative label.

In this book, the word *American* is used to refer to residents of the United States.

RELIGION

The primary religion in the Riviera Maya is Catholicism, though many of the ancient rituals of the Mayans are alive and well, oftentimes intermingling with traditional Catholic practices, giving the region a bit of its own religion and associated customs. Services are offered in various denominations, and the larger hotels maintain a list of current services and worship schedules. Tourists are welcome at all ceremonies, provided they dress and act appropriately, and show respect for the local customs.

TRAVELING WITH PETS

Mexico allows the temporary importation of dogs and cats into the country, provided that the owner has an official letter from a veterinarian stating that the animal is healthy and current on all vaccinations. Most vets have a standard form that they can provide for such uses. Each airline has its own regulations, so it's best to check ahead if you are compelled to bring your pet on your trip.

Even if you figure out how to do it, taking your pet on a trip to the Riviera Maya may not be a great idea, anyway. Few hotels are equipped to accommodate travelers with pets, there are stray dogs that could carry disease, the weather can be quite hot, and unless you're able to babysit your pet at all times, you could run into trouble.

Las Palapas beach is an ideal spot for a casual wedding ceremony.

WEDDINGS IN PARADISE

If your idea of the perfect wedding is exchanging vows during a beachside ceremony with the sun going down, tropical flowers forming the aisle, a Mexican trio providing romantic music, and your guests dancing the salsa while they sip tequila, then getting married in the Mayan Riviera may be for you.

Though most weddings in the region are fairly casual outdoor affairs, the facilities and services exist to put on a spectacular formal ceremony for hundreds of guests, complete with all the traditions and comforts of a wedding in your own hometown. Both civil and religious ceremonies can be planned, depending on the preference of the bride and groom.

There are several independent wedding planners in town, in addition to the on-staff planners at the larger hotels. They can assist with all of the details, from cakes to flowers, from hotels to photography, and from rehearsals to receptions. Due to the legal requirements for foreigners getting married in Mexico, it is recommended that the couple arrive in Playa del Carmen at least three business days prior to their wedding day to file the necessary paperwork.

Legal Requirements for Getting Married in Mexico

At least two days before the ceremony, the couple must go to the local courthouse and present:

1. A valid tourist card (your temporary visa, issued at the airport).
2. A notarized copy of each person's birth certificate (must have a raised seal).
3. An official Spanish translation of the birth certificate (should be done locally by a court-approved translator).

4. A health certificate certifying blood type and AIDS/STD status. (The tests must be performed and certified by a court-approved facility.)
5. The proper court documents if either person is divorced or widowed.
6. Two witnesses, with valid passports showing name, age, address, and nationality.
7. Basic fees, which total about $475.

BEACH ETIQUETTE

All of the beaches in the Riviera Maya and throughout Mexico are federal property. No hotel can restrict access to the beach (from the water) or make up their own regulations about what you can and can't do. That being said, hotels do not have to allow you to cross their private property to get to the beach, and they can prevent access to the hotel from the beachfront. Many hotels set up a cordoned-off area or supply beach chairs or shade umbrellas for the exclusive use of their guests, and this is allowed by law.

Going nude or even topless is not permitted by Mexican decency laws. Topless sunbathing is tolerated (and sometimes appreciated) by the local police in many areas, though, and many visitors to Playa del Carmen and the Riviera Maya—

Top Five Places to Pop the Question
• The cliffs at the Mayan ruins of Tulum
• On a private sailboat in Soliman Bay
• On the beach at Playa Maroma
• On top of the rocks at the Xaman Ha Beach in Playacar
• In the canals of the Sian Ka'an Biosphere
(List courtesy of Brenda Alfaro, owner of Ajua Weddings in the Riviera Maya. For more information log on to www.ajuaweddings.com.)

Top Five Places to Host a Wedding Reception or Other Special Event
• **Ajua Maya Lobster & Steak House**, Playa del Carmen: Great food, playful waiters, live music (see chapter 2)
• **Hotel Básico**, Playa del Carmen: Choose the patio seafood restaurant or the exclusive rooftop terrace (see chapter 2)
• **Kartabar**, Playa del Carmen: A trendy spot for food and drinks in the middle of Playa's party zone (see chapter 2)
• **Maroma Resort & Spa**, Punta Maroma: Hosts upscale events that your guests will be proud to attend (see chapter 1)
• **Rancho Punta Venado**: A private beachfront ranch with all the necessary facilities (see chapter 4)

particularly Europeans—enjoy this freedom. To avoid any trouble with the law, it is best to restrict such European-style sunbathing to times and places when there are other people doing the same. In Playa del Carmen, for instance, the beaches adjacent to the ferry dock are popular with local families and children, and tourists should be respectful of the local customs and refrain from going topless in these areas. Farther south of the dock, closer to the Hotel Gran Porto Real, topless tanning becomes more of the norm, and visitors should not have any problem, except for an occasional passing gawker. To the north, most of the beaches are topless-friendly, though it is more uncommon in front of the more family-oriented hotels.

Elsewhere in the Mayan Riviera, the local attitude will dictate whether or not topless sunbathing is acceptable. On most beaches it is no problem, though in some areas it is frowned upon. The general rule is that the more locals or families, the less appropriate it is to go topless. Full nudity is generally frowned upon in all but a few specific areas, namely in front of the nude resorts, such as Hidden Beach, Desire Resort, and Playa Secreto.

The Mayan Riviera still has some relatively deserted beaches, accessible only by a four-wheel-drive vehicle and a bit of courage. Though these beaches do see occasional patrols from the Mexican Army or local police, discreet travelers can generally enjoy the freedom of being one with nature, however they choose to define it.

YEARLY EVENTS CALENDAR

January 1, New Year's Day.

January 6, Day of the Three Kings. A traditional day of Christmas gift giving, marking the Christian holiday of Epiphany, and the day when the three wise men arrived to give gifts to the baby Jesus.

January 10, Constitution Day for Quintana Roo. Banks are closed, but not much else happens.

January 11, Anniversary of the Reinstatement of Quintana Roo as a Territory.

February 5, Constitution Day. A federal holiday, but there's not much social celebration.

February 14, Day of Lovers and Friends. Similar to Valentine's Day in the United States. Street vendors sell flowers and balloons; restaurants offer special romantic meals for couples.

February 24, Flag Day. A ceremony is held in Cancún and Cozumel at the site of their super-size flags.

February–March, Carnaval. Fluctuates with the Christian calendar. It's mostly celebrated in Cozumel and Playa del Carmen, where school children dress in colorful costumes and parade through the streets. In Playa, there's a week of festivities and impromptu parades, capped by a long procession down Quinta and up 12th Street to the municipal park, where a live music stage, food vendors, midway games, and revelers keep the party going late into the night. Mostly locals, but tourists are welcomed.

March 20 or 21 (depending on the year), Vernal Equinox. This marks the first official day of spring, when daylight and night are the same length. It's celebrated at Chichén Itzá, where the shadow of the serpent Kukulkán snakes down the side of the temple when the sunlight hits it just right.

March 21, Birthday of Former President and Reform Movement Leader Benito Juárez. Juárez's name pops up frequently in the Riviera Maya, in street names, building names, and statues. The name of Playa's main highway connector road, for instance, is Benito Juárez Avenue. All banks and government offices are closed, but most tourist businesses stay open.

March or April, Easter and Holy Week. This is a very popular travel time for Mexican families since schoolchildren get two weeks' vacation. The holiday, which celebrates Christ's resurrection, is traditionally celebrated even more than Christmas.

April 21–May 2, Sol a Sol Regatta. Yearly sailboat race from St. Petersburg, Florida, to Isla Mujeres, north of Cancún. Live music, street festival, and celebrations.

May 1, Labor Day. National holiday.

May 5, Cinco de Mayo. Celebration of Mexican independence from France during the 1862 Battle of Puebla. Not as widely celebrated as the September 16 holiday marking independence from Spain.

Some Things Are Cheaper South of the Border

Though the price of meals, drinks, and many everyday purchases are relatively close to what you'll find back home, some services are still a bargain south of the border. Here are a few ideas of how you can save some money while you're in the Riviera Maya:

Get new eyeglasses. Bring a written prescription or even a pair of well-calibrated glasses, and the technicians at area eyewear shops can match your prescription in a wide variety of frames and lenses for a fraction of what you'd pay at home.

Manicures and pedicures. Want acrylic nails or just need a fresh mani/pedi? Prices are half or less of what you'd pay back home at salons catering to locals.

Watch repair. If you have an old watch that needs fixing and you've been putting it off, bring it on vacation. Drop it off one day and pick it up the next, and it'll be ticking like it was new. Watch shops in Playa are common a few blocks back from the beach, and the skilled craftsmen can fix almost anything.

Shoe repair. Shoes falling apart? Stop by a local shoe repair shop, and you can have new soles, heels, or other repairs done while you're away enjoying the ruins at Tulum. The price will be significantly less than back home, and the craftsmanship is top-rate.

Prescription medications. Local pharmacies will gladly fill prescriptions from US doctors. Don't have a prescription? In many cases, one can be issued on the spot, for a limited charge.

May, Cancún Jazz Festival (date varies). Annual music festival sponsored by the Cancún Hotel Association.

June 1, Navy Day. Honors sailors lost at sea. Celebrations vary by municipality.

Last weekend of June, Playa del Carmen Sportfishing Tournament. This major fishing tournament helps to fill the hotels and restaurants, but the town doesn't get too involved.

July, Reggae Fest (date varies). Reggae bands from Mexico and around the world meet in Playa for a weeklong beach party, with concerts, food, and drink.

August, Dia de la Asuncion Festival, Oxkutzcab, Yucatán (date varies). Weeklong Assumption Day celebration near Loltún Cave, about three hours from Playa del Carmen.

Second weekend of August, Ferragosto Italian Food Festival (date varies). Restaurant specials and a yearly "largest pizza in the world" exhibition, where restaurants on Quinta pitch in to create (and then serve) a pizza that spans some 6 blocks through town. Coincides with a similar celebration in Italy, so the town's Italian population celebrates all weekend at the many Italian-owned restaurants and bars.

August 17, Isla Mujeres Founding Day. Locals celebrate the date of their town's founding with parades, parties, live music, and street dancing. Underwater ceremony at Los Manchones Reef, where a large bronze cross is attached to the coral.

September 1, Presidential State of the Union Address. Mexicans love politics, and many stay riveted to their TVs to watch the speech. Bars and stores are not allowed to serve alcohol until it's over, but it usually turns into a party afterward.

September 16, National Holiday Marking Mexico's Independence from Spain in 1821. Widely celebrated with parades, fireworks, and street parties. Much more important to locals than Cinco de Mayo.

September 22 or 23, Autumnal Equinox. Marks the first day of fall. Date varies according to the year.

September 27–October 13, Fiesta de Cristo de las Ampollas in Mérida. Religious festival honoring a sacred relic housed in the main cathedral.

October 12, Dia de la Raza, or Columbus Day. Celebrated throughout Mexico as a day to honor the many types of people that make up the country's population.

October, Isla Mujeres International Music Festival (date varies). Twelve-day event with music and dance performances featuring locals and invited guests from around the world.

October 31, All Souls' Day. Festivities inspired by the American Halloween celebration.

November, Latin Jazz Fest (date varies). This three-day festival brings together jazz musicians from around the world for concerts, dancing, and all-night parties.

November 1–2, Day of the Dead. Mexico's larger Halloween-time holiday to honor the dead. Friends and relatives gather at the graves of loved ones to celebrate their lives and honor their deaths.

November 20, Mexican Revolution Day. Marks the 1910 Revolution of Mexico. It's mostly a federal holiday, with little local observance.

December 8, Feast of the Immaculate Conception. Religious holiday celebrated through-out the Riviera Maya.

December 24, Nochebuena, or Christmas Eve. A religious and social holiday with parades and street parties.

December 25–January 2, Christmas Week. Weeklong festival with candlelight processions, Catholic mass, nightly parties, and religious ceremonies.

December 31, New Year's Eve. Many bars offer drink specials and all-you-can-eat specials. At the stroke of midnight, it is good luck to eat 12 grapes, one for each month of the new year. Nightclubs stay open until dawn.

IMPORTANT TELEPHONE NUMBERS

Lost credit cards:
American Express, 1-800-333-3211 (U.S.)
MasterCard, 1-800-307-7309
Visa, 1-800-847-2911 (U.S.)

Long-distance service:
AT&T, 1-800-288-4472 (U.S.)
MCI, 1-800-021-8000 (U.S.)
Sprint, 1-800-877-8000 (U.S.)

Airlines:
Aerocaribe, 998-884-2000
Aerocozumel, 998-884-4000
Aeromexico, 1-800-021-4000 (U.S.) or 998-287-1860
Allegro (charter), 998-887-3459
American, 1-800-904-6000 (U.S.) or 998-886-0086
British Airways, 998-866-0554
Magnicharters (charter), 998-884-0600

1

The Riviera Maya— North of Playa del Carmen

The cities and towns of the Yucatán Peninsula and the Riviera Maya are covered in this book following a north-to-south orientation. Many of the locations are found along Highway 307, which parallels the coastline as it traverses the region from Cancún to the north down to Tulum and beyond in the south. Whenever possible, addresses are given using Highway 307 as a primary reference point, which is especially useful for self-guided travelers who choose to explore the region on their own.

The region north of Playa del Carmen is highlighted by the islands of Isla Holbox, Isla Contoy, and Isla Mujeres, plus the resort city of Cancún and the growing town of Puerto Morelos, which marks the official start of the Riviera Maya and is the midway point between Cancún and Playa del Carmen. Isla Cozumel is also included in this section, though the island's main town, San Miguel, is located due east of Playa del Carmen.

Most travelers to the Riviera Maya arrive via Cancún, which is one of the world's most popular mega-resorts. The small islands to the north of Cancún offer an abundance of relaxation, sunshine, and pristine beaches without the crowds so often associated with tropical vacations. Cozumel, meanwhile, is a scuba diver's dream, where shore dives, wall dives, and night dives can all be done in a single day.

Isla Holbox (105 miles northwest of Cancún)

Holbox (Mayan for "black hole"), a long, narrow island 7 miles off the northern coast of the Yucatán, is one of the region's lesser known and underappreciated destinations. It has a year-round population of less than 750, including descendants of the island's original eight families. It is said to have been settled by pirates who used it as a hideout and then ended up making friends with the local population and decided to stay.

The island is a come-as-you-are hideaway for ultracasual vacationing. If you consider the Riviera Maya to be the land of *mañana* (tomorrow), then Holbox would be sometime next week. It's doubtful that anyone has ever worn a tie here, unless it was some kind of joke. Most locals don't even wear shoes since the roads are powdery sand. In fact, the mayor led an effort to pave the streets a few years ago, but the locals voted it down.

Since the island faces the Gulf of Mexico, it does not have the turquoise water that is

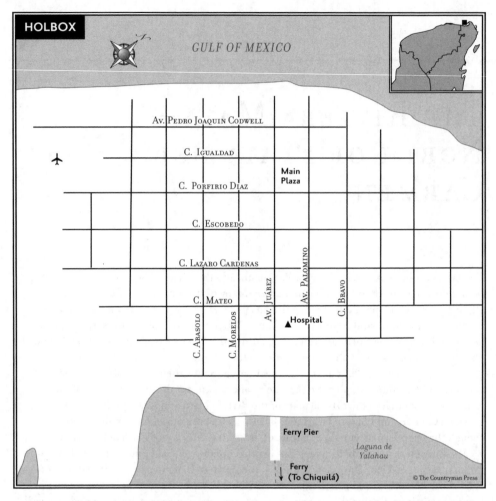

common in the Riviera Maya. It is more of a greenish murky color, though there are some areas clear enough for snorkeling. Because of the currents and the island's location, thousands of shells wash on shore at each high tide. Many of them are complete, with no breaks, making them highly prized for gatherers.

The island has no cars, just electric carts, bikes, and mopeds. Locals operate the handful of restaurants, bars, and inns. There's also a basketball court, playground, church, general store, and even an Internet café. Others go fishing and lobstering and sell their catches each day at the beach. There are no banks or ATMs, and most businesses accept only cash. From May to September, whale sharks pass by just offshore of the island, and tour boats can take you close enough to see them frolic in the water, or you can even don your mask and snorkel and swim right with them. Tourists while away the day on the beach or go windsurfing, sailing, fishing, snorkeling, and diving; several dive sites are reachable via a short boat ride. Local dive and fishing guides can be hired at the boat dock, and rental equipment is available.

Yalahán Lagoon, on the sheltered side of the island, features a mangrove swamp, flamingos, schools of dolphins, and a freshwater spring just up from the beach. It is a popular gathering spot for locals and tourists alike. In the times of the Mayans, it was believed to have curative properties, and natives would come from miles away to rejuvenate and refresh.

Holbox was hit particularly hard by Hurricane Wilma, which pounded the tiny island for hours when it slammed through the region in late 2005. The hotels, restaurants, and shops were flooded and the wind damage was extensive.

GETTING THERE

The island of Holbox is about a three-hour drive from Cancún and then 7 miles offshore. If you're lucky enough to fly there, the airstrip is just a few blocks from the town plaza. (For more information about plane tours to Holbox, log on to the Web site for **Aerosaab**, which has an office in Playa del Carmen, at www.aerosaab.com.) Otherwise, you must first get to the village of Chiquila and then take a ferry to the island. Chiquila can be reached by bus or car from the Riviera Maya. If you're in your own car, a secured lot is available for only $2 a day.

To drive to Chiquila from Riviera Maya, go north on Highway 307, which parallels the coast. Once you pass through Cancún, take Highway 180 west to the town of El Ideal, and then start watching for signs to Holbox, which will lead you to an unnamed road going north to Chiquila.

If you're traveling there by bus, buses depart from the main Cancún bus terminal for Chiquila daily at 8 AM, 12:30 PM, and 1:30 PM. The bus ride takes three hours and costs $6. Once you've reached Chiquila, ferry service to Holbox is available at 6 AM, 8 AM, 10 AM, noon, 2 PM, 4 PM, 5 PM, and 7 PM. Return trips to Chiquila depart at 5 AM, 7 AM, 9 AM, 11 AM, 1 PM, 3 PM, 4 PM, and 6 PM. The trip takes 30 minutes and costs $4 per person. A water taxi is available also and costs $20 for up to seven passengers, departing whenever you want.

LODGING

Accommodations in Holbox are not luxurious. If you're looking for Italian sheets, cold air-conditioning, a Jacuzzi in the bathroom, and a terry cloth robe, you're best off just visiting the island as a day trip and then returning to Cancún or the Riviera Maya. But if you're comfortable sleeping on a hammock and taking quick showers before the water runs cold, you'll do just fine in Holbox.

The cheapest way to stay the night is to rent one of the Mayan-style beach *palapas* available on the island's north side. For around $10, you can get a place to put your things and a hammock to sleep in, either under the stars or in a small hut.

Bathrooms are communal and not in the best of shape. Another low-budget solution is to rent a room in a local house. To go this route, just ask any cab driver or waiter or pretty much any local, and they are sure to know someone who has a room for rent. The cost for doing this ranges from $15 to $25 and includes a private room, shared bathroom, and usually a meal or two with the host family.

Lodging Prices

$	less than $75 per night
$$	$75 to $125 per night
$$$	$126 to $225 per night
$$$$	$226 to $350 per night
$$$$$	more than $350 per night

AMIGO HOUSE

www.isla-holbox.net
Two blocks from the beach, by the volley-ball courts

Opened in 2004, this bright and cheery house features king or double beds, air-conditioning, ceiling fans, tile floors, CD player, color TV with DVD player, and shared kitchen. Accommodates up to eight guests. $$

ESMERALDA HOTEL

www.esmeralda-hotel.com
Cancun office 998-845-4234
Playa Blanca

Rooms have tropical décor, with wooden furnishings, pastel colors, air-conditioning, and ocean-view balconies. $$

HOTELITO CASA LAS TORTUGAS

www.holboxcasalastortugas.com
998-875-2129
Playa Blanca

Swing in a hammock and watch the day go by at this ultra-relaxing inn on the beach. Stay in a two-story bungalow, a junior suite with refrigerator, or the romantic suite with king bed and private balcony with hammock. $$ to $$$. Air conditioning can be added for an extra $10/night.

HOTEL PUERTO HOLBOX

On the beach, 3 blocks from town

This lodging has four simple rooms, hot water, air-conditioning, and a balcony. $ to $$.

VILLA FLAMINGOS

Playa Blanca

On the beach, Villa Flamingos is composed of 10 thatched-roof bungalows with ceiling fans, double beds, and private bathrooms. There is also a pool, kayaks, and bikes for guest use. $$.

XALOC RESORT

800-508-7923 or 1-800-728-9098 (U.S.)
Playa Norte

With 18 rustic rooms and a public living room, Xaloc also has air-conditioning and a pool. Rates: $$ to $$$; including breakfast.

DINING

EDELYN

On the main tourist street

If you're looking for lobster, Edelyn is the top place in town. It is known for having the freshest and best, nearly year-round. Moderate.

PINOCCHIO'S

On the main plaza

Popular with the island's European, Canadian, and American ex-pats, this restaurant serves grilled steaks and fresh seafood. Moderate.

VIVA ZAPATA

On the main tourist street

This two-story open-air restaurant has a thatched roof and serves lobster, whole fish, shrimp, and traditional Mexican fare. Inexpensive.

Isla Contoy (25 miles north of Cancún, by boat)

This bird sanctuary and wildlife refuge is offshore from the northeastern tip of the Yucatán Peninsula. There are no bars or restaurants, no hotels, no roads, and very few facilities. A

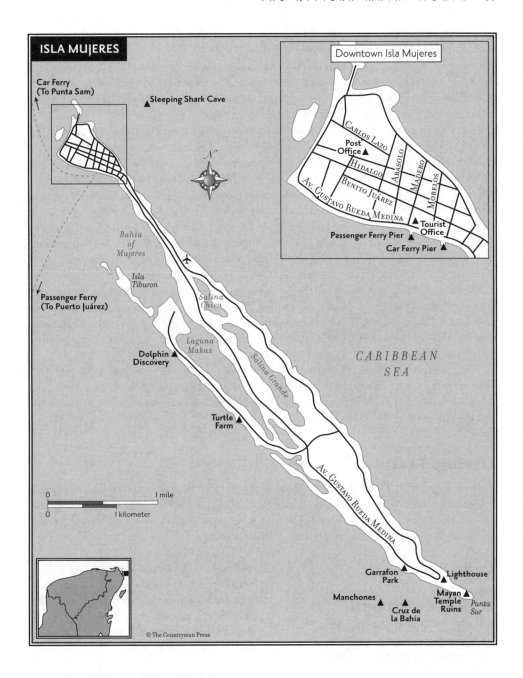

ISLA MUJERES

Car Ferry
(To Punta Sam)

Sleeping Shark Cave

Downtown Isla Mujeres

CARLOS LAZO
Post
Office
HIDALGO
BENITO JUÁREZ
Av. GUSTAVO RUEDA MEDINA
ABASOLO
MADERO
MORELOS
Tourist
Office
Passenger Ferry Pier
Car Ferry Pier

Bahía
of
Mujeres

Isla
Tiburon

Passenger Ferry
(To Puerto Juárez)

Salina
Chica

Laguna
Makax

Dolphin
Discovery

Salina Grande

CARIBBEAN
SEA

Turtle
Farm

Av. GUSTAVO RUEDA MEDINA

0   1 mile
0   1 kilometer

Garrafon
Park
Lighthouse

Manchones
Cruz de
la Bahia
Mayan
Temple
Ruins
Punta
Sur

© The Countryman Press

small group of Mexican Marines runs a lighthouse, museum, lookout tower, and outpost, but there are no other full-time inhabitants. It is a popular nesting ground for sea turtles, and occasionally naturalists will camp out and care for them and watch for poachers, backed by the Marines. There are a few rolling hills and a long deserted beach, ideal for strolling and snorkeling. Visitors can arrive by private boat or with a tour group.

Isla Mujeres (15 miles north of Cancún, by boat)

Once a sacred pilgrimage site for the Mayan natives, 5-mile-long Isla Mujeres is now a top spot for travelers seeking sunny days, pristine beaches, good food, tropical bars, and a casual lifestyle that you just can't get on the mainland. The island was named by Spanish conquistador Francisco Hernandez de Cordoba, who visited the island in 1517 to look for gold and other riches. Though he didn't find precious metals, he did discover a large number of Mayan statuettes of women, which had been used in religious ceremonies. It was then that he named the spot Isla Mujeres, which translates to "Island of the Women." Other visitors included pirates, among them Jean Lafitte, and then later the island was discovered by hippies and bohemians who used it as a place to get away from civilization and commune with nature and all it has to offer. Today, the island's few narrow roads are best explored in golf carts, which are available for rent by the hour or by the day. The top tourist attraction is Garrafon Park, a snorkeling paradise with a shallow protected cove and a coral reef heavily populated with fish and other marine life. Other draws include a Spanish fort, a museum, the town square, shopping boutiques, and tranquil beaches. Snorkeling, fishing, and diving are the main activities, and boats leave from the municipal pier throughout the day on various excursions. The island was partially destroyed by Hurricane Wilma in 2005. The infrastructure was badly damaged and the entire island was incommunicado for nearly a week. It has been rebuilt and is once again welcoming guests to its tropical shores.

There is an HSBC Bank across from the ferry dock, and there are several ATMs and money-exchange houses in the downtown area. There is a clinic near the town square (Centro de Salud, 998-877-0117), and the Red Cross provides ambulance service throughout the island (998-877-0280).

GETTING THERE

Ferries depart from Puerto Juárez to Isla Mujeres every 30 minutes from 6:30 AM to 8:30 PM, and again at 11:30 PM. They return from Isla Mujeres to Puerto Juárez every 30 minutes from 6 AM to 8 PM, and again at 9 PM. The cost is $3.50 per person. The boat departs from the main dock in Puerto Juárez, 5 miles north of Cancún.

LODGING

✪ CASA DE LOS SUEÑOS

998-877-0651 or 1-866-705-1691 (U.S.)
www.casadelossuenosresort.com
On the road to Garrafon, Isla Mujeres

This exclusive property offers 8 rooms with ocean views, private terraces, air-conditioning, premium bedding, and original decorations. There is a gym, yoga instructor, bicycles for guest use, pool, snorkeling, kayaking, and hiking. The on-site Spa Zenter offers a range of traditional and regional treatments, including an aloe vera body wrap, a seaweed detox wrap, and a nourishing ocean mud wrap. Rates: $$$$; include complimentary morning coffee delivered to your room, continental breakfast, and a stocked minibar.

CIELITO LINDO BEACH STUDIOS

998-877-0585
78 Rueda Medina

Right across the beach and just 4 blocks from the ferry dock, Cielito Lindo, once a private residence, is divided into two separate guest apartments, each with air-conditioning, satellite TV, ceiling fans, living room, kitchenette, coffeemaker, and ocean-view balcony. It's a great place if you want to stay a while and don't want the hassle of dealing with a standard hotel. $$. Three-night minimum; cash only.

HOTEL & HOSTEL POSADA DEL MAR
998-877-0044
www.posadadelmar.com
Avenue Rueda Medina, #15

If you're looking for a beachfront hotel but don't need anything big and fancy, try the Posada del Mar. It has 50 contemporary-style rooms with bright tropical decor, air-conditioning and fans, phone and TV, private balcony, and in-room safe. There's even a pool and beach club with *palapa* bar. The on-site Pinguino's restaurant serves three meals per day. Rates: $. The hotel also operates a few rooms a couple blocks away as a hostel, with safe rooms for budget travelers for $9 per person per night.

HOTEL BUCANEROS
998-877-1222
www.bucaneros.com
Downtown Isla Mujeres

With only 16 rooms, Bucaneros is a friendly inn with a local feel. The staff is helpful and friendly and is happy to recommend restaurants and bars located nearby. The beach is a 10-minute walk from the hotel. Rooms are simple, but they are attractive and clean, and some have air-conditioning. The on-site restaurant serves quality Mexican food and seafood. $. Recommended for budget travelers.

HOTEL NA BALAM
998-877-0058
www.nabalam.com
Calle Zazil-Ha, #118, Playa Norte

Na Balam, which means "house of the

jaguar" in Mayan, is an exclusive beach-front hotel with 28 rooms decorated as traditional Mayan cabañas. Rooms are located around the pool or next to the beach and have air-conditioning, ceiling fans, safes, and private balconies or terraces. The hotel gardens offer shade from the Caribbean sun and hammocks ideal for napping in the warm breeze. An on-site restaurant serves local and regional specialties. The hotel specializes in weddings, yoga retreats, and other special groups. Rates: $$$.

HOTEL OSORIO
998-877-0294
Madero Avenue near Benito Juárez Avenue

This family-run downtown hotel is a block from the beach and offers budget accommodations that are clean, but not luxurious. Rooms have ceiling fans, private bathrooms, and a place to hang your hammock. Rates: $.

✪ HOTEL SECRETO
998-877-1048
www.hotelsecreto.com
Punta Norte

On a secluded cove of Halfmoon Beach with a great shoreline, this upscale Mediterranean-style boutique hotel offers luxurious accommodations and a sense of privacy and exclusivity that can be hard to find on Isla. Rooms feature original artwork, air-conditioning, CD players, satellite TV, safes, and refrigerators. Each room has an outdoor terrace with patio furniture. Great spot for a romantic hideaway. Rates: $$$. Recommended.

✪ HOTEL VILLA ROLANDI
998-877-0500
www.rolandi.com
East beach

Your stay starts off with a trip across the Cancún straits in a private yacht. Once at the resort, you'll be treated to uniquely decorated rooms with air-conditioning, satellite TV, contemporary furnishings, superior linens, private balconies, and ocean views. There is an infinity pool overlooking the beach and a gourmet restaurant on a dock over the ocean, where meals can last for hours as you savor a glass of wine or cup of coffee and watch the stars after your meal. Tony Blair stayed here on his last visit to Mexico. Rates: $$$$. Highly recommended.

✪ UNIK RESORT ISLA MUJERES
877-888-UNIK (U.S.)
www.unikresort.com
South beach

Located near the southern tip of the island, the 84-room Unik is 10 minutes from the airport and about 4 miles from the Blue Bay Club Marina. Most guests, though, arrive on the resort's private yacht, which picks guests up from a dock in Cancún and takes them directly to the hotel pier, a 25-minute trip. The hotel is designed for sophisticated travelers looking to rest, visit the spa, dine on gourmet foods, and be treated with world-class service. Rooms are spacious and are outfitted with feather-top duvets, laptop safes, flat-screen TVs with DVD/CD players, marble bathrooms, jetted tubs, and great views of the Caribbean. The spa has a fully-equipped fitness center, yoga and Pilates classes, personal trainers, and several treatment rooms for a variety of holistic and modern treatments. Guests can choose a room-only plan or can have meals and drinks included for an additional charge. Don't expect tacos and burritos, the food is gourmet quality and freshly prepared at each meal, with no buffet lines in sight. Rates: $$$$, without meals.

VILLA LAS BRISAS
www.villalasbrisas.com
2.5 miles from Playa Norte

This seaside bed & breakfast has six rooms and caters to adults only. The house offers a relaxing respite from the hurried world and has no phones, TVs, or alarm clocks, but the rooms have ocean views, air-conditioning, ceiling fans, and minibars. The common areas include a spacious open-air living room, a terrace with hammocks, a swimming pool, and a bar. From May to July, sea turtles nest on the hotel beach. Rates: $ to $$ depending on the room and time of year; breakfast included. Recommended.

DINING

CASA O'S
998-888-0170
www.casaos.com
Playa Sur, near Garrafon

One of the top restaurants in town, Casa O's has waterfront dining, candlelit tables, a garden courtyard, and a boat dock for diners arriving by water. The service is excellent, and the tables face west, affording views of the sunset and the lights of Cancún. The kitchen serves mainly seafood, with shrimp and squid ceviche, lobster bisque, and grilled shrimp. There is also steak and a wide assortment of after-dinner drinks. Moderate.

CHI-CHI & CHARLIE'S
Playa Norte

Isla's traditional spot to watch the sunset, Chi-Chi & Charlie's serves burgers and Mexican snacks, along with ice-cold beers and cocktails. Inexpensive.

CHILES LOCOS
Avenue Hidalgo, downtown

This hot spot has affordable lunches and dinners, plus live music nightly. The rather simple menu is highlighted by burgers, tacos, and fajitas. Inexpensive.

LA ADELITA
Avenue Hidalgo, downtown

Open for dinner and drinks, La Adelita is the spot to sample your choice of 150 tequilas. For dinner try the grilled shrimp, steak, or fajitas. Moderate.

ROLANDI'S
998-877-0500
www.rolandi.com

This gourmet restaurant is on a dock behind the Villa Rolandi hotel. The Cancún elite are known to boat over on occasion, just for dinner. The menu features seafood, steak, shrimp, and Mexican specialties. There are also selections from around the world and an excellent wine list. Expensive.

ZAZIL HA RESTAURANT
998-877-0058
www.nabalam.com
Calle Zazil-Ha, #118, Playa Norte

This romantic spot under a large *palapa* roof serves vegetarian and regional specialties, including shrimp, rice and beans, and grilled chicken. Inexpensive.

NIGHTLIFE

BUHO'S
Avenue Carlos Laza, Playa Norte; by the Maria del Mar hotel

Isla's happy hour bar, popular with locals and tourists, has a *palapa* roof and swinging bar stools. It is known for cocktails made with tropical fruit, and the bartender is happy to mix-and-match to create your own unique drink. The music is a mix of reggae and American rock, with an occasional Mexican standard thrown in to spice things up.

MAMACITA'S
Avenue Hidalgo at Matamoros Street

Isla's party crowd packs Mamacita's after dinner for drinks and live music.

OM BAR
Matamoros Street, downtown

A Playa del Carmen native, OM Bar offers beer, wine, and cocktails along with live jazz music and an upscale lounge atmosphere.

SERGIO'S
Adjacent to the town plaza

This sports bar is a popular hangout when there's a big game on. Other times, visitors munch on burgers or tacos and play pool.

ATTRACTIONS

GARRAFON PARK
www.garrafon.com
Punta Sur, km 6

On the southeast tip of Isla Mujeres, Garrafon is the easternmost point in Mexico. Each New Year's Day, locals flock to this spot to be the first of their countrymen to see the sun in the new year. The park also has the Yucatán Peninsula's highest cliff, which leads down to the beautiful Caribbean. Visitors arrive by the boat on day trips from Cancún or can arrive by land from downtown Isla. The park gets its name from the Spanish word for "canister," either because the site was once used as a fuel depot or because the bay off the coast is shaped like the curved neck of a water bottle, depending on which version of the story you believe. The park has several restaurants, souvenir shops, an ice cream parlor, a swimming pool, a protected snorkeling area, a sundeck, and a hammock area, and there is also a museum and an ancient Mayan lighthouse relic. Visitors can rent clear-bottom kayaks ($6) and a Snuba ($39) or Sea Trek ($39) suit to experience the underwater realm. The park is open 9–5 (until 6 in the summer), and the entrance fee is $15 for adults and $8 for children (5–12 years old). For $29 for adults and $15 for kids, the trip includes a round-trip cruise to Cancún, admission, and a downtown tour, and for $54 for adults and $27 for kids, you can also get unlimited food and drinks. Snorkeling gear is available for rent for $10.

Cancún (45 miles north of Playa del Carmen)

Though officially it is too far north to be considered a part of the Riviera Maya, many visitors choose to stay a night in Cancún for a taste of the world-class shopping, great restaurants, powdery beaches, and over-the-top nightlife. The hotel zone is about 14 miles long, with dozens of hotels and every tourist service imaginable. There is a less commercial downtown area with great local restaurants, large bus station, many Internet cafés, shops, and nightspots. The main tourist area is at the elbow of the seven-shaped tourist strip, near the convention center. Within a short walk, there are two malls, a Hard Rock Café, 20 restaurants, more than a dozen nightclubs and bars, pharmacies, cigar shops, grocery stores, souvenir shops, and—yes—even strip clubs. An 18-hole waterfront golf course is just a few minutes away, and there are even some impressive Mayan ruins just miles from the convention center.

Hurricane Wilma battered the hotel zone with 150 mph winds, 25-foot waves, and an 11-foot storm surge when it stalled out over the city for nearly 12 hours in late 2005. The beachfront resorts suffered major damage and there was some serious beach erosion, but the hotels immediately went to work to rebuild and Mexico's number-one tourist town reemerged. One of the last hotels to reopen, the AQUA Cancún, opened to great fanfare in February 2008, marking the end of the Wilma era and the beginning of the new Cancún.

LODGING

CANCÚN PALACE

998-881-3600
www.palaceresorts.com
Boulevard Kukulcan, Km 14.5
Cancún hotel zone

With nearly a dozen resorts in the region, Palace is one of the most major brands you will come across. This Cancún beachfront outlet is one of the liveliest in the chain and appeals to spring-breakers, singles, and young couples, though many families make it their homebase also. The resort was completely renovated following hurricane repairs and reopened in February 2007.

A huge pool winds across the back of the hotel, with poolside games and dozens of people wading through the water to and from the swim-up bar with plastic cups full of exotic cocktails. Rooms are contemporary and offer cold air-conditioning and all expected amenities. Rates: $$$$ to $$$$$, all-inclusive.

CARISA Y PALMA CONDOS

998-883-0211 or 1-866-521-1787 (U.S.)
www.carisaypalma.com
Boulevard Kukulcán, km 11
Cancún hotel zone

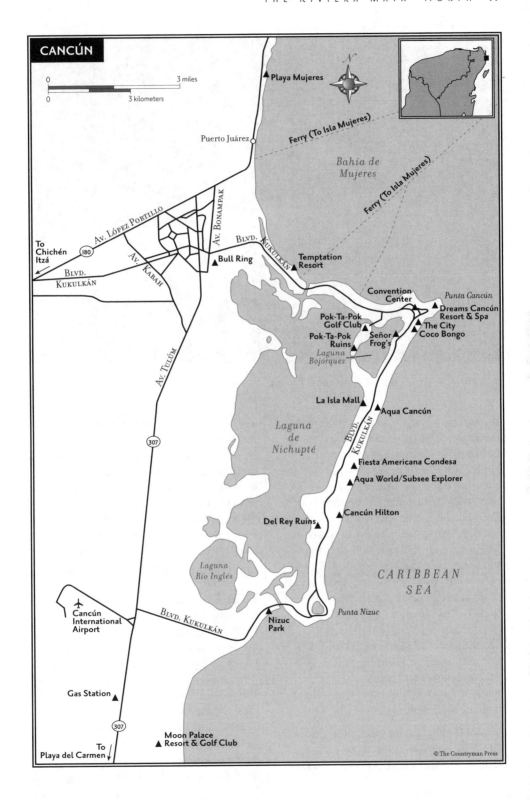

CANCÚN

0 ——————— 3 miles
0 ——————— 3 kilometers

▲ Playa Mujeres

N

Puerto Juárez

Ferry (To Isla Mujeres)

Bahía de Mujeres

Ferry (To Isla Mujeres)

Av. LÓPEZ PORTILLO

Av. BONAMPAK

BLVD. KUKULKÁN

To Chichén Itzá

180

BLVD. KUKULKÁN

Av. KABAH

▲ Bull Ring

Temptation Resort

Convention Center

Punta Cancún

Dreams Cancún Resort & Spa

Pok-Ta-Pok Golf Club

Pok-Ta-Pok Ruins

Señor Frog's

The City
Coco Bongo

Laguna Bojórquez

Av. TULÚM

La Isla Mall ▲

▲ Aqua Cancún

Laguna de Nichupté

BLVD. KUKULKÁN

307

▲ Fiesta Americana Condesa

▲ Aqua World/Subsee Explorer

Del Rey Ruins ▲

▲ Cancún Hilton

Laguna Río Inglés

CARIBBEAN SEA

✈ Cancún International Airport

BLVD. KUKULKÁN

Nizuc Park

Punta Nizuc

Gas Station ▲

307

To Playa del Carmen

Moon Palace Resort & Golf Club ▲

© The Countryman Press

The Dreams Resort, at the northeastern tip of Cancún. Courtesy of Dreams Resorts & Spas

If you're on a budget but want to be close to the action of Cancún's main tourist center, Carisa y Palma offers a good value. The beachfront buildings are showing their age a bit, but if you just need a place to crash that's walking distance from Señor Frog's, Coco Bongo, and dozens of other restaurants and bars, it may be worth it. Rooms have air-conditioning (not the best) and kitchenettes, and there's an on-site restaurant, tennis court, swimming pool, convenience store, and gym. Rates: $ to $$; breakfast included.

✪ DREAMS CANCÚN RESORT & SPA
998-848-7000 or 1-866-237-3262 (U.S.)
www.dreamsresorts.com
Boulevard Kukulcán, km 10, Punta Cancún
Cancún hotel zone

Known for its great location, this large-scale all-inclusive resort is on the beach and is walking distance to the convention center and main tourism entertainment district. It was badly damaged during Hurricane Wilma in late 2005 but reopened again in early 2006. It's one of the few resorts in Cancún where you could pass a week without getting in a car or bus and still get to see some of the town's main attractions. Of all the hotels within the convention center area, it has the best beach, which is hidden in a sheltered cove next to the Hyatt Regency. There is no easy public access to the beach, making it especially safe and relaxing. Though it's all-inclusive, guests are not required to wear wristbands, and instead sign all meals/drinks to their room. There are several restaurants and bars, including a seaside sushi bar, an air-conditioned buffet, a seafood grill, and a beach bar. There are nightly themed shows and meals, including a Mexican fiesta complete with mariachi bands and folkloric dancers. Accommodations include all food and drinks, nonmotorized water sports, gym,

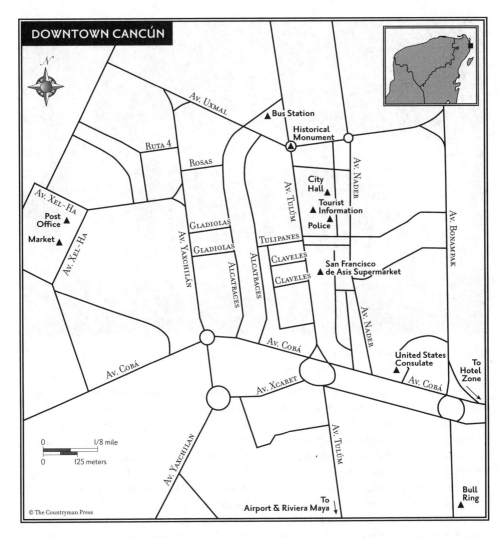

DOWNTOWN CANCÚN

business center (including Internet access), stocked minibar, and even 24-hour room service. The staff goes out of their way to provide great service, even though tips are included in the room price. Highly recommended. Rates: $$$$ to $$$$$, all-inclusive.

ELAN RESORT & SPA
998-891-4080
www.elanresort.com
Boulevard Kukulcan, Esq. Galeon St km 3.5
Cancún hotel zone

Elan opened in the summer of 2007 after a $15 million renovation of the former Club Las Velas, one of Cancún's original hotels. It is located on a private beach facing the Nichupté Lagoon on the Cancún mainland, just a few miles from the main entertainment district. The hotel was designed by Mexican architect Tomas Aunon to resemble a 17th century Mexican village, and the staff works hard to maintain a gracious Old World sense of warmth and service. Strolling mariachis, Mexican folklore shows, cooking classes, and history lessons also help to set the tone.

Fiesta Americana Grand Condesa Cancún. Courtesy of Fiesta Americana

The hotel has several restaurants and in the evening, the on-site Café Mystic is the spot for live piano music, fortune-telling exhibitions, and billiards. The resort is operated as an all-inclusive, with all food, drinks, and non-motorized water sports included. There is a fitness center, two pools, two tennis courts, and a full-service day spa, offering ancient Mayan healing treatments, facials, massages, and a number of ayurvedic treatments. There are steam rooms, a Temazcal sweat lodge, massage, yoga, Pilates, aikido, body wraps, facials, Reiki, reflexology, and a host of salon treatments. Accommodations include a half-hour massage on the day of arrival. Rates: $$$$$, all-inclusive.

✪ AQUA CANCÚN

998-840-6010
www.fiestaamericana.com
Boulevard Kukulcán, km 13
Cancún hotel zone

Located a couple of miles from the central tourist area and on a perfect beach across from a new shopping center, the Aqua is a new concept for the Grupo Posadas brand, normally known for its traditional Mexican-style resorts, Fiesta Inn and Fiesta Americana. The hotel is thoroughly contemporary in every way, from the aromatherapy kits available in each room and the 24-hour lounge music to the phosphorescent pillows at the beachside lounge. The rooms are spacious and feature premium bedding, marble bathrooms, and private balconies with an ocean view. The on-site restaurants feature celebrity chefs and have become the hip spots in town for the see-and-be-seen crowd. Guests, however, get preferential reservations. Other highlights include an upscale spa, a "garden of secrets" nature walk, wine and mescal bar, and poolside lounge area with sun cabanas. The hotel lost nearly every ocean-facing window during Hurricane Wilma in 2005 and had to completely rebuild, not opening again until early 2008. Rates: start at $$$$ to $$$$$. Highly recommended.

FIESTA AMERICANA GRAND CONDESA CANCÚN

998-881-4200
www.fiestaamericana.com
Boulevard Kukulcán, km 15.5
Cancún hotel zone

With the tallest *palapa* in all of Cancún, the Condesa (named for the chain's hotel on Condesa beach in Acapulco) is hard to miss. It was recently renovated, giving it a slick mix of traditional Mexican hacienda decor combined with a bevy of local accents and upgrades. The lobby is cooled with ocean breezes, and the beach is composed of flourlike sand. The buildings are reminiscent of a Mexican village, with subdued earth tone colors and cool stucco. There is a great Mexican restaurant on-site, plus several pools, a hip lobby bar, and a modern fitness center. For those who complain that Cancún has lost its charm, the Fiesta Americana Condesa may make them change their mind. Rates: $$$ to $$$$

HOTEL GRAND OASIS CANCÚN

998-881-7000
www.oasishotels.com
Boulevard Kukulkán, km 16.5
Cancún hotel zone

The Grand Oasis Cancún is a luxury all-inclusive resort in the heart of the Cancún hotel zone. The main attraction is the picture-perfect beach, ideal for sunbathing, strolling, sightseeing, building sand castles, and playing in the water. The hotel is less than 30 minutes from the Cancún International airport and half that from the main nightlife, shopping, and entertainment district of the city. The Grand Oasis is easy to spot from the street, thanks to its massive glass pyramid, rising above the green grass of the golf course and gardens that front the hotel. Once inside, guests are surrounded by hanging plants and tropical flowers, which ring the interior atrium and help create an exotic and faraway ambience.

Guest rooms feature contemporary styling with aspects of Mexican design, including earth-tone walls, native print linens, and decorative headboards. All rooms feature shower/tub combos, cable TV, direct-dial phones, hair dryer, minibar, and private terrace or balcony with views of the Caribbean or lagoon. Suites have separate sitting areas and spacious bathrooms with jetted tubs.

The Grand Oasis Cancún has more food and beverage options than nearly any other hotel in the Cancún area, giving guests plenty of options at mealtime. There are bounteous buffets served at a couple of different restaurants, plus specialty à la carte restaurants serving Italian, Asian, Tex-Mex, gourmet Mexican, sushi, Mediterranean, Brazilian rodizio, seafood, and more. Between meals, guests can hit up the poolside snack bar or a snack bar next to the beach.

Nightlife options are nearly as numerous. There is a lively lobby bar serving exotic cocktails, a sports bar with several TVs, and the Up & Down Nightclub, a cocktail lounge for relaxation and making friends, home to the Thursday night Foam Party, which draws revelers from all across Cancún. There are also theme parties and live music each evening to keep guests entertained.

The hotel pool is famous all across Cancún. It is more than .25 mile long, with waterfalls, tropical gardens, several swim-up bars, and plenty of room to lounge in the sun. The beach in front of the hotel is huge also, with lounge chairs and umbrellas for guest use. Most days the water is calm and clear, making it a great place to play in the water. The sand is powdery white and is so fine that it doesn't get hot, even in the middle of the day.

Active guests can enjoy a wide variety of activities and recreational opportunities without leaving the resort. There are two lighted tennis courts, a soccer field, basketball court, and fitness center with workout stations, free weights, and treadmills. Guests can also visit the hotel's water sports center, which offers free kayaks, paddleboats, and surfboards. They also offer a variety of local fee-based tours, including scuba diving, snorkeling, fishing, adventure tours, and visits to Mayan ruins.

Guests can play golf for free at the resort's own nine-hole course, located just in front of the property. The holes are short, but still present a fun challenge for all levels of play. There are sand traps, water hazards, and glimpses of the Caribbean and the Nichupté Lagoon. The hotel maintains a corporate membership at Cancun's Pok-Ta-Pok Country Club, located about 20 minutes away. Guests get great discounts on fees and can make reservations through the hotel concierge desk.

You can't keep going at high-speed your whole vacation, though. When it's time to relax, guests head to the on-site day spa and salon. Popular treatments include massages, sunburn relief, body wraps, facials, waxings, and visits to the Temazcal, which is a Mayan-style sweat lodge. Rates: $$$$, all inclusive.

MOON PALACE GOLF & SPA RESORT
998-881-6000
www.palaceresorts.com
Highway 307, km 338

Most flights out of the Cancún airport fly over the all-inclusive Moon Palace, which gives everyone a view of the magnificent beach and huge lagoon pools. It's the closest resort to the Cancún airport and is about 30 minutes from the main Cancún hotel zone. It's a massive complex, with nearly 2,000 feet of beachfront, 123 acres of jungle, more than 2,100 rooms, 10 restaurants, seven bars, six tennis courts, two basketball courts, and two gyms, giving it a sort of Las Vegas-on-the-beach feeling. The rooms are housed in three-story villas, most with an ocean view, and all with air-conditioning, satellite TV, private balcony, in-room safe, minibar, coffeemaker, and liquor dispenser. Accommodations include all meals and drinks, local and imported liquor, nonmotorized water sports (such as snorkeling, kayaking, and paddleboating), activities program, volleyball, mini golf, bicycles, and even a daily round of golf at the resort's 18-hole Jack Nicklaus golf course. The resort provides complimentary transportation to the Cancún hotel zone, where guests have privileges at the other Palace resorts. At night, guests head to the on-premises theater for live entertainment, then to the dance club, where everything is included. Rates: $$$$.

DINING

✪ LA HABICHUELA
998-884-3158
www.lahabichuela.com
25 Margarita Street, downtown Cancún

Though the indoor air-conditioned dining room is quite pleasant and suitably upscale to impress any date, the true joy of this place is the back patio, where the trees, plants, Mayan replicas, and twinkling lights create a majestic setting for a long, slow meal. The specialty of the house is the *Cocobichuela,* which features a coconut stuffed with lobster in a cream sauce. It has a unique flavor and goes great with ice-cold beer. The restaurant also has a respectable wine list. Expensive.

LORENZILLOS LOBSTER HOUSE
998-883-1433
Boulevard Kukulcán, km 13

Built on stilts over the water in the Nichupté lagoon, across the main road from the beach, Lorenzillos advertises its lobster all over town, and it lives up to the promotion. Choose from tails or whole, live lobster and pick your meal from the tank. It's a great place to watch the sunset, and at night you can see the city lights and the stars at the same time. The dining room fills up nearly every night, so go early or call ahead if you want one of the coveted water-side tables on the outer deck. In addition to lobster, there are some great fish and shrimp dishes. Blown to bits by Hurricane Wilma in 2005, this long-time Cancún favorite rebuilt quickly. Expensive.

✪ PERICOS
998-884-3152
www.pericos.com.mx
Yaxchilán 61, downtown Cancún

Okay, so it's not really an authentic Mexican cantina, but the fiesta that Pericos throws every night sure is fun. There are folkloric dancers, funny skits, conga lines, a live mariachi band, and even dancing masked midgets. The menu features a selection of Mexican standards, including fajitas, tacos, enchiladas, and grilled steak or shrimp. Moderate.

THE PLANTATION HOUSE
998-883-1254
Boulevard Kukulcán, km 13

Seafood specialties are served up in style at the Plantation House. The waitstaff has a well-practiced Southern sense of service, and the food is prepared fresh. Top dishes include grilled shrimp and lobster. Adjacent to Lorenzillos, it offers a more buttoned-up approach to the over-the-water dining experience. Expensive.

NIGHTLIFE

✪ COCO BONGO CANCÚN
998-883-5061
www.cocobongo.com.mx
Boulevard Kukulcán, km 10.5

Nightly acrobatic shows at Coco Bongo Photo courtesy of Coco Bongo

Located across from the convention center, this is one of the city's top nightspots. But to call Coco Bongo a bar would be woefully inadequate—to even call it a nightclub is somewhat of a joke. It's more like an entertainment center, where travelers congregate to celebrate life and get a little bit crazy. There's often a line wrapping around the corner, but it goes fast, and you can start making friends before you even get inside. The cover charge ranges from $30 to $60 depending on the night, but it includes all drinks. Once inside, you'll find a central bar area ringed by stadium-like seating, an upper deck with another bar and more seating, and an elevated stage, where most of the club's nonstop action happens. From celebrity impersonators and high-flying acrobats to live rock music, there's always something happening on stage or hanging from the rafters above the main bar. The atmosphere is very convivial, with a strong spirit of communal fun.

THE CITY CANCÚN
998-848-8380
www.thecitycancun.com
Punta Cancún, Boulevard Kukulcán, km 10.5

This megaclub features a swanky Miami Beach–style cabana bar and a massive indoor discotheque complete with laser light shows, smoke machines, and live performances. There are nine bars, big-name DJs, and a four-level dance floor. The whole place can accommodate more than 4,000 partyers, making it one of the largest night spots in all of Latin America. Cover charge is normally around $40, but it's all-you-can-drink. Check the sign out front for specials, including ladies' night, where females enter (and drink) for free.

✪ SEÑOR FROG'S
998-883-1092
www.senorfrogs.com
Boulevard Kukulcán, km 9.5

This legendary bar keeps packing in the partyers, night after night. No matter what time of the year or what day of the week it is, you'll find a mix of young and old, locals and visitors, partying hard and dancing even harder. The bar host keeps things moving with games, contests, and sing-alongs, while the waiters and shot-girls make sure nobody goes thirsty. It's open for meals during the day, and then around 10 PM the tables get pushed back and the dancing starts. Cover charge is around $10, but for $40 it's all you can drink. Specials vary depending on the night. Wear your bathing suit if you'd like to try out the indoor swimming pool built above the bar, or the waterslide that starts on the second floor and dumps out into the lagoon.

Isla Cozumel (11 miles from Playa del Carmen by boat)

Isla Cozumel was once considered the sacred home of Ix-Chel, the Mayan goddess of fertility and childbirth, and Mayan women from around Mesoamerica would travel to pay homage and pray for their unborn children. Several religious shrines have survived over the years and can still be visited today. Measuring 28 miles by 10 miles, Cozumel is only 5 percent developed and is mostly open land, ripe for exploration on Jeep, horseback, or moped. It is a mecca for scuba divers and snorkelers, who revel in the amazingly clear waters, easily accessible reefs, and first-class dive operators.

The ferry from Playa lands at the town square of the town of San Miguel, the island's only town, which is on the island's western shore. From nearly every beach hotel on this side of the island, guests have a spectacular view of the sunset as it slowly goes down into the Caribbean. There are dozens of shops, restaurants, bars, and other attractions within

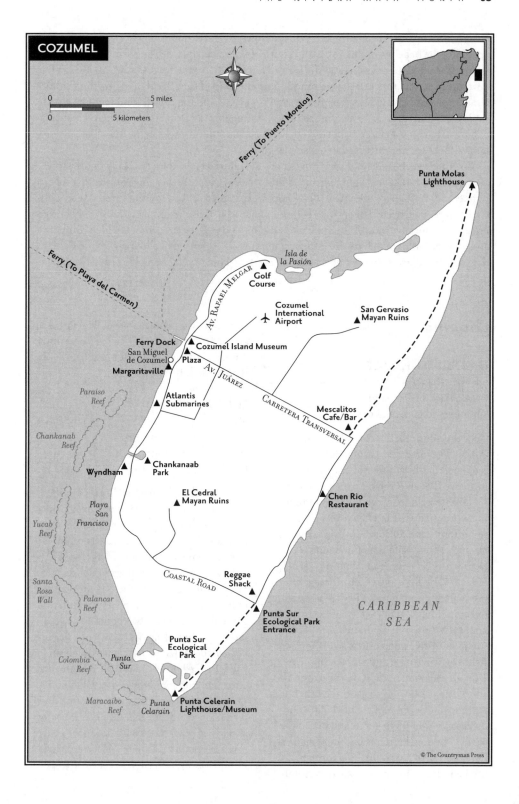

COZUMEL

N

0 _____ 5 miles
0 _____ 5 kilometers

Ferry (To Puerto Morelos)

Ferry (To Playa del Carmen)

Punta Molas
Lighthouse

Isla de
la Pasión

Golf
Course

Av. Rafael Melgar

Cozumel
International
Airport

San Gervasio
Mayan Ruins

Ferry Dock
San Miguel
de Cozumel
Margaritaville

Cozumel Island Museum

Plaza

Av. Juárez

Atlantis
Submarines

Carretera Transversal

Mescalitos
Cafe/Bar

Paraiso
Reef

Chankanab
Reef

Wyndham

Chankanaab
Park

El Cedral
Mayan Ruins

Chen Rio
Restaurant

Playa
San
Francisco

Yucab
Reef

Santa
Rosa
Wall

Palancar
Reef

Coastal Road

Reggae
Shack

CARIBBEAN
SEA

Colombia
Reef

Punta
Sur

Punta Sur
Ecological Park
Entrance

Punta Sur
Ecological
Park

Maracaibo
Reef

Punta
Celarain

Punta Celerain
Lighthouse/Museum

© The Countryman Press

an easy walking distance of the ferry dock. There are a few hotels downtown, and the rest are along the beaches to the north and south of the town square. The eastern side of the island faces the open ocean, and the water is much rougher, with less reef, and much less development. Visitors can drive around the south side of the island, hugging the shoreline almost the entire way. This is a great way to get away from the crowds and feel like a real explorer, though you are never more than 15 minutes away from a cold beer and tasty plate of food. There are a few Mayan ruins that are run as federal parks, with information centers, gift shops, and certified multilingual guides.

Cozumel was heavily damaged during the dual hurricanes of 2005. Many of the street signs, *palapa* roofs, and light poles were blown down, and the beachfront was severely flooded. More than a dozen dive-boat piers were ruined and two of the three cruise-ship docks were destroyed. The island received major assistance from the federal and state governments (the governor of the state of Quintana Roo was from Cozumel, which didn't hurt) and was rebuilt to match its pre-storm splendor. The opening of a Margaritaville Café, in the summer of 2007, helped boost morale on the island and it hasn't looked back since.

LODGING

✪ COZUMEL PALACE
987-872-9430
www.palaceresorts.com
Southern hotel zone, km 2.5

Once the site of the Plaza Las Glorias, Cozumel's famed dive resort, this hotel reopened in the summer of 2005 as the all-inclusive Cozumel Palace, which is about a 15-minute walk to town. A complete renovation spruced up the pool, guest rooms, lobby, restaurants, and all common areas. The hotel has 176 rooms; each is a junior suite with Jacuzzi tub, safe, air-conditioning, ceiling fan, satellite TV, stocked minibars, and private balcony with ocean views. Guests enjoy unlimited food and drinks, snorkeling gear, pool activities, and 24-hour room service. An on-site dive shop offers scuba tours, fishing excursions, and snorkeling trips. Though the hotel is right on the water, the shoreline is exposed reef, so the beach is built up above the rocks. Snorkelers and divers use ladders to get in and out of the water. The snorkeling is excellent right at the hotel, with barracuda, parrot fish, colored coral, sea anemone, sea urchin, lobster, and other things to see. Boats pick up guests from the hotel dock for excursions. A kids' club is available for children 4–12. Rates: $$$$. Recommended.

EL COZUMELEÑO
987-872-9530 or 1-800-437-3923 (U.S.)
www.elcozumeleno.com
Northern hotel zone, km 4.5, Santa Pilar Beach

One of Cozumel's original hotels is still one of the most popular spots for families and others looking for an affordable, all-inclusive beach vacation. Guests enjoy unlimited meals, snacks, drinks, cocktails, and nonmotorized water sports. Recreational activities include mini golf, tennis, beach soccer, Ping-Pong, billiards, giant outdoor chess, two pools and two Jacuzzis, snorkeling, intro to scuba lessons, bicycle tours, windsurfing, aerobics, and volleyball. At night, guests head to the on-site nightclub for karaoke and DJ dancing. The resort's 252 rooms have spacious floor plans, air-conditioning, satellite TV, safes, and private balconies with ocean view. The Cozumel Country Club is just a couple of minutes away, and guests receive a 30 percent discount on fees. There is also an on-site workout room, and dive and tour shop, where guests can schedule scuba diving, fishing, WaveRunner rental, parasailing, and other activities. A kids' club provides complimentary supervision and children's activities during the day. Rates: $$$ to $$$$.

FIESTA AMERICANA COZUMEL DIVE RESORT
1-800-FIESTA1 (U.S.)
www.fiestaamericana.com
Southern Coast Road, km 7.5

Located on the southern end of the island, this 224-room hotel is popular with families, serious scuba divers, and other guests who value ready access to the best dive sites over proximity to downtown, which is a 20-minute car ride away. The hotel is very casual and features traditional Mexican decor. There are two swimming pools, a beauty shop, massage service, and a video arcade and playground for the kids. The rooms have air-conditioning, coffeemakers, and an ocean or garden view. There are two restaurants and a popular bar, where guests congregate at night for live music, billiards, karaoke, and other entertainment. The beach is across the street from the main part of the hotel, where there is a swimming pool, restaurant, lounge chairs, and a boat dock, where divers, snorkelers, and anglers depart. Rates: $$ to $$$.

IBEROSTAR COZUMEL RESORT
987-872-9900
www.iberostar.com
Southern Coast Road, km 17

If you value proximity to the reefs more than convenience to town, the all-inclusive Iberostar Cozumel could be the choice for you. There are 306 rooms built alongside a massive pool. Guests have complimentary use of catamarans, sailboards, kayaks, tennis courts, fitness center, and snorkeling gear. A private boat dock makes getting to the nearby dive sites a breeze. The drive into town, though, can take 30 minutes or more, so it's much more of a remote getaway than a homebase for exploring downtown and other local environs. Rates: $$$ to $$$$.

PLAYA AZUL BEACH RESORT
987-872-0033
www.playa-azul.com
Northern hotel zone, km 4, San Juan Beach

This beach and golf resort is just a few miles north of the town square. It has 50 rooms in a contemporary hacienda style, with a beachside swimming pool and plenty of beach chairs. The rooms feature tropical decor, living room, air-conditioning, satellite TV, coffeemaker, safe, and ocean-view balcony or terrace. Guests receive unlimited play at the Cozumel Country Club golf course, just a couple of minutes away. Rates: $$$.

✪ SAFARI INN
987-872-0101
www.aquasafari.com/safariinn.html
Rafael Melgar, between 5th and 7th Streets

Located behind the Aqua Safari dive shop, the Safari Inn is a favorite for divers and other guests who don't need to be on the beach but want the convenience of being near downtown and area nightlife. The hotel is about a five-minute walk from the town plaza and is across the street from a rocky beach. Guests use the Aqua Safari pier, across the street, for meeting boats for excursions. The hotel has 12 rooms with cold air-conditioning and spacious floor plans sleeping up to five guests. Rates: $ to $$, depending on the season and occupancy. Highly recommended for the value.

SUITES COLONIAL
987-872-9090
www.suitescolonial.com
North side of the town square, overlooking the plaza

If you want to be in the downtown area and near the ferry dock and you don't need to be right on the beach, the Suites Colonial is an affordable option. Rooms are not fancy, but they are clean and convenient to everything in town. Activities can be booked through any local dive shop, and arrangements can be made for hotel or pier pickup. The 28 rooms and suites all have air-conditioning, cable TV, and safes. Rates: $ to $$; Continental breakfast included.

✪ WYNDHAM AURA GRAND BAY COZUMEL
987-872-9300
888-293-0293 (U.S.)
www.auraresorts.com
Southern Coast Road, km 12.9

When it opened in early 2008, this 87-room all-inclusive adults-only boutique hotel became the first newly constructed hotel on the island in more than a decade. With its South Beach chic style, modern architecture, and trendy vibe, it significantly ups the ante on resorts on the island. Guest rooms are all suites and some have swim-up terraces. There are two nice restaurants, a couple of swanky bars, and a solarium bar with two Jacuzzi tubs looking over the beach—the ultimate sunset spot. Guests enjoy 24-hour room service, unlimited food and top-shelf drinks, watersports, activity program, and they have full privileges at the adjacent Wynhdam Cozumel (reverse privileges do not apply). The next-door Islander Spa is the biggest and nicest on the island. This is by far the most sophisticated and luxurious resort in Cozumel. Highly recommended. Rates: $$$$ to $$$$$.

WYNDHAM COZUMEL
987-872-9300
888-293-0293 (U.S.)
www.wyndhamcozumel.com
Southern Coast Road, km 12.9

The former site of the Cozumel Reef club, about 15 minutes south of town, turned into a Wyndham and was completely refurbished to become the island's largest resort hotel in the summer of 2007. It offers 312 luxurious rooms and suites, a .5 mile beach, several pools, restaurants, bars, watersports center, kids club, fitness center, and large European day spa. The hotel's Sabor section is adults-only, with its own guest rooms and pool area. The adjacent Reef Plaza Shopping Center has more than a dozen shops and eateries. Rates: $$$.

DINING

✪ CASA DENIS
Town square, downtown Cozumel

If you're facing the clock tower with the ocean behind you, follow the walkway that leads straight back from the plaza on the right-hand side. The first restaurant you run into is Casa Denis. It has been there for more than 20 years and offers up some of the best food in town, particularly if you're looking for traditional Mexican fare. They have fish, tacos, enchiladas, shrimp, and steak. They also have *sopes,* a traditional dish from Acapulco served on thick, soft corn tortillas with lettuce, cheese, refried beans, and meat toppings. Inexpensive.

CHEN RIO RESTAURANT
Seven miles up the coast on the island's east side

Most of the island's east side has rough water and somewhat less-than-inviting beaches, but at Chen Rio the reef is just offshore, which cuts down the waves and makes the water shallow and calm. There is a long stretch of white-sand beach, some small waves, tide pools, and a casual beachfront restaurant. The menu is limited, with fried whole fish the main specialty. The

A typical street scene in Cozumel.

drinks are cold, and the shallow cove makes for a great place to take a dip and cool off from your journey. If you have packed a picnic lunch, you can just buy drinks at the restaurant and then lay out your blanket on the beach. Inexpensive. No credit cards.

LAS PALMERAS
Town square, downtown Cozumel

Located on the west side of the town square, facing the ferry dock, Las Palmeras is the traditional place to pass the time while waiting for the boat to Playa del Carmen. It is famous for its fishbowl margaritas, which are served ice-cold, potent, and delicious. The restaurant serves breakfast, lunch, and dinner and has seating indoors with open windows and walls, allowing the ocean breezes in and giving diners a great view of the waterfront and the bustle of the ferry dock. Moderate.

MEZCALITOS
At the intersection of the cross-island road and the northern end of the road that goes along the eastern shoreline

This local favorite is the northeastern-most public restaurant on the island. If you take the southern route around the island, this is where you will turn left to head back to the town of San Miguel. If you take the eastern route, this is where you will turn right and start paralleling the coast. The restaurant serves Mexican dishes and snacks and has a full bar. There are tables in a shaded indoor area and also outside on the waterfront patio. The beach is not good for swimming, but it is great for exploring since it is undeveloped and natural. This is a great place to meet other travelers because everyone here is doing the same thing—cruising around the island. It's a nice way to get tips on hidden beaches and good places to go. The restaurant shares a parking lot with a couple of souvenir stands selling T-shirts, trinkets, Mexican blankets, and other goods. The restaurant was destroyed during Hurricane Emily but has since been rebuilt. Inexpensive.

PASTA PRIMA
Town square, downtown Cozumel

From the center of the plaza, take the walkway to the right that heads south, and Pasta Prima will be on the northeast corner of the first intersection. Owned by a native of Dallas, Texas, this Italian terrace restaurant is a favorite for visiting diving clubs, honeymooners, and even locals searching for an authentic Italian meal. Visitors enter from the street level and climb a stairway so narrow it seems like a replica from a Mayan ruin. The dining room is on an open-air patio overlooking the city streets, with the ocean just beyond. It bustles most nights, and there is frequently a wait for a table, though it is always worth the time. The menu features pastas, spaghetti, and a heavy dose of seafood, including live Caribbean lobster, prepared a variety of ways. There is also a respectable wine list. Moderate.

✪ PEPE'S GRILL
One block south of the town square, downtown Cozumel

One of the fancier and more expensive restaurants on the island, Pepe's Grill is the traditional spot for a first or last meal during a Cozumel visit. The chef prepares tender steaks, fresh seafood, and Mexican specialties. It may be best known, however, for its Mayan coffee, which contains a locally made orange schnapps called Xtabentun. The waiters make the after-dinner drinks tableside, and whenever one is being prepared, the whole restaurant watches as the liquor is lit on fire and poured into the coffee. Expensive.

PLAZA LEZA
Town square, downtown Cozumel

This casual outdoor café is on the south side of the main plaza, facing the clock tower. It specializes in fajitas and steak, and the smell from its grills will catch you as you walk by. If the waiter's offering you a table wait and take a seat at one of the covered sidewalk café tables or in the small indoor dining room. After dinner, linger a while with a cup of coffee or a tropical drink and watch the people walk by. On Sunday nights, this is a great place to watch the music and festivities that take place at the plaza's gazebo. Inexpensive.

NIGHTLIFE

HARD ROCK CAFÉ
On Rafael Melgar Avenue, the road along the coast at 2nd Street
987-872-5271
www.hardrock.com

Located just a block south of the town square, this is one of the international chain's smallest locations. Live music is featured most nights and visitors enjoy buying T-shirts and checking out the rock memorabilia.

✪ JIMMY BUFFET'S MARGARITAVILLE CAFÉ
On Rafael Melgar Avenue, the road along the coast, south of the town square, by the cruise-ship dock, where the overhead walkway empties into the shopping plaza

Built on the water a few blocks south of the town square, this outlet of Jimmy Buffett's chain of cafes is a Parrothead paradise, with beachfront tiki bar, beach music (including plenty of Buffett hits), burgers, seafood, and an open-air dance floor. Patrons are passionate about their beach-bum hero and impromptu sing-alongs are commonplace.

Cozumel's Hard Rock Café

few hammocks for snoozing and a couple of tables set up in the sand, right next to the water. The reef here is exposed and the water is rough, so there is no swimming. If you walk to the left, there is a deserted beach ideal for walking and tanning. There is a handmade NUDE BEACH sign, but it is not an official nude beach, and nudity is not recommended, though topless is generally fine. Though the facility was wiped out by Hurricane Emily, it was quickly rebuilt and is as popular as ever.

SEÑOR FROG'S AND CARLOS 'N CHARLIE'S
On Rafael Melgar Avenue, the road along the coast, south of the town square, by the cruise-ship dock, where the overhead walkway empties into the shopping plaza

With one built right on top of the other, these two main tourist bars make barhopping easier than ever. Just take the escalator down from Señor Frog's, and you're at Carlos 'n Charlies. Señor Frog's is more nightlife oriented, with a stage, dancing waiters, and full-time party atmosphere, while Carlos 'n Charlie's is more of a restaurant, with a more subdued atmosphere, at least until late at night, when it transforms into more of a bar. Depending on the day and how many cruise ships are in town, these tourist havens can be packed or empty, raucous or tame. They both serve consistently good Mexican food, seafood, and pasta.

✪ REGGAE SHACK
Southern Coast Road, where the coastal road turns east at the southern tip of the island

This come-as-you-are beach bar has no electricity (and doesn't accept credit cards) and is rather ramshackle, but it is a must-see waypoint for travelers circumnavigating the island by Jeep or moped. It is at the southwest end of the island, where the highway reaches a stop sign and all traffic must turn to the left. Go straight instead and park along the street. Each day, the bartender brings a cooler of ice and drinks from San Miguel and serves them up cold and cheap to passing visitors. There are a

ATTRACTIONS

✪ CHANKANAAB PARK

987-872-0914
www.cozumelparks.com.mx
Southern Coast Road, km 9.5

Created in 1980 to protect the marine life in the region, plus the flora and fauna along the shoreline, Cozumel's main beach and nature park is just south of the Fiesta Americana hotel on the coastal road. The water is crystal clear, with more than 100 feet of visibility on most days, making for excellent snorkeling and scuba diving. The beach offers easy water access, slow currents, and exciting shore dives, where statues of Christ and the Virgin Mary beckon from the shallows. There is a botanical garden with 60 species of palm trees, orchids, water lilies, and dozens of tropical flowers, plus birds and iguanas. An archaeology area features 60 Aztec, Mayan, and Toltec replica temples and a replica of a Mayan *choza,* or hut, where visitors can witness how the indigenous inhabitants of Cozumel and the Riviera Maya once lived and worked. There is also a dolphin and sea lion discovery lagoon where visitors can pay to swim with these creatures in their natural habitat. Underwater videos of the encounters are available for purchase. Open 7–6 daily. Admission is $16 for adults and $6 for kids ages 3–11.

✪ COZUMEL ISLAND MUSEUM

www.cozumelparks.com.mx
Rafael Melgar and 4th Street

The island's history museum is on the coastal road just a couple of blocks north of the town square. Through a series of displays (re-creations, drawings, and artifacts) it tells the history of the island from the days of the Mayans to the 16th-century discoveries by Juan de Grijalva and Hernan Cortez, through the pirate years and the War of the Castes, and to the present day. There is a gift shop, library, and snack bar, and bilingual guides are available for hire. Open 9–5 daily. Admission: adults $3, kids eight and under free.

✪ PUNTA SUR LIGHTHOUSE PARK

987-872-0914
www.cozumelparks.com.mx
Southern Coast Road, km 27

This 247-acre ecology reserve and beach park is at the southeastern tip of Cozumel Island. It encompasses white-sand beaches, mangrove swamps, lagoons, and thick jungle. The crowning feature is the Faro Punta Sur, the famed lighthouse where the former caretakers would host a weekly fish fry and invite everyone on the island—locals and tourists alike—to the party. The $10 entrance fee (for all visitors nine and up) includes transportation through the park and access to the museum, lighthouse, and other attractions. There is also a souvenir shop and snack bar. A catamaran tour is available for $25 extra. Open 9–6 daily.

SAN GERVASIO MAYAN RUINS

987-872-0914
www.cozumelparks.com.mx
Cross-Island Road, km 7.5

Located about halfway between the town square and the east side of the island and Mezcalito's restaurant, San Gervasio is Cozumel's largest and most historically significant Mayan site. It was inhabited from A.D. 200 until the Spanish conquest and was a major political, spiritual, and social center for the natives; it was also an important pilgrimage site for women who traveled to the island to pay homage to Ixchel, the goddess of fertility. The site, which spans more than 2 square miles and has several different temples and small pyramids, is home to many tropical birds and iguanas. Visitors can walk among the ruins by themselves, reading the interpretive signs, or they can hire a guide. There is a gift shop, bookstore, and snack bar. Open 7–4 daily. Admission is $5.50 for adults and free for children under eight.

COZUMEL MINI-GOLF
1st Street South at 15th Avenue
987-872-6570
www.czmgolf.com

This U.S.-owned minigolf course is open until 11 PM, making it a fun place to enjoy the outdoors, sip a cocktail, listen to music, and practice your putting skills. Fee is $5 per round.

RANCHO BUENAVISTA
987-872-1537
www.buenavistaranch.com

This outlet offers two-hour horseback tours through some of the island's most rugged and picturesque landscapes. Individual and group tours are available.

BEACH CLUBS

✪ MR. SANCHO'S BEACH CLUB
Southern Coastal Road, km 13
987-876-1629
www.mrsanchos.com

A lively beach club on a picture-perfect white-sand beach south of town. Visitors can swim, snorkel, take an ATV or motorcycle into the jungle, ride the banana boat, ride horses, shop, relax at the bar, eat in an open-air restaurant, get a massage, take a tequila tour, and make friends in the beachside 30-person Jacuzzi. The beach is public property, but facilities have a fee.

NACHI COCOM BEACH CLUB
Southern Coastal Road, km 16.5
987-872-1811
www.cozumelnachicocom.net

A relaxing beach club for playing on WaveRunners, going parasailing, playing beach volleyball, swimming, and tanning.

Underwater Mayan city at Playa Mia Grand Beach Park Courtesy of Playa Mia

✪ PLAYA MIA GRAND BEACH PARK

Southern Coastal Road, km 15.5
987-872-9030
www.playamia.com

This well-established beach club is like a tropical island recreation paradise. Visitors pass the day kayaking, sailing, parasailing, sunning, swimming, and applying sunblock. There is a little zoo, restaurant, beach bar, and even a floating climbing wall. It's also a great place to snorkel, thanks to the underwater replica Mayan relics that have been laid out especially for snorkelers.

PLAYA SAN FRANCISCO

Southern Coastal Road, km 15
987-872-0754

Long considered the island's best beach, Playa San Francisco is still one of the most popular. It has been the site of thousands of weddings and remains a favorite place for watersports, seafood, and cold beers.

THE RIVIERA MAYA BEGINS

Puerto Morelos

(HIGHWAY 307, KM 320; 20 MILES NORTH OF PLAYA DEL CARMEN)

If you want to know what Playa del Carmen was like 20 years ago, just take a look at modern-day Puerto Morelos, which is the official beginning of the Riviera Maya, and its northern border. The quiet town square ringed by a few restaurants and shops, the natural beach, the unpaved roads, the encroaching jungle—it's almost exactly how Playa used to be. The

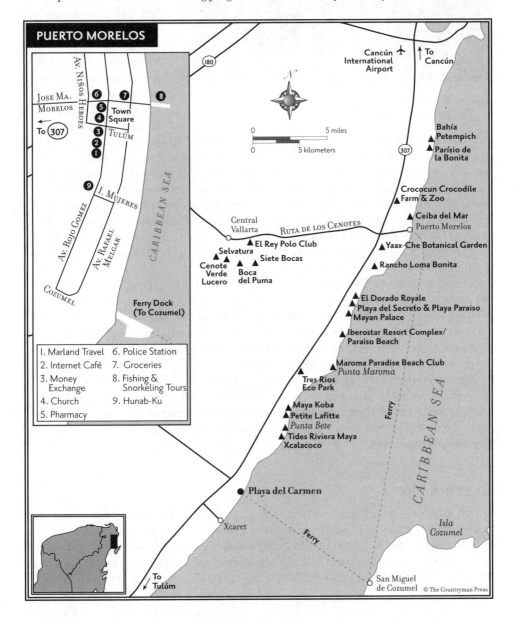

PUERTO MORELOS

1. Marland Travel
2. Internet Café
3. Money Exchange
4. Church
5. Pharmacy
6. Police Station
7. Groceries
8. Fishing & Snorkeling Tours
9. Hunab-Ku

© The Countryman Press

Souvenir shops line the town square in Puerto Morelos.

road from the highway to town is a straight shot through 2 miles of scrub brush and mangrove swampland before ending at the town square. Most of the development is within a couple blocks of the square, which has a beachside restaurant, several open-air sidewalk restaurants, a couple of Internet cafés, a coffee/pastry shop, and a few souvenir stores, pharmacies, money exchange offices, and dive shops. Along the beach you'll see a leaning lighthouse and a fishing pier where the boats dock when they're not pulled up onto the beach. Less than .5 mile offshore is the barrier reef, and you can see the waves breaking where the coral meets the surface, which indicates a great spot for snorkeling when the seas are calm. The roads leading north and south from town are dusty and unpaved, but they lead to some of the nicest natural beaches in the area. To the north is a collection of rental homes and small hotels, plus a couple of recently developed large-scale resorts. To the south the road curves behind an Army base and then a shipping and industrial area before meeting the beach again near the entrance to a laid-back budget hotel and a clothing-optional "lifestyle" resort.

The town was hit hard by Hurricane Wilma in late 2005. The storm pushed a thick layer of sand 200 yards inland, flooded the mangroves, tore down *palapas,* destroyed an elementary school, and heavily damaged most beachfront establishments. The town received less government support than Cancún and struggled to regain its services. The townspeople worked together to clean up the mess and repair the damages. By the spring of 2006, tourists were returning in droves and the town marched onward.

A gambling-boat operator had petitioned to operate a casino boat from the port to take travelers to international waters, but the petition was denied, and the area retains its calming and relaxed feeling. A ferry transfers vehicles from Puerto Morelos to Cozumel at 5 AM, 10:30 AM, and 4 PM, with return trips at 8 AM, 1:30 PM, and 7 PM. For more information call 998-871-0008.

GETTING THERE

Puerto Morelos is located at the midpoint between Cancún and Playa del Carmen. The turnoff from Highway 307 was marked with just a speed bump only a few years ago, but now there's a traffic light, turning lanes, several shops, and even a road sign, so you can't miss it. Another road, just north of the Crococun Zoo, leads to the north end of town and the Secrets Excellence and Paradisus hotels. From there the road winds and turns as you head south, passing by private homes and small family-run hotels. In several spots, heavy marine rope has been laid across the street as a sort of makeshift speed bump. After a few miles, the road ends at the town square. There are frequent buses from the Cancún and Playa del Carmen bus stations that will drop you off at the crossroads, and from there it's a 2-mile hike to town or a $3 taxi ride. A new bus station was built in 2008 on Highway 307, just south of the main crossroads next to the 7-Eleven convenience store, with regular departures to Tulum, Playa del Carmen, and Cancun. Though it may not be generally encouraged, it's also fairly easy to hitch a ride along the road that leads to town. Since the road basically goes to only one place, it's a pretty fair bet that anyone headed down that road is going somewhere close to where you are.

Lodging

Bahia Petempich

AZUL HOTEL & BEACH RESORT
998-872-0808
www.karismahotels.com
Highway 307, km 330

To get to Azul, go through the gated entrance to Bahia Petempich, and then turn left where the main road meets the beach road. Once in the gated entrance, you'll be met by a greeter and a glass of champagne. The feng shui–friendly hotel is an up-market all-inclusive boutique resort located on an idyllic beach just a few miles north of Puerto Morelos. The lobby has marble floors and minimalist decor, with lots of whites and blues, and calming music playing in the background. The hotel welcomes families and even has an activities program for kids. It has fewer than 100 rooms, all of which are very close to the beach and have cold air-conditioning, minibars, coffeemakers, DVD players, and a private balcony or patio. There is a beautiful pool with attendants at the ready to bring you fresh towels, drinks, magazines, or whatever else you need. Since it's all-

The courtyard of the Azul Hotel

Hurricane Wilma—Mexico's Costliest Natural Disaster in History

Three months after Hurricane Emily tore through the Riviera Maya in July 2005, Tropical Storm Wilma formed in the Atlantic Basin and churned and sputtered for a couple of days without much strengthening or fanfare. On Wednesday, October 19, though, things changed quickly. Within 24 hours, the storm had developed into a massive category 5 hurricane, reaching a minimum central pressure of 882 millibars and sustained winds of 175 mph, making it the most intense hurricane on record in that part of the world. The U.S. State Department issued an urgent evacuation notice for all U.S. citizens in the region. By the morning of Thursday, October 20, the MTV Latin Music Video Awards in Xcaret had been canceled and music performers and celebrities crowded the Cancún airport with thousands of tourists, all trying to get a flight back home. Meanwhile, the storm was poised offshore, forecast to veer to the east and spare the region, but not yet showing signs of the turn.

By late afternoon, winds from the outer bands of Hurricane Wilma began lashing the coast of Cancún and the Riviera Maya. Palm trees were bending and the waves were crashing, even though the storm was still 150 miles offshore. At dawn on Saturday, October 21, 10-foot waves were pounding into the seawall on the western shore of Cozumel, shooting sprays of water 30 feet into the air. The outer bands were tearing at the trees and rooftops and some signs had already blown down. Up and down the Riviera Maya and Cancún, hotels prepared for the worst and visitors and residents were bused to shelters while the military patrolled the streets, ensuring everyone had a place to ride out the storm. As the hurricane's eye neared the coast, the area braced for a direct hit, with landfall predicted to be somewhere between Playa del Carmen and Cancún.

At 10 AM on Friday, Cancún police reported the city's first death. A local woman was on her roof cleaning debris and a power line fell and electrocuted her. At 2 PM, the wall of the eye passed over the northern tip of Cozumel, while all across the region, the situation deteriorated rapidly. Gary Walten, an Akumal resident and owner of LocoGringo.com, was seeking shelter in his home while talking on the phone to CNN, which broadcast the conversation to the world. Wolf Blitzer asked him to hold his phone near the window so the audience could hear the sound. The noise was howling at a near-deafening volume, described by one survivor as "one thousand cats, screaming in pain." Water was washing across the main street through the Cancún hotel zone, and Quinta Avenida in downtown Playa del Carmen was a shallow river, with whitecaps cresting between storefronts. Most of the windows were boarded up; the ones that weren't were shattered. Cars were washing down the street in downtown Cancún and in the back streets of Playa and Puerto Morelos.

By sundown, the eye had stalled over the Cancún hotel zone, creating the worst-case scenario for the region, as the rainfall continued relentlessly. The wind created a 50-mile-long wall the strength of a Force 2 tornado, and the storm surge inched higher and higher. Reports of an exploded gas tank and associated injuries made their way across the Internet, with readers praying for the safety of their loved ones, stranded in shelters across the area. Water was waist-deep along the Cancún hotel zone and had completely washed out the road leading from Tulum to Punta Allen. Through the night, things only got worse. Witnesses in Playa del Carmen reported seeing 200-gallon water tanks, stoplights, plate glass, and even automobiles flying through the air. Water had washed completely over Kukulcán Boulevard in Cancún, connecting the ocean and the lagoon and making one solid sea of water.

At sunrise on Saturday, October 22, weary-eyed residents and tourists, many of whom were kept awake by the screeching winds and rising waters, peeked out the windows and were horrified by what they saw. The devastation was worse than anyone had imagined. Mexico's President Vicente Fox had already declared the entire region a disaster zone. To make matters worse, the storm was still stalled, meaning the misery would last at least another 12 hours. Nearly every hotel in Cancún had lost

Puerto Morelos rebuilds after Hurricane Wilma.

dozens, if not hundreds, of windows, while the ocean in Playa del Carmen had risen to meet Quinta Avenida, forming a sea of water 3 feet deep along the town's main tourist district. By 3 PM, the winds had receded to below hurricane strength for the first time in 24 hours, though the conditions were still too severe for anyone to leave the shelters. Food and water were running scarce and reports of looters being arrested in Cancún did little to calm any fears. Across the entire region, waves of up to 25 feet continued to crash ashore, ripping apart everything in their path.

By Sunday, rumors of "total devastation" swept across the Internet, while Hurricane Wilma left the Yucatán and made a beeline for the Florida coast, where it went on to cause $11 billion in insured damages. Back in the Riviera Maya, thousands of travelers were stranded, with no way to get home. The Cancún airport was damaged, and some tourists paid up to $400 for a taxi to Mérida to catch a plane out. Tour operators scrambled to take care of their passengers and get them home. Some stranded survivors waited in line for two hours to use a pay phone to tell their loved ones that they were alright. Over the next week, the Mexican government passed out roofing materials for rebuilding houses and thousands of bottles of water, and also cleared the streets. Generous locals prepared food for hungry tourists. Residents and visitors banded together to start cleaning up.

Within weeks, most of the damaged buildings had been cleared or were in the process of being rebuilt. The Capitan Lafitte, just north of Playa del Carmen, was declared a total loss and has since been replaced by a trendy new property, the Petit Lafitte. Cozumel's beachfront and Cancún's hotel zone took the brunt of the storm, with some hotels having to replace hundreds of windows and replace soft goods in all of their rooms. But over the following months, the beaches regained their natural splendor. Restaurants along Quinta in Playa put on fresh coats of paint and rebuilt their palapas (open-sided dwellings with thatched roofs). The large all-inclusive resorts along the Riviera Maya built back bigger and better than ever.

Thankfully, Hurricane Wilma claimed only five lives in all of Mexico. Once again, the region proved itself to be incredibly resilient, even in the face of great challenges. By 2006, the crowds were returning in droves, proving that the Riviera Maya is not only a destination full of history and stories of a splendid past, but also a world-class travel destination with unlimited potential for the future.

inclusive, guests can indulge all they like at a variety of on-site restaurants and bars. There is a special menu for kids, an all-lobster menu, a stylish sushi bar with tatami tables, and a healthy diet menu, plus 24-hour room service. Unlike many all-inclusives, the bars serve premium liquors. Rates: $$$$ to $$$$$, all-inclusive.

DESIRE RESORT & SPA

998-872-8280
www.desireresorts.com
Highway 307, km 326

Two minutes south of the town square in Puerto Morelos, the narrow road enters a swampy area renowned for its crocodiles and other wild animals. The aptly named Desire Resort sits on the ocean side of the moatlike swamp, connected by a wooden bridge. Songbirds fill the air, and the palm trees sway a welcoming wave. Once past the

Keep Puerto Morelos clean—no "K-K" allowed on the beach! "K-K" is a Spanish play on the slang word "caca," in this case suggesting beachgoers clean up after their dogs.

lobby, you'll realize that Desire is not for the prudish. In fact, if you're not a swinger or at least open to the swinger lifestyle, you're best off choosing another place to spend your vacation. If, however, you're into that kind of thing, this stylishly done resort deserves a serious look. It is known in the "lifestyle" circles as one of the best hotels around for swingers who enjoy traveling to the tropics to meet others, have fun, and cast away their inhibitions, assuming they had any to begin with.

The 110-room all-inclusive resort accepts only adult couples, and minutes after arrival it's obvious why that is. Billed as "clothing optional," the hotel caters much more to the sexually liberated set than the run-of-the-mill nudist or "naturist." Public displays of affection, even extreme affection, are allowed and, in some designated areas, encouraged. And even though there's a strict "no means no" policy, it's clear that there are lots of yeses going on.

There is a great beach, and the local officials look the other way (literally), allowing guests to be on the beach in the buff, though it's generally frowned upon in most other areas. There are three restaurants, four bars, a dance bar, a fitness room, a beauty parlor, and a spa with steam room and several treatment rooms. There are two pools and a huge Jacuzzi with room for 30 people (I'm sure you could fit more if you tried), which seems to be the center of attraction most days. Next to the dance bar there is a "play room" where the most sexual activity takes place.

The rooms are spread out in low-rise thatch-roofed buildings, and each has a garden or ocean view, bathrobes and slippers, CD player, and fully-stocked minibar. Room rates include all meals, snacks, 24-hour room service, premium liquors, entertainment, and nonmotorized watersports. Rates: $$$$ to $$$$$.

Top 10 See-and-Be-Seen Hotels of the Riviera Maya Area

BLUE PARROT, PLAYA DEL CARMEN: With an open-air dance floor and fire dancers at your back door, you can't go wrong. (See chapter 2.)

FAIRMONT MAYAKOBA, PUNTA BETE: The huge stone entryway makes you wonder what's inside; only the privileged few know for sure. (See this chapter.)

AQUA CANCÚN: Cancún's one and only lounge hotel, with 24-hour DJ and luminescent bar pillows. (See this chapter.)

HOTEL BÁSICO, PLAYA DEL CARMEN: The prosperous days of 1950s Latin America glorified with a rooftop bar, oil-tank swimming pools, and rooms with neon lights. (See chapter 2.)

HOTEL DESEO, PLAYA DEL CARMEN: Up the unmarked stairs, it's the hip hangout for the Playa elite. (See chapter 2.)

HOTEL ESENCIA, XPU-HA: The former estate of an Italian duchess can be yours, for a price. (See chapter 3.)

MAROMA RESORT & SPA, PUNTA MAROMA: If it's good enough for Tom Cruise and Katie Holmes, you'll probably enjoy it also. (See this chapter.)

MEZZANINE HOTEL, NORTH OF TULUM PUEBLO: Swanky digs, topless beaches, and DJ parties in the shadow of the Tulum ruins. (See chapter 3.)

OCCIDENTAL ROYAL HIDEAWAY, PLAYACAR: Playacar's premier hotel proves all-inclusive resorts can be luxurious, too. (See chapter 3.)

PARAISO DE LA BONITA, NORTH OF PUERTO MORELOS: With a $3,000-a-night penthouse, you never know whom you may rub shoulders with at the swim-up bar. (See this chapter.)

✪ PARAISO DE LA BONITA RESORT & THALASSO SPA

998-872-8300 or 1-866-751-9175 (U.S. reservations)
www.paraisodelabonita.com
Highway 307, km 330

The turnoff for Paraiso de la Bonita is a few miles north of the town of Puerto Morelos; there is a gated entry marked Bahia Petempich. The road to the resort is not paved, but it is fairly smooth, with no major potholes, though there are large speed bumps every .25 mile or so. When the road reaches the beachfront, turn left and head north a short spell, and you'll arrive at the entrance to the hotel. With fewer than 100 rooms and suites, this very high-end, all-suite property has 1,100-square-foot standard rooms with ocean views. The service is impeccable, and the staff does an excellent job of making guests feel special. The architecture and decor are unusual, with a combination of African, Asian, Balinese, Caribbean, European, and Mayan inspirations. Guests enjoy a Jacuzzi, a sauna, tennis courts, a pool bar, and saltwater swimming pool. For an extra fee, there is a Mayan steam bath (temazcal), sailing tours, and full-service restaurant. Room rates include complimentary airport transfers, yoga and Pilates classes, daily breakfast, and a welcome gift. The beach is raked clean, but the tides are full of seaweed, making swimming less than pleasant. Rates: $$$$$; penthouse $3,000/night.

PUERTO MORELOS PROPER

CEIBA DEL MAR

998-872-8060
www.ceibadelmar.com
Highway 307, km 320

Halfway between the Cancún airport and Playa del Carmen, the Ceiba del Mar is a newer property spawned from the La Ceiba hotel in Cozumel, a longtime favorite of scuba divers. Along the beach just north of the town of Puerto Morelos, this 126-room resort is ideal for guests who want to get away from the city and the bustle of Cancún but don't want to be too far from the activities and fun of the Riviera Maya.

The architecture is a combination of traditional Mayan and contemporary Mexican. Set on a large plot of land surrounded by jungle, the resort is laid out with meandering paths in a sort of villagelike atmosphere, so guests never feel too crowded. There are two large, beautiful pools, rooftop sundecks, an upscale lobby, a gift shop, a beauty salon, and a European spa that uses organic spa-care products. Amenities include a water sports center, yoga classes, Jacuzzis, and a fitness center with free weights and exercise stations. There are three on-site restaurants and bars. Rates: $$$$, including continental breakfast; $$$$$, including a food and beverage plan.

SECRETS EXCELLENCE RIVIERA
998-872-8500
www.secretsresorts.com
Highway 307, km 323; northern end of Puerto Morelos

The most direct route to get to this adults-only resort, the sister property of Secrets Capri, is to take the turnoff just north of Crococun and follow it to the beach. Designed as a place of tranquility and relaxation, with an emphasis on privacy, personal service, and romance, Secrets Excellence's 446 suites feature a Jacuzzi tub, coffeemaker, and stocked minibar, which can make spending time in the room just as enjoyable as venturing out. There are six swimming pools, a fitness center, three outdoor Jacuzzis, a beauty salon, and a 35,000-square-foot full-service European spa, which has indoor and outdoor treat-

ment rooms and a soothing, gardenlike atmosphere. There are six theme restaurants (Mexican, Japanese, steak, seafood, gourmet, continental), plus a buffet. There are also nine bars, including a coffee bar, piano bar, swim-up bar, lobby bar, *palapa* bars, sports bar, and show bar. Snacks and drinks are available 24 hours a day, and everything is included. Rates: $$$$$.

H10 OCEAN CORAL AND OCEAN TURQUESA
998-287-2100
Supermanzana 12, Manzana 05, Lote 1-05, Puerto Morelos
www.h10hotels.com

Opened in early 2008, this all-inclusive resort complex is located just north of the "downtown" area of Puerto Morelos, at Punta Coral Beach. There are several pools, a day spa, activities program, kid's club, tennis courts, and great snorkeling just off the hotel beach. All 576 rooms are junior suites or larger and come with private balconies, Wi-Fi, stocked minibars (daily beer, water, sodas), safe, and ceiling fan. There are six restaurants: Japanese, Italian, beach, American, buffet, and Mexican. There's also a coffee shop open until midnight. The property appeals mostly to divers, families, and couples who want to be in a central location to explore nearby attractions. Rates: $$$$.

SOUTH OF PUERTO MORELOS

EL CID
www.elcid.com
Highway 307, km 316; southern end of town

The 350-room El Cid sits on a beach a couple miles south of town on a sheltered cove, with a marina that offers mooring for up to 200 boats. The resort is all-inclusive and operates much like the chain's resort in Mazatlan, with a strong emphasis on time-share sales. Rates: $$$$ to $$$$$.

HOTEL OJO DE AGUA

998-871-0202
www.ojo-de-agua.com
Highway 307, km 321; Avenue Javier Rojo
Gómez at the beach

On a northern beach between Bahia
Petempich and the town square, Ojo de
Agua serves as somewhat of a home base for
beachfront activity. It has beach toys for
rent, a swimming pool, a full-service
restaurant, and an on-site tour office. The
hotel's 36 rooms, decorated in contemporary Mexican style, have air-conditioning
or fan and kitchenette. The hotel was dev-
astated by Hurricane Wilma in 2005 but
rebuilt and even improved its facilities.
Rates: $

RANCHO LIBERTAD SAK OL

998-871-0181
www.ranchosakol.com
Highway 307, km 318; southern end of
Puerto Morelos, past the Army base and
shipping facility

Sak Ol, formerly known as Rancho
Libertad, offers an alternative to the large
corporate-owned hotels for travelers who
value simplicity and serenity over luxury
and pampering service. There are 14 minimalist rooms with suspended beds, air-
conditioning (downstairs units), purified
drinking water, and a rocky yet calm and
natural beach that is practically deserted—a
good spot for more hotels. You can look to
the north and see a half-sunken barge at
the shipping facility that has been there for
years. Rates: $ to $$; includes a large buffet
breakfast each day, plus wireless Internet
access.

✪ HACIENDA TRES RIOS RESORT

800-224-4231
www.haciendatresrios.com
Highway 307, km 300, 7 miles north of

Playa del Carmen

Located next to the 326-acre Tres Rios ecopark, this ultra high-end all-inclusive
resort opened in the summer of 2008. It
features 273 suites with ocean or canal
views, two-person Jacuzzis, flat-screen
TVs, sitting area with sofabed, Internet
access, concierge service, and a private terrace or balcony. There are two swimming
pools, three outdoor Jacuzzis, a 500-seat
theater, kids club, six restaurants, three
bars, and a European day spa with a Mayan
temazcal. The property has 10 freshwater
lagoons, two rivers and a mile-long beach.
$$$$

DINING

CAFÉ FINCA
South side of the town square

Open for breakfast and lunch, this
European-style café serves fresh coffee,
crêpes, and homemade sandwiches. The
staff can also prepare meals to go for excursions and tours. Moderate.

CAFFETTO
One block north of the town square

This small café serves coffee, crêpes, pastries, full breakfasts, and fruit and snacks.
Open for breakfast and lunch. Inexpensive.

COCINA ECONOMICA
Northwest corner of the town square

This ultracasual restaurant, popular with
locals and budget travelers, offers super-
cheap lunches of typical Mexican and
Yucatecan foods, including tacos,
empanadas, and enchiladas. Inexpensive.

EL PICUDO AZUL
South side of the town square

With an extensive menu for these parts,

this casual eatery offers fresh fish, salads, steaks, enchiladas, and fish tacos. The bright and airy dining room is a nice spot to seek shelter from the sun. Moderate.

EL TIO
Northeast side of the town square

Sometimes open, sometimes not, this hole-in-the-wall eatery offers typical local fare. It's good if you're in a pinch: The staff will wrap up your sandwich or tacos to go, if you ask. Inexpensive.

LA MARINA
On the Marina El Cid
998-871-0184

Offering a view of the luxury yachts docked at the marina, this casually elegant restaurant serves lobster, fresh fish, and other seafood specialties. It also has steak, chicken, and upscale Mexican food. Sit in the shaded indoor dining room or the alfresco patio. Moderate.

LE CAFÉ D'AMANCIA
Southwest corner of the town square

This small café, with a few tables in a small dining room, serves sandwiches, fresh breads, cheesecake, fruit, espresso, cappuccino, and coffee. Open 8–3 and 5–10 daily. Inexpensive.

LOS GAUCHOS
Across from the church, near the town square

This sidewalk café serves pizza, pasta, empanadas, and Continental breakfast. Inexpensive.

MONCHIS
Southeast corner of the town square

Monchis (get it?) sells coffee, sandwiches, ice cream, and other snack items, as well as a selection of T-shirts and other souvenirs.

(You won't find items that are much different than at other area shops, but many of them are made locally, so you can feel good about your purchase.) There are a couple of small tables, but most diners get their food to go. Inexpensive.

OJO DE AGUA RESTAURANT & BAR
998-206-9179
Avenue Javier Rojo Gómez; on a northern beach, close to Secrets Excellence hotel

This casual beachfront restaurant, bar, and beach club offers a daily breakfast buffet, fresh seafood, and Mexican dishes, as well as a daily happy hour from 3 to 4. Inexpensive.

THE OLD FISHERMAN
North side of the town square

This second-story restaurant offers fresh lobster, chiles rellenos, hogfish in butter, grouper, and other seafood dishes, plus grilled steak and chicken. The dining room is air-conditioned, and the waiters are longtime local residents who can give you advice on tours and activities. Moderate.

PELICANOS RESTAURANT
Southeast corner of the town square

The most prominent restaurant near the town square, it's also the largest. It offers a selection of Mexican and American breakfasts for less than $5, and for lunch and dinner, it's seafood or nothing. Try the fried whole fish, the shrimp ceviche, or the grilled shrimp, and you can't go wrong. There are tables inside, but there's no air-conditioning, so your best bet is to find an empty *palapa*-covered table facing the beach to catch a bit of breeze. Moderate.

PORTO BELLO
South side of the town square

Good Italian food, including pasta, pizzas, salads, and lasagna, is served here in a fan-cooled dining room or at sidewalk tables. Open for lunch and dinner. Moderate.

RESTAURANTE EL MUELLE
South of the town square, just west of the Army station

Turn back toward the highway instead of the ocean, and you'll find this bustling restaurant. It is popular with workers from the shipping facility and gets busy at shift change. Very inexpensive lunch items are served, including ceviche, chicken tacos, and rice and beans. Inexpensive.

✪ YAX-CHE RESTAURANT
At the back side of the La Ceiba Hotel, facing the main street

A second location for the restaurant of the same name in Playa del Carmen, it offers traditional Mayan cuisine for lunch and dinner, including turkey, *tikin chic* (baked fish wrapped in banana leaves), and great steak. The upscale, relaxing dining room is decorated with replicas of Mayan relics, tropical plants, and carved stone. It's also one of the few places around with air-conditioning. Expensive.

SHOPPING

ALMA LIBRE BOOKSTORE
South side of the town square

This shop sells newspapers, magazines, used books, maps, regional books, and paperbacks.

HUNAB-KU
Half block south of the town square

Offering crafts, blankets, hammocks, T-shirts, and souvenirs, the shop is owned by a group of 18 families in a sort of co-op, where they work together on arts and crafts and then sell them direct to the public, without a middleman. You can watch the artists working on hammocks, jewelry, wood carvings, native clothing, and other creations.

GROCERIES & SERVICES

ATM MACHINE
North side of the town square, next to Casa Martin

CASA MARTIN GROCERIES
North side of the town square

If they don't have it at the mini-super, they probably don't have it here, either. But at least it gives you some hope.

INTERNET CAFÉ
Southwest corner of the town square

They offer Internet connection for $1.50 an hour, long-distance phone calls to the United States and Canada for 50 cents, fax service, office supplies, and stationery.

MARAND TRAVEL
998-871-0162
www.puertomorelos.com.mx
Southwest corner of the town square

This full-service travel agency offers airline ticketing, hotel reservations, car rental, and flight confirmations. They can also book any of the tours in the area, including snorkeling, fishing, diving, Chichén Itzá, Xcaret, Xel-Ha, and Tulum. They have free local maps high-lighting area attractions, plus a few computers with Internet access.

MINI-SUPER
Northwest corner of the town square

Open daily, it sells groceries, snacks, and basic supplies.

MONEY EXCHANGE
Southwest corner of the town square

Open daily 8–6.

PHARMACY
West side of the town square

Sells snacks, over-the-counter and prescription medicines, sunblock, water, Gatorade, and batteries and film.

POLICE STATION
Northwest corner of the town square

PUERTO MORELOS CHURCH
West side of the town square

Service in Spanish only; service times are posted on the door. The doors are usually open for vistors; however, the church is fairly humble and without any historical significance, and it may not be of interest unless you're looking to attend a service.

TOURS & ATTRACTIONS

EL REY POLO COUNTRY CLUB
8 miles down the Ruta de Cenotes Road in Puerto Morelos

Part traditional polo field, part real estate development, this project encompasses 73 rustic home lots, clubhouse with restaurant, dressing rooms, golf driving range, horse stables, and children's play area. It seems wildly out of place deep in the Mayan jungle, but it is an interesting place to visit and ponder what it may become, if the region keeps growing so rapidly. The facility hosts regular polo tournaments that are quite high in quality and draw players and spectators from around the country.

FISHING & SNORKELING TOURS
Northeast side of the town square, next to the beach

The friendly folks at this tour office can arrange fishing and diving trips along the Puerto Morelos coastline, and because they have their own fleet of shaded 25-foot boats and local guides, they can custom-create a trip that suits your fancy. Basic tours include a four-hour fishing trip (including trolling and bottom-fishing), which includes beer, water, sodas, and all equipment and bait for $225 for up to four people. Common catches include dorado, tuna, barracuda, and even marlin and sailfish, if the timing is right. Snorkeling trips are $22 per person for a two-hour trip covering two different sites. For custom trips, the boats can be chartered for $40 an hour—which is common for sightseeing and sunset cruises. It's preferred that you make your reservations the day before so the staff can get all the necessary equipment and supplies, though impromptu trips can be arranged as long as you're flexible.

PUERTO MORELOS ADVENTURE TOURS
998-884-2316
www.snorkelincancunrivieramaya.com

Operating out of the Ojo de Agua hotel, this tour company offers active tours in and around Puerto Morelos. Top trips include a two-hour snorkeling trip for $35, which includes lunch, beer, equipment, and a visit to a handicrafts market. An ATV tour ($58 for one ride, $48 each for two) departs each day at 9 AM, returning at 2 PM, and includes visits to two cenotes, a Mayan village, and a market; swimming; and lunch and beer. There's also a $69 cenote and reef snorkeling excursion, which includes visits to caves, cenotes, and a marine park, plus gear, snacks, and drinks. It departs at 9 AM and returns at 5 PM.

✪ SELVATICA
Ruta de Cenotes, km 19
998-847-4581
www.selvatica.com.mx

This park runs adventure tours from hotels in Playa del Carmen and the Riviera Maya. The trip includes a visit to a 247-acre preserve, with bike riding, zip-lining, canopy tours, and lunch. Impromptu visits can also be accommodated. The park boasts a zip-line circuit that has 24 platforms and is more than 2 miles long, making it the longest circuit in North America. There is also a 160-foot-wide cenote, perfect for cooling off and swimming. Adults $59, children $42, including transportation; adults $42, children $29, entry only. Admission includes the zip-line canopy tour, biking, cenote swimming, lunch, drinks, and lockers. This trip was named, "one of the 35 great adventures of the world" by *Travel & Leisure* magazine. Highly recommended.

Playa del Secreto & Playa Paraíso (Highway 307, km 308–312)
Playa del Secreto and Playa Paraíso combine to form one of the largest stretches of mostly undeveloped beach remaining in the area. Several spots along the shoreline are frequented by sea turtles, which lay their eggs in the balmy summer months. The area is dominated by the massive Iberostar resort complex, which includes four separate but connected all-inclusive resorts, totaling more than 1,200 rooms. There is a convention center operated

Dried seaweed lines some of the deserted beaches in Playa del Secreto.

by Iberostar and an 18-hole golf course, which opened in mid-2005 and features 18 holes designed by P. B. Dye, the son of renowned course designer Pete Dye.

LODGING

PLAYA DEL SECRETO & PLAYA PARAÍSO

EL DORADO ROYALE—A SPA RESORT
998-872-8030
www.karismahotels.com
Highway 307, km 312, Playa Paraíso

This 432-room, all-inclusive, adults-only resort bills itself as "laid-back luxury," and it seems to be an appropriate description for a resort best known for its in-room hot tubs and patio hammocks. Spanning 450 acres of prime beachfront land, the hotel has a mile-long beach (called Punta Brava) marked by white sand, a few rocks, and hundreds of palm trees. All rooms have indoor Jacuzzis,

cold air-conditioning, private terrace with hammock and chairs, and a coffeemaker and stocked minibar. At mealtime, guests choose from international, Italian, gourmet Mexican, Pan-Asian, or grilled cuisine. There are also six bars, ranging from secluded and romantic to lively and sociable. Recreation options include paddleboats, sauna, steam baths, yoga classes, fitness center, tennis, kayaking, or even free scuba clinics. The on-site European day spa offers a variety of traditional European and regional Mayan treatments. At night, guests can head to the outdoor *palapa*-covered discotheque for live entertainment and dancing. Rates: $$$$ to $$$$$.

IBEROSTAR PARAÍSO BEACH
984-887-2800 or 1-888-923-2722 (U.S.)
www.iberostar.com
Highway 307, km 309, Playa Paraíso

Part of the massive five-resort Iberostar complex, the Paraíso Beach property has

The beach in front of the Iberostar complex is one of the area's best.

388 rooms and suites with satellite TV, stocked minibar, coffeemaker, and private balcony. There are six restaurants, two pool bars, lobby bar, cigar bar, sports bar, and a theater with nightly live shows put on by the staff. There is a huge meandering pool and large sundeck, and a kids' pool and kids' club keeps children ages 5–12 entertained during the day. Other activities include aerobics, archery, sailing, table tennis, tennis, volleyball, water polo, and windsurfing. Internet access, scuba diving (there is an on-site PADI dive school), spa services, and tours are available for an additional fee. This is the most affordable of the Iberostar properties, making it most popular with families and those seeking package deals. Rates: $$$$ to $$$$$; package deals can bring the price down.

IBEROSTAR PARAÍSO DEL MAR

984-877-2800 or 1-888-923-2722 (U.S.)
www.iberostar.com
Highway 307, km 309, Playa Paraíso

Stretched out along nearly a mile of idyllic beachfront, the 388-room Iberostar Paraíso del Mar is an all-inclusive resort popular with budget travelers who are looking for an active vacation full of fun water sports and tours, with plenty of relaxation mixed in. Since the resort is only 9 miles from Playa del Carmen, many guests go into town for shopping and nightlife, though with the nightly shows and on-site restaurants and bars, it's not really necessary. Rooms are housed in 11 low-rise buildings clustered along the beach, giving all guests ready access to the soft sand and clear water. There is a PADI dive shop, which offers diving and snorkeling trips to nearby reefs (for an extra fee). The grounds are amazing, with several pools emptying into a central canal. Amenities include tennis courts, a fitness room, a day spa, an outdoor Jacuzzi, and a swim-up bar. The main nightclub that services all the Iberostar hotels is at this resort. Rates: $$$$ to $$$$$.

Hotel Choices: All-Inclusive or European Plan

One of the first decisions travelers need to make when planning their trip is whether to stay in an all-inclusive (AI) or European Plan (EP) hotel. AI resorts generally include all food and drinks consumed on-site, plus a variety of non-motorized watersports, activity programs, and fitness centers. Some even include premium alcohol, gourmet a la carte meals, stocked minibars, and other amenities. European Plan (EP) hotels frequently have their own restaurants and bars also, but guests have to pay for any meals or drinks that they have.

The Riviera Maya has a growing number of all-inclusive resorts, practically pioneering the concept in Mexico. Most of the large-scale full-service beachfront resorts are operated as AIs, while the smaller independently run hotels along the beach and near Playa del Carmen's Quinta Avenida are operated on an EP basis.

Overall, the decision on whether to choose for an AI or an EP is up to the traveler. There are positives and negatives to both choices.

AI resorts are generally good if:

You don't want to do much planning. AIs are generally higher priced than hotels because you are getting all meals, activities, and alcohol included. However, the food and activity choices can get tiresome, and some guests complain that mixed drinks are watered down, though this is certainly not always the case.

EP hotels are generally good if:

You are a little more adventuresome. You will pay less on average but will need to make arrangements for food, activities, and alcohol yourself. Since you'll likely be spending more time away from the hotel, you will get a more authentic Mexican experience.

Now let's get into the details.

Food

Obviously, meals are included at AIs while they are extra for those staying in EP hotels. AIs generally have limited choices and unless you go for the very expensive resorts, the quality of the food can range from poor to very good. Most AIs have a main dining room where meals are served buffet style and a small selection of a la carte restaurants on-site available for little or no extra charge. Reservations are usually required for the a la carte restaurants and can be difficult to get if the resort is busy. It is not unusual for those who stay at AIs to report that they get tired of the food choices by the end of their stay.

On the other hand, most Playa hotels have limited menus, meaning you'll either have to go grocery shopping at the local super market or eat out at the surrounding restaurants. The quality and prices of the restaurants varies widely, but exploring the town looking for a good place to eat can also be a lot of fun.

Drinks

All-inclusives include unlimited drinks, including water, juices, sodas, beer, and mixed drinks, which is

IBEROSTAR PARAÍSO LINDO

984-887-2800 or 1-888-923-2722 (U.S.)
www.iberostar.com
Highway 307, km 309, Playa Paraíso

The Paraíso Lindo has 448 rooms and offers midrange lodgings for travelers looking for comfort, elegance, and beautiful surroundings. The all-inclusive accommodations include

one of their main selling points. This is unfortunately not always as good a deal as it sounds. In Mexico, the same brands of liquor are available in different "grades," where each grade carries a different level of alcohol. The liquor you find in the all-inclusives is generally of the lowest grade, and some guests report that drinks sometimes taste watered down.

If you stay at an EP hotel, you will generally purchase your drinks at local bars, restaurants, or from the in-room minibar. The prices for liquor differ according to location, but you are generally assured of quality. If you really want to save money, take a trip over to Wal-Mart and stock up on the cheapest liquor in town.

Activities

Most AIs have a variety of activities tailored to their clientele: sports, exercise classes, dance classes, arts and crafts, pool games, and team sports are common offerings. It is less common for EP hotels to have these options available.

One problem with AI-sponsored activities is that these resorts tend to draw a very diverse crowd. Visitors are encouraged to research their resort fully, since you will generally spend most of your time there and you will likely end up socializing with other guests.

Bringing the Family?

Although parents should always know where their children are, the set-up of an AI resort, with their kids' clubs and activity programs, may allow parents to give children more freedom than they would get in a hotel that has a lot of casual traffic. This can be a big plus for AIs when parents and children have different ideas of what activities they are interested in. Again, parents should never get too lax with their children's safety while on vacation.

Convenience

Many people like the convenience of not having to carry money to pay for meals and activities. This is a nice perk of AIs.

Rooms

There is a wide range of room quality at both AI resorts and EP hotels. If having a very nice room is important, you should make sure you do your research carefully. Don't make the mistake of thinking that an AI will automatically be nicer than a nearby EP hotel; the quality of both varies greatly.

Cost

Although many believe that AIs are cheaper than EP hotels, this may vary depending on the vacationer and what kinds of activities they do while on vacation. Travelers who spend most of their time at the resort and partake in the free activities will probably find that an all-inclusive is the more economical choice. Vacationers who plan to take several tours and spend a lot of time outside the resort will probably find that an EP hotel is the lower-cost alternative.

Still not sure? Here's a helpful rule of thumb: if you have read this far, it means you like to do your research and enjoy learning about new things and should almost certainly stay at an EP hotel.

Content provided by SeePlaya.com, a great online source for insider's information on the Riviera Maya.

meals at the 12 restaurants (gourmet, Italian, Cajun, Asian, steak, and others), 14 bars (lobby, theater, pool, beach), plus 24-hour room service. Guests can also eat at any of the other Iberostar resorts in the area. There is even a wave pool—the only one in the Riviera Maya. This property is a big hit for honeymooners, families, and singles. Rates: $$$$ to $$$$$.

The main pool at Iberostar Paraíso Maya.

IBEROSTAR PARAÍSO MAYA

984-887-2800 or 1-888-923-2722 (U.S.)
www.iberostar.com
Highway 307, km 309, Playa Paraíso

The 432-room Paraíso Maya is laid out like a Mexican village, so guests never feel crowded. The rooms have TVs with DVD players, in-suite Jacuzzis, large marble bathrooms, and premium bedding. There are several pools, a lazy river tube slide, a large gym, a spa, a shopping plaza, and a kids' club. There are several specialty restaurants (Japanese, steak, Mexican, seafood), plus dining privileges at 16 others, 17 bars, and 24-hour room service. At night, guests head to the theater for live entertainment and then to the disco, located at the Paraíso del Mar. Rates: $$$$$.

✪ IBEROSTAR GRAND HOTEL PARAISO

984-887-2800 or 1-888-923-2722 (U.S.)
www.iberostar.com

Highway 307, km 309, Playa Paraíso

The newest and most luxurious resort in the Iberostar Playa Paraiso complex opened in March 2007. It offers an adults-only all-inclusive environment to counter the often-rambunctious family atmosphere found at the other hotels. The Greco-Roman architecture of the hotel blends with the jungle-like terrain, full of tropical gardens and flowering trees. Guests are warmly greeted at check-in with a cold towel and glass of champagne, setting the tone for an indulgent vacation, where nearly everything is included in the room price, including nightly theatrical shows, premium brand liquors, golf, sailing, wine tastings, and gourmet à la carte meals. Guests at the Iberostar Grand have access to the facilities at the other resorts within the Playa Paraiso complex, including 19 restaurants and 19 bars. Even for guests who prefer to stay on property, there are many dining options, including a beachfront international buffet, a steakhouse, Japanese restaurant, Italian restaurant and 24-hour room service.

There are three swimming pools, including a huge saltwater pool, a lake-like freshwater pool and a heated indoor pool. The beach is nearly .5 mile long and is dotted with sunbeds, ideal for taking a snooze in shaded comfort. Active guests can head to the fitness center and hit the workout stations, treadmills and free weights, or even take advantage of the included yoga, Tai Chi, Spinning, and dance classes.

The Playa Paraiso Resort Spa services all the hotels in the complex. It offers 32,000 square feet of Zen-like luxury and specializes in couples treatments, thalasotherapy, and beauty treatments. There are Jacuzzis, saunas, Turkish baths, Roman baths, and a Mayan temazcal sweat lodge. Massages are offered in the spa, on the beach or in the guest rooms. Guests have playing privileges at the adjacent 18-hole championship golf course, designed by P.B. Dye. Hotel guests get one round of golf per person for a stay of 4 nights or less, and two rounds for longer stays. A full-scale convention center welcomes groups with more than 15,000 square feet of space, ideal for upscale meetings, conventions, and expositions.

Guest rooms are housed in modern buildings spread out around the complex. All rooms are actually suites, with one king or two double beds, spacious floor plans, two-person jetted tubs, satellite TV, CD/DVD player, MP3 docking station, safe, coffeemaker, ceiling fan, premium linens, stocked minibars (including beer, wine and liquor), premium bedding, and private terrace or balcony, depending on location. Bathrooms are large, with marble fixtures, luxury amenities, bathrobes, and slippers. Nightly turndown service is complimentary. Rates: $$$$$.

MAYAN PALACE RIVIERA MAYA
984-206-4000
www.mayanpalace.com.mx
Highway 307, km 310, Playa Paraíso

Home to what may be the largest and most impressive entryway of any hotel in the Riviera Maya, the aptly named Mayan Palace is equally inspiring once you're inside. With such a grand entrance, it's a bit surprising that the resort has only 336 rooms. Though the architecture may be inspired by the traditional Mayan building style, with thatched-palm roofs, low-rise buildings, and heavy use of local materials, the standards of luxury are significantly higher than even the Mayan gods could have imagined. The rooms are thoroughly contemporary, with tropical colors, soothing earth tones, cold air-conditioning, great views, bold artwork, and marble floors. The beach is beautiful but rocky, so be prepared to pick your way through the rough terrain if you want to go swimming. There is an on-site 18-hole Jack Nicklaus golf course, tennis courts, and an on-site kids' club, which provides complimentary child care in a fun environment. Since the property is so large, some guests complain about the walking distances from one attraction to another, but the landscaping and the natural beauty seem to keep most happy. Rates: $$$$$.

PUNTA MAROMA
Six miles south of Playa Paraíso, quiet Punta Maroma has the kind of sugar-sand beach so often featured in postcards and travel agency brochures. The beach, more than 100 feet wide in many parts, is bordered by coconut palms and sea oats, and there are very few rocks and light waves, making it a great place for swimming and snorkeling. There are a few upscale resorts, villas, and private homes, but it has an uncrowded, timeless, and faraway feel to it, making it an ideal spot for a tropical escape.

CLUB EL MANDARIN

984-873-4700
www.clubelmandarin.com
Highway 307, km 299, Xcalacoco

This 320-room all-inclusive resort has a private entrance from the highway. Once inside, guests enjoy a calm and isolated beach, a big pool and Jacuzzi, three restaurants, several bars, a nightclub, live entertainment, two tennis courts, a gym, pool tables, a fitness area, and spacious rooms with private balconies. A kids' club keeps children entertained during the day while parents relax by the pool or take a tour. Guests can take a free shuttle to Playa del Carmen. Scuba diving, shopping, and Internet access are available for an additional fee. $$$.

✪ MAROMA RESORT & SPA

998-872-8200 or 1-866-454-9351 (U.S.)
www.maromahotel.com
Highway 307, km 305; enter through the Venta Club entrance

Recognized as one of the top hotels in the world, the 65-room Maroma Resort deserves its stellar reputation, with repeat guests making up a large percentage of the monthly reservations. The resort occupies some 25 acres of land, giving it an uncluttered and private feeling that can be hard to find in the area. Unlike many Riviera Maya resorts, Maroma is not the kind of place where visitors hang out in their cutoffs and tank tops, swilling margaritas and playing volleyball in the pool. Guests are much

Maroma's Lomi-Lomi Massage

The Lomi-Lomi massage is one of the oldest and most powerful forms of healing. It works gently yet deeply into the muscles with continuous, flowing strokes, offering a complete nurturing of the body and gifting the recipient with a deep sense of relaxation and well being. This flowing massage allows for a very close bond between the energy of the therapist and the client's energy, using long and slow movements and a very loving touch to relax you to the inner core, helping you to let go of old beliefs, patterns, and behaviors. Some people cry, others laugh, and others have a near out-of-body experience as they descend into a very deep state of relaxation.

Celebrity Guests at Maroma Resort

Tim Allen • Tony Blair • Tom Cruise • Claire Danes • Danny DeVito • Cameron Diaz • Matt Dillon • Minnie Driver • Farrah Fawcett • Enrique Iglesias • Brad Paisley • Sean Penn • Robert Plant • Prince Charles • Sharon Stone

more subdued, and there is even a dress code at the restaurant for dinner, with no jeans, sandals, or T-shirts allowed. Don't get the feeling that it's stuffy, though. It's definitely still relaxed, just classy.

The resort is down a gravel road and on an absolutely perfect beach. The jungle encroaches from all sides, and jungle animals seem ever present, including iguanas, birds, and even arboreal turkeys, which call loudly from the trees at dusk. At night, a thousand candles line the walkways, giving the hotel a romantic and faraway feeling. The buildings feature thatched roofs, furniture made on-site from native hardwoods, and original artwork throughout. Rooms have hand-painted tiles, wool rugs, oversize tubs, and cold air-conditioning, which gives each room a blend of the old and the new, the traditional and the contemporary, the simple and the sublime. The beach is dotted with shaded cabañas, and a refreshing pool is next to the terrace, overlooking the beach. Sunbathing guests are tended to by a pool concierge, who is always ready with a cold drink, warm towel, or refreshing bottle of water. The on-site Maya/Zen spa specializes in Reiki, facials, mud

There's plenty of room to roam at Playa Maroma. Courtesy of Maroma Resort

baths, aromatherapy, body scrubs, crystal therapy, and other types of body treatments. Massages are also offered at a beachside hut or in the hotel's lookout tower, perched four floors above the jungle canopy, making it one of the tallest points around.

A beachside *temazcal* (sweat lodge) is the place to be at dusk, when guests are led through a 90-minute sweat-lodge ceremony, followed by a refreshing dip in the sea. Another treatment, a flotation chamber, allows guests to float weightless in a hyper-salted water tank. A 45-minute rest in the chamber is supposed to be equivalent to an eight-hour sleep. An on-site gym has a full-time personal trainer, yoga and Pilates classes, and modern equipment. The restaurant, next to the beach, serves grilled fish, fresh seafood, lobster, salads, natural fruit juices, ceviche, and nightly specials. Try the *agua de chaya* for a refreshingly sweet alternative to water. Guests just give their room number when making purchases at the restaurant or other hotel installations, rather than signing a check each time.

Maroma has a variety of activities for

Jorge of the Jungla

Picture yourself in the virgin jungle of the Riviera Maya. Imagine a landscaped dotted with freshwater cenotes and subterranean rivers, caverns with exquisite rock formations and stalactites, and exotic foliage complete with rare orchids and bromeliads. Now add colorful birds, monkeys, deer, and the occasional jaguar.

The 300-acre Selva de Aluxes real estate development was created to offer residents and visitors access to this jungle, combined with a community cultural center, private beach access, a yacht club, landing strips for small aircraft, facilities for holistic wellness, and an organic produce market. The development is committed to protecting the environment, with the use of windmill turbines, solar panels, air generators, and a host of other environmentally-friendly techniques.

Property is available for purchase and can be used for a vacation home or a even a permanent residence. The community is moderately priced compared to nearby oceanfront developments. Lots start at 2.4 acres and at press time were available for a starting price of $105,000. www.selvadealuxes.com

The temazcal at Maroma Resort   Courtesy of Maroma Resort

guests to enjoy. From an early-morning nature walk (jaguars have been spotted in the past), and snorkeling and scuba diving, to trips to area cenotes and Mayan ruins, the on-site tour desk can help you plan any activity. At the resort, there are tequila tastings, chili tastings, cooking classes, and a Spanish immersion program, in which guests receive a colored bracelet that lets staff members know to speak to them only in Spanish.

The resort is closed for upgrades each August. Rates: $$$$ to $$$$$. The four-bedroom Villa Pisces has its own private pool and feels much more like a beachouse than it does part of a hotel.

✪ MI HOTELITO

998-872-8038
www.karismahotels.com
Highway 307, km 297

With only 24 rooms, including two spectacular honeymoon suites, Mi Hotelito is a very private resort, and it prides itself on offering personal service and luxurious accommodations. All rooms have an ocean view, plus minibar, coffeemaker, CD/DVD player, and private balcony or terrace with hammock. Even though there are only 24 rooms, there is a full-service restaurant and bar on-site serving international, Italian, and Asian food. Rates: $$$$ to $$$$$.

✪ SECRETS CAPRI

987-873-4880
www.secretsresorts.com
Highway 307, km 298

A lavish resort complex on 71 acres of pristine beach just south of Playa Maroma, the 285-room Secrets Capri is for adults only and all-inclusive. It appeals to active cou-

Playa Xcalacoco

Some small Mayan ruins and a coconut grove mark the small, secluded beach of Xcalacoco, which is just south of Punta Bete. There are a couple of *palapa* restaurants that serve seafood and Mexican dishes, and campers can set up their temporary home at the Xcalacoco campsite, which has solar power and public showers.

ples who want to experience a broad range of recreational options while being surrounded in the comfort of a high-end resort. The architecture is a combination of Mediterranean and colonial Mexican, with graceful arches, tile work, and tropical plants throughout. Guests are welcomed into the lobby with a glass of champagne and a chilled towel and then descend a grand staircase to the pool deck area. There is a European day spa offering more than 30 different treatments, a swim-up bar, a poolside Jacuzzi, and drink service at the pool and on the beach. Rooms all have private balconies, jetted tubs, CD/DVD players, high-speed Internet access, coffeemakers, stocked minibars, and marble bathrooms. There are meeting and special-event facilities, plus a full-service business center with Internet access. This is a popular spot for weddings and honeymoons, and it offers an on-site wedding planner. All meals, drinks, and nonmotorized water sports are included. Rates: $$$$ to $$$$$.

Punta Bete Region

Marked by the large wood-and-stone entrance of the Mayakoba megadevelopment, Punta Bete is just 4 miles north of Playa del Carmen, at km 296–298, making it popular for visitors who want to stay somewhere out of the way but still be close to the action of town.

LODGING

FAIRMONT MAYAKOBA
1-800-441-1414 (U.S.)
www.fairmont.com
Highway 307, km 297

Crowning the Spanish-owned Mayakoba development near Playa del Carmen, this family-friendly 401-room resort opened in May 2006. It features 90 two-story bungalows with only two to four rooms each, giving it a spread-out and spacious feeling (the resort spans 45 acres). The decor is home-style Mexican, with dark wood, stone, and a palette of gold, soft reds, and oranges throughout. The rooms have air-conditioning, ceiling fans, premium bedding, oversize tubs, high-speed Internet access, LCD TVs, DVD/CD players, and private balconies. The property has two infinity pools, a great beachfront, and a 20,000-square-foot Willow Stream spa, with treetop treatment rooms, mineral pools, and steam rooms. Guests are shuttled through the resort on boats and in golf carts, and bicycles are also available for guest use. Mayakoba will eventually have six self-contained hotels, two golf courses, and private homes. Given its remote location, many guests would assume that the hotel is all-inclusive, but it isn't. There are, however, several excellent restaurants and bars on-site. Rates: $$$$ for a standard room and $$$$$ for a suite.

✪ ROSEWOOD MAYAKOBA
Highway 307, km 298
Mayakoba
984-875-8000

Opened in 2008, this uber high-end resort and spa is located within the exclusive Mayakoba development. It has a couple of gourmet restaurants, golf course access, the world-class Sense Spa, fashionable tequila bar, and lush grounds. The 128 guest rooms (all suites, of course) are on par with what you'd expect at a Ritz-Carlton or Four Seasons, but its location along the waterfront and lagoon-like canals makes it all the more romantic and unique. All rooms are outfitted with superior linens, marble bathrooms, LCD TVs, stereo system, work desks, high-speed Internet access, and a private pool and sundeck. The more expensive waterfront rooms even have their own private boat dock. $$$$$.

MANDARIN ORIENTAL RIVIERA MAYA
984-877-3888
www.mandarinoriental.com
Highway 307, km 298

The 128-room Mandarin Oriental Riviera Maya opened in late 2007, bringing a new level of sophistication to the ultra-luxury all-inclusive category in the region. Fine artwork and sculpture gardens replace the Corona beer signs and water volleyball nets that seem so ubiquitous at other area resorts. The Mandarin is located on 36 acres of lush beachfront within the master-planned Mayakoba luxury development. The architecture is thoroughly modern, with smooth lines and cool colors. Interiors utilize native hardwoods, stone, and other local accents. Guests have easy access to three championship golf courses, including the El Cameleon course, operated by the neighboring Fairmont hotel.

The guest rooms are housed in two-story villas scattered through the resort grounds. All rooms feature water views, either of the ocean, a freshwater lagoon, a saltwater lagoon, or the canals that wind through the property. They are outfitted with high-speed Internet access, safe, satellite TV, minibars, premium bedding, and a private terrace or balcony. Many rooms have outdoor garden tubs or private plunge pools.

There are several on-site restaurants, multiple bar scenes and 24-hour room service. Guests enjoy exclusive access to three swimming pools and can go snorkeling, kayaking, and windsurfing at the hotel beach. There is also a fitness center, tour desk, kids club, and massive spa, known for its Watsu pool, where you can get a floating massage. Room rates: $$$$$. Suites are $1,365 to $15,500.

PETIT LAFITTE
(984) 877-4000
www.petitlafitte.com
Highway 307, km 296

Built on the site of the Capitan Lafitte hotel, one of the region's long-time favorites before Hurricane Wilma did it in, the Petit Lafitte is once again making this perfect stretch of beach a popular spot for families, divers, rich hippies, and honeymooners. There are only 30 rooms, half with garden views and half with ocean views. The buildings are crisp, modern, and white but the vibe still reflects the relaxed atmosphere that guests of the original hotel enjoyed so much. It's a bit remote and slow-paced for young singles, but it's still a fine place to relax and get away. $$$.

BLUE BAY GRAND ESMERALDA
984-877-4500
www.bluebayresorts.com
Highway 307, Km 300

This massive complex was originally built as the Gala Grand Esmeralda but opened as a Blue Bay in 2007. It is situated on a huge 180-acre complex with a .25 mile beach. The resort's 986 rooms host familes in an upscale family-friendly environment, with multiple swimming pools, nightly shows, varied restaurant options, five bars, a litany of land and water sports, and kids' club. Rooms are modern and tropical with stocked minibars, private outdoor spaces, satellite TV, DVD players, and PlayStation game systems. $$$.

THE TIDES RIVIERA MAYA

987-877-3000 or 1-866-332-1672 (U.S.)
www.tidesrivieramaya.com
Highway 307, km 294, Playa Xcalacoco (just
south of Punta Bete)

To get to The Tides Riviera Maya, follow
Highway 307 south just past the Tres Rios
resorts and ecology park and look for the
turnoff to the left. The 1.5-mile gravel road
leads to the hotel entrance, and only registered guests are permitted access.

Formerly known as the Ikal del Mar,
The Tides is small and very upscale, making it one of the more likely places to spot a
vacationing celebrity or business tycoon.
Far from pretentious, though, the resort
strives to harmonize with nature rather
than completely shut it out. The hotel
prides itself on the fact that no trees were
cut down during construction. At night,
tiki torches line the paths from the rooms
to the restaurant and along the beachfront.
Though the service, amenities, and price
clearly place it in the luxury category, there
are no marble bathrooms or video check-
in kiosks. Here the privileged setting, simple indulgences, and personal service
define luxury. A thatched palm pavilion at
the hotel entrance passes as the lobby, and
the 30 guest rooms and royal villas are
housed in freestanding modernized versions of Mayan-style huts scattered along a
winding sand trail that leads from the
powdery white beach to the jungle. The villas and furnishings are made from local
stones and hardwoods. While the setting is
exotic, don't expect iguanas and hermit
crabs to sneak in between the thatched
twig walls like they surely must have done
in the days of the Mayans, however. Rooms
are upgraded from the days
of old with sealed walls, imported linens,
private bathrooms, and—yes—even air-
conditioning. Each villa also has a private
terrace with plunge pool, hammock, and
an outdoor moon shower.

The hotel beach is wide and cleaned
daily. Guests relax under shady *palapas*,
sipping tropical drinks and snacking on
fresh ceviche. A long pier extends into the
Caribbean, giving guests a shortcut to the
good snorkeling spots. The pool and sundeck are just steps away. At mealtimes, the
two-level gourmet restaurant serves a
blend of Mediterranean and Mexican cuisine dubbed "Mexiterranean." There are
also Asian-inspired selections and Mayan
specialties. The wine list spans from
French to Spanish to Italian.

The hotel spa is where the real pampering happens. It offers a steam room,
Jacuzzi, Swiss showers, and several treatment rooms. A local Mayan shaman leads
guests in spiritual healing sessions at the
beachside stone sweat lodge, called a
temazcal. Other services include massage,
facials, body scrubs, and yoga lessons.
Rates: $$$$$.

2

Playa del Carmen

Playa del Carmen is in the geographic center of the Riviera Maya and is the region's principal city. It is the seat of the municipal government and is home to the area's primary lodging, dining, nightlife, and shopping options.

Playa, as the locals call it, is the only town in the region whose development fills the land between Highway 307 and the beach. Within the past few years, it has even spilled onto the west side of the highway, an area that is seeing more and more development, including major shopping centers and housing developments for the local population.

No longer a sleepy fishing village, Playa has grown into a cosmopolitan beach resort, while somehow staying true to its roots—typified by its laid-back lifestyle, low-density development, international flavor, and casual come-as-you-are vibe. Visitors will find small local inns next to luxury villas, taco shacks next to steakhouses, and dusty cantinas next to stylish lounges. The mix of people and cultures, the variety of tourist offerings, and the welcoming spirit of the locals make it a unique travel destination, not just in Mexico, but in the entire world.

Looking toward Cozumel from Playa's lighthouse

Put on Your Comfy Zapatos for a Walking Tour of Playa del Carmen

Take a walk through some of the older parts of Playa del Carmen and glimpse samples of the town's Mayan past, its dynamic present, and its international-flavored future. It makes a great introduction to the town and would be great to do as soon as possible after you arrive, as it will give you a good sense of the lay of the land and will introduce you to most of the key components of the downtown area.

Approximate time required: Two to three hours, including breaks.

If you're susceptible to heat, consider going early in the morning.

Be sure to bring: camera, water (or buy along the way), sunscreen, hat.

Note: This is not a loop. The walk ends about a mile north of where it starts.

Remember: Fifth Avenue is called Quinta Avenida locally.

The Beginning: 600 Years of Arrivals & Departures

Start at the very center of the Riviera Maya—the gazebo in the middle of the town square where Quinta Avenida (Fifth Avenue) meets Juarez Avenue. Stand in the center of the gazebo and gaze out at the bustling plaza, with its park benches, flowering plants and shade trees (notice the tree trunks, painted white for decoration only, though some will claim it's there to prevent insect infestation). Walk toward the water and consider buying a cup of fresh fruit (cantaloupe, watermelon, mandarins, mangos, cucumbers, and coconuts), topped with chili and lime for $1.50. If you're already thirsty for a cold beer or frosty margarita, the La Palapa bar at the beachfront is a good place to watch the action on the beach while sitting in the shade. With the beach on your left, head south from the bar and you'll see a low-rise cement building set back on your right, serving as military barracks and topped with radio antennas. The soldiers at the entrance are armed with machine guns and are usually willing to pose for a picture.

Keep going south to the ferry dock, which was first built in 1969-70 and has regular departures for Cozumel Island, located 11 miles offshore. Peek inside the Sr. Frog's Bar and check out the VW bus turned into a DJ booth and the swinging barstools modeled after lifeguard throw buoys. Out of Sr. Frog's, **turn away from the beach and head uphill**. One store up from Sr. Frog's, **cut left between the storefronts and then pass through the arched passageway** to the other side of the block. **Walk through the courtyard toward** the Playacar Palace hotel. Once you get to the cobbled street, you'll see a small Mayan shrine on a little ridge to your right, but **keep following the street up and around the hotel**, walking parallel to the dry creek bed. Keep the hotel on your left until you come to where the road takes a sharp left toward the beach. **On your right** are the remains of three more Mayan shrines, collectively called Xaman-Ha.

This site, which means "Waters from the north," is an important ceremonial shrine discovered in 1528 by Francisco de Montejo (the same Montejo whose name was given to a local beer from Merida that's sold around town). Mayan women would pray here before heading across the straits to Cozumel in their dugout canoes to worship Ixchel, the goddess of fertility. A placard at its base tells more of the story. After viewing all three shrines, **head toward the tennis courts behind and to the right of the ruins**, then **head back toward the town plaza**, but on the road that's just inland from the one you came in on. This street is called Coral Negro and it passes through a quiet residential area with million-dollar homes straddling the wet-weather creek. **Go past the guard post and veer left**. Before you get to the restaurant, peek over the rail to your left to see a cave that has been carved into the creek bed. Access was blocked off in the late 90s, but it's still interesting to look down and ponder what sort of ancient Mayan rituals may have taken place there 600 years ago.

On the corner of Coral Negro and 10th Avenue, you'll see a local sports bar with a Spanish fountain at the corner. The Playa del Carmen airport (airstrip, really), built in 1979, is just another block inland, but

Playa del Carmen Municipal Park

there's not much to see. **Turn right at the fountain onto 10th Avenue** and **head back to the north**. On the right is the Paseo del Carmen outdoor shopping mall, with its trendy shops, local artists, human statues, and strolling musicians. Once you pass the mall, **make a left onto 1st Street South.** If you're here during business hours, you'll likely see a mule hanging out on the sidewalk, advertising the souvenir shop on the corner. **Walk for 1 block along 1st Street and then turn right onto 15th Avenue**. As you walk north you will be flanked by an elementary school on your right. The first intersection is Juarez Avenue and there's a tourist information office directly opposite of where you're standing if you're interested in picking up some brochures on tours and other attractions. **Turn right onto Juarez and head back in the direction of the beach**. This is a hectic stretch of road with mopeds and taxis buzzing by, plus buses arriving and departing at the small ADO bus terminal, (former site of the town's original tortilla factory) that will be on your left as you approach Fifth Avenue.

    Kitty-corner from the bus station is the tiny Playa del Carmen chapel, which was erected in 1964 and underwent major renovations in 2007 to add the water bridge, rear glass wall, and resurfacing of the exterior whitewash. Respectful visitors are welcome to step inside the church and enjoy the ocean view behind the altar and a calming respite from the bustle of the town square. No padded kneelers are present, as worshippers simply kneel on the floor. No photography is allowed and donations placed in the receptacle by the door are appreciated to help with regular upkeep.

    This may be a good time to stop at the Playa Mart shop, located at the same intersection as the bus station, for a bottle of water, quick snack, or maybe an enormous velvet sombrero and a bottle of mezcal with a worm at the bottom. Next, you'll want to **head north on Quinta (away from the town square)**.

This is the main pedestrian thoroughfare through the heart of the tourist zone. On your right, you'll see a religious shrine of another kind—the local McDonald's. Take note, though, even this American hamburger joint has a thatched-palm roof, as if that somehow helps it blend in. There is an ATM under the McDonald's and two more inside the ADO station, so this may be a good time to get some extra pesos if you're feeling low on cash. **Stay on Quinta for 2 blocks**, enjoying the rush of locals mixed with guests of nearby hotels, day-trippers from the all-inclusive resorts along the coast, and cruise ship escapees stretching their legs. Chances are good you'll be offered fake Cuban cigars, drink specials, a date with someone's sister, or a prescription for Valium if you hang around very long. You might also see flute-toting musicians, a parrot "driving" a remote-control car, or a tiny colorful monkey on someone's shoulder—all of whom are willing to pose for a picture for a few pesos.

The Middle: Sneaking Around
The second intersection is 4th Street and you'll want to turn right here, heading downhill toward the beach. On your left, you'll pass a scuba shop, a convenience store, and an old painted sign for the Yan-Tem Beach Club. The facility is mostly defunct now but has avoided the condo rush because it hides a large freshwater cenote, making it nearly impossible to build around. **Enter through one of the corridors leading behind the convenience store, or even go straight into the Yan-Tem entrance** to catch a glimpse of the cenote, currently occupied by a family of resident turtles and used as an aqua playground for the families living on the property. If you're due for a break, you can take a seat at the Yan-Tem beach bar and enjoy the waterfront view.

Hidden cenote at Yan-Tem

Next, **backtrack a bit up 4th Street and cross over Quinta this time**. On this block, you'll discover a castle-like structure that was built as the town's first indoor shopping mall in the early 2000s, though it was so ill-conceived, with no parking and a maze-like interior, that it only lasted a few months before closing down. On the left is the Ajua Maya Cantina, a popular restaurant featuring nightly live music and playful Mayan waiters that entertain you during your meal. Be sure to shout "Aaa-hooo-waaa" as you walk by, and if you're hungry, take a lunch break here and show them this book for a free round of tropical drinks. **Keep heading uphill on 4th Street to 20th Avenue and turn right**. A small nearly unmarked shop on your left sells taxi driver uniforms, Playa del Carmen firefighter ballcaps, school uniforms, and other apparel and accessories that aren't meant as tourist items, but that really do make for fun souvenirs.

Keep going another block to the city hall municipal building. Turn **into the main structure on your left and enter the courtyard** to view a nice fountain backed by a huge colorful mural depicting life through the years in Playa del Carmen. The park across the street has a walkway with goalpost-like arches with the names of various towns within the Playa del Carmen municipal district, plus upright rocks displaying the state song and others showing how to count to 20 in the native Mayan language. Depending on the day, there may be a free show going on at the amphitheater on the northeast corner of the park. **Head back toward the beach on 10th Street and look for the Hotel Basico 2 blocks up on your right**. This hotel has garnered tons of media attention for its avant-garde design and daring use of materials, including cement walls infused with Caribbean sand, tire tread floors, latex window coverings, and twin rooftop swimming pools made from petroleum tanks.

Pass through the lobby with an, "it's OK, I know what I'm doing" nod to the handsome desk attendants and **take the industrial-style elevator to the top floor**. Here you'll be graced with an awe-inspiring view of the ocean, the lighthouse, and Fifth Avenue. Order a cocktail (I recommend the pear martini or the signature Basico cocktail) and linger for a bit in one of the swanky poolside sundeck cabanas, while enjoying the view. On your way back through the lobby, check out the selection of art and history books for sale, **then turn right back onto 10th Street and head toward the lighthouse** that crowns the El Faro condo complex.

Walk out on the beach and look beyond the waves and you can see the hotels that make up Cozumel's northern hotel zone. **Walk to your left on the beach and you'll find the Blue Parrot Beach Club**, where you'll see topless sunbathers of every shape and size and maybe catch a glimpse of the fire dancers rehearsing for their nightly show, which takes place each night after the beach club turns into a night club. **Cut through the complex next to the dance floor, past the reception area, and out to the street where you'll see OM Nightclub**.

El Fin: Playa's Past & Present

You're now at the eastern end of the 12th Street Party Strip, as I like to call it, though locals haven't progressed from calling it simply "la doce." **Head uphill on 12th Street past OM, Classico, Las Dioses, Kartabar, Il Divino, and the other patio lounges** that make up Playa's trendiest district. **Turn right back onto Quinta and head north for a couple of blocks. Look for a sign on your left for Calle Corazon**. This **angled alley is worth a short loop** to look at the shops and sit for a while in one of the hand-carved wooden chairs.

When you get back on Quinta, look across the road for a statue of a Mayan god with feathered headdress, which marks a small passageway that leads to a nearly forgotten Mayan ruin, about the size of a Volkswagen Beetle. It sits behind a chain-link fence, marked with a signpost from the National Institute of Archaeology, but is otherwise nondescript, with no placard explaining the history or other fanfare. Still, though, it's fun to see, and to try to envision what it may have been used for by the native Mayans. Perhaps

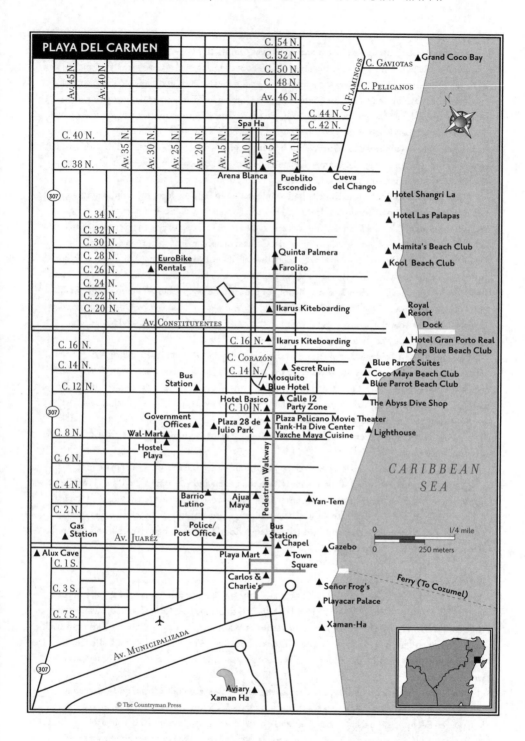

it had something to do with the gulley that you can see if you follow the hallway to the right of the ruin, past some of the town's least-trafficked storefronts. A single picnic table at the bottom of the ditch seems to serve as a workbench of some sort and it's possible that this area was once a freshwater lagoon, perhaps even used as a recreational swimming hole, and the temple served as an ancient lifeguard stand, though maybe not.

Go back to Quinta and head north again and you'll approach a tree on your right that is heavily adorned with glass orbs and rings of lights, first put there when the UltraFemme and UltraJewels shops opened in late 2007. It's especially nice to see at night, when it provides a warm glow visible from blocks away. **The big intersection ahead is Constituyentes Avenue,** marked with a large Olmec head (the predecessors of the Maya) statue in the center of the traffic circle. Across the street is Aca Los Tacos, which serves good tacos and great margaritas. Consider taking a picture with the giant cow, which is Playa's version of Kip's Big Boy. The structures to the north of here didn't exist 10 years ago and now constitute the area known as the "New Playa," "Little Italy," or the "International District," depending on who you talk to.

If you're not tired yet, **just keep walking north on Quinta**. The primary tourist district continues for another 10 blocks or so, with dozens of restaurants, bars, and shops ripe for exploring. Turn right anywhere along this stretch and you're only 2 blocks from the beach. This is where Mamita's Beach Club, KOOL Beach, and the other popular wave-watching and people-watching spots can be found.

After all that walking, I think it's time for a Corona. Or a margarita, or a piña colada ...

LODGING

For some travelers, selecting a hotel is part of the fun of a visit to Playa del Carmen. There are more than 350 hotels offering some 30,000 rooms in the Riviera Maya, with many of them in the greater Playa area. Within a 2-mile radius, visitors can see more than 70 hotels, many of which, while not necessarily large, would be perfectly suitable for most needs. (Many of the area's hotels—about 75 percent—have 30 rooms or fewer.) Though many people choose to book a hotel prior to arriving, most of the year it's completely possible to show up without a reservation and take a stroll around town looking at different properties and current prices before making a final decision. Most hotel operators will happily give travelers a quick tour of their property and rooms, and sometimes they will be willing to negotiate a discounted price. Accommodations range from student hostels and inns with very few amenities that cater to budget travelers, to large self-contained resorts with first-class facilities and services. There is also a new wave of "concept hotels," such as Hotel Básico and Hotel Deseo, which offer trendy accommodations in uniquely designed surroundings. Many hotels offer a wide range of room choices, with simple beach cabañas, modern hotel rooms, and luxury villas all at the same resort. The most important considerations are location (on the beach, on Quinta, or in town), budget, and desired atmosphere (romantic, singles, quiet, traditional). The selections in this chapter are organized into three different budget categories—budget, midrange, and luxury—and within each category there are a wide range of choices to please a wide range of tastes.

Lodging Prices

$	less than $75 per night
$$	$75 to $125 per night
$$$	$125 to $225 per night
$$$$	$226 to $350 per night
$$$$$	more than $350 per night

Antigua Posada Barrio Latino hotel Courtesy of Posada Barrio Latino

Budget Hotels

These properties are generally located a couple of blocks from the beach, between the town square and 30th Street. They are considered to be clean and safe but do not have many of the amenities that many travelers are accustomed to. Most do not have swimming pools, beautiful views, or on-site restaurants, and the rooms may not have in-room bathrooms, air-conditioning, or balconies. Prices range from $15 for a bed in a hostel dorm room to $65 for a well-kept room in a family-run inn with ceiling fan, purified water, and in-room safe. These hotels are popular with budget travelers, students, and short-term visitors who just need a place to stay for a couple of days while traveling through.

✪ ANTIGUA POSADA BARRIO LATINO

984-873-2384
www.posadabarriolatino.com
4th Street between 10th and 15th Avenues

This is the namesake hotel for the Barrio Latino neighborhood from 2nd to 6th Streets, between the beach and 30th Avenue. The area is reminiscent of the way that Playa used to be, with traditional hotels and a slower pace than the rest of town. The 16-room Italian-owned hotel is a popular home base for Europeans, student travelers, and others who may have money to stay at one of the more luxurious properties around town but choose to stay at a smaller hotel for the local charm, traditional character, and family-like service. The hotel is just 1.5 blocks from Quinta, providing quick access to the town's restaurants and nightlife. Rooms are secure and clean, with private bathrooms, tile showers, ceiling fans, and in-room safes. Many also have air-conditioning. The owners can book most of the same tours that the larger tour agencies can, but they return their sales commission to their guests, resulting in a nice discount. An Internet station is located near the front desk, and complimentary wireless Internet access reaches most rooms. Rates: $; including complimentary

Continental breakfast and free international calls. Highly recommended.

COLORES MEXICANOS HOSTEL

984-873-3701
15th Avenue between 2nd Street and Juarez Avenue

This affordable and safe hostel offers private rooms and four-person dormitories. They are located just 3 blocks from the beach, 2 blocks from the downtown bus station, and across from a park. Guests can access the Internet from a desk in the reception area and can watch TV in the lounge. It's a great place to meet other travelers. Rates: $, ranging from $40 for a private room to $12 in the dormitory.

COPA CABAÑA

984-873-0205
Quinta between 10th and 12th Streets
www.thecopacabanahotel.com

At the Copa Cabaña, located next to 100% Natural (see Cafés and Light Fare), lounging in the courtyard and going to the beach are always in fashion. The rooms are built around a shady central garden decorated with potted plants, tropical flowers, and Mayan-inspired artwork. The simple but comfortable rooms have air-conditioning, ceiling fans, and Mexican furnishings. There is a rooftop sundeck with Jacuzzi, hammocks, and a massage room. Rates: $ to $$. Recommended.

DON EMILIONE

984-873-2073
www.donemilione.com
Quinta at 2nd Street

Opened in 1999, this 12-room, three-story hotel has a modern feel to it. The rooms are large and have air-conditioning, wicker furnishings, tile floors, safes, TVs, private bathrooms, and purified tap water. The hotel is just a block from the beach, and guests have seating privileges and dining discounts at a nearby beach club. The on-site Mexican restaurant has sidewalk tables and an indoor dining room, and the bar has a nightly happy hour from 5 to 7. Rates: $ to $$, depending on the view (courtyard or beach) and the time of year.

Peso-Pinching Activities

Traveling on a budget? Try these free and fun activities:

- Take free salsa lessons Tuesday and Thursday at 7 PM at La Bodeguita del Medio (see Dining).
- Walk along the interpretive nature trail at the back of the parking lot of the Las Palapas hotel (see Luxury Hotels).
- Visit the Xaman-Ha ruins in Playacar, just south of the Playacar Palace hotel (see chapter 3).
- Head to the beach and build a sand castle in the shape of the great pyramid at Chichén Itzá.
- Get up early to watch the sun rise over the Caribbean. Some people like it even more than watching a sunset.
- Take advantage of the free appetizer/drink coupons offered by many restaurants along Quinta in Playa del Carmen.
- Stroll the park across from the municipal building and learn to count in Mayan from the educational displays.
- Grab your snorkel and take a dip in Manatee cenote, across from Blue Sky Resort in Tankah (see chapter 3).
- Watch the fire dancers perform their nightly show on the beach of the Blue Parrot bar (see Drinks & Dancing) at 11 PM or at the next-door El Pirata bar (see Casual Drinks) at midnight.
- Join the locals for a street party in Cozumel, complete with live music, each Sunday evening in the town square.
- Snorkel the protected cove at Akumal Bay and see moray eels, stingrays, and barracuda lurking in the shallows.

The Riviera Maya: A Land of Business Opportunity

Contributed by Brenda Alfaro

Great business opportunities abound in the Riviera Maya, and with careful consideration and planning, foreigners can invest successfully in this growth. Doing business in Mexico is not for the faint of heart, however. It requires moxie and experienced advice to be successful. Having a local on your side is always a plus, especially in Latin America, where polite business relationships guide you through the maze of paperwork, labor relationships, and license requirements. Patience is also a must-have virtue to survive the relaxing mañana Latin style.

Where do you start to create a business in Mexico? Well, not with the "slick talker and aggressive salesperson" attitude, would be my advice. First, look for someone who has been successful in a quiet way, who obviously has learned the ropes and has created the business and official relationships that have kept her in business. Seek her advice and be wise enough to listen to it.

Second, before stepping into the business community with a substantial investment, research and understand the legal system and labor relationships in Mexico. This is easily done on the Internet. Mexican laws are based on the Napoleonic Code, similar to the laws of France or Louisiana in the United States. Labor relationships are based on the "employee is always right" philosophy, and Mexican employees know their rights and use them effectively—as do the lawyers who represent them.

Third, understand the importance of a Mexican notary, which is a powerful appointed position in Mexico. Notaries create most of the official legal documents in Mexico, including establishment of corporations, buy-sell agreements, and real estate transactions. No transaction or legal agreement is considered legal in Mexico unless it has been officially registered. All parties to an agreement must sign it in front of a notary, and that agreement must be registered in the municipality's official records.

Fourth, before completing a business transaction, seek the advice of a person who is completely independent of the parties involved in the transaction and one you trust to translate the agreements to you accurately. I am always amazed when I hear that someone is using a lawyer or notary who was recommended by those who stand to benefit from the transaction, such as a seller or a real estate agent. A good rule of thumb is "If you would not do this in your country, you should not do it here."

FIESTA BANANA
984-803-0201
www.fiestabanana.com
Quinta at 32nd Street

With less than 20 rooms, a common terrace, and a rooftop sundeck, this three-story inn has the feel of a large and friendly home. Its location near the northern end of Nueva Quinta puts it in the middle of the action, and it's just a couple of blocks from Kool and Mamita's beach clubs. Rooms are spacious and offer traditional Mexican decor, air-conditioning, and tile floors. The staff is young and outgoing and can help provide local information and plan day trips. Rates: $. Recommended for budget travelers that still want to be in the middle of the action.

✪ HOSTEL PLAYA
984-803-3277
www.hostelplaya.com
25th Avenue at 8th Street

Located about .5 mile from the beach and directly across from the Wal-Mart, this inexpensive lodging alternative is a good spot for students and budget travelers who want a safe spot to stay but don't need much luxury. Rooms feature a natural wood motif and have mosquito netting, orthopedic mattresses, and clean bedding. There is a fully-equipped kitchen for guest use, plus a

Fifth, contract an accountant to keep you current with your tax filings and license requirements. Be careful whom you contract, and seek the advice of those who have experience here.

Sixth, avoid all lawsuits and labor board actions. Swallow your pride or anger and settle with an employee who is leaving or involved in a legal situation. In the end, it will save you money and stress and allow you to focus on your business at hand and not on revenge or a compelling desire to "win." If you do end up needing a lawyer, find one who actually knows the law and has strong legal contacts as well.

Seventh, be polite and patient—always! Mexican people are intelligent and are part of a formal, polite society. Do not underestimate their abilities or insult them. Stop, listen, and think before you answer or react. Directness is not a business asset in Mexico. Talk, smile, and never argue or raise your voice. If you do, the costs will be great.

Eighth, follow the rules. It is so much easier when you are always in compliance, which means no extra favors need to be made to run your business. Remember, the person who receives a favor will be out of power in a few months or years, and the new official will expect the same or more—so why begin? And get your FM3, our resident work visa. Don't risk deportation.

Ninth, treat your employees with respect, learn the labor laws, and use employee contracts. Talk with business owners in your field and understand your employee base. Call for references before hiring someone. Find out who the "professional labor board employees" are who move from business to business to collect a labor settlement. Look prospective employees in the eye—if they do not look back or seem distrustful, do not hire them. Trust your instincts.

Tenth, enjoy the experience. When your patience begins to wear thin, escape to the beach to relax, recharge, and remember why you chose to live and work in this paradise in the first place. Brenda Long Alfaro and her Mayan husband, Jorge Luis Alfaro Mérida, are successful restaurateurs in Playa del Carmen. They own the widely acclaimed Ajua Maya restaurant (see **Dining**), a seafood and Mayan grill; the Hacienda Maya restaurant (see **Dining**), featuring 19th-century French-influenced Mayan and Mexican cuisine; and Ajua Weddings, which offers custom-designed weddings and event services on the Riviera Maya. They also established the Fundación América Maya to provide health care, education, and economic programs to Mayan families and children.

common living room with sofas, TV, and DVD player. There is free coffee every morning and purified water all day long. At night, the central lounge area takes on an almost magical atmosphere, conjuring visions of a granola-traveler's version of the Hogwarts dining room, as small groups gather around tables drinking beer (available at the on-site bar), digging through guidebooks, and sharing tales from the road. Rates: $; male, female, or mixed bunkrooms $13 per night; private rooms with double beds $20 to $25 per night. All guests receive a large locker with padlock. No credit cards; no children. Recommended.

HOTEL ALUX
984-803-2482
www.hotelalux.com
14th Street between 10th and 15th Avenues

This small, 16-room, inn-style hotel has contemporary Mexican design and hacienda-inspired furnishings. All rooms have air-conditioning and private bathrooms. It's a good choice for visitors who don't mind being a couple blocks removed from the action. Rates: $; standard double rooms start at $35; rooms with kitchenettes and ceiling fans $40 to 50.

A Sunset Facing East?

Since the Riviera Maya faces east, it is not known as a good place to witness a tropical sunset. If your beach vacation just won't be complete without watching the golden orb disappear into the horizon, there's still hope. Try these five tips for catching a sunset in the Riviera Maya.

• Take a champagne sunset cruise aboard the Fat Cat 41-foot catamaran in Xaac Cove near Puerto Aventuras and watch the sun sink into the Caribbean (www.fatcatsail.com).

• Walk to the point at the north end of Playa del Carmen Cove, in back of the Gran Porto Real hotel, and watch the sun go down next to the El Faro lighthouse.

• Climb to the top floor of the Paseo del Carmen mall, next to the Area Body Zone and enjoy a rare sunset over downtown Playa and the jungle beyond.

• Take a day trip to Isla Cozumel and stay for sunset, then take a late ferry back to the mainland. Since the town's main beaches and town square face west, the sun sets over the ocean, just like in the postcards.

• For the ultimate unobstructed sunset view, schedule a sundown skydive and look down, not up, at the setting sun (see chapter 4).

HOTEL AZUL

984-873-0562
www.hotel-azul.com
Quinta between 10th and 12th Streets

This hotel, in the center of the main tourist strip, has 20 rooms with private bathrooms and traditional Mexican ambience. It may not be fancy, but you can't beat the location if you want to be near the action. There is no pool, but there is a shady courtyard, and the hotel is just 1.5 blocks from the beach. Rates: $ to $$$.

HOTEL DELFIN

984-837-0176
www.hoteldelfin.com
Quinta at 6th Street

A no-frills budget hotel in the heart of the older part of Quinta, the Hotel Delfin has simple but clean rooms with air-conditioning, TV, minibar, and safe. Rates: $.

HOTEL LAS MOLCAS

984-873-0070
www.molcas.com.mx
1st Street at Quinta

This hotel is at the west end of the town square, making it especially convenient to the Paseo del Carmen mall and Quinta, as well as the ferry dock. There are 25 rooms with private bathrooms, air-conditioning, and minifridges. It was one of Playa's very first hotels, opened in 1974, and is clean but a bit dingy and not especially charming. Rates: $ to $$.

HOTEL RIVIERA CARIBE MAYA

1-800-822-3274 (U.S.)
www.hotelrivieramaya.com
10th Avenue between 28th and 20th Streets

This local-style inn is a budget hotel but doesn't feel like one. Its 22 rooms have contemporary design, air-conditioning, ceiling fans, cable TV, minifridge, and safe. There is also a pool, Jacuzzi, and restaurant. Rates: $ to $$, depending on room class and time of year.

HOTEL VISTA CARIBE

984-873-0349
www.hotelvistacaribe.com
Quinta at 6th Street

A longtime favorite for budget travelers, this 36-room hotel has a great location on Quinta and is only a block from the beach. All rooms have air-conditioning, ceiling

Pension San Juan

fans, TVs, and safes for storing valuables. Some rooms have an ocean view, and others face the street. There is a small swimming pool and a flower garden. Rates: $ to $$.

JUNGLA CARIBE

984-873-0650
www.jungla-caribe.com
Quinta at 8th Street

Full of local charm, this hotel has been around a while and has developed a loyal following. Though it may not be trendy, it has a lot more character than many of the newer hotels. The winding staircases, shaded courtyard, small pool, and tile work all add to the ambience. The on-site Jaguar restaurant and bar serves Mexican dishes and seafood in a funky and fun setting overlooking Quinta. Rates: $ to $$, depending on air-conditioning and terrace availability.

LA ZIRANDA

984-873-3933
www.hotellaziranda.com
4th Street between 15th and 20th Avenues

With its stucco walls, *palapa* roof, green grass, and stone walkways, La Ziranda charms from the moment you see it. There are 16 rooms with air-conditioning or ceiling fan, and purified water. Each opens onto a grassy courtyard. Rates: $ to $$, depending on the time of year. No credit cards.

✪ MAYA BRIC/ TANK-HA HOTEL

984-873-0011 or
984-873-0302
www.mayabric.com or www.tankha.com
Quinta between 8th and 10th Streets

This family-owned hotel has two names and two Web sites, but it's really the same place. Maya Bric is the original name of the hotel, and Tank-Ha is the on-site dive shop and the name that is used when marketing the hotel to divers. There is a shaded pool for basic dive instruction, and the 29 simple rooms have private bathrooms and air-conditioning. Divers can learn about area dives and book their trips at the dive shop, a good spot to meet other divers if you need a dive buddy. Rates: $ to $$.

OM HOTEL & LOUNGE

984-879-4784
www.omplaya.com
12th Street between the beach and Quinta

Built above the ultra-hip red-and-black OM Lounge, this 17-room hotel is great for travelers more concerned with proximity to the party scene and the beach than they are with posh accommodations and service. The smallish rooms are fairly plain, with simple furnishings, walk-in shower stalls, and small TVs, but they also have multiple candles, powerful window-unit air condi-

tioning, ceiling fans, mini-fridges, and
refillable pitchers for purified water (dispenser on the second floor). Given their
unbeatable access to the 12th Street
nightlife scene (including the Blue Parrot,
just across the street), the rooms themselves somehow seem to remain fairly
quiet, especially on the upper floors. Guests
can secure their valuables in a safety box at
the front desk, which is manned sporadi-
cally through the day. Rates: $$ to $$$.

✪ PENSION SAN JUAN
984-873-0647
www.pensionsanjuan.com
Quinta between 6th and 8th Streets

This friendly, family-run, 12-room inn is
located right on Quinta. Rooms have traditional Mexican decor, ceiling fans, safes, and
private bathrooms, and some also have air-
conditioning, TVs, minifridges, and a view of
Quinta. There is an incredibly charming
outdoor kitchen for guest use on a terrace
overlooking Quinta, which gives you the
sense that you're in your own private café.
Rates: $; include complimentary coffee and
cooking supplies. Highly recommended.

HOTEL CIELO
984-873-1382
www.hotelcielo.com
4th Street between 10th Avenue and Quinta

Across from the Ajua Maya restaurant (see
Dining), this simple 18-room hotel has a
great location close to the action. Wind your
way through the maze of stairs and you'll
find the units are clean and bright, with air
conditioning, TVs, and walk-out balconies.
Complimentary Continental breakfast is
served at the Carboncitos restaurant downstairs. Rates: $ to $$.

✪ SIESTA FIESTA
984-803-1166
www.siestafiestahotel.com
Quinta between 8th and 10th Streets

There's always something going on at this
hot spot in the middle of Playa's busy
pedestrian walkway, which can be a good
thing or a bad thing. There is a restaurant
and bar in the cozy courtyard, featuring
several hours of live music each night, plus
sidewalk tables and a large-screen TV for
live sporting events and recorded concerts.
Vacation camaraderie is especially strong
here, making it a great spot to meet and
socialize with other travelers. Rooms have
private terraces with hammocks, air-
conditioning, private bathrooms, and
mini-fridges. Rates: $.

URBAN HOSTEL
10th Avenue between 4th and 6th Streets

Topped with a *palapa* and filled with budget
travelers from around the globe, this student favorite has bunk rooms, private
rooms, communal bathroom, basic kitchen
and laundry facilities, and a lounge area
with TV, dinette set, and even a computer
with free Internet access. Rates: $; Bunks
go for $10/night and private rooms are $25
each. Breakfast is included.

Midrange Hotels
Located on or near Quinta or even on the
beach, these hotels are sufficient for most
travelers. Many have swimming pools,
restaurants, bars, and other amenities.
They generally have air-conditioning, and
all have private bathrooms. Prices range
from $60 for a standard hotel off the beach
to $120 for a property with a premier
location (on Quinta or the beach), air-
conditioning, and upgraded amenities.
They are popular with travelers who want to
stay somewhere comfortable and with a
local feel, without spending too much money.

✪ ACANTO HOTEL & SUITES
984-873-1252 or 631-898-3026 (U.S.)
www.acantohotels.com
16th Street between 1st Avenue and Quinta

10 Tips for Enjoying Your Trip

Rent a car. Being mobile and free gives you a whole new perspective on a destination. You won't need it the whole time, but get one for a few days and explore the coast on your own. Pack a cooler, beach towel, map (freebies are available at the airport and most hotels), and mask/snorkel, and hit the road. Make sure to hit Tulum, hidden beaches, and lost-in-time villages.

Learn a Little Spanish. A little goes a long way, and it helps you feel like you belong. It's also a nice gesture to make to your Mexican hosts, who will appreciate the effort and are usually happy to take some time to teach you new words. For bonus points, learn a little Mayan. Even saying "hello" or "thank you" in the native language is a sure way to get smiles from the locals, many of whom speak it fluently.

Take Care of Yourself. Don't get dehydrated or sunburned. Drinking plenty of purified water will keep your energy level up and can prevent serious illness. Don't be stingy with the sunscreen, either: A trip-ruining sunburn can happen in less than an hour if you're not used to the sun and you don't protect yourself. And while you're at it, put on insect repellent before heading out at night. While others are scratching their ankles, you'll be enjoying your margarita.

Order the Whole Fish. Native to the region, this dish has been a favorite for hundreds of years. The fish is scaled and gutted but left whole, and it is then lightly fried and usually served with tomatoes and onions. It's a good dish to share, with each diner forking off the pieces he or she wants. Even the skin is crispy and tasty, full of healthy fish oils.

Request a Mariachi Song. Sure, you can hear them playing at the table across the way, but there's nothing like being surrounded by the band as they play at your very own table. It makes for great photos, also, so request a song, try to sing along, and take some fun pictures. Remember to tip $3 to $5 per song.

Check Out the Late-night Scene. Sitting at a rope-swing bar stool and dancing under the stars is a longtime Playa tradition, and it's alive and well at the Blue Parrot (see Drinks & Dancing). The party gets going at around 11 PM, when the fire dancers put on their show, followed by DJ music and dancing on the wooden dance floor, on the beach, or in the chic *palapa*-covered lounge room. More into a relaxing scene? Linger over a glass of wine at the Glass Bar (see A Classy Night on the Town), savor mojitos at Diablito or practice your lounging skills at Kartabar (see Trendy Lounges). Not tired yet? Head to Santanera (see Drinks & Dancing) and learn to dance like a local.

Stroll Along the Beach. Leave your sandals behind and take a long walk on the powdery white-sand beach. If you're staying in Playacar, head south toward Xcaret and follow the beach until a rocky point bars your way, and you'll find a secluded and picturesque spot to rest before heading home. If you're staying near Quinta, head north past Mamita's Beach Club all the way to the Reef Club hotel and the deserted beach beyond (Playa Chun-Zumbul).

Visit a Cenote: These freshwater sinkholes, unique geographical features, are a whole lot of fun. The refreshingly cool water feels great after a day in the sun, and the virtually unlimited visibility makes you feel like you're floating in space. **Hidden World** (see chapter 4) is the most expensive, but it's also the best.

Snorkel or Scuba Dive on the Great Mayan Reef. Take the plunge for a chance to see colorful corals, tasty-looking lobsters, stern-looking barracuda, slippery eels, majestic turtles, and hundreds of tropical fish.

Get Up Early. Though the sun sets over Quintana Roo mainland, it rises over the Caribbean. Combined with the solitude and quiet of the early-morning hours, watching the sunrise is a spiritual and calming way to start your day. Next, head to your favorite café for a cup of coffee and some *pan dulce* (sweet pastries) as you watch the shops open up and the tourists start their rounds.

Southern end of Quinta/Fifth Avenue

This small complex is on a quiet side street just off an upscale part of Quinta. The grounds have tropical gardens, a swimming pool, and a rooftop terrace with grill for guest use. The seven one-bedroom villas, in a modern hacienda-style setting, have a decidedly Asian/Zen influence and include a private bedroom with queen bed, romantic bedding, candles, ceiling fans, and a large tiled shower. Each unit also has air-conditioning, a full kitchen with appliances and supplies, cable TV, a dining room, and a living room with sofa bed and stuffed chair, as well as a terrace or balcony with table and chairs and a hammock. Rates: $$ to $$$; include complimentary wireless Internet access. The New York owner also has several private apartments around town and near the beach available for weekly/monthly rental.

ADELIA MARIA SUITES

984-879-3393
www.adeliamaria.com.mx
1st Avenue between 24th and 26th Streets

This condo-style hotel has 18 rooms with traditional Mexican decor, air-conditioning, and cable TV. It's a bit reminiscent of *Melrose Place,* with a courtyard pool and a friendly, social atmosphere. Rates: $ to $$$; range from $70 for a studio with kitchenette up to $190 for a two-room deluxe suite with living room, sofa bed, and kitchen.

ALHAMBRA HOTEL

984-873-0735
www.alhambra-hotel.net
8th Street at the beach

With 23 rooms right on the beach, Alhambra is part of the old Playa, before the development of large-scale condo projects that pushed the density restrictions to the max. Don't expect luxury, but you will find clean accommodations, air-conditioning, friendly service, in-room TVs, and a

New Age atmosphere with an emphasis on peace and tranquility. There is a small pool and sundeck, massage service, and yoga classes. The best thing about Alhambra, though, is staying on the best beach in town, with close proximity to the town's best restaurants and nightlife. Rates: $$ to $$$.

AQUALUNA HOTEL

984-873-1013
www.aqualunahotel.com
10th Avenue between 12th and 14th Streets

The 12 charming rooms have clearly received lots of love and are immaculately maintained to always have a fresh and modern vibe. Rooms have air-conditioning, safes, minibars, fans, phones, arched doorways, rain showers, and cable TV. The blue and white décor gives the property an almost Mediterranean feeling, and there is a relaxed garden courtyard where time melts away and guests tend to linger and reflect on their day. Rates: $$$.

BLUE BEACH HOTEL

984-873-1204
www.bluebeachhotel.com
On the beach between 12th and 14th Streets

This part of the beach is a bit rocky, and the shallows have many fishing boats with their anchors stretched to the beach. It's more relaxed than nearby beaches, though, and the hotel is set back from the ocean, giving guests plenty of room to stretch out and relax. This complex has 28 units in all, ranging from simple but contemporary beachside bungalows and a hotel building to a three-bedroom beachfront villa with all the luxuries. Rates: $$ to $$$$, depending on the type of unit and time of year.

CASA TUCAN

984-873-0283
www.casatucan.de
4th Street between 10th and 15th Avenues

Looking everything like a quaint European hideaway from the street, the Casa Tucan is a charming alternative to the corporate-run resorts that have led the explosive growth in the Riviera Maya. There is a small pool, some tropical gardens, and a street-facing café that was built around the trunk of a large tree. The rooms don't have air-conditioning, but they are usually clean and cozy. Its location in the Barrio Latino district puts it just a block from the excitement of Quinta. Rates: $.

COSTA DEL MAR
984-873-0850
www.hotelcostadelmar.com
1st Avenue between 10th and 12th Streets

One of the original beach hotels in Playa, the modest Colonial-style Costa del Mar has kept up with the times but retained its simple and relaxing nature. It has a small pool, a great beach, and 38 rooms, most with air-conditioning, safes, ceiling fans, and TVs. At the beach, the on-site El Pirata bar and restaurant serves draft beer and snacks, and has a wooden bar with swinging bar stools. It's directly adjacent to the Blue Parrot bar (see Drinks & Dancing), so guests have ready access to the nighttime revelry. Rooms near the beach can be a bit loud at night, so choose one near the street if you want to go to bed before the clubs close. There's also an on-site dive shop offering trips to the nearby reefs, Cozumel, and the freshwater cenotes of the Riviera Maya. Rates: $$ to $$$, depending on amenities and time of year.

DA GABI HOTEL
984-873-0048
www.hoteldagabi.com
12th Street at 1st Avenue

This nine-room hotel is built above a trendy lounge in the middle of Playa's 12th Street Party Strip. During the day, the property seems quaint and charming, but the street noise at night indicates that it's a better place to stumble home to at sunrise than expect to use as a quiet romantic retreat. Rooms were renovated in 2007 with a bright tropical décor and feature air-conditioning, mini-fridge, tiled baths, and 21-inch TVs. The suites have thatched roofs and private terraces. Rates range from $ for a standard room in low season to $$$ for a suite in high season.

ECLIPSE HOTEL
984-873-0629
www.hoteleclipse.com
1st Avenue between 12th and 14th Streets

This artsy 18-room hotel has themed rooms, including the two-story Robinson Crusoe Suite, the De Luxe Suite, and the Caribbean Palapa Suite. Each eclectic and casually rustic room features original decor and artwork, a unique floor plan, wooden furnishings, ceiling fan, satellite TV, and other extras, depending on the room. Some have air-conditioning. The courtyard has some large palm trees, hammocks, and gardens. It is a favorite of traveling artists, young couples, backpackers, and others who like some character and charm in their accommodations. An attached convenience store and Native Deli café (known for quality inexpensive breakfasts) are open to the public. Guests can borrow bicycles for free. The German owner speaks several languages, has been in the area for years, and is happy to dispense excursion-planning advice. Guests can book airport transfers at the hotel front desk. Rates: $ to $$$, depending on the room selected.

FUSION HOTEL
984-873-0374 or 1-800-224-6250 (U.S.)
www.fusionhotelmexico.com
6th Street at the beach

Formerly known as the Hotel Alejari, the 29-room Fusion Hotel has a great location on the beach and is just a block from the most bustling part of Quinta. The rooms are oriented around a central courtyard and are reminiscent of a Spanish villa, with winding staircases and meandering sidewalks. Units are decorated in a traditional Mexican style and face the courtyard or the open ocean. Each room has a mini refrigerator, cable TV, and ceiling fan. Many also have air-conditioning and a private balcony and some are beachfront. The on-site international restaurant serves tropical drinks and snacks on the beach, plus seafood, Mexican food, and pasta dishes. At night, the beachside lounge offers a relaxing alternative to the nightclub atmosphere of the Blue Parrot and other beach clubs. Rates: $$.

HOTEL COCO RIO
984-879-3361
www.hotelcocorio.com
26th Street between Quinta and 10th Avenue

This 15-room hotel features colonial architecture and spacious rooms with air-conditioning, cable TV, in-room safes, and mini-fridges. The decor is tropical, with bright and airy rooms, and the staff works to make guests feel welcomed and secure. There is an on-site restaurant serving gourmet Italian food. Rates: $ to $$$, depending on the size of the room and time of year.

✪ HOTEL LUNATA
984-873-0884
www.lunata.com
Quinta between 6th and 8th Streets

Though it's right on Quinta, Lunata seems somewhat secluded given its narrow entrance through a private hall, which lends an air of privacy and sophistication not found in other downtown hotels. The decor is contemporary hacienda style, designed by architect Angel Isles, with archways, earth tones and blues, river stones, dark woods, iron, and tile. The

hotel has the feeling of an old-style guest house, with only 10 rooms, each with its own style and charm. All rooms have air-conditioning and private balcony with ocean, garden, or street views. Rates: $$ for a standard in low season to $$$ for a junior suite in high season; includes Continental breakfast. Highly recommended.

HOTEL QUINTO SOL
984-873-3292
www.hotelquintosol.com
Quinta at 28th Street

A Mediterranean/Mexican hacienda-style hotel in the heart of Quinta's international section, the midsize Quinto Sol has much of the same style and class as some of the area's more expensive hotels, yet its prices are more moderate. Rooms and suites have air-conditioning, minibars, cable TV, safes, and phones, and some have kitchenettes, balconies, terraces, living rooms, Jacuzzis, and business desks. Rates: $$ for a standard room and $$$ for a suite, depending on the time of year.

LA RANA CANSADA
984-873-0389
www.ranacansada.com
10th Street between Quinta and 10th Avenue

Open in 1984, this is one of Playa's oldest and beloved hotels. Loyal guests return year after year for the consistently comfortable Colonial-style accommodations, central location, true beachtown ambience, and friendly service from the Swedish hosts and Mayan staff. The hotel is just a couple blocks from the beach and is just a half-block from the joyful bustle of Quinta. The hotel's 15 rooms are individually designed, with simple Mexican decor, private bathrooms, and ceiling fans. Upgrades with air conditioning and TVs are available. Guests can use the community kitchen and lounge area. The owners are affiliated with the

Hit the Beach

Playa, plage, spiaggia, beach: However you say it, and in whatever language, the white powdery beaches of the Riviera Maya are undeniably—and justifiably—the region's main draw. Though not quite as flourlike as the shoreline in Cancún, the crushed-shell beaches in and around Playa del Carmen are world renowned for their softness, white color, and cleanliness.

All ocean beaches in Mexico are considered federal property and are open to the public. No hotel, landowner, beach bar, or other entity may legally restrict access to the beach. That being said, it is common for hotels to cordon off an area for the exclusive use of their guests, and this is generally accepted as it seems to do more good than harm for the most number of people. All-inclusive hotels, for instance, may serve food and drinks on the beach, and it is helpful to their servers if their guests are slightly removed from other beachgoers. Some beach bars set up a perimeter around their beach-front tables and do not allow minors to enter and can even have a cover charge, but the area cannot extend all the way to the water line, so nonpatrons can still freely pass by without being hassled. In some spots, resorts have set up a roped-in area where their guests can use beach chairs and beach umbrellas without being hassled by passing vendors or other nonguests.

Licensed vendors can set up chairs and shaded *palapas* and can legally charge for their use. The general rule is, unless you're staying at the hotel that owns the facilities, you are not allowed to use them. Still, though, many tourists successfully beach-hop and visit a number of different beaches and rarely have problems using any lounge chair they happen by. Sometimes ordering a drink can earn you access to a good beach spot, and having a beach towel that matches the color of the ones the hotel provides helps, too.

Many of the main beaches, including the beach just north of the ferry dock in Playa, and along the shallow cove of Akumal, are secured by federal lifeguards, who are well equipped and well trained to handle most emergencies. The nature parks, including Xcaret, Xel-Ha, and Tres Rios Resort (see chapter 4), have private guards on duty to keep an eye on bathers and assist with any problems. With the lack of undertow, little poisonous marine life, clear water, and well-marked swimming areas, accidents are relatively uncommon, though, and the beaches are considered quite safe.

Some areas, though, do require a bit more caution. Keep an eye out for submerged rocks, shallow reefs, and off-course WaveRunners. Be careful also to avoid the black spiny sea urchins, floating debris, and diving into shallow water. If you're exploring remote areas, it's a good idea to stay in a group and not wander off alone. It's also important to keep in mind that although the Riviera Maya is generally safe and most of the people are friendly and welcoming, every town has its bad apples, and you don't want to encounter them. Even though the beaches are government property, locals may not take too kindly to tourists wandering too far from the beaten path and encroaching on their home territory. Be careful not to enter private property that is adjacent to the beach and be respectful of locals who have claimed a beach area for themselves.

Petty theft can be a problem anywhere, including on the beach. Keep a watchful eye on your belongings if you stray from them or, better yet, take turns playing in the waves and leave someone on the beach to watch your things. And don't assume that just because you're on a remote spot and can't see anyone that no one can see you. Stories abound of snorkelers who come back to their beach blankets after a stint on the reef only to find their bags pilfered. Though some may choose to deny that there could be crime in paradise and instead blame the pesky and ever-curious white-faced monkeys, the thieves' penchant for cash, MP3 players, and digital cameras leads me to believe the culprits are looking for more than bananas.

The city police in Playa del Carmen sometimes patrol the popular beaches of town on ATVs. They

Courtesy of Mike Stone

are mainly looking for rowdy drunks and local drug users, so the average tourist, even a Corona-guzzling one, is almost never bothered. In some areas, generally remote beaches, the Mexican Navy performs foot patrols, presumably checking for drug runners and drop-off sites. Be respectful, and they will pass by with just a friendly wave.

To the north of Grand Coco Bay (described later in this chapter), the beach known as Chun-Zumbul is still mostly deserted and is great for exploration and relaxation. Parking is available next to the Reef's main parking lot. Though there are other developments planned for the area, there's still a lot of virgin beach available, and intrepid adventurers will always be able to find a secret spot in which to enjoy the sand and the waves in relative seclusion.

Living the Dream

Four years ago, Tony and Cheri Head had enough of the concrete jungle in San Francisco. They quit their jobs as an attorney and business analyst to pursue a lifelong dream of living in the tropics. After buying a small, dilapidated hotel in Playa del Carmen, they packed their belongings and drove 4000 miles from northern California to start a new life in Mexico's Riviera Maya.

Their plan was to renovate the old hotel and in its place create a small inn for people with a love of travel like themselves. Of course, things didn't go as easily as planned. Construction problems, crooked contractors, the Third World bureaucracy, the mañana way of life, and Hurricane Wilma were some of the obstacles they had to face.

But Tony and Cheri refused to give up. They renovated the buildings and filled them with custom-made furniture and local artwork. Eventually they finished the project and reopened as the Luna Blue Hotel & Garden. Next, they turned the cenote beside the hotel into a garden with tropical flowers, a waterfall, decks and terraces, hammocks, and a sensuous mural of a Mayan goddess. Later they added a tropical swing bar overlooking the garden. Since then they have received many awards and accolades from travel writers, websites, and guests.

It is clear they enjoy what they're doing. You can usually find them in their hotel chatting with visitors about the joy of life in the tropics. "We love it here," they always say. "Life is unhurried and sweet. We start each day swimming in the Caribbean Sea and end it by toasting the great luck that brought us to this magical place. We know we are living the dream of a lot of people."

The Three Questions

Everybody seems to ask Tony and Cheri the same three questions when they hear their story:

Was it harder than you thought it was going to be?

"Sometimes. Moving to a new country has a lot of challenges. There is not only a new language, new food, and new customs, but an entirely different attitude. The mañana life that is so much fun on vacation can be a little frustrating when you live it every day. And of course, there are those pesky hurricanes on occasion."

Do you have any regrets?

"No. Sure there are difficulties and problems. However that is true for everyone's life, everywhere. We have found that living on the edge of the Caribbean offers a life that is unhurried with days full of wonder, surprises and magical moments. We love it here."

Do you know you're living my dream?

"Yes, we do! We consider ourselves very lucky to have been able to pursue a dream shared by so many people. We think it's a dream worth having and worth following. We always tell people, 'Keep dreaming. You never know when those dreams just might come true.' They did for us."

Next time you're in Playa, stop by their hotel and look around, or enjoy a drink in their tropical bar.

Tony & Cheri, Owners
Luna Blue Hotel & Garden
www.lunabluehotel.com

playa.info site and know a lot about the area. Look for the metal frog on the sidewalk; it houses the Webcam that's streamed live on the playa.info site. Rates: $ to $$. Recommended.

LOS ITZAES HOTEL

984-873-2373
www.itzaes.com
10th Avenue between 6th and 8th Streets

A block back from Quinta, Los Itzaes is a haven from the rush of the downtown entertainment district. The hotel's 14 rooms and suites are casual, but quite soothing and even a tad elegant, at least for the price. Each has air-conditioning, ceiling fan, satellite TV, mini-fridge, safe, and private balcony. There's a well-stocked book exchange behind the front desk. The complex has a rooftop swimming pool with a view of the city and the beach. Rates: $$; Continental breakfast included.

✪ LUNA BLUE HOTEL & GARDENS

984-873-0990
www.lunabluehotel.com
26th Street between Quinta and 10th Avenue

Formerly known as the Zanzibar, this hotel was completely renovated in late 2005, partly with the help of Hurricane Wilma and partly with the help of the ambitious new owners from San Francisco (see sidebar). There are shaded hammocks and a lagoonlike Mayan-themed sunken garden and waterfall, and the whole place is surrounded by jungle and tropical flowers, giving it a lost-in-time quality that's not always easy to find in a modern resort destination. Each of the 18 rooms at Luna Blue is a little bit different. All rooms have ceiling fans, safes, air-conditioning, private bathrooms, locally made furnishings, and some have a private porch with hammock. The deluxe units are large double rooms that sleep four and have a full kitchen. The treetop terrace penthouses have a private deck, air-conditioning, and refrigerator. Guests receive complimentary in-room purified water, a free VIP discount card valid for special offers at nearby bars and restaurants, and daily access to Mamita's Beach Club with chairs and an umbrella. Complimentary wireless Internet access reaches the public areas, terraces, and most guest rooms. Rates: range from $ for a stan-

Ocean Safety

Many beaches along the Riviera Maya use a colored flag system to alert swimmers of the ocean's condition:

Black: No swimming allowed. Used to denote swift current, dangerous tides, lightning, or other serious problems. Seldom seen and should be taken very seriously.

Red: Caution urged. Dangerous conditions possible. Used to mark crashing waves, presence of rocks, or other potential hazards. Common at high tide or on windy days. Good swimmers can still enter the water but should be careful.

Yellow: Stay alert. No known issues, but swimmers should stay aware. Most common flag flown in the area. Used on all but the calmest of days. Competent swimmers should not be dissuaded from enjoying the water.

Green: Ideal conditions. Safest swimming possible. Seen only on the best of days.

dard room in low season to $$ for the deluxe rooms in high season—still one of the best deals in all of the Riviera Maya. The on-site bar serves free coffee to guests in the morning and is a relaxing spot to sip a beer or tropical cocktails in the afternoon and evenings.

PLAYA DEL KARMA HOTEL

984-803-0272
www.hotelplayadelkarma.com
15th Avenue between 12th and 14th Streets

With only 16 rooms, this traditional-styled hotel has a very high charm factor. The simple tropical décor of the rooms is enhanced with a thatched roof, air-conditioning, cable TV, celing fan, digital safe, minibar, coffeemaker, and private patio or terrace. Several room types are available, ranging from a simple room with one king bed to a double room with one king and two doubles, perfect for a family or mixed group. A candle-lit pool, court-yard, and small restaurant add to the coziness and help it stand above other similarly priced hotels. Highly recom-mended. Rates start at $$.

PLAZA MARIACHI HOTEL
16th Street at Quinta

Located just to the beach side of Quinta, this well-located hotel has a nice pool and sundeck and spacious rooms with kitch-enettes, air-conditioning, and ceiling fans. There is an on-site bar, Internet access, and a snack bar. It's not particularly fancy, but if you want to be in the center of the action and don't want to pay too much, it can be a good alternative. Rates: $.

❂ POSADA FREUD
984-873-0601
www.posadafreud.com
Quinta between 8th and 10th Streets

Located above a busy restaurant and bar, the 14 rooms and penthouse suite at Posada Freud define funky chic. Rooms have two double beds or one king, tile floors, bal-conies, and traditional Mexican decor, and some also have air-conditioning. The multi-level, three-bedroom penthouse has a living room with entertainment center, air-conditioning, several private terraces, coffeemaker, sofas, and dining area, and it feels more like a private home than a hotel room. Rates: range from $ for a single room with no air in low season to $$$ for the penthouse in high season (four-night min-imum). Highly recommended.

RIVIERA DEL SOL HOTEL
984-873-3100
www.rivieradelsol.com
1st Avenue and 40th Street

At the northern end of the tourist section of downtown Playa del Carmen, this 23-room

family-run hotel is easy to spot, with a Mediterranean-influenced cupola crown-ing the main lobby. The hotel has Mexican decor and tropical furnishings, and it's a quiet respite from the bustling Quinta commercial district. There is a swimming pool and relaxing waterfall, plus an on-site international restaurant. The rooms have air-conditioning, ceiling fans, minibars, satellite TV, mosaic tile work, safes, and private balconies. Some also have kitch-enettes. Rates: $$.

❂ HOTEL TROPICAL CASABLANCA
984-873-0057
www.tropicalcasablanca.com
1st Avenue between 10th and 12th Streets

Billing itself as "The Feel Good Hotel," this property is just a block from the beach and also just steps from the heart of the 12th Street Party Zone. It has been open for more than 20 years but new Canadians owners mounted a major renovation start-ing in 2007. The hotel was upgraded with a slew of improvements and modernizations to give it a more boutique feeling through-out. Locally sourced building materials (limestone concrete, natural white cement, fresh water rocks, recycled glass, indige-nous woods, and sand), natural fibers, a natural swimming hole, and earth-tone decor give the property a soothing vibe, while amenities like WiFi, beach towel service, cold air-conditioning, private balconies/terraces, ceiling fans, morning coffee, and cotton robes lend an air of modern luxury. The property includes 20 hotel rooms, plus a six-bedroom villa, equipped with a full kitchen, entertainment center, a slew of comfort and convenience amenities. There is an on-site dive center and the hotel can assist with all manner of tours, spa services, and even weddings and special events. Guestroom rates are $$. The villa rate is $$$$ and includes services of a private chef and varies through the year.

Luxury Hotels

The best of the best, these hotels and resorts cater to international travelers who are accustomed to the finer things in life. Most have multiple swimming pools, restaurants, bars, fitness rooms, business centers, and concierge service. They generally have efficient air-conditioning, satellite TV, spacious rooms, well-designed bathrooms, guest balconies, and on-site restaurants, and many also have room service, Internet access, and other amenities associated with a first-class hotel. Room rates range from $125 per night for a highly rated tourist-class hotel up to more than $500 per night for a room at a top-of-the-line all-inclusive resort.

AVENTURA MEXICANA
984-873-1876
www.aventuramexicana.com
22nd Street at 10th Avenue

With 25 rooms, this boutique hotel is large enough to have a nice pool, two outdoor Jacuzzis, a gourmet restaurant, and other facilities, but still small enough to benefit from personal service, a tranquil atmosphere, and a dose of class. The decor is reminiscent of a Mexican hacienda, but with many modern upgrades. All rooms have stylish modern decor, air-conditioning, ceiling fan, satellite TV, Internet access, garden/pool views, and room service. It has multiple sundecks and is particularly popular with gay travelers. Rates: $$$ to $$$$.

BLUE PARROT FIFTH AVENUE
984-879-4781; 1-800-435-0668 (U.S.)
www.blueparrot.com
Quinta between 10th and 12th Streets

This is the spot formerly occupied by Pancho's Hotel & Frida Bar, which was one

The Blue Parrot on Quinta is more subdued.

of the most popular spots in town before being shut down by the government for not paying taxes. Open in late summer of 2005, Fifth Avenue is the newest location of the popular Blue Parrot franchise. Guests traverse a wooden bridge to get to the lobby, and there are 18 boutique-style upscale hotel rooms as well as a Thai-influenced restaurant and bar perched above a decorative pool and adorned with ornate *palapas*. The scene is much more serene and sophisticated than at Blue Parrot's beachfront location. The spacious Asian-inspired rooms have cold air-conditioning, satellite TV, and safes. Guests have privileges at the nearby Blue Parrot beach club. Rates: $$$. Recommended.

PLAYA PALMS

984-803-3908
www.playapalms.com
12th Street at the beach

The Playa Palms is the hotel that used to be
known as the Blue Parrot until 2007. It is
essentially the operating name for the hotel
at the Blue Parrot bar. As such, it offers the
quintessential Playa del Carmen experience.
Owned by the individual owners of the units
themselves, it's more of a tropical community center than a hotel. Even if you're not
staying here, you'll most likely end up here
at some point. Whether it's to eat breakfast
at the beachfront restaurant, lounge in a
beach chair and sip a cold drink, visit the
Abyss dive shop to plan a tour, or stop by for
a late-night swing at the bar to watch the
fire dancers (show starts at 11 PM) and dance
the night away, nearly all Playa visitors are
touched by the Playa Palms and the surrounding Blue Parrot complex in some way.
The hotel's 39 luxury rooms are housed in a
condo-style complex a block away from the
reception and bar area. There are spacious
studios and one-bedroom suites with
wicker furniture, contemporary/tropical
decor, kitchenettes, patio hammocks,
Internet access, and soothing colors. A few
have oceanfront views, but most are set back
a bit from the beach, looking across at other
units, with a partial ocean view to one side.
There is a narrow pool between the buildings and a welcomingly shady courtyard.
There is also a small group of rustic beachfront bungalows just north of the beach bar.
Rates: $$ to $$$. Recommended.

✪ BLUE PARROT SUITES

984-873-0083
www.blueparrot.com
1st Avenue at 14th Street

Though guests use the reception desk at the
Blue Parrot Hotel on 12th Street, the Suites
are in a separate building 1.5 blocks away.
The 22 units have modern amenities and
name-brand furnishings, kitchenettes, and
a Bahamas-like contemporary rattan decor.
Since it is a bit removed from the rest of the
Blue Parrot property, it is quite calm and
relaxing. There is a small pool, and the
beach is only a block away. Rates: $$$.

✪ BLUE PEARL SUITES

1-888-898-9922 (U.S.)
www.thebluepearl.com.mx
1st Avenue between 10th and 12th Streets

This collection of eight villas feels more like
a private apartment complex than it does a
hotel. It's located just a half-block from the
main 12th Street party zone, but somehow
retains its privacy and serenity. The owners,
a charming couple from Mexico City, moved
to Playa to live out a stress-free life focusing
on conservation, recycling, and natural liv-
ing. The units range from a simple one-
bedroom apartment to a two-level two-
bedroom villa, complete with sitting room,
patio splash tub, and fully stocked kitchen.
All units feature local handcrafts, natural
fibers, garden or terrace, hammocks, flat-
screen cable TV, air-conditioning, ceiling
fans, kitchenettes, sofa beds, and wireless
Internet access. Guests can call ahead to
have their kitchens stocked to their liking.
Rates: $$$, usually rents weekly.

✪ CASA TICUL HOTEL

984-267-3501
www.casaticul.com
Quinta between 38th and 40th Streets

Located in the newly bustling northern
part of Quinta Avenue, this independently
owned adults-only boutique hotel opened
in early 2008. It is named after an old
Yucatan city 60 miles south of Merida
known for its clay pottery and leather
shoes, but the environs here are decidedly
more contemporary. There is a cozy lobby
that feels like a stylish home in 1940s
Europe, and the quaint courtyard with
small pool and sundeck looks especially

charming after the sun goes down. The 20 rooms are thoroughly modern, with dark wood furnishings, luxury bedding with pillow-top mattresses, large flat-screen TVs, safes, powerful air-conditioning, minibars, nice bathrooms with rainshowers and plenty of hot water, bedside slippers, radio alarm clocks, diffused lighting, and complimentary wireless Internet access, even by the pool. Across the street is a large condo complex and there are many shops, restaurants, and bars within easy walking distance. A great stretch of beach, backed by luxury hotels and beach clubs, is just 2.5 blocks away and the ferry dock and town square are about 1.5 mile to the south. Rates: $$$.

DEEP BLUE HOTEL

14th Street at the beach

This beachfront boutique hotel has 35 rooms and features tropical decor, a trendy ambience, and a see-and-be-seen attitude. The vibe is positive, though, and the ready access to the backyard beach club makes it a great place to stay. Rates: $$$ to $$$$.

GRAN PORTO REAL

984-873-4000
www.realresorts.com.mx
Constituyentes Avenue at the beach

Constructed on the site of Playa's original nudist beach, the Gran Porto Real was the first large-scale hotel built on the town's main tourist strip. It has Italian and Mediterranean decor and overlooks a waveless cove at the southern end of Playa's central beach. Guest have their choice of all-inclusive or European plan accommodations. There are five restaurants, four bars, a nice pool, a car rental desk, a day spa, and a kids' club. Rooms have satellite TV, premium bedding, minibars, and private balconies. Rates: $$$ to $$$$.

✪ HOTEL BÁSICO

984-879-4448
www.hotelbasico.com
Quinta at 10th Street

Básico is a concept hotel owned by the same company that runs Deseo, just down the road. It has 14 rooms, including three suites, housed on three floors and built above Quinta with an entrance on 10th Street. The beige facade owes its unusual color to the Caribbean sand that was mixed with concrete to form its solid walls. The design was conceptualized by a well-known avant-garde design firm in Mexico City called Omelet, since, as its owner says, it takes "*huevos*" to do the kind of design they do. The theme is rooted in 1950s Mexico and Latin America, when oil production and construction boomed and beach vacations were a sign of prosperity. The building shines with the creative use of tile (imported from Mérida), glass, rubber, and latex. Rooms have high beds with built-in minibar and lighting system, exposed plumbing, corner rain shower, TV with DVD player, and colored neon accent light, plus air-conditioning and a security safe. The ground-level juice bar doubles as the front desk. The patio level features a Veracruz-style seafood restaurant, and the visually striking rooftop terrace features canopy sunbeds, a trendy bar, a projection movie screen, ocean views, hammocks, and two smallish plunge pools, modeled after holding tanks commonly found at Mexican oil fields. Rooms that overlook the street can get a bit loud, so consider this when choosing yours. Guests have complimentary use of the hotel's three-wheeled bicycles during their stay. Rates: $$$ and vary with patio or ocean view.

HOTEL COHIBA

984-873-2080
www.hotelcohibaplaya.com
1st Avenue and 12th Street

The lighthouse at El Faro Condos Courtesy of Mike Stone

If you want to be close to the party zone and prefer boutique style over a large full-service resort, Cohiba is a good choice, provided you don't mind the street noise and don't plan on going to bed early. The three-story hotel's 20 rooms are tropically swanky, with decorative lighting, wood furnishings, and an intriguing sense of fashion. Standard rooms feature air-conditioning, ceiling fan, cable TV, and private balcony. There's also a thatched-roof rooftop suite with a spacious bedroom, kitchenette, and large terrace. Rates: $$$; breakfast is included.

✪ HOTEL DESEO
984-879-3620
www.hoteldeseo.com
Quinta and 12th Street

Think Miami Beach meets Beverly Hills meets the Riviera Maya. Built around a central pool and swanky bar, the hotel's 15 rooms are very minimalist, but very cool. The walls are a crisp white, and lounge music is piped in from the hotel bar. On the nightstand, you'll find incense, earplugs, and condoms. The beds are amazingly comfortable, and the rooms have stage lighting, so you can create your own shadowbox show, if you're so inclined. It's a good place to meet other travelers, and it's always a plus when there's a happening bar right outside your door. Best bet for the young and single crowd. Rates: $$$.

ILLUSION BOUTIQUE HOTEL
1-866-460-3604 (U.S.)
www.illusionhotel.com
8th Street between Quinta and 10th Avenue

Opened in 2005, this swanky Mediterranean-style hotel has a central location and clean rooms opening into a central courtyard. The decor is decidedly European, and everything looks crisp and neat. Rooms have air-conditioning and ceiling fans, and some feature terraces with a partial ocean view. There is a rooftop pool and *temazcal*, plus an on-site spa and dive shop. Rates: $$$ to $$$$.

✪ QUINTA PALMERA BOUTIQUE HOTEL
984-803-5007
www.quintapalmera.com
Quinta at 30th Street

Built above a restaurant in Playa's happening international district, this upscale Argentinean-owned executive-style hotel is great for guests that prefer the urban loft-like lifestyle over the scrubby beach ambience that pervades many of the town's lodging options. There are only six rooms, three with balconies and Jacuzzis and three with indoor jetted tubs. Each unit has modern Mexican architecture with rockwork, marble, work desk, and modern bathroom. They feature cold air-conditioning, iPod docks, 26-inch plasma TVs, laptop computers with fast wireless Internet access, electronic safes, and telephones. Guests can order room-service breakfast and get complimentary access to a Mamita's Beach Club with chairs and umbrellas. Room rates: $$$.

PUEBLITO ESCONDIDO
984-803-5108 or 866-473-4421 (U.S.)
www.pueblitoescondidoresort.com
38th Street at 1st Avenue

Crowning a fast-growing section of "New Playa" on the north side of town, this hulking hotel is part of a "resort residences" movement that is bringing in a wave of high-end condo-style accommodations. The rooms are spacious, with sitting areas, terraces, kitchens, and private bedrooms. The property has a dozen pools, plus an adults-only rooftop infinity pool next to the swanky Sky Bar Lounge. There's also an on-site Mexican restaurant and wireless Internet access in public areas. The best thing about the property, though, is the easy access to Kool Beach, just a half-block away. $$$. Recommended.

Beach wedding setup in front of Las Palapas

✪ ARENA BLANCA

38th Street between Quinta and 10th Avenue

Though located on a fairly busy intersection just blocks from the heart of downtown Playa's busy International District, solitude and relaxation await just inside the locked gates and stone walls. A small table seems to float like an island in the center of the swimming pool, which is visible from each of the 11 rooms housed in a three-story building featuring classic Spanish architecture. Units have domed brick Catalan ceilings, premium linens, tile floors, marble countertops, Internet access, full kitchens, spacious living rooms, CD stereos, TVs, and cold air-conditioning, and feel more like private homes than hotel rooms. One- and two-bedroom units are available. The units are individually owned, so there's no central reservations number, but they are easy to find on sites such as VRBO.com and HomeAway.com. Rates: $$$

✪ LA TORTUGA

984-873-1484
www.hotellatortuga.com
10th Avenue and 14th Street

On a corner, just a block off Quinta and around the corner from the Calle Corazon district, this 45-room boutique hotel offers stylish rooms, an exclusive welcoming pool, a pool table, and a private and upscale ambience. Rooms have air-conditioning, safes, fans, satellite TV, wireless Internet access, and phones. Many also have a mini-bar, private balcony, and views of the court-yard pool. The hotel has an entrance into the Spa Itzá Mayan-themed day spa (see Spas, Gyms & Body Work), and the hotel restaurant, Agora, serves Italian and international food in a casual sidewalk café atmosphere and boasts the best cappuccino in town. Rates: $$$; complimentary beach club access and the use of a beach towel included. Recommended.

LAS PALAPAS

984-873-0616
www.laspalapas.com
34th Street at the beach

One of Playa's original hotels is still one of its most revered. It's a bit north of the main strip, so the beach is a touch more secluded, and there are no rocks, making it a great place to play in the water. There is a

Temazcal

The word *temazcal* means "bath house" in the Nahuatl language of the ancient Aztecs, and the centuries-old *temazcal* sweat-lodge ceremony hasn't changed much over the years. The ritual, performed by a shaman or trained healer, is designed to serve both spiritual and medical purposes. Native women were known to give birth inside the dark, warm environment of the *temazcal*, thus making the transition from the womb more gradual. The sweat-lodge ceremony takes place in a stone or adobe hut, dug into the earth and forming a dome large enough for about a dozen participants. Before entering the *temazcal*, all those who will participate reflect on the four cardinal points and are cleansed with incense. Volcanic stones are heated in a wood fire, carried into the *temazcal*, and placed in the center of the floor.

Each participant sits behind a clay pot full of water, and the door is closed and sealed, making the inside completely dark and very hot. The leader pours water onto the rocks, creating steam that fills the *temazcal* and helps partakers to liberate their minds, bodies, and souls. Ancient chants are repeated, songs are sung, and participants are led through a cleansing ritual. In some versions, regional fruits are passed around to be tasted and rubbed on the skin. Modern-day participants generally wear their bathing suits and can splash water on themselves to regulate their breathing and prevent overheating.

Many people have visions and even see an animal or other creature rising from the glowing rocks. The ceremony leader can help interpret whatever you may see. At the end of the ceremony, it is customary to run to the ocean and bathe in the shallows, letting the cool water wash away the sweat and complete the renewal process. Next, a soothing herbal tea helps lock in the benefits reaped during the ceremony. It's a wonderfully spiritual experience that can leave you energized and refreshed for hours afterward.

Places in the Riviera Maya with *temazcal* facilities include Maroma Resort & Spa, Punta Maroma (see chapter 1); Ceiba del Mar, Puerto Morelos (see chapter 1); Tulum Dreams/Resort & Spa, Tulum (see chapter 3); Ikal del Mar, Playa Xcalacoco (see chapter 1); Ana y José Charming Hotel & Spa, south of Tulum (see chapter 3); Cabañas Copal, south of Tulum (see chapter 3); and Oasis Akumal, Akumal (see chapter 3).

Spiritual healing awaits in the temazcal. Courtesy of Maroma Resort

Mosquito Blue Hotel Courtesy of Mosquito Blue Hotel

shady pool, Mayan-inspired lawn art, and an interpretive walking trail through the jungle. The hotel's 75 rooms are housed in spacious individual cabañas near the beach or in two-story villa-like buildings with *palapa* roofs and private porches, built around a pair of grassy courtyards. The beachfront rooms don't have air-conditioning, but most of the rest do. Rates range from $$ for a standard room in low season up to $$$$ for a beachfront cabaña in high season. Make sure you check ahead if you plan on staying here; rumors of a condo development were rampant at press time.

✪ MOSQUITO BEACH HOTEL

984-873-1245
www.mosquitobeachhotel.com
On the beach between 12th Street and 14th Street

Sister property to the Mosquito Blue just up the road, this boutique beachfront property sets itself apart with an on-site Mayan spa, sleek furnishings, premium bedding, and an exclusive style that exudes a sense of privilege and superiority, right down to the trendy red and black lounge chairs along the hotel beach. On-site restaurant and beach bar available. Rates range from $$ to $$$$ depending on room class and time of year.

✪ MOSQUITO BLUE

984-873-1245
www.mosquitoblue.com
Quinta between 12th and 14th Streets

Though Mosquito Blue carries a Quinta address, it fronts 12th Street, and the entrance is not especially visible from Quinta. Composed of a mix of Mexican and Mediterranean architecture, it oozes a hip and cool style that you'll notice as soon as you enter the lobby. The 45 rooms in the two-story building face the interior courtyard and nautical-themed entrance. Amenities include a library, a lounge area, a courtyard pool, and an on-site restaurant that specializes in Italian cuisine and has imported wines. It's a great choice for couples and singles who may want to impress a guest. Rates: $$$$ to $$$$$.

GRAND COCO BAY

984-877-2880
www.grandcocobay.com
40th Street at the beach

This all-inclusive resort has a privileged location on the northern end of the last beach in Playa del Carmen. To the south are the two main coves of Playa, and to the north is a for-now deserted beach ideal for walking, swimming, and exploring. There are 200 rooms with air-conditioning, minibars, large-screen TVs, and private balconies. At mealtime, guests head to the

Playa Maya Hotel Courtesy of Paul Yamagata-Madlon

buffet restaurant or the Latin or Italian specialty restaurants. There are two pools, a kids' pool, a kids' club, a teens' club, nightly shows, a gym, pool tables, a tennis court, a basketball court, and a wide variety of water sports. Rates: $$$$.

MAGIC BLUE BOUTIQUE HOTEL

866-505-9121 (U.S.)
www.magicbluehotel.com
10th Avenue between 10th Street and 12th Street

This hip and stylish hotel offers 45 highly contemporary rooms built around a courtyard pool, garden, and sundeck. Rooms have flat-screen TVs, superior bedding, minifridge, digital safes, and patio or terrace. Rates: $$$ to $$$$$, depending on the room type and time of year. Rate includes buffet breakfast and access to a nearby beach club, with towels, lounge chairs, and umbrellas.

✪ PLAYA MAYA HOTEL

984-803-2022
www.playa-maya.com
On the beach between 6th Street and 8th Street

Appearing a bit Mediterranean, with its cool blues and whites, the Playa Maya can only be reached by the beach, making it one of the few places in town where you get to feel the sand each time you come and go. The hotel is family owned (by an American and his local bride) and only has 20 rooms, giving it an intimate and relaxed feeling absent at some of the more-trendy options nearby. A small pool makes for a nice dip, though the main attraction is the hotel beach, one of the best in the area, with sandy water access, generally calm waves, and plenty of bikini-clad (or not) people-watching. A casual beachfront restaurant serves up delicious coconut shrimp, fish ceviche, and other seafood and

Mexican dishes. Massage service is available on-site and a PC is set up in a small lounge area for complimentary guest use. Wireless access for laptop users carries a nominal fee. Rates range from around $$ to $$$, depending on the room type and time of year. Rooms with Jacuzzis are available, as are two-room connecting suites.

ROYAL RESORT PLAYA DEL CARMEN

987-873-4000
www.realresorts.com.mx
Constituyentes between Quinta and the beach

This is the sister property to the Gran Porto Real, just across Constituyentes. With 418 rooms, it is by far the largest hotel on the Playa del Carmen side of town. It has a grandiose portico reminiscent of Cancún or even Las Vegas. A large concrete dock stretches out from the beach in front of the hotel, which can be a bit distracting, but the sand itself is great, the water is calm, and it's one of the better beaches in the area. Rooms have flat-screen TVs, cold air-conditioning, Jacuzzi tubs, and private balconies with hammocks. It has six restaurants, four bars, a nice pool, a day spa, and a fitness center. Next door is Mamita's Beach Club, a popular day-tripping site for cruise passengers. Rates: $$$$.

SANDOS CARACOL VILLAGE

984-873-4444
www.caracolvillage.com.mx
Highway 307, km 295

A couple of miles north of Playa del Carmen, this 362-room, all-inclusive resort offers a contemporary Mexican atmosphere, lots of green space, two lively pools, three restaurants, three bars, a kids' club, volleyball, tennis, sailing, windsurfing, bocce ball, archery, nightly shows, and other activities. Rooms have cold air-conditioning, TVs, and private balconies. It

is most popular for vacationing and honeymooning couples, young families, and singles who want to be a bit removed from the bustle of downtown Playa del Carmen. Rates: $$$$.

SHANGRI-LA CARIBE

984-873-0611
www.shangrilacaribe.net
38th Street and Quinta

This beachfront hotel is laid out like an old Mayan village, with low-rise, thatched-roof cabañas housing most of the rooms. One of the original hotels in the area, it retains its local charm while keeping the facilities up-to-date. It is one of the last hotels on the northern edge of town, giving it a sense of privacy and remoteness. Each room has a ceiling fan, private porch with hammocks, and bottled water, and some rooms have air-conditioning. There are two pools, three restaurants, and a beachfront bar. Rates: $$$ to $$$$. This property is rumored to be on a list to be turned into condos, so check ahead.

✪ VILLAS SACBE

984-879-3918
www.villasacbe.com
1st Avenue between 12th and 14th Streets

Villas Sacbe offers privately owned one- and two-bedroom condos, each with its own unique and very trendy decor. All condos have air-conditioning, full kitchens, living rooms, purified water, indoor parking, linens and towels, and satellite TV with DVD players. The complex has a narrow, meandering pool and Jacuzzi, and it's a great place to stay in luxury and still be close to the 12th Street party zone. Rates: range from $$$ for a one-bedroom unit up to $$$$ for a two-bedroom villa; three-day minimum. Discounted weekly rates are available. Highly recommended.

DINING

Playa del Carmen offers an incredibly wide variety of cuisine types and dining establishments. From hole-in-the-wall taco shacks offering complete meals for less than $3 and traditional Mexican steakhouses serving fine cuts of Angus beef and live lobster, to stylish lounge-style restaurants serving Mediterranean and international cuisine, Playa is sure to please.

Breakfasts are normally inexpensive, with many restaurants posting their specials on a chalkboard out front. Choices include traditional Mexican dishes such as *pan dulce* (sweet pastries), *huevos rancheros* (ranch-style eggs) and *huevos Mexicanos* (Mexican-style eggs), and there are also American favorites such as pancakes, omelets, and steak and eggs, and European choices such as bagels and lox, croissants, and crêpes.

Lunch is generally quite casual, with many travelers choosing to eat fresh seafood, sandwiches, or burgers on the beach or next to their hotel pool. Most restaurants in town are open for lunch, too, with happy-hour specials starting early and plenty of seats available at the sidewalk restaurants along Quinta.

Once the sun goes down and the stars come out, the lights of the restaurants, bars, and shops of Playa's main street start to twinkle, and candlelight glows from many eateries. The town begins to feel a bit like an international bazaar, with the restaurants competing for your business, hawking their specials, offering free drinks with a meal purchase, and tempting diners with live music, wafting smells, and attractive hostesses.

Fresh tortillas in downtown Playa
Courtesy of Philip Gammon

Choosing where to eat is sometimes half the fun, with many visitors making several laps along the entire 2-mile-long street, checking out the night's offerings and taking in the scene. Many restaurants put together sample entrées and place them on display next to their menus, showing you the exact size of their plump steaks, lobster tails, giant shrimp, or fish fillets. Each block has several options to choose from and one famous block, on Quinta between 28th and 30th streets, there are 12 restaurants, including 7 intimate eateries in a row, each three tables wide and two or three rows deep, ranging from a Mediterranean restaurant offering lamb and hookah pipes, to an Asian noodle house to an Argentinean steakhouse.

If you're not sure what you're in the mood for or if you have a group of travelers with varied tastes, you're in luck, since many of

Playa del Carmen offers a wide variety of cuisine.   Courtesy of Riviera Maya Tourism Authority

the restaurants have extensive menus, spanning the range from tacos to pasta, from fish to steak, and from pizza to burgers.

Restaurants in this book are labeled as inexpensive, moderate, or expensive. The average meal price at an inexpensive restaurant is less than $7 per person. Moderate restaurant meal prices range from $7 to $20. Expensive restaurants offer meals starting at $21 and higher.

Dine for Less Than $15/Day

Breakfast—Tequila Barrel: Huevos rancheros served with refried beans, toast, and coffee–$5.

Lunch—Cart next to the town square bus station: Plump chicken tamales steamed in banana leaves–$1.50/each.

Dinner—La Portena: Amazing burgers and fries; dine on the sidewalk stools or take home to the hotel–$4.50.

Drinks—Pick up a quart of beer from a grocery store or convenience store and sit on the seawall in the town square, watching the world go by.

All of the locations in the Budget Dining section are ultracasual eateries catering to locals, students, and other budget travelers. They are good places to sample the local fare and use your Spanish. They typically do not accept credit cards and may have restrooms that are not up to the cleanliness standards expected by some travelers. They are still regulated by the health department and serve only purified ice and water.

Budget Dining

ACA LOS TACOS
984-803-3482
Constituyentes at Quinta

This popular taco spot is located on a busy street corner between the old and new sections of town. Like the busy taco stands near where the locals live, Aca serves fresh, hot tacos *al pastor* (cut right from the fire), beef tacos, and cheese tacos. There are tables along the patio, overlooking the traffic circle near the Royal Resort. Open 11 AM–1 AM daily.

Aca Los Tacos

Hungry but don't want to go out? Delivery Express offers restaurant food delivery to hotels, condos, and other locations throughout Playa del Carmen. The service works with many local restaurants, including Hot Baking Company, Il Baretto, Maktub, Kabuki, 100% Natural, El Oasis, and Dr. Taco. There is a 15 percent service fee, and tips are not included. Delivery is available from 11 AM–9 PM. For more information call 984-803-5986.

BAMBU
8th Street between Quinta and 10th Avenue

This is the place for inexpensive Mongolian stir-fry. Pork, beef, shrimp, and vegetarian options are available. There are a few shaded tables facing the street, making it a fun spot to sit and watch travelers walk from the hotels west of Quinta to the beach.

BIP BIP PIZZAS
984-803-2888
Quinta at Constituyentes

Open for three meals per day, this casual spot is close to the traffic circle. It offers traditional breakfasts, smoothies, pizza, nachos, tacos, pasta, and seafood. Tables are covered by a shady *palapa*. Open 7 AM–11 PM daily.

CHICAS GRILL & BAR
Quinta between 28th and 30th Streets

This casual restaurant opens for lunch and serves until midnight. There are only six tables, each with a front-row seat of the parade of people along Quinta in the New Playa district. Menu faves include pasta, steak, sandwiches, and carpaccio. There is a huge cocktail menu.

COCTELERÍA EL PAISANO VERACRUZ
Avenue Juárez, just west of Highway 307

Eat seafood with the locals. The restaurant specializes in shrimp cocktail but also serves fried fish, ceviche, and other dishes. It is located away from the tourist zone and you're likely to be the only travelers during your meal. Most of the waiters don't speak English, but don't let that dissuade you from going. Chances are you'll be able to communicate enough to order or someone at the restaurant will be able to help translate.

DR. TACO
10th Avenue between 8th and 10th Streets

In front of the Plaza Pelicano movie theater and mall, this tiny outlet serves tasty and inexpensive tacos and quesadillas. Diners sit on bar stools at the counter or at one of a handful of plastic tables along the sidewalk. Many locals stop by on their way to or from work. Recommended.

EL AMENDRO
984-803-1473
4th Street between Quinta and 10th Avenue

This typical Mexican restaurant is popular with area workers and budget travelers. The shaded dining room has plastic tables, and the menu includes selections from around the country, including *panuchos* (thick corn tortillas topped with chicken, lettuce, and cheese), quesadillas, and fried Mexican sandwiches called *tortas*. Daily lunch specials ($4) include a main dish, small salad, rice, beans, and fruit drink.

✪ EL FAISÁN Y EL VENADO
Highway 307, just north of Avenue Juárez

This is a popular local spot for tacos, quesadillas, and seafood. At midday workers fill the plastic tables and order from the *comida corrida* menu, which offers hearty meals prepared and served quickly (just like you'd find in a typical Mexican home).

Meals are served with fresh corn tortillas and spicy *pico de gallo*, a mixture of onions, tomatoes, cilantro, and jalapeno.

EL FOGON
30th Avenue between 4th and 6th Streets, in front of Harmon Hall

Located along the busy 30th Avenue strip of local restaurants, El Fogon serves a mixed-grill plate *(parrillada mixta)* big enough to serve three people. Also try the fried nopal cactus. Highly recommended.

✪ EL FOGONCITO
30th Avenue between 28th and 30th Streets

Where do the bartenders and restaurant workers go when their shifts are over? Chances are, you'll find them at El Fogoncito, which is open 24 hours. Top dishes include tacos *al pastor* (cut right from the fire) and fried meat sandwiches served on a toasted bun called *tortas de carne*. Very inexpensive and very good.

EL TROPICAL-ITO
10th Avenue between 6th and 8th Streets

This hole-in-the-wall lunch spot serves cheap tacos, fajitas, nachos, and sandwiches. Nothing on the menu is more than $4. Diners order at the counter and sit at plastic tables along the sidewalk.

LA LONCHERIA DE LA QUINTA
Quinta between 22nd and 24th Streets

This tiny restaurant has only four tables and does not serve alcohol, though they don't mind if you bring a drink in with you. Sit outside at a shaded table and watch the crowd go by on Quinta while enjoying tasty $1 fish or shrimp tacos.

KILLER TACO
1st Avenue between 10th and 12th Streets

Located next to Litros bar, it's a good place

The Playa del Carmen Children and Family Services Department accepts donations for its health and literacy programs, so if you can save a bit of space in your luggage to bring donations, the residents of Playa would greatly appreciate it. For medical items, please do not bring outdated medicines or equipment.

Requested items include:
Kindergarten and primary school workbooks (in Spanish)
Number 2 pencils, colored pencils, crayons
Coloring books
Children's books (in Spanish)
Educational toys (no batteries required)
Glucometers and glucose test strips
Stethoscopes
First-aid kits
Lumbar-sacral body supports
Neck collars
Tension wraps/bandages
Fiberglass cast kits
Arm slings
Infant and children's clothing
Blankets/children's blankets
Children's toothpaste
Eyeglasses (children's and adults', including prescription lenses)
Vitamins (children's and prenatal)

Items can be dropped off at the Ajua Maya restaurant on 4th Street between Quinta and 10th Avenue. For more information call 984-803-1118 (Playa del Carmen) or 804-201-4142 (in the United States), or log on to www.americamaya.org.

for cheap tacos on the way to or from the 12th Street party zone. The menu is written on a chalkboard and features beef tacos, quesadillas, burritos, and even pork tacos *al pastor,* cut right from the spit. Everything on the menu is $5 or less. They don't sell alcoholic drinks, but feel free to stop next door and get a beer to go. No credit cards accepted. Open late.

✪ LAS ARRACHERAS
1st Avenue South between 15th and 20th Avenues

One of Playa's original taco restaurants is still one of the best. Located on 1st Avenue South, just a few blocks up from the town square, this hole-in-the-wall local restaurant has some of the best grilled meats in all of Playa, and for a price that makes you want to go back every night. Sit on plastic tables and sip a cold drink while you pile your sliced meats high on corn tortillas, add spicy salsas, and enjoy the taste and atmosphere of the "real Mexico"—all while only a five minute walk from the start of the main tourist district. Inexpensive, highly recommended.

PIZZA BANANA
984-803-1249
12th Street at 10th Avenue (and other locations)

Here you can get inexpensive pizza by the slice or pie, as well as combo deals with drinks and multiple pieces. Open late; delivery available noon–6 AM.

PIZZA PAZZA
Quinta at 14th Street
10th Avenue between 8th and 10th Streets

At Pizza Pazza, which has a good reputation and seems to open more stores all the time, slices go for $1.50. (The gourmet pizzas are slightly more.) There are also combos with slices and drinks included. Open late, they are a favorite for satisfying after-party munchies.

PIZZA 16
Quinta between 10th and 12th Streets

Open from lunch until very late at night, this is an inexpensive spot for pizza by the slice. There are a few stools at the counter, but most customers sprinkle on some Parmesan cheese, red pepper flakes, and hot sauce, grab a few napkins, and eat their pizza on the go.

SUPER PANADERIA AGUILAR
Quinta between 2nd and 4th Streets

This is a great spot for inexpensive pastries, pizza, sandwiches, cold drinks, coffee, and snacks, and they also sell convenience-store items.

TANGO TACO
984-803-1859
10th Street between 10th Avenue and 15th Avenue

This casual Argentinean-owned restaurant serves up Argentinean meats, Mexican tacos, and amazing prices (huge grilled steaks go for about $10). Its location just a block off Quinta makes it a great place to go when you want a bargain meal but don't feel like walking too far from the tourist strip. Other options include cheesy empanadas, European-style tapas, grilled beef fajitas, and even baked potatoes. Closed on Mondays. Highly recommended.

✪ VAGABUNDA
Quinta between 24th and 26th Streets

A favorite with locals and ex-pats, this *palapa*-shaded restaurant serves traditional American and Mexican breakfasts, crêpes, omelets, pastas, and cappuccino. Recommended.

Mexican & Mayan

✪ AJUA MAYA LOBSTER & STEAK HOUSE
984-873-2523 or 818-581-4075 (USA)
www.ajuamaya.com
4th Street between Quinta and 10th Avenue

With a great mix of authentic food, entertaining waiters, good service, and a great location, Ajua has become very popular with repeat guests. The owners are on-site

Carlos 'n Charlie's

most of the time and are great at remembering the names of customers they may see only once or twice each year. Food ranges from traditional Mayan dishes to lobster, fish, Black Angus beef, flambes, Caesar salads, pasta, fish tacos, and Mexican favorites. This is a popular place for wedding receptions and special-event meals. There is live Latin jazz music nightly and free wireless Internet access. An upstairs *palapa*-covered deck offers a more upscale dining and special-events room with hacienda-style furnishings. Check with the staff to find out about their Mexican and Mayan cooking demonstrations and tequila tasting events. Prices range from $5.50 for fish tacos to $20 to $25 for larger dishes. Open 11 AM–2 AM daily. Highly recommended.

ASADO DE MANOLO

Quinta between 24th and 26th Streets

This bustling local café features traditional Mexican lunches, sandwiches, coffee, and fruit juices. It is located in the international section of Playa and has a varied clientele, from hotel workers to the owners of the nearby nightlife hot spots. Great prices and a varied menu.

CARLOS 'N CHARLIE'S

984-803-3953
www.carlosandcharlies.com
10th Avenue at 1st Street

Occupying a prime corner at the northern edge of the Paseo del Carmen Mall, Carlos 'n Charlie's could be called the anchor tenant of the entire shopping plaza. This Mexico standard offers consistently good Mexican food, seafood, and pasta, though the main draw is the lively atmosphere, unique decor, and friendly waiters. There are several seats along the window, affording nice views of the plaza. Unlike some of the chain's other locations, this is more of a restaurant than a bar, so don't expect too much in the way of vacation revelry, drinking contests, or wet T-shirts. For that scene, check out C&C's sister property, Señor Frog's, located on the ferry dock, just a block away. Opens at 10 AM daily.

DON DIEGO
984-879-4493
Quinta at 22nd Street

This medium-size sidewalk café in the heart of "New Quinta" offers contemporary Mexican food (or "Modern Mex," as they call it), steak, and seafood. Open for dinner only, 5–midnight daily.

DON EMILIONE
984-873-2073
www.donemilione.com
Quinta at 2nd Street

Near the bus station and the town square, this restaurant is part of the Don Emilione hotel. There are tables along the sidewalk, plus an air-conditioned dining room. Popular dishes include soup, pasta, lobster tacos, calamari, steak, and shrimp, and vegetarian dishes are also available. A Latin or jazz band plays on some nights, and there's a nightly happy hour from 5 to 7. After your meal, order a flaming Mayan coffee and homemade cheesecake.

DOÑA MARY
30th Avenue at 28th Street

A local fave, it opens at 8 PM daily and stays open until the wee hours. Good pork tacos *al pastor* (cut right from the fire), quesadillas, and fajitas are served in a casual setting with traditional Mexican decor. It is located several blocks from the tourist strip and is frequented by expatriates and others who need a break from the standard tourist joints.

EL FAROLITO
Quinta between 28th and 30th Streets

Step into the type of urban taqueria you might find in Guadalajara or Monterrey or other metropolitan Mexican city. Munch on tacos and sip on cold beer and margaritas with a mixed crowd of locals and tourists.

EL JARDÍN DEL JAGUAR
984-873-0650
Quinta at 8th Street

With a red, black, and white color scheme, Jaguar seems to be stuck in the 1970s, except for the fact that almost none of Playa del Carmen even existed then. The restaurant serves seafood, steaks, and Mexican food. The tables border Quinta, making it good for people-watching.

EL PASTORCITO
30th Avenue between 28th and 30th Streets

White plastic tables and glowing yellow lights welcome diners to this local taqueria in the busy commercial district a few blocks from the tourist zone. True to the restaurant's name, tacos *al pastor* are the featured menu item, and they are served on small corn tortillas and topped with a slice of fresh pineapple. Other items include quesadillas, steak, guacamole, and hot salsa. Unlike many local taco restaurants, El Pastorcito offers a full bar.

EL TEMPLO
8th Street between Quinta and 10th Avenue

Serving typical Mexican dishes on a large second-story terrace on a busy side street, El Templo's dining area overlooks the pedestrian plaza, where travelers scurry to and fro. Since it's off the main road, it's an ideal spot for relaxing and sipping a cold beer.

GUADALUPANA
984-879-3717
10th Avenue at 12th Street

Popular with locals, this stand-alone restaurant has a two-for-one happy hour and traditional Mexican food such as tacos and fajitas, plus burgers, grilled fish, and shrimp. It also has cold air-conditioning, which patrons are grateful for on the hottest of days.

HACIENDA MAYA
984-873-2523
www.haciendamaya.com
4th Street between Quinta and 10th Avenue

Hacienda Maya offers upscale dining on a *palapa*-covered balcony above the Ajua Maya restaurant, which is run by the same owners. The menu features 19th-century French-influenced Mayan and Mexican cuisine, with dishes featuring Angus beef, venison, Cornish game hens, breast of duck, and prawns. The candlelit restaurant is a great spot for a romantic date or a group meal and frequently hosts wedding receptions. Recommended.

✪ LA ADELA
Quinta between 6th and 8th Streets

Feeling more like a private party at a stately hacienda in rural Mexico than a beachtown restaurant, La Adela offers some of the town's best Mexican food and a warm and inviting atmosphere that makes diners want to linger and soak it all in. Upscale Mexican cuisine, mole enchiladas, and seafood top the menu. Diners are drawn to the combination of traditional and whimsical décor, but it's the food that brings them back for a second time. Seating is available indoors or outside on the pedestrian walkway. Highly recommended.

✪ LA CUEVA DEL CHANGO
984-804-9190
38th Street between Quinta and the beach

The "Monkey Cave" restaurant is an eclectic spot that somehow manages to be rustic,

funky, and romantic all at the same time—perfect for a special occasion or just a night out. The menu features several cuts of steak, fish, shrimp, fajitas, and other Mexican specialties. The candlelit tables are in a junglelike setting, making it very soothing and exotic. Highly recommended.

LA DIEZ
984-803-5829
10th Avenue at 8th Street

Known for having self-service beer taps at some of its tables, this cantina offers all-inclusive meal packages with all you can eat and drink, as well as a daily brunch. Menu items include traditional Mexican food, plus grilled meats, seafood, and pork. There are pool tables, board games, Foosball, and other games. Open 1 PM–2 AM daily.

LA PARRILLA
984-873-0687
Quinta at 8th Street

With its Spanish-tiled roof and strolling mariachi bands, La Parrilla puts diners in the mood for good Mexican meals, and it delivers. The best dishes include beef fajitas, grilled shrimp, and chiles rellenos, and there are also fresh salads and vegetarian dishes. Save room for the flambé desserts and flaming coffees, prepared tableside. Open noon–1 AM daily. Highly recommended.

LA TABERNA
984-803-0447
5th Street between Quinta and 10th Avenue

With a good mix of locals and tourists, this bar and restaurant combo is especially popular when there are live sporting events on TV. One wall has computer workstations, with Internet access going for $1.50 an hour. It's a good spot for cooling off since it's one of the few restaurants in the area

Requesting a Mariachi Song

The strolling mariachis you see in the restaurants, walking down Quinta, or sometimes even on the beach, work for tips. The typical price per song is $3 to $5, but ask ahead to be sure. Duos can cost less, and larger groups cost more. Not sure which song to request? Here are a few longtime favorites to choose from:

"El Son de la Negra." This raucous song is often the first song played when the mariachis make their grand entrance; it's also a lively, uplifting song to play anytime the room needs a lift.

"La Bamba." Everybody knows the words—at least some of them. This is an uplifting song of hope and can really get the crowd going.

"La Cucaracha." The sad tale of a bad day for a cockroach. It's a funny and entertaining song that's easy to sing along with. Kids love it, too.

"Las Golondrinas." A sad song known to bring grown men to tears. It tells the tale of the swallows flying on and is often played when someone is gone or going away.

"Las Mananitas." This is the song played for birthdays and celebrations. Request it for a friend who is celebrating something special.

"Maria Isabel." An easy song to sing along to, it tells the story of lovers on the beach. It has a happy tropical sound that you'll remember for a long time and is especially popular in Cozumel.

food with a bit of Caribbean influence. The menu includes grilled shrimp, spicy pork tacos, and fried fish. Order beer by the bucketful for the best value. Open noon–11 PM daily. Inexpensive.

LAS MANANITAS
984-873-0014
Quinta between 4th and 6th Streets

This jovial spot in the original part of Quinta serves traditional Mexican food (such as tacos and fajitas), plus seafood (shrimp, fish, octopus), spaghetti, baked pasta, steak, tuna tartare, carpaccio, and fresh salads. Open 7 AM–midnight daily.

LAS DIOSES
12th Street between 1st Avenue and the beach

Occupying a prime piece of real estate on the 12th Street Party Strip, this lively contemporary Mexican restaurant has a somewhat traditional menu but an ambience and look that are far from plain. Tables are spaced apart to allow diners a good view of the parade of revelers passing by on their way to the beach clubs for a night of partying. It's a good place to try sipping a smoky shot of mescal.

LIMONES CAFÉ
984-873-0848
Quinta at 6th Street

This subdued restaurant has an entrance on Quinta, but the eating area is down a flight of stairs and tucked in a sheltered courtyard away from the hustle of the street. The menu features traditional Mexican dishes, fish, shrimp, lobster, steak, and grilled chicken. Mayan replicas, candlelit tables, and a fountain add to the warm and welcoming ambience. Open noon–11 PM daily.

with air-conditioning. It serves tacos, burgers, grilled chicken, nachos, steak, quesadillas, and seafood cocktails. Open 10 AM–4 PM daily. Recommended.

LAS DELÍCIAS
984-803-1214
Quinta at 22nd Street

Located in the newer part of Quinta, this casual restaurant offers traditional Mexican

Mayan Cuisine

Contributed by *Destination Riviera Maya* magazine

Traditional Mayan cuisine integrates the delights of land and ocean. The beans, vegetables, and fruits are cultivated, then mixed with the products of fishing and hunting as part of the customs of a centuries-old society. Corn, chocolate, honey, and turkey not only are the main ingredients of delicious meals and beverages but also are an integral part of Mayan religious rituals, where chocolate became known as the "drink from the gods." Numerous spices such as peppercorn, coriander, *achiote* (similar to paprika), and cinnamon are used to make *recados*, special seasoning pastes that enliven chicken, fish, or beef dishes. Some traditional Mayan dishes include the following:

Cochinita pibil. The word *pibil* means "to roast in a hole," and luckily, modern cooks have devised a method that requires no shovel. The dish is typically made with pork and marinated with red *recado* and bitter orange. It is wrapped in banana leaves with onions and steamed or roasted, and then served with onions marinated in vinaigrette.

Poc chuc. Char-grilled pork marinated in sour orange with black beans, purple onion, tomato, and Mayan spices.

Papadzules. Tortillas stuffed with hard-boiled eggs and covered in a pumpkin seed and tomato sauce. *Frijol con puerco.* Pork and black bean stew served with chopped radish, onion, tomato, and pieces of lime, eaten with a corn tortilla.

Relleno negro. Turkey, ground beef, and hard-boiled eggs in a blackened chile sauce.

Tikinxic. A whole fish marinated in *achiote* and sour orange with tomato, white onion, and green pepper slices, then wrapped and grilled in a banana leaf.

Panuchos. A fried tortilla filled with refried beans, pieces of turkey or chicken, lettuce, tomato, onion, and avocado.

LOS ALUXES
Quinta at 16th Street

Across 16th Street from Natural Spa and above a liquor store, Los Aluxes offers a quiet place to enjoy a good meal while still being near the hustle of Quinta. It has good happy-hour drink specials, and at night several tiki torches illuminate the alfresco dining area, giving the place an exotic and romantic vibe. The menu features such classic Mexican specialties as fajitas and tacos, plus seafood and steaks. Recommended.

LOS COMALES
984-873-0982
Quinta between 2nd and 4th Streets

This cozy Mexican restaurant features steaks, fajitas, tacos, quesadillas, and some seafood. The waiters are longtime Playa residents who know a lot about the area and are happy to make suggestions and recommendations—on your dinner and on your tours.

✪ PEZ VELA
984-873-0999
Quinta at 2nd Street

This sports bar and Mexican cantina has several settings in one spot: There is a bar with swinging bar stools, a central dining area with plastic tables, a few sidewalk tables, and some TV-front tables, perfect for watching live sports games, which seem to always be on. There's even an upstairs Internet café. The menu, which includes tacos, grilled shrimp, and burgers, is inexpensive and good for the price. For the best deal, order beer by the bucket (five bottles). Recommended for the casual ambience, bar scene, and unbeatable views of Quinta.

TECOLOTE

984-803-1249
North side of the town square

This sidewalk restaurant offers traditional Mexican food, such as tacos, burritos, and quesadillas. It has frequent beer specials, and it's a great spot for watching the pedestrian traffic on the main square.

XLAPAK

Quinta between 14th and 16th Streets

This small but friendly restaurant with whimsical Mayan decor is tucked in a narrow lot facing Quinta. Menu selections include chicken, fish, beef fajitas, spaghetti, and squid.

✪ YAXCHE

984-873-2502
www.mayacuisine.com
8th Street between Quinta and 10th Avenue

With seating along the sidewalk or in a gardenlike interior, Yaxche is one of Playa's most respected restaurants. It serves authentic Mayan cuisine, including fish, chicken, and turkey, all cooked with native methods and using traditional spices. Yaxche is the Mayan name for *la ceiba,* a green-leafed tree believed to bring good luck. Try the Mayan Kiss after-dinner drink, made with Xtabentun and Kahlúa. Dishes range from $15 to $25. Open noon–midnight daily. Recommended.

Italian

AGORA

10th Avenue between 12th and 14th Streets

Located on the ground floor of the La Tortuga Hotel (see Lodging), this casual restaurant serves Italian food, pasta, fish, and inexpensive breakfasts under shaded *palapas* next to a busy street. It is Italian owned, and the food is authentic and good.

CAFÉ DE LA LUNA

4th Street at 15th Avenue

Owned by the same folks who run the Posada Barrio Latino hotel, this authentic Italian eatery has great pastas, pizza, lasagna, cold beer, and a decent wine selection. There's also a pleasant outdoor seating area.

IL BARETTO

Quinta at 26th Street

Serving three meals a day, this sidewalk café and restaurant is somewhat of a headquarters for the Italians making the international part of Quinta their home. More than just ex-pats appreciate Il Baretto's pasta, pizza, seafood, and beef menu items, though. The restaurant also serves imported coffee drinks, espresso, and cappuccino and is known for sumptuous desserts.

✪ LA FE RESTAURANTE

Quinta between 26th and 28th Streets

You'll think you've been transported to an Italian beach town and stumbled upon a friendly neighborhood restaurant where everybody knows each other. Tables line the sidewalk and covered terrace and are filled each evening with local and visiting Italians, sipping imported wines, munching on fresh bread, and feasting on pizza, pasta, and seafood dishes. The late-night crowd is boisterous and spills well into the blocked-off road, turning the bar scene into a bit of a street party, with techno music booming and gelato, cappuccino, wine, and tequila each being enjoyed in abundance. Italian and French voices are much more common than English or Spanish, but everyone is welcome to join in the fun.

LUNA MAR
984-873-0526
Quinta between 12th and 14th Streets

Upstairs from a busy shopping area, this nice, yet casual, spot offers pasta, fish, grilled chicken, and other favorites. Daily specials are written on a chalkboard on the street level and a warm glow and carved wooden chairs beckon diners to take the stairs up for a meal.

✪ RISTORANTE DA BRUNO
984-873-0048
Quinta at 12th Street

This is a longtime Playa favorite, for both its authentic Italian menu and its premium people-watching perch in the heart of Quinta. The owners and chefs are Italian, the pasta is made in-house, and the food tastes fresh and hearty. Top dishes include gnocchi, pizza, ravioli, antipasti, proscuitto, mahimahi, lobster, and, of course, tiramisu. Open 5 PM—1 AM daily. A typical entrée is $16. Recommended.

ROLANDI'S
984-803-4121
Paseo del Carmen Mall

Long a favorite in Cozumel and Cancún, Rolandi's now has a location in Playa del Carmen. There is indoor and outdoor seating, and the ambience is casual but with an upscale flair. Wood-oven pizzas highlight the menu, along with pastas and desserts. Open noon—midnight daily.

✪ ROMAGNA MIA
Cozumel Avenue (1st Avenue) between 30th and 32nd Streets

A favorite with locals, this tiny out-of-the-way sidewalk restaurant near Mamita's Beach serves traditional Italian cuisine, including pasta carbonara, strozzapretti, gnocchi, and lasagna. Also try the ham and cheese piaditas—an easy dish to share.

International

AMARIS
984-803-4050
Paseo del Carmen Mall

Boasting an "eat, drink, lounge" concept, this fusion restaurant features decor and cuisine from Asia, Central America, and the Mediterranean. It has a marble bar, plasma TV, and indoor/outdoor seating. Best bets are the chicken satay—grilled chicken strips with peanut sauce. Open noon—midnight daily.

APASIONADO
984-803-1100
Quinta at 14th Street

This terrace restaurant, above the Zoo Café (see Cafés and Light Fare), has unique lighting that gives it a bit of a magical quality. The decor truly adds to the dining experience, letting patrons know they are in for something special. Menu faves include grilled octopus in garlic sauce, sizzling beef fajitas, lobster, filet mignon, and grilled shrimp. Open noon—1 AM daily, with live jazz music nightly.

ARRACHERA'S GRILL
Quinta at 30th Street

Take a seat on the shaded patio at this Latin American restaurant specializing in Argentinean grilled meats and wines. Additional menu items include pasta, steak, chicken, and seafood.

APHRODESIAC
12th Street at 1st Avenue

Flowing curtains, glowing candles, exotic music, and a delectable menu typify this unique Playa restaurant, located below Squid Roe in the 12th Street entertainment district. It may be one of the only places in all of the Yucatán to sample traditional African dishes. There is also a wide variety of desserts, after-dinner drinks, and coffees that tempt diners to linger when the meal is done.

✪ BYBLOS
984-803-1790
14th Street between Quinta and 10th Avenue

A French-owned gourmet restaurant and wine bar, Byblos is one of the few spots in town where you can enjoy a delicious dinner in an air-conditioned dining room with white linen tablecloths, not to mention exceptionally high service levels. There's also an alfresco patio. Menu highlights include carpaccio, foie gras, pasta, risotto, grilled fish, flambéed lobster, veal chops, rabbit, New Zealand beef and lamb, duck, apple tarts, and crêpes flambéed with Grand Marnier. Open 6 PM–1 AM; closed Sunday. Highly recommended.

✪ CASA MEDITERRANEA
984-876-3926
Quinta between 6th and 8th Streets

Though its address is officially on Fifth Avenue, you'll need to look for the arched doorway labeled Hotel Marieta and head down a sheltered corridor to the back courtyard to find this tucked-away eclectic gem of a restaurant. Italian owners Maurizio and Maria have been pampering Playa dinners for years and it's easy to see why their restaurant continues to prosper, even though you can't see it from the street when you walk by. Upscale locals have made a habit of coming here when they want to pretend they're not in Playa for a few hours. The homemade pasta is a crowd favorite, as are the insalata fruit da mare, and other regional dishes from Northern Italy. Wine is more common than Corona, which can be a welcome change from the daily grind. Though the atmosphere is decidedly more subdued and mature than many area restaurants, casual attire is still accepted. Closed on Sundays. Highly recommended.

✪ CHICAGO DON JOSE'S
6th Street between 5th and 10th Avenues

A favorite spot for local hotel executives, this casual sidewalk restaurant has an unusual menu for the area and may prove a welcome taste of home for many travelers. Top menu items include BBQ ribs, imported Certified Angus steak, lamb, lobster, and grilled shrimp.

EL 10
Quinta at 32nd Street

Argentineans are moving into Playa in a big way and this restaurant is one of their many contributions. Seating is available in an indoor dining room or an outside terrace that wraps around the front and side. Feast on delicious steak that's served hot off the grill like only the South Americans can do. Though the menu is mostly Argentinean, the atmosphere makes you feel like a bit like you're in Italy.

EL ZOCALO
8th Street between Quinta and 10th Avenue

The interior at this restaurant has a strong Mexican theme, but the menu is international fusion. The food is good, and the waiters are professional and accommodating. Popular dishes include chiles rellenos (stuffed peppers), Caesar salads, steak, and pasta.

✪ THE GLASS BAR
Quinta at 12th Street

An elegant bar and eatery on the Quinta side of Mosquito Blue hotel (see Lodging), the Glass Bar has cushioned chairs, linen tablecloths, and personable waiters. The menu features Italian and Mediterranean food, pasta, fish, and steak. Dishes range from $15 to $20. The outdoor seating is slightly less exclusive but still very upscale and comfortable, offering a great view of the goings-on along Quinta. There is an extensive wine list, featuring selections from Mexico, the Mediterranean, and beyond. Highly recommended.

DI VINO
984-803-1270
Quinta at 12th Street

A swanky lounge/restaurant with indoor seating, candlelit tables, comfy sofas, and sidewalk tables facing Quinta, Di Vino's menu offers such upscale options as grilled fish, steak, and lobster. (See also Trendy Lounges.) Open 1 PM–2 AM daily. Credit cards accepted.

KAREN'S
Quinta between 2nd and 4th Streets

This lively sidewalk restaurant not far from the town plaza has nightly live music and one of the most varied menus in town. Diners can sample fish, shrimp, lobster, pasta, pizza, and all sorts of Mexican cuisine. Crowds tend to linger and enjoy the atmosphere, so getting there early for a good table is recommended.

✪ KARTABAR
984-873-2228
www.kartabar.com
12th Street at 1st Avenue

Cool colors, flowing tapestries, dim lamplight, and flickering candles highlight the decor at this Mediterranean-style restaurant and lounge. The menu features Lebanese and Mediterranean cuisine and seafood, including beef carpaccio, Provincial Mussels (baked with Parmesan, garlic, olive oil, bread, olives, and parsley), calamari, falafel, stuffed grape leaves, tabouli, shrimp stew, lobster ravioli, and mahimahi. It's also a great spot for an after-dinner drink or for a romantic tête-à-tête. Meals average $21. Open 6 PM–3 AM daily. Recommended for its varied menu, sexy atmosphere, and prime location.

LA CAPRICHOZA
984-801-8034
Quinta between 12th and 14th Streets

A newer addition to the Quinta cuisine scene, this upscale eatery offers fish, lobster, steaks, pasta, and fresh salads. The restaurant is upstairs, and the decor is soothing and welcoming, making you want to take a break from Quinta and stay a while. There is live music most nights.

LA PALETTE
984-879-4802
8th Street between Quinta and the beach

Opened in late 2006, this upscale French fusion restaurant in front of the Mosquito Beach hotel is owned and operated by a couple from Toronto, Canada. It has subdued lighting, excellent service, and it is quite romantic. They offer great French and international food, including an extensive tapas menu that makes for easy sampling and sharing of multiple dishes. Highlights on the rotating menu include foie gras, escargot, duck confit, lamb, ostrich, wild boar, and other wild game. Expensive, credit cards accepted.

LA TASCA
984-803-2891
Constituyentes between 10th and 15th Avenues

La Tasca offers typical Spanish food, including paella, tortes, and seafood, in a casual setting. There are several outdoor tables facing the street, which usually bustles with traffic and tourists walking through town.

LE BISTRO
2nd Street between 5th and 10th Avenues

This casual French bistro serves seafood and vegetarian offerings, and there's live music. It's just off the main plaza, making it a good stopping point while waiting for the Cozumel ferry.

LOS TULIPANES

984-873-1255
Quinta at 14th Street

Come for dinner, and then stay for the loungelike atmosphere and soothing decor. Soft music beckons passersby to stop in and stay for a while. The candlelit tables and icy margaritas add to the appeal and make it harder to leave. The menu features steak, fish, and pasta selections, plus a house specialty, Molcajete Azteca, which has chicken, beef, octopus, and baby onions. Another favorite is the grilled chicken with Xtabentun liqueur. Open 7 AM–11 PM.

MAKTUB CAFFE

Quinta between 28th and 30th Streets

Located in the international section of Quinta, in a strip with other sidewalk restaurants, Maktub is known for its authentic Arabic menu. Highlights include couscous, hummus, pitas, gyros, and grape-leaf rolls. An indoor hookah bar has six low tables surrounded by pillows for lounging and smoking. Recommended.

MANDARINA'S PIZZA & CHAMPAGNE

984-803-1249
Quinta at 14th Street

The decor at this Argentinean-owned restaurant and nightspot is more reminiscent of champagne than of pizza, with a decidedly upscale look and feel. The tables are lit by flickering candles and are deftly arranged to give diners an extra bit of privacy. There is live music nightly, which adds to the timeless, faraway ambience. The menu ranges from Mexican breakfasts and crêpes, pizza, and pasta to octopus, mussels, and lobster. Most diners choose to lengthen their stay with dessert and coffee —or perhaps another mojito cocktail, a house specialty.

NEGROSAL

984-803-2448
www.negrosal.com
16th Street between 1st Avenue and Quinta

Sample Mediterranean, Latin American, African, and Mexican cuisine at this upscale climate-controlled restaurant just off the main strip. The dining room will make you think you're in Europe and the varied menu will make you almost certain you're not in Mexico. Favorites include fish, pasta, and beef. The wine cellar stocks more than 100 labels. Recommended.

PALAPA HEMINGWAY'S

984-803-0003
Quinta between 12th Street and Calle Corazon

One of the few air-conditioned restaurants on Quinta, Hemingway's is known for its varied menu and interesting decor. The interior is decorated with bold paintings and Cuba-inspired accessories. The food is Mexican and Cuban, with salmon in three cheeses, grilled steak, Caribbean shrimp, and lobster tail among the favorites. There are also patio tables for those who would rather people-watch than cool off. Open 8 AM–midnight daily.

✪ PLAYASIA

984-879-4781
Quinta between 10th and 12th Streets

This inspired "jungle-chic" courtyard restaurant at the front of Blue Parrot Fifth Avenue has a scenic waterfall, and Ewok-esque treehouse seating over a jewel-tone pool. Crystal chandeliers, glowing orbs from Morocco, and candles set a decidedly romantic tone to the entire space. The menu ranges from traditional sushi favorites to Japanese, Thai, and Vietnamese specialty dishes. The two Bangkok-inspired bars play chill-out music and are a great place to hang out, even if you're not having dinner. Expensive. Highly recommended for its faraway feel.

RISTORANTE ANTICA–OSTERIA DEL MAR
Quinta at 32nd Street

Italian specialties like gnocchi, caprese, seafood, and pasta are served up alongside a great selection of imported wines.

SOL FOOD
Quinta between 20th and 22nd Streets

Sol, in this case, means "sun," as in, "fresh food from the sun," rather than a misspelling of soul food, an ethnic cuisine popular in the southern United States. The dining room is sharp and modern, and the menu features dishes from Italy and the Mediterranean. Favorites include cold salads, baked linguine, and grilled shrimp.

SUR PIZZERIA, GRILL & WINE BAR
984-803-3285
Quinta at Calle Corazon, between 12th and 14th Streets

This two-level restaurant offers fan-cooled dining overlooking Quinta. The decor is slick and mod, with indirect lighting, soothing lounge music, and a strong Mediterranean vibe. The affordable menu includes pizza, grilled steaks, fish, chicken, and steamed shrimp. Open noon–midnight daily.

✪ ULA GULA
984-879-3727
Quinta at 10th Street

Highly recommended for its gourmet Argentinean cuisine and extensive wine list, Ula Gula features white linen tablecloths, candlelit tables, and a sultry but casual terraced dining room over Quinta. It is a favorite of trendy locals, American expats, and visiting diners from around the world. Downstairs from the restaurant, there's a tiny bar on the street corner decorated in white and tan. It has a trendy vibe and a nice view of Quinta. Open 6 PM–midnight daily. Recommended.

WINE & CIGARS BAR
Quinta at 14th Street

Fifth Avenue is a little less rushed on this block and the sidewalk cafes have a little more room, making it easier to linger at your table and, well, maybe have a cigar. This restaurant/bar is set below a canopy of trees and has live music, a swing bar, and a handful of candlelit tables spilling out to the curb, making it one of the more relaxing spots along this busy strip.

ZAS
Quinta between 12th and 14th Streets

The varied menu at this local upscale fave includes vegetarian dishes, fresh salads, pastas, fish, steak, and chicken. The dining room is air-conditioned, and in the evening there are candles on each table.

Asian & Sushi

✪ BABE'S NOODLE HOUSE
Quinta between 28th and 30th Streets
10th Street between Quinta and 10th Avenue

This sidewalk restaurant, which has two locations, offers inexpensive and well-portioned Asian and Thai dishes for lunch and dinner. It serves chicken, beef, pork, vegetarian dishes, coconut rice, spring rolls, and egg rolls. Open noon–midnight daily. Recommended for its good prices, tasty dishes, and local vibe.

KABUKI
984-803-5816
8th Street between Quinta and the beach

Located on the beach side of the El Jardín del Jaguar hotel (see Lodging), Kabuki is one of the best spots in town for sushi. It's a small affair, with a couple of sidewalk tables and a small sushi bar. Delivery is available. Open 1 PM–11 PM daily.

SUSHI ITTO

984-803-4127
Paseo del Carmen Mall
10th Street at 1st Avenue

With only a few seats at the sushi bar, most diners sit at one of the sidewalk tables, where they can watch the goings-on of the busy mall. (There's also a second location on 10th Street.) The restaurant offers fresh sushi, plus a variety of cooked rice and noodle dishes. The shrimp and rice is especially good. Delivery is available. Open 1 PM–11 PM during the week and until midnight on weekends.

SUSHI TLAN

984-803-3838
14th Street at Calle Corazon, between Quinta and 10th Avenue

Quinta between 28th and 30th Streets Sushi Tlan serves artistic and well-presented sushi dishes. You'll find such sushi standards as tuna, salmon, and California rolls, plus special dishes made from local fish. Dine in or call for delivery.

THAI MID

984-879-4186
Constituyentes at 10th Avenue

Located in a small shopping plaza just up from the traffic circle on Constituyentes, this moderately upscale restaurant serves traditional Thai noodle and rice dishes, soups, and spring rolls. It also has a decent wine list and a street-side patio ideal for lingering. The restaurant is part of a chain, with other locations in Mérida and Los Cabos.

Steak

✪ JOHN GRAY'S PLACE

984-803-3689
www.johngrayrestaurants.com
Quinta at Calle Corazon, between 12th and 14th Streets

This dark restaurant, popular with ex-pats and regulars, has a first-floor bar and lounge area and an upper-level dining room with cozy tables, candles, and a subdued, upscale atmosphere. The menu is international, with great steak and seafood. Open 6 PM–midnight daily. Highly recommended for its romantic interior and high-quality food.

PANCHO VILLA

4th Street at 1st Avenue

This casual patio restaurant at the Hotel Plaza (see Lodging) offers surprisingly good steaks and seafood, considering its unassuming setting and budget-friendly menu. Since it's on 1st Avenue it's close to the beach, making it perfect for a quick bite between sunning sessions. Recommended.

Seafood

BIG LOBSTER

984-873-2026
Quinta between 4th and 6th Streets

This casual eatery offers two-for-one beers, whole fish, fajitas, surf and turf, and, of course, lobster. The waiters are friendly and provide a bit of entertainment during your meal. Sample dishes are on display at the front, allowing diners to preview the meals before they enter.

✪ BLUE LOBSTER

984-803-2651
Quinta at 12th Street

The Blue Lobster opened in 1991 and is one of Playa's older restaurants. The two-story eatery just off Quinta specializes in live lobster and seafood (including a daily $14.95 lobster special), plus such unusual dishes as octopus puffs and fish with curry and anisette, as well as coconut shrimp. The Key lime pie is a popular dessert. Open 11 AM– midnight daily; happy hour is noon–4:30 PM. There's live music in the evenings. Recommended.

✪ EL OASIS

984-803-2676
12th Street between Quinta and 10th Avenue

Across from the Santanera nightclub (see Drinks & Dancing), this inexpensive eatery has shrimp tacos, fish tacos, and other seafood and Mexican dishes. The dining room is large and softly lit, and the decor is decidedly Mexican. It is always lively with a preparty crowd. Recommended.

HOTEL BÁSICO SEAFOOD RESTAURANT

984-879-4448
www.hotelbasico.com
Quinta at 10th Street

Even if you're not staying at Hotel Básico, you'll want some excuse to visit and experience the hotel's unique design, and the second-floor patio restaurant provides the perfect opportunity. Run by a staff brought in from a small town outside of Veracruz, the restaurant serves authentic Mexican Gulf Coast seafood in a style they call *maiz mariscos,* which means "corn and seafood" (though it sounds better in Spanish). The patio has a timeless quality, with 1950s-style concrete floors, lights twinkling in the trees, candles and lanterns around the tables, a market kiosk housing the food-prep area, and seating along a balcony overlooking the street. Menu favorites include shrimp empanadas, seafood cocktails, ceviche, stuffed blue crabs (*jaibas rellenas*), fried whole fish, grilled octopus, and lobster. It's also a good spot to sample some traditional Mexican desserts, such as *cocada con helado* (coconut ice cream), flan, and *budin de elote* (corn pudding). To make things more authentic, order your beer as a *michelada* and savor the salt and lime. Depending on the night, there are dance classes, tortilla-making demonstrations, or a marimba band. Highly recommended.

LA BAMBA JAROCHA

984-803-0965
30th Avenue between 36th and 38th Streets

Eat with the locals at this vibrant seafood eatery, a bit off the main tourist trail. It's safe and friendly, and the waiters will be happy to help you order. Favorites include fried or grilled fish, seafood cocktails, fresh oysters, and paella. A traditional baked rice dish called *arroz tumbada* is served on Sunday only. Recommended.

✪ LA CASA DEL AGUA

984-803-0232
Quinta at 2nd Street

Located next to the Playa town square, this gourmet restaurant features European and Latin fusion cuisine, including fresh fish, shrimp, and shellfish, plus Angus beef and a few traditional Mexican dishes. Water features decorate the dining room, and the candlelit tables are covered in white linen, giving it a contemporary yet romantic feeling. Open 11 AM–11:30 PM daily. Highly recommended.

LAS BRISAS

4th Street between Quinta and 10th Avenue

Popular with locals, this seafood restaurant specializes in shrimp cocktail and ceviche, and it also serves fried fish and grilled shrimp. Seating is in a covered dining room with open walls, allowing the breeze to flow through. Open 1 PM–11 PM daily.

Fast Food

BURGER KING
984-873-1523
South side of the town square, by the ferry dock

This walk-up eatery serves the same flame-broiled faves you're used to back home, using most of the same ingredients. Prices are comparable.

JOHNNY ROCKET'S
Paseo del Carmen Mall

Mostly undistinguishable from the American chain's stateside locations, this casual fast-food joint serves up cheese-burgers, hot dogs, onion rings, french fries, and malts.

MCDONALD'S
984-879-3450
Paseo del Carmen Mall
Quinta at 2nd Street
Highway 307 by Chedraui
On the ferry dock, across from Señor Frog's (take-out only)

Face it: After a few days of beer drinking,

taco eating, and sensory overload, it's nice to be in the familiar confines of a McDonald's. The location near the town square and across from the bus station may be one of the only McDonald's locations with a *palapa* roof. The entry is up a flight of steep stairs. The quality is comparable to the locations back home, and the prices are a bit better.

SUBWAY
984-879-4553
Constituyentes at 10th Avenue
Paseo del Carmen Mall

Just like back home, this lunch spot has fresh bread, a varied menu, and custom-made sandwiches.

Cafés and Light Fare

✪ AH CACAO
984-803-5748
www.ahcacao.com
Constituyentes at Quinta

Facing the Olmec statue and fountain at a busy intersection, this small sidewalk spot makes all sorts of chocolate delicacies, including hot/cold drinks, to-die-for brownies, ice cream, cookies, and old-fashioned chocolate bars. It also has gour-met coffees from around Mexico. Stop by and ask for a sample taste of chocolate every day between 7:45 AM and midnight. Free wireless Intenet with a good strong signal. Highly recommended.

CAFÉ CORAZON
Quinta between 28th and 30th Streets

This relaxing sidewalk café has a whimsi-cal menu that's worth trying. Open 8 AM–midnight daily.

Even the McDonald's has a palapa *roof!*

Living Our Dream in Playa del Carmen

What do you do when you have a dream that is so big and bold that to live it you need to move to another country?

The dream for my husband and I was to live in a tropical place with palm trees and beautiful beaches. Mexico beckoned to us invitingly. "Come play here," is what we kept hearing.

So my husband and I moved to Playa del Carmen with our two children in the fall of 2002 and that is when life became a real adventure. Adding immensely to the journey is the fact that our children are now teenagers. We are Canadian, but they consider themselves Mexican. I hope Mexico can handle that!

We came expecting to have many things be different for us and they were. We suddenly had a new home, a new culture, a new climate and a new language. It was a lot of change, but we had made a very deliberate choice to live this adventure. We wanted our children to gain a new perspective on the world. We all gained immensely.

Playa, to me, is not typical Mexico. It has a very diverse culture. We have Mexican, Mayan, European, Caribbean, American, and Canadian influences here all mixing together. I like that as it adds even more variety. We are enjoying every day in our new tropical paradise. I hope that you enjoy your visit too.

My suggestions for the top 10 things to do in Playa del Carmen

10. Sit at a café on Fifth Avenue and count the sunburned tourists. Look for the men wearing socks with sandals as they are obviously Canadian.

9. Go to the beach and eat ceviche, fried fish with tortillas, and guacamole. You can even try to make new friends and try the food on the table next to you.

8. Visit Xcaret—it's a natural theme park. Plan to spend all day and night to enjoy it all!

7. Go to the movies because they are air-conditioned, have great seats, popcorn with hot sauce, and they are cheap. Playa del Carmen has three different movie theaters now with about 19 viewing options.

6. Go swimming—in the ocean, a pool, or a cenote. Why? Go because it feels so good.

5. Go to the beach in the evening (when it is really quiet), walk barefoot on the sand, and look out at the ocean in the moonlight and know what it is like to live here.

4. Have a party—any reason is a reason for a party! You can invite the new friends you made at the beach.

3. Go shopping just for fun—Playa has three big malls now, plus all the shops on Fifth Avenue. Buy a big Mexican sombrero to wear on the plane home.

2. Dine at Playasia restaurant on Fifth Avenue. It is a tropical oasis and a culinary delight.

1. Still my number one—let yourself fall asleep in a hammock!

Enjoy the Adventure! —Suzanne

Suzanne Marie Bandick is a Life Coach and the author of: *Only in Mexico, You Say? The Humorous Side of Living in Mexico.* Visit www.SuzanneMarieBandick.com or www.OnlyinMexicoYouSay.com. Suzanne's husband Shawn is co-owner of One Stop Real Estate in Playa.

CAFÉ SASTA
Quinta between 8th and 10th Streets

Complete with espresso bar and sidewalk tables with seemingly permanent smoking patrons, this very European café has good coffees, pastries, and snacks. Recommended.

CAFÉ TROPICAL
984-873-2111
Quinta between 8th and 10th Streets

In front of the Maya Bric/Tank-Ha Hotel (see Lodging), this sidewalk restaurant serves inexpensive breakfasts and lunches. The menu features traditional American and Mexican egg dishes, smoothies, pastries, croissants, sandwiches, fruit, salads, hummus, falafel, and seafood. Open 7 AM–midnight daily.

CAFFE-INA
Quinta between 20th and 22nd Streets

This whimsically named kiosk café serves Illy-brand coffee, sandwiches, pastries, cookies, and other goodies. It is in the new stretch of Quinta, surrounded by boutique shops and restaurants.

CASA TUCAN RESTAURANT
4th Street between 10th and 15th Avenues, on the ground level of the Casa Tucan hotel (see Lodging)

At Casa Tucan, where a large banyan tree grows up through the middle of the restaurant, they serve an inexpensive breakfast that includes eggs, toast, coffee, and orange juice. Crêpes, sandwiches, steaks, and international entrées are also available. A small shop within the restaurant sells used books, perfect for beach reading.

✪ COFFEE CAFÉ
984-803-4290
Quinta at 34th Street

Tucked under the portico of a large residential and commercial building in Playa's International District, this cozy coffee shop is open daily from 7 AM to 11 PM. There are fresh pastries, fruit, and a good menu of hot and cold coffee drinks. Sit inside at a quiet table or one of the handful of sitting areas on the covered sidewalk. Highly recommended. $

EL ESPACIO
10th Avenue between 6th and 8th Streets

Located in the Los Itzaes Hotel (see Lodging), this small café with wooden sidewalk tables serves coffee, pastries, and sandwiches. The staff can prepare a meal to go for the beach or for a car trip.

FRESH CAFÉ & PAN
Quinta at 2nd Street

This small café offers fresh-ground coffee, gourmet pastries, homemade desserts, natural fruit smoothies, omelets, waffles, baguette sandwiches, and salads. Open 6 AM–11 PM daily.

FRUTI YOGURTH
Paseo del Carmen Mall

This eatery in the well-maintained Paseo del Carmen outdoor mall features fresh-squeezed juices, *torta* sandwiches, salads, and yogurts. Open 9 AM–10 PM daily.

✪ HOT BAKING COMPANY
984-806-0781
10th Street between Quinta and 10th Avenue
Calle Corazon at 14th Street

This casual café serves tea, coffee, fresh-squeezed juice, eggs, omelets, muffins, bagels, banana bread, carrot cake, cookies, pastries, and sandwiches. Open 6 AM–3 PM daily.

✪ JAVA JOE'S
984-876-2694
10th Street between Quinta and 10th Avenue

A good spot for espresso, cappuccino, and iced mochachino, Java Joes also serves bagels, cakes, pastries, sandwiches, and boxed lunches, perfect for a day trip.

Top Spots for Late-Night Dining

There's nothing better after a night at the bar than a greasy, spicy plate of food. Try these spots, and you'll never go to bed hungry:

El Fogoncito, 30th Avenue between 28th and 30th Streets. Eat with the locals who head straight for tacos and cerveza after their late shift working at the hotels.

La Taberna, 5th Street between Quinta and 10th Avenue. Check your e-mail and have a hamburger before calling it a night.

Pizza Banana, 12th Street at 10th Avenue. Grab a cheap slice of pepperoni and mushroom pizza and strike up a conversation with others doing the same.

Pizza 16, Quinta between 10th and 12th Streets. Near the top nightlife spots, this pizza joint gets busy when the bars let out. It's a good place for a last chance at romance.

NATURE DELI

984-873-0629
www.hoteleclipse.com
1st Avenue between 12th and 14th Streets

Located at the entrance to the Eclipse Hotel (see Lodging), this casual sidewalk café is run by a chef who has put in time at some of the area's top hotels. He now enjoys the more relaxed life of preparing meals for only a handful of tables, which are generally filled by regulars and hotel guests who have discovered the well-priced meals and gourmet tastes.

✪ 100% NATURAL

984-873-2242
Quinta between 8th and 10th Streets

Open for breakfast, lunch, and dinner, this is one chain restaurant that doesn't feel like it. There are several different eating areas, from the sidewalk and tables next to a waterfall to covered tables with ceiling fans upstairs. The menu has omelets, enchiladas, sandwiches, seafood, steak, and other dishes. The fresh fruit juices and smoothies are delicious and good for what ails you. Special concoctions exist for lowering cholesterol, boosting energy, curing hangovers, improving memory, and others. The prices are good, and the food is always fresh and delicious. Open 7 AM–11 PM daily. Highly recommended.

SABOR

Quinta between 2nd and 4th Streets

With its location close to the town square, this natural-foods café is popular with locals and others waiting for their bus or ferry. The menu offers homemade *pan dulce* (sweet pastries), sandwiches, juice, and coffee.

STARBUCKS

Quinta at 10th Street
Quinta at 28th Street

If you just have to get your Starbucks fix, you're not alone. This place is usually packed, with the familiar coffee drinks, comfy furnishings, and snacks available. An open-air patio overlooks Quinta, making it a nice spot to linger over a hot cappuccino or cold Frappuccino.

TUTTO DOLCE

984-803-4936
20th Avenue at 10th Street

Providing a nice air-conditioned respite from a hot day, this is a good spot for fresh breakfasts and lunches. The menu features empanadas, quiche, pizza, lasagna, fresh fruits, and coffee. Open 7:30 AM–8 PM daily.

Fire dancers practicing for the nightly show at the Blue Parrot.

ZOO CAFÉ
984-803-2377
14th Street at Quinta

A lively Internet and sports bar, Zoo is surprisingly inexpensive for how hip and stylish it looks. A bank of computers fills the center of dining room, while tables ring the outer edges, affording great people-watching along Quinta. Zoo offers Internet access, long-distance phone calls, newspapers, coffee, smoothies, sandwiches, and light meals. Open 7:30 AM–1 AM daily. Recommended.

Ice Cream & Gelato

BASKIN ROBBINS
Quinta between 2nd and 4th Streets

They have a good selection of ice cream (not quite 31 flavors) available in cups and cones, as well as frozen drinks and juices.

CIAO GELATO
Quinta at 26th

This popular chain seems to be opening new locations as fast as Starbucks. Several flavors are available, with a small sitting area.

HÄAGEN-DAZS
Quinta at 4th Street
Quinta at 10th Street
Quinta at 32nd Street
Paseo del Carmen Mall

This international chain offers its signature ice creams, shakes, and other cold concoctions. The quality is the same as back home.

Go for the Experience

✪ ALUX
984-803-0703
Avenue Juárez between 65th and 70th Avenues, just west of Highway 307

You've heard of cave diving, but this is cave

The beach at Señor Frog's

dining: This restaurant and bar is housed deep within a natural cave, formed thousands of years ago. There is live music nightly, and it makes for a romantic spot for dinner or a drink. The food is not the best, but the novelty of eating in a cave more than makes up for it. Local promoters occasionally host all-night rave parties here, which can get extremely crowded and are best avoided if you're prone to claustrophobia.

BLUE PARROT RESTAURANT
984-206-3350 or 800-435-0668 (U.S.)
www.blueparrot.com
12th Street on the beachfront

This is Playa's premier party location, but it's also a fun spot for a lively meal. Traditional American and Mexican breakfasts are served at the beachside *palapa*, and for lunch or an early dinner, there are tacos, juicy burgers, grilled chicken, and seafood. Meal and drink service is also available at the chairs and bedlike lounges along the beach. At night, the lights go down and the music goes up as visitors fill the swinging bar stools that ring the bar. There is also a covered lounge area with DJ dancing. Food is served until 6 PM. At around 11 PM, fire dancers descend on the main stage and beach area and the restaurant turns into overflow bar seating. Recommended.

✪ LA BODEGUITA DEL MEDIO
984-803-3950
Paseo del Carmen Mall

A Cuba-themed restaurant, bar, and late-night dance club (originally founded in Cuba in 1942) at the back end of the Paseo del Carmen shopping plaza, La Bodeguita del Medio has a few sidewalk tables and a fairly large indoor dining room. The slightly kitschy decor features Cuban artwork, flags, and a wall of fame with signatures and messages from previous diners. Ask for a marker and leave your own comments. A Cuban salsa band plays most nights. There is a back patio overlooking a steep, rocky arroyo. There are daily drink specials, free wireless Internet access, and free salsa lessons Tuesday and Thursday at 7 PM. Open 9 AM–1:30 AM daily.

✪ MAMITA'S BEACH CLUB

984-803-2867
www.mamitasbeachclub.com
28th Street at the beach

This bustling beach club, on Playa's best beach, just north of Constituyentes, is a hot spot to be during the day. It's usually packed with day-trippers, cruise passengers, and sun worshippers staying in Playa, but not on the beach. Mamita's rents lounge chairs and umbrellas and offers beachside drink and meal service, with fish, shrimp, tacos, and other Mexican specialties topping the menu. There are lots of beach activities to enjoy, including WaveRunners, parasailing, banana boat rides, and more. Recommended.

SEÑOR FROG'S

984-873-0930
www.senorfrogs.com
Plaza Marina, at the ferry dock

You can't get off the ferry from Cozumel without first passing by Señor Frog's, situated at the end of the ferry dock and with a seating area on stilts right near the water's edge. It is very casual, and the waiters keep things lively. There is live music nightly and DJ dancing until the wee hours, and there are many audience-participation opportunities, including sexy body contests, drinking contests, and sing-alongs. The menu features Mexican standards, plus pasta, seafood, and burgers. It was completely destroyed by Hurricane Wilma in late 2005 but was rebuilt bigger and better than ever. Recommended.

NIGHTLIFE

When the sun goes down, the action on Quinta heats up. Tourists hit the town with their sun-kissed skin and newly purchased tropical outfits to enjoy the evening breeze, have dinner, gaze at the twinkling lights, and then, quite frequently, have a few drinks. Fortunately, there are plenty of options for nightlife on and around Quinta and the beach. Whether you're looking for a casual beach bar, live tropical music, TV sports, or a cosmopolitan discotheque, you'll find what you're looking for in Playa. There are clubs and bars all along Quinta and at various spots along the beach. Many travelers will take a few laps around town to see what's going on before settling on a place to go. As the night goes on, the crowd thins a bit, becomes less populated with Americans, and funnels to the after-hours clubs, some of which continue serving drinks until sunup.

The most popular area for nightlife is 12th Street, where bars and clubs line both sides of the road all the way from 10th Avenue to the beach. As the night gets later, the crowd moves up the hill toward Coco Bongo, Santanera, and Bali nightclubs, which are all open until sunup. An eclectic crowd assembles from midnight to 2 am at the tiny hole-in-the-wall bar between the main entry to Santanera and the pizza shack next door. They serve beer in giant Styrofoam cups and have only a couple of tables, with the crowds spilling over into the street for a nightly impromptu street party.

Drinks & Dancing

✪ BALI CLUB

984-803-2864
www.baliclub.com.mx
12th Street between Quinta and 10th Avenue

You might think you took a wrong turn and

ended up in Cancún when you make your way through the narrow entrance at this late-night spot, only to find a dark and cavernous dance club, large enough to accommodate up to 1,200 partyers. A 15-foot Buddha crowns the stage, where live artful performances happen every hour or so. The whole place seems to be a dance floor, with the throngs gyrating to Latin pop, rock, and international music. Open 10 PM–4 AM daily. Cover is $10 on busy nights, with all-you-can-drink available for $35. Stop by early in the evening for a free-cover coupon, given out before the crowd settles in.

BANG NIGHT CLUB
984-803-0066
www.bangclub.com.mx

On the beach between 4th and 6th Streets
This dance club is open very late, with the main scene not even starting until 2 AM or so. Entry is via a somewhat dark stretch of beach and visitors should be particularly careful as the night gets later. International DJs spin a variety of house, deep house, and techno music. The crowd is very national, with few American tourists finding their way here. The sound system is quite good, however. There is a cover of at least $10 on most nights.

✪ COCO BONGO PLAYA DEL CARMEN
998-883-5061
www.cocobongo.com.mx
12th Street between Quinta and 10th Avenue

One of Cancún's most popular clubs since 1997 opened this sister club in Playa in 2008, marking the city's unofficial departure from its hippie heyday and ushering in a new era of mass international tourism that continues to change this once-sleepy fishing town. Though somewhat smaller than its sister club up the coast, it is still Playa's largest, most modern, and most

Help Support the Playa del Carmen Fire Department
The local fire department, Bomberos de la Riviera Maya, frequently sets up a kiosk in the Playa del Carmen town square near the ferry dock. They sell hats and T-shirts with the department logo to raise funds to buy updated equipment for the rescue squad. The department's various firehouses are welcoming to guests who want to take pictures and are eager to exchange patches with other fire departments around the world. Make donations and purchase souvenir merchandise online at www.bomberosdelarivieramaya.org.

extravagant nightspot. In fact, it should be viewed as much more of a tourist attraction that you've just got to experience than it should be a regular club or bar. Live performances, including lip-syncing celebrity lookalikes, flair bartenders, DJs, dancers, and most notably—high-flying acrobats—keep the audience entertained all night long, making it feel like New Year's Eve every night of the year. Smoke machines, a video wall, laser light show, balloon drops, confetti explosions, and compressed air blasts help ensure that there's always something pumping energy into the crowd. Cover charge ranges from $30-$60, depending on the night, and includes open bar with domestic beer and liquor drinks. Open nightly from 10:30 PM to 5 AM.

✪ BLUE PARROT DRAGON BAR
984-206-3350 or 1-800-435-0668 (U.S.)
www.blueparrot.com
12th Street at the beach

The king of *palapa* bars in Playa, Blue Parrot is a sort of community center, with a hotel, popular beachfront with lounge chairs, and flowing beers, and at night, it's one of the best parties in town. The main oval-shaped bar is about 100 feet long and

Cancún Pub Crawl Tour

If you're staying in Playa but want to check out the nightlife in Cancún, there's an easy way to do it without having to worry about the drive, finding the good places to go, or having friends to party with. Melsea Tours offers a Cancún party tour for $67, which includes round-trip transportation from your hotel, VIP cover charge, all-you-can-drink open bar, and guide at four Cancún clubs: The City, Dady O, Bulldog Café, and Daddy Rock. For more information call 984-803-3085.

is ringed with swinging bar stools, plus several tables and chairs leading all the way to the water's edge. Around 11 PM, local fire dancers perform, flinging sparks and ash dangerously close to the thatched roof, not to mention the entranced crowd, made up of Americans, Canadians, locals, and people from around the world. The show is amazing, though, with attractive young performers showing off their skill and daring. A covered lounge area offers romantic cushioned seating areas on top of the sandy beach and a stage, where a DJ spins throbbing electronic beats sure to set the mood for a fun night.

As if the dual hurricanes of 2005 were not enough, the Blue Parrot burned to the ground in February 2006, when a fireball from one of the fire dancers landed on the thatched-palm roof and quickly spread throughout the club and surrounding structures. To the delight of Playa revelers, the bar rebuilt once again. Open 11 AM–4 AM daily.

LA BODEGUITA DEL MEDIO
984-803-3950
Paseo del Carmen Mall

La Bodeguita del Medio is a restaurant during the day and evening but its crowd gets more rowdy and the music gets louder as the night goes on. Live salsa music is fea-

tured most nights. For a break from the crowd, seek respite on the back patio and ask for a marker to add your name to the wall of fame. There are daily drink specials, free wireless Internet access, and free salsa lessons Tuesday and Thursday at 7 PM.

Open 9 AM–1:30 AM daily.

CLASSICO
12th Street between 1st Avenue and the beach

Renowned cocktail lounge chain with super-popular outlets in Acapulco and Mexico City makes a go in Playa del Carmen with this swank nightspot resembling a high-end supper club, with dark red furnishings, black walls, and low ceilings. There are three bars, a small dance floor, VIP lounge, outdoor terrace, and DJ playing electronic, rock, and pop music. The ground floor entry leads up a set of stairs to the club. Cover is $5 most nights.

COCO MAYA BEACH CLUB
14th Street at the beach, Playa del Carmen

Beach club by day and night club by night, Coco Maya is an alternative to the hyped-up scene at the Blue Parrot next door. No fire dancers here, just hip DJ music, a handful of couches arranged around the dance floor, and a few additional sitting areas set up in the sand. At the main bar, drinkers vie for the bartender's attention while a movie projector plays old Mexican classics on a wall nearby.

✪ MAMBO CAFÉ
984-803-2656
www.mambocafe.com.mx
6th Street between Quinta and 10th Avenue

With live salsa music every night, Mambo Café has developed quite a following with the local crowd. Tourists are more than welcome to join in the fun, but some dancers

The stylish Tacombi taco truck

take their moves very seriously, so try to keep up or at least stay out of the way. There's a $5 cover charge, depending on the day of the week and the band. All-you-can-drink, open bar available. On Wednesday, ladies enter and drink free 10 PM–midnight.

PLAYA 69

984-879-3217
Quinta between 4th and 6th Streets

This is the top gay bar in town: Look for the rainbow flag while walking down Quinta, and you'll know you've found it. There's live and recorded male entertainment, and it's a great spot to meet locals, ex-pats, and travelers from around the world. The scene gets going around midnight and lasts until about 4 AM.

✪ SANTANERA

984-803-2856
www.lasantanera.com
12th Street between Quinta and 10th Avenue

Look for the brightly lit Vegas-style sign facing 12th Street and you'll find Santanera, the closest thing Playa has to the raging discos in Cancún. But don't worry, even this place has an unpretentious and down-to-earth atmosphere, and a patio bar. The club's decor seems to pay equal homage to Mexican professional wrestling and the Catholic Church. Downstairs, it's like a traditional nightclub, a bit reminiscent of the House of Blues, but without a stage. Upstairs, a large *palapa* roof contains the crowd of dancing, socializing, and margarita-drinking patrons. DJs spin the latest tunes, including American pop, Mexican rock, tropical music, and a bit of funk. The crowd is a good mix of locals and visitors, gay and straight. Opens at 8 PM, but it doesn't start hopping until at least midnight. Last call is 4 AM. The VW bus Tacombi is permanently parked outside the front door, making it easy to grab a bite for the walk back to your hotel. Highly recommended.

SEÑOR FROG'S

984-873-0930
www.senorfrogs.com
At the ferry dock in the Plaza Marina center

Popular with day-trippers, cruise passengers, Mexico first-timers, and vacationers at hotels in the adjacent Playacar development, Señor Frog's is always a good bet for good cover bands, reggae music, audience-participation gags, goofy contests, and a bit of risqué fun. It is built out over the sand and has a great view of the Palace resort beach and the ferry dock. The restaurant serves Mexican food, seafood, and pasta and is open for lunch and dinner. It makes a good spot to dine while waiting for your ferryboat to Cozumel. Open 10 AM–2 AM daily.

Trendy Lounges

✪ BÁSICO TERRACE BAR

984-879-4448
www.hotelbasico.com
Quinta at 10th Street

Enter through the hotel lobby on 10th Street and take the elevator to the top floor. If you're there in the daytime, you'll be treated to a breathtaking view of the ocean, and at night you can see the twinkling lights of Quinta. There are several seating areas, hammocks, canopy sunbeds, and unique aboveground pools.

✪ DESEO BAR

984-879-3620
www.hoteldeseo.com
Quinta between 10th and 12th Streets

Here you can indulge in ultra-hip lounging in an atmosphere as nontraditionally Mexican as the $8 martinis they serve. You'll feel cool as soon as you crest the top stair that leads to the bar from Quinta. It's a lot like being in L.A. or Miami when you're at Deseo, but without the attitude that comes along with it. The glimmer of the pool, the glowing lights from the rooms ringing the deck, and the projection TV on the wall next door set a surreal stage for some serious lounging. Most of the patrons are hipsters from Mexico City, and they all seem to know each other, but find your spot at the bar, at a poolside bed, or at one of the lounge chairs near the hotel rooms, and you'll fit right in.

✪ DIABLITO CHA CHA CHA

12th Street at 1st Avenue

See and be seen at this swanky open-air bar while you sip mojitos, cuba libres, daiquiris, and other tropical drinks. The lights are dim, but the people-watching is still second-to-none as the well-heeled international set grooves to African and Latin rhythms while showing off their trendy vacation duds.

EL CIELO

12th Street at 1st Avenue

During the day it may look like it closed down a month ago, but at 10 pm, the red leather couches are pulled from storage and set up along the street and the fiber optic chandelier is turned on, making this one of the hipper places to linger over cocktails. Owned by South Americans, it's popular with revelers from around the world, with a vibe that's more Miami-beach chic than it is Playa casual. The centerpiece is a large square bar, surrounded by barstools and filled with a sexy crowd that's far less pretentious than one would guess by appearance alone. Open 10 PM to 3 AM daily.

DI VINO

Quinta at 12th Street
984-803-1270

As the night goes on, diners swap out for drinkers, and the lounge scene begins. The swank factor multiplies and the indoor couches become the favored seats, making

The trendy rooftop bar at Hotel Básico

an ideal spot for candlelit kanoodling. Food is served until late at night, but you'll see more swizzle sticks than butter knives as the night goes on. Di Vino is not so much a singles' scene as it is a conspiratorial hideaway for folks who may have been single the night before. It's also a great spot to woo a date or show your feelings for your special someone.

KARTABAR

984-873-2228
www.kartabar.com
12th Street at 1st Avenue, across from the Blue Parrot (see Drinks & Dancing)

This must be what lounge bars in the Mediterranean would be like. Cool colors, flowing tapestries, dim lamplight, flickering candles—it has all the trappings of a secret romantic escape. The scene is somewhat social, but folks tend to keep to their groups more than not. The dinner menu features Mediterranean and Lebanese cuisine, but things really get going around midnight, when the dinner crowd yields to the late-night lounge scene, steeped in style and exclusivity. An upstairs boutique inn, Hotel Cohiba (see Lodging), plays on a similar theme. Open 6 PM–3 AM daily.

MUSHROOM BAR

Quinta between 28th and 30th Streets

This stylish bar offers a unique serene and trendy atmosphere for lounging with locals and ex-pats. The music is a mix of electronic, funk, reggae, rock, and soul. There is a tiny "Kabaret" stage with live musical performances most nights and occasionally other shows. Thursday nights, ladies drink free for the first part of the evening. Open 6 PM–2 AM daily.

Party like a pirate at OM Bar Courtesy of Mike Stone

✪ OM BAR & LOUNGE

984-745-0584
www.omplaya.com
12th Street at 1st Avenue

Located just across the street from the entrance to the Blue Parrot (see Drinks & Dancing), this nightspot gets more busy as it gets later. The decor foretells what may happen if Martha Stewart were to make over a pirate ship, with dark wood furnishings, flowing red sails, candles, and well-maintained fixtures. International DJs spin lounge and chill-out music while patrons dance on the tables, conspire at dark tables, and enjoy watching the busy street scene. Open 5 PM–4 AM daily.

ZENZI BAR AT THE CORTO MALTES

10th Street at the beach

A long chapter in Playa's history came to an end when the original Corto Maltes hotel closed down in 2007. One of the town's original hotels, it kept its lost-in-time vibe, with thatched roofs, sandy floors, no air-conditioning, and slow pace until the very end. But with its incredible location in the absolute center of town, it was only a matter of time until the inevitable happened and the hippie hotel going for $18 a night was shuttered and in its place went up a complex of 16 modern condos starting at $700,000 for a one-bedroom. The development's public beach bar, the Zenzi, is 180 degrees from what it used to be, though it still holds some appeal—not for its sense of

Local Lingo—Out on the Town

2 x 1. Look for this sign at the entrance to a bar, and you'll know that their two-for-one happy hour has begun!

Anejo con coca. *Anejo* is a golden blend of aged rum, and it goes great with Coke, making it a bit of an upgrade from a standard rum and Coke. To order one in a loud bar, grasp your chin and move your hand downward, as if stroking a beard. Then, with the same hand, hold your pinkie under your nose for a moment, then wipe it away, as if you're snorting a powdered Colombian export from under your fingernail.

Barra libre. Some bars offer *barra libre* nights, where your cover charge includes open bar, or basically all you care to drink. This normally includes bottled water, so it's a good chance to hydrate as well.

Cantinero. Spanish for "bartender."

Chela/chelada/michelada. *Chela* is colloquially used to mean "beer." A *chelada* is a beer served in a glass of fresh lime juice and salt. For a real local treat, try a *michelada*—a *chelada* plus Worcestershire, Tabasco sauce, and tomato juice.

Consumo minimo. Translating from Spanish into "minimum consumption," it's a common policy at popular bars and clubs, where instead of a cover charge, your entry fee includes drink coupons equivalent in value to the amount you pay to get in. Such a policy keeps out patrons who just want to socialize and dance but not buy anything.

Cuba libre. "One revolution is still necessary: the one that will not end with the rule of its leader," wrote Cuban spiritualist Jose Marti, describing his desire for a free Cuba, which in Spanish is *Cuba libre*. It's also the name used locally for a rum and Coke, served with a wedge of lime. In the Riviera Maya, bartenders will still understand if you just order a "Cuba."

Desechable. Remember, no bottles on the street, so if you want your drink to go, ask for it in a *desechable*, and it will come in a Styrofoam cup. Many bars also have a stack of them at the exit, so if you've got one for the road, leave your glass behind.

En las rocas. Spanish for "on the rocks." Try your margarita *en las rocas* and earn a bit of respect from your *cantinero*.

Frog's/Carlos. Abbreviated versions of Señor Frog's and Carlos 'n Charlie's, it's how the locals refer to the popular drinking establishments.

Lager. Used when ordering a Dos Equis (XX) beer in the green bottle, as opposed to the XX Amber, which is the dark beer in the tinted bottle. You can also hold your index fingers together to form an "X" in front of you, then pump your hands twice, indicating dos equis, or "two Xs." To order two or more Dos Equis, first flash the number of drinks you want with your fingers, then proceed to make the "X" sign.

Nohoch. The Mayan word for "big." Order your favorite cocktail *nohoch*, and it'll be served in a tall glass.

history or laid-back lifestyle, but for its trendy vibe and lively beach scene. Tropical drinks and tasty fusion-style appetizers are served in a Mediterranean-inspired setting, with stained woods and stone accents on a huge terrace or in fancy chaise lounges on the beach itself. It's a fairly casual beach bar during the day but the swank factor turns up a notch after sundown, with resort wear being more common than shorts and T-shirts.

Bourbon Street

Casual Drinks

✪ BAD BOYZ BEACH CLUB

On the beach between 2nd and 4th Streets

Owned by the proprietor of the former Captain Dave's bar a few blocks up, this ultra casual beach bar has live jazz music in the late afternoon, plus sun chairs, good food, ice-cold beer, and a good mix of ex-pats, regulars, and folks just walking by on the beach who see the pirate flag flying proudly and want to see what the commotion is all about. Recommended.

BOURBON STREET
984-803-3022
Quinta between 6th and 8th Streets

This New Orleans–themed bar has live music, projection TV, beer specials, and a crowd of ex-pats and regulars who always make for good conversation. You'll hear much more English than Spanish here, making it a nice respite when you need a taste of home. The music and crowd tend to be a bit more mature than other places along this stretch.

BOTICA
Quinta between 22nd and 24th Streets

Boasting a menu of 20 types of mescal, this tiny bar is in the heart of the International District and buzzes in the evening with locals and visitors snacking on inexpensive food, sipping their drinks, and watching the world go by.

CASA TEQUILA–LA TEQUILARIA
984-873-0195
Quinta between 4th and 6th Streets

This is primarily a liquor store, with hundreds of bottles ranging from $7 to $250. Most can be purchased by the shot, which makes for a fun experiment in tequila sampling. There are a few sidewalk tables, plus an upstairs balcony with a couple of tables overlooking Quinta—perfect for people-

Casa Tequila on Fifth Avenue Courtesy of Philip Gammon

watching. Open 9 AM–1 AM daily.

EL BUEY
4th Street at 15th Avenue

This most untouristy bar a couple blocks from the main strip is not for the timid. Ranchero music blares through the tree trunk walls and hard-drinking regulars sit at plastic tables swilling $1 beers. The menu is surprisingly extensive, with soups, Mexican food, and seafood. The deal of the day is $5 and comes with a main course and two beers.

✪ EL PIRATA
On the beach between 12th and 14th Streets; enter through the Costa del Mar hotel (see Lodging)

Next door to the Blue Parrot, El Pirata has its own sound system, own crowd, and own vibe. The drinks are cheaper, the lines at the bar go faster, and the scene is a lot more relaxed. Kick back with a cold beer on a plastic table just feet from the Caribbean and ponder the stars, or join the crowds near the bar for some first-class mingling and friend-making. Not to be outdone, El Pirata has its own fire dancers, performing nightly at the water's edge around midnight. Open 9 PM–3 AM daily.

GEORGE & DRAGON PUB
Quinta between Constituyentes and 18th Street

Watch sports games and music videos on a projection-screen TV while sipping actual draught Guinness beer, one of the very few places to do so in the Riviera Maya.

KARAOKE BAR
6th Street between Quinta and 10th Avenue

This hole-in-the-wall karaoke bar is a fun spot to have a few beers and do something you wouldn't do back home—sing in front of a crowd of strangers! The song list features popular hits in English and Spanish.

Dancing on the Sand: Top Spots to Have Sand between Your Toes and a Drink in Your Hand

Blue Parrot, 12th Street at the beach. Get there early to reserve a coveted waterfront table. If you fall out of your chair, you'll land on powder-white sand. Dancers spill out from the wooden dance floor all the way to the water line.

El Pirata, on the beach between 12th and 14th Streets. This no-frills beach bar offers a laid-back alternative to the Blue Parrot next door. The music is loud, the bar stools swing, and the tables on the beach are just steps from the lapping waves of the Caribbean. Fire dancers perform on the beach behind the club most nights at around midnight.

Mamita's Beach Club, 28th Street at the beach. Who says you can't go dancing during the day? The folks at Mamita's prove that getting your groove on by sunlight can be just as fun as by moonlight. The party gets going in the early afternoon and peaks just before sundown, then quickly dwindles. Arrive early to claim a coveted beach bed.

Señor Frog's, Plaza Marina, at the ferry dock. Built above the beach at the base of the ferry dock, this resort-town stalwart packs in a primarily American clientele in search of good Mexican food, pop music, and sometimes love. Dancing patrons can get their drinks to go and boogie on the beach below.

There are plenty of beachfront restaurants and bars in Playa.   Courtesy of Mike Stone

LA RANITA BAR

984-873-0389

www.ranacansada.com

10th Street between Quinta and 10th Avenue

Guests of the La Rana Cansada hotel and others looking for a shady spot to sip a cold one in a traditional rustic Mexican setting that says "beachtown cantina" as well as any bar in town will, find themselves at home at this small bar a half-block up from the buzz on Fifth Avenue. Patrons can sit at the bar, in the lounge area, or out in the courtyard, surrounded by flowering tropical plants. Recommended.

LA CREMA

4th Street between Quinta and 10th Avenue

A good spot to sit and talk, this funky bar specializes in inexpensive draft beer. The interior is decorated with colorful tapes-

Common Beers of the Riviera Maya

Bohemia. Served in a dark bottle with gold foil on the neck, Bohemia is a bit more expensive than other beers, but it has a robust taste and is a bit of a status symbol.

Bohemia Dark. Introduced to the Riviera Maya in 2008, this darker cousin of Bohemia offers a richer head and creamier, almost stout-like finish.

Corona. Though it's brewed in Mexico, it seems to be more common in the States. Not all bars carry it, so if you're normally a Corona drinker, it may be time to expand your horizons. Normally served with a slice of lime.

Dos Equis. Advertised on billboards throughout the region, Dos Equis (XX) comes in lager (green bottle) and amber (tinted bottle). The lager is much more common and goes better with lime.

Leon Negra. A bit of a microbrew, this dark and flavorful beer is locally brewed in Mérida, the capital of the state of Yucatán. Sometimes hard to find.

Modelo Especial. Sold by the bottle or in single cans in the convenience stores, this light-bodied lager is favored by many locals and goes nicely in a cooler at the beach.

Montejo. Crafted at the same Mérida brewery as Leon Negra, this beer adds a touch of class to your bar visit. Not always available, though.

Negra Modelo. A dark beer sometimes sold at a slightly higher price than other beers. It's normally served in a glass and goes great with steak.

Noche Buena. From the makers of Bohemia, this dark seasonal brew is only available in the winter holiday season. The name means, essentially, "Christmas Eve."

Sol. Commonly found at beach bars and nightclubs, Sol is what most Corona drinkers opt for when their usual beer is not on the menu. Frequently served with lime.

Superior. Served in a dark tinted bottle, which helps keep it from getting skunked in a cooler on a sunny day, this full-bodied beer is sold at a discount in grocery stores and is available mostly at bars favoring locals.

Tecate. Most commonly served in cans, Tecate is best enjoyed with plenty of salt and lime. Popular at sports bars.

Victoria. Brewed by Grupo Modelo, the same company that makes Corona and other local favorites, this is a hoppy pilsner that is not generally exported, so it's fun to see it and try a few.

tries along the walls and hanging from the ceiling.

LA HORA FELIZ
Quinta at 26th Street

It's always happy hour at this casual bar in the heavily Italian part of Quinta. Two-for-one drinks all day long, plus snacks and desserts.

LA JARRA
10th Avenue at 4th Street

This local hangout, known for draft beer and rock music, is a good place to ask locals about lesser-known area attractions.

LA PALAPA BAR
Town Square near the ferry landing

If you're just off the ferry from Cozumel and need a drink, this is the place to go. It's a round bar offering a great view of the lively scene of Playa's main beach zone. Watch the soccer games, sunbathers, lifeguards, and local families while sipping a tropical cocktail. It's the perfect way to say, "Hola," to Playa del Carmen. Also makes for a good resting point if you've been exploring the town and you want to get out of the sun.

LA TABERNA
984-803-0447
5th Street between Quinta and 10th Avenue

A good spot to watch a live sporting event on TV, La Taberna has a wall of computer workstations, with Internet access going for $1.50 an hour. There are dart boards, pool tables, and multiple TVs, and there's also cold air-conditioning, so it's a good spot to go after a long day at the beach, when you just can't bring yourself to sit at a patio bar. They serve good tacos, burgers, grilled chicken, nachos, steak, quesadillas, and seafood cocktails. Open 10 AM–4 AM daily. Recommended.

LITROS
1st Avenue between 10th and 12th Streets

This primarily local hangout offers 33-ounce beers for $3 and equally large mixed drinks for $7. It's a good spot to sit on the sidewalk and watch the crowd gather for the Blue Parrot (see Drinks & Dancing). The small indoor area has funky lighting and Mexican rock music. Can't finish your drink? It's okay to get it to go, as long as it's in Styrofoam.

✪ LIVING GARDEN BAR
Quinta between 14th and 16th Streets

Giving a little taste of the jungle to the sidewalk bar scene, this bar opened in 2007 and quickly developed a loyal following. Some tables front Fifth Avenue but others are set back in a tree-covered setting, surrounded by tropical plants, dappled lighting, and jungle décor. It's a nice place to chill out for a while and grab a snack. The temperature seems to drop about 10 degrees as soon as you step inside.

LUNA BLUE BAR
984-873-0990
www.lunabluehotel.com
26th Street between Quinta and 10th Avenue

Opened in March 2008, this tropical-themed bar is tucked into the front of the popular Luna Blue hotel. It clearly shows its Jimmy Buffet-style inspiration, with swinging bar stools, thatched roof, and Caribbean vibe. The convivial atmosphere is shared by hotel guests, regulars, and others who happen to walk by and find themselves drawn to the laughter and upbeat music. Recommended.

PERLA NEGRA
984-803-4430
Quinta at 32nd Street

Famous home of the "20 snacks," this sports bar, night club, hookah lounge, and tapas bar offers indoor and outdoor seating, large-screen TVs, and a home atmosphere. The main draw though is their offer of free appetizers with every drink. And the best part is you get to choose the freebie. The nightclub portion opens at 9 PM and has nightly specials: no cover Wednesdays, free open bar for ladies on Thursday, and bikini contests on Fridays.

PURO BUENO
Quinta at 30th Street

This contemporary indoor bar is air-conditioned and relaxing, while its patio is more casual and kicked back. It's a good spot to sip a cold one and watch the endless parade of chic Italians along Quinta's international section.

✪ BEER BUCKET
10th Street between Quinta and 10th Avenue

This American-dominated happy-hour favorite offers loud pop and rock music, beer specials, mixed drinks, and a come-as-you-are attitude. Seating is on the ground floor or on an upper deck overlooking the street. While not a great place to impress a date, it's a fun place to party with friends and make some new ones. As the

Mucha Ropa, Mucha Ropa!

The equivalent to the English "take it off, take it off," *mucha ropa, mucha ropa* is just as cliché and out of fashion. In the Riviera Maya, the main gentleman's clubs are in Playa del Carmen, along Highway 307. They are generally considered safe for tourists, though like anywhere, it's best to keep your wits and not do anything that you think could get you in trouble. That being said, the law allows for quite a bit, and you're sure to find your choice of willing participants—for a price.

One such club is Baby's Hot (Highway 307 at 6th Street). It's a small hangout for locals and doesn't see many gringos, so it can seem a bit rough around the edges to many foreigners. Cover charge is posted at $25, but they are flexible if they think you'll spend some money once you're inside, especially if you threaten to go down the road to visit their competitors instead. A few blocks south is Marlin Men's Club (Highway 307 at Avenue Juárez, www.marlinmensclub.com, 984-110-5082). Open Monday to Saturday from 1 PM to 7 AM, it's the most stylish of the area clubs and features a pool table, laser light show, massages, escort girls, show girls, table dances, private dances, and multiple stages. Cover charge is negotiable. Farther down Highway 307, across from the southernmost entrance to Playacar, is Chilly Willy's, a palapa-roofed sister club to the longtime nudie institution in Cancún. Cover charge is posted at $20, and the club seems to open only certain times of the year.

Each club offers table dances in a private curtained room for $15 to 20, payable directly to your dancer of choice, waiter, or floor manager (who is eager to assist with your selection). More intimate encounters can be arranged for an additional fee (around $200 for the complete package), and each club has private rooms for rent by the hour.

Drinks are relatively inexpensive, though if a dancer asks you to buy her a drink, the fee is significantly higher—up to $15 for a single cocktail—so unless you're ready to drop a lot of money, you're probably best off saving your pesos for a dance since it's roughly the same price. Cash is the preferred payment method, so bring some bills and stay aware of your surroundings.

All taxis know these clubs well and will often recommend one to you since they get a kickback for dropping people off there. Negotiate your price in advance (it shouldn't be more than a few dollars from any Playa del Carmen or Playacar hotel), and if you want to try to get in without paying a cover, have them drop you off a block or two away so you're not obligated to your taxi driver in any way. No need to have your cabbie wait for you; there are plenty waiting outside when it's time to leave.

Be smart. Be safe. Have fun.

---

night goes on, the scene gets a little crazier, making for a fun night on the town. They play U.S. sports on TV for the playoffs and other key games.

✪ SIESTA FIESTA

984-803-1166
www.siestafiestahotel.com
Quinta between 8th and 10th Streets

This courtyard bar and restaurant is a popular meeting spot where travelers congregate to watch live sporting events on the big-screen TV and listen to live music (several bands per night). After the live music, the staff puts live sports or recorded concerts on the TV, and the party keeps going. There are tables near the stage, several bar stools, and sidewalk tables for those seeking a bit more peace and quiet. Vacation camaraderie is especially strong here, making it a great spot to meet other travelers. Food is available all day long. There is also a quaint hotel offering comfortable and affordable accommodations (see Lodging).

It May Be Paradise, but It's Still the Jungle

Don't forget, even though Playa del Carmen and the Riviera Maya are exotic and wonderful beach vacation destinations, they are still relatively undeveloped and are in close proximity to the jungle, and you should set your expectations accordingly. You should also remember that there are hassles and frustrations inherent to any travel situation. You're on vacation to have fun and celebrate life, so try not to let little challenges you encounter bother you.

If a chicken walks into your beachfront restaurant and pecks at your crumbs, don't get mad—take a picture. If a gecko streaks across the wall of your hotel room, don't call the front desk—give him a name and consider him your pet. If your shower runs out of hot water, don't complain to the concierge—it's good for your sunburn. And most importantly, if you find yourself at odds with your travel partner, it's time to hit the nearest bar, order a margarita, feel the warm breeze, and remember why you came here in the first place.

✪ TEQUILA BARREL

984-873-1061
www.tequilabarrel.com
Quinta between 10th and 12th Streets

A popular meeting point for message-board groups, the Texan-owned Tequila Barrel is a Playa classic. A dark wood bar gives a traditional hacienda feeling to the interior, while a large-screen TV near the back plays sports and news. When nothing good is on TV, there is live music. Sidewalk tables spill out onto Quinta, making this a great spot to sip a cocktail and watch the parade of people walk by. The bartenders are friendly and welcoming, and the bar stocks more than 85 types of tequila (the owner's favorite is Centenario Anejo), plus a huge selection of imported cognacs, whiskeys, and Scotches. An air-conditioned sports bar on the bar's back side has a pool table and several TVs. The kitchen serves up traditional Mexican and American breakfasts, plus burgers, wings, fajitas, and other bar foods. The bar's Web site has a live Webcam and archives photos taken at the bar each night. Open daily from 7 AM to 2 AM.

2 DOLLAR DRINKS

984-803-3895
10th Avenue between 6th and 8th Streets

Despite the American name, this spot is popular mostly with locals who come for the cheap drinks (beer is $1, mixed drinks are $2), the soccer games on TV, and the camaraderie of friends. Tourists are welcome, though, so feel free to give it a try and maybe make a local friend. Open 11 AM– midnight daily.

VIVA MARGARITA

Paseo del Carmen Mall, by Johnny Rocket's
(see Dining)

This casual sidewalk bar features live and recorded music and serves tasty Jose Cuervo margaritas in a variety of flavors. Mango is a favorite of the regulars, and it comes with a salted and limed rim and light dusting of chili powder. Patrons can order sushi from the neighboring Sushi Itto location (see Dining).

A Classy Night on the Town

THE GLASS BAR

984-803-1676
Quinta at 12th Street

An elegant bar and eatery on the Quinta side of Mosquito Blue hotel (see Lodging), Glass has cushioned chairs, linen tablecloths, and personable waiters. The menu features Italian and Mediterranean food, pasta, fish, and steak. (Dishes range from

Lightweight clothes are recommended year-round in Playa.

$15 to $20.) The outdoor seating is slightly less exclusive but still very upscale and comfortable, offering a great view of the goings-on along Quinta. There is an extensive wine list, featuring selections from Mexico, the Mediterranean, and beyond. Credit cards accepted. Highly recommended.

ULA GULA
984-879-3727
Quinta at 10th Street

This small lounge on the corner serves drinks until past midnight in a tiny covered area and at a few sidewalk tables fronting 10th Street. The interior is decorated with candles, making for a romantic spot to sit and watch the people walk by. There's also a much larger upstairs dining room. Open 6 PM—midnight daily.

SHOPPING & SERVICES

Watches, Jewelry, Sunglasses & Cosmetics

DIAMONDS INTERNATIONAL
984-873-1611
www.diamondsinternational.com
Avenue Juárez at Quinta
Quinta at 14th Street

Especially popular with the cruise-ship crowd, this international chain retails rings, necklaces, watches, pendants, and gifts with a variety of gemstones and metals, including diamonds, emeralds, pearls, topaz, rubies, sapphires, tanzanite, silver, gold, and platinum.

EFFY JEWELRY FACTORY
984-803-4100

Top 10 Songs to Load on Your iPod

The right song can help secure a memory, make good times even better, and share an experience with friends. Try some of these to capture the spirit of the Riviera Maya:

"Margaritaville" by Jimmy Buffett. Said to have been written on a flight from Cozumel to Houston, it's a song about a mythical island at the bottom of a Cuervo bottle.

"Mexico" by James Taylor. This is a classic tale of an extended vacation: "The sun's so hot, I forgot to go home."

"Stays in Mexico" by Toby Keith. A countrified reminder to keep your vacation exploits to yourself.

"Mexico" by Nash Girls. Young women having fun at the beach.

"Married in Mexico" by Mark Wills. A south-of-the-border romance complete with beachfront nuptials.

"I Got Mexico" by Eddy Raven. Sometimes, that's all you need.

"Blame It on Mexico" by George Strait. "Too much guitar music, tequila, salt, and lime." I know I've used this excuse before.

"Ten Rounds with Jose Cuervo" by Tracy Byrd. Crazy things can happen with tequila, especially after 10 rounds.

"Mail Myself to Mexico" by Buddy Jewell. Vacation fantasies go postal.

"One Step Closer to Cancún" by Elmer Thudd. Inspirational song about an upcoming vacation.

---

www.effycollection.com
Paseo del Carmen Mall, 10th Avenue at 1st Street

This international brand has locations in Alaska, Aruba, Cozumel, Curaçao, New York, and St. Martin. The shop has cold air-conditioning and a broad selection of gold, silver, and diamond jewelry.

ETENOHA
Quinta between 8th and 10th Streets

This shop, which carries jewelry and accessories made from local amber, also has unusual lamps and interesting houseware.

QUARZOS
Quinta at 4th Street

This brightly lit shop has silver and gold jewelry, pre-Columbian re-creations, and souvenir jewelry.

SOL DEL MAR
Quinta between 6th and 8th Streets

Sol del Mar sells jewelry and clothes from major designers, and also local brands.

SUB CHRONO
Paseo del Carmen Mall

At the back end of the mall, this upscale watch shop sells name-brand watches from leading designers, dive watches, and fashion watches.

SUNGLASS ISLAND
Quinta between 8th and 10th Streets

Offers decent prices on eyewear by Ray-Ban, Gucci, Chanel, Prada, Armani, and others.

ULTRAFEMME
www.ultrafemme.com.mx
Quinta between 10th and 12th Streets

Duty-free prices, outside the airport. UltraFemme offers great deals on name-brand perfumes, cosmetics, and other merchandise. It carries Rolex, Cartier, Tiffany & Co., Brequet, David Yurman, Mikimoto, Tag Heuer, Omega, Ebel, Roberto Coin, Mont Blanc, Corum, and Movado. Cosmetic brands include Lancôme, Estée Lauder, Clinique, Clarins, Chanel, La Prairie, Shiseido, Hugo Boss, Ralph Lauren, and Calvin Klein.

For the Beach

BAZAR AZUL
Quinta between 10th and 12th Streets

This large air-conditioned shop offers sportswear, hats, bathing suits, sandals, jewelry, picture frames, and souvenirs.

BEACH COMPANY
Quinta at 12th Street

A popular stop for cruise-ship passengers, this stylish shop has bathing suits, summer wear, hats, sandals, bags, and other accessories you may find useful on a tropical vacation,

BIKINI PALACE
Quinta between 10th and 12th Streets

Here you'll find trendy name-brand bikinis, thong bathing suits, and cover-ups.

BLUE PLANET
Quinta between 10th and 12th Streets

This boutique shop sells wraps, bathing suits, casual wear for men and women, bags, hats, sandals, and accessories.

CRUSH
Quinta between 6th and 8th Streets

This is the place for hip sunglasses and sportswear to help you look good at Playa's beaches and lounge bars.

MARE SWIMWEAR
Quinta between 6th and 8th Streets

Mare sells just what you'd expect from its name: bathing suits for men and women. National and local brands are available.

MARTI
984-803-4083
Paseo del Carmen Mall

This large national chain store offers high-quality sporting goods, including diving and snorkeling gear, running shoes, water shoes, water toys, games, apparel, hats, jerseys, and other equipment.

MIRO
Quinta at 4th Street

Known for its "everything is $10" prices, this chain store has T-shirts, shorts, sportswear, and other summery clothing.

TANK-HA DIVE SHOP
Quinta between 8th and 10th Streets

While Tank-Ha offers dive trips and equipment rental/sales, and there is an electronic kiosk out front with information on area dining and nightlife, it's also a good spot to purchase masks, fins, and other gear for snorkeling and diving.

ZINGARA SWIMWEAR
Quinta between 8th and 10th Streets

Here you can get name-brand and off-brand swimsuits, cover-ups, and accessories, mostly for women.

Clothing & Accessories

CARACOL
Quinta between 6th and 8th Streets

This small boutique store offers women's apparel, sandals, bags, hats, jewelry, and accessories.

Caracol

DIESEL
Quinta between 8th and 10th Streets

This medium-size showroom has casual wear, bags, shoes, sunglasses, and accessories. Its hip clothing can help you look like one of the stylish Europeans walking the streets of Playa.

GOLD DUCK
Quinta between 2nd and 4th Streets

You can't miss the big logo on the front of the building. This chain store offers mostly leather and canvas goods, including bags, backpacks, and hats.

HARLEY DAVIDSON
Paseo del Carmen Mall

This shop has Harley-branded merchandise and apparel, including shirts, hats, jackets, leather goods, sunglasses, sport bags, and more. Harley Davidson motorcycle rentals are available at the rental office located on Highway 307 at Constituyentes Avenue.

KIN MAYAB
Quinta between 10th and 12th Streets

Kin Mayab has traditional men's and women's clothing, Mayan-inspired apparel, and clothing made of natural fibers.

LA CASITA
984-803-1249
Quinta between 10th and 12th Streets

Sells tropical apparel, *guayaberas* (Mexican wedding shirts), *huipiles* (traditional embroidered Mexican dresses), and hand-stitched garments for men and women. There is also a selection of kids' clothing, silver jewelry, and accessories.

PYGMEE'S
Quinta between 8th and 10th Streets

Here you'll find a funky selection of tropical sportswear, shoes, lamps, and accessories.

ROGER'S BOOTS
2nd Street between Quinta and 10th Avenue

A popular regional chain, Roger's offers handmade leather boots starting at around $100. Custom boots are also available, if you're going to be around a while. They also sell leather bags, belts, fancy belt buckles, hats, holsters, and rifle cases.

TITA SANDALIAS
20th Street between 1st Avenue and Quinta

This unique boutique has a sand floor with wooden stepping-stones and cheery decor. On display are a wide variety of mostly handmade sandals for the beach, the disco, or strutting along Quinta. Bags and other accessories are also available.

WAYAN NATURAL WEAR

984-803-3543
www.wayan.com.mx
Paseo del Carmen Mall
Quinta at 2nd Street
Quinta at 16th Street
Quinta at Constituyentes

This successful chain, with stores in Cancún and Playa del Carmen, sells wraps, shirts, and other Mayan-inspired apparel, plus jewelry, bags, housewares, crafts, and accessories.

Handicrafts & Gifts

CARIBBEAN PUZZLES

Calle Corazon
Quinta at 20th Street (kiosk only)

This shop offers games, books, puzzles, and other fun stuff for kids. It's a good spot to find a gift for a child left at home or to find something to help keep a vacationing kid busy in the hotel room. Most of the stock is of the educational variety—nothing here makes loud noise or goes fast.

JELLYFISH LAMP SHOP

4th Street at Quinta

This shop spills well onto the sidewalk and sells the tropical lamps that you'll see in many restaurants and bars. They are made from coconuts and similarly shaped gourds and are adorned with jewels, whimsical designs, and streamers that make them look like jellyfish with their dangling tentacles. They range from baseball-sized ones selling for a few dollars to basketball-sized works of art selling for more than $100.

LE BEST

Quinta between 2nd and 4th Streets

This large and well-stocked shop offers good liquor prices, souvenir bottles, T-shirts, lighters, tons of souvenirs, and—no joke—even a variety of hand-painted sinks.

PACHAMAMA

Calle Corazon

On the south side of the short Calle Corazon strip, this shop offers Mayan and Mexican artwork, handicrafts, postcards, books, religious art, and great gift items.

PLAZA LA FIESTA

Quinta between 4th and 6th Streets

This popular chain store is the largest souvenir store in town. It offers a vast array of gifts, personal items, and fun reminders of the area. There are T-shirts, sportswear, boots, sandals, leather goods, pottery, jewelry, hats, ashtrays, keychains, Mayan replicas, sculptures, and hundreds of other items.

Bargains abound in the Riviera Maya. Courtesy of Mike Stone

Bargain Hunting in Playa

Contributed by Donna Loera

Playa del Carmen is a shopper's dream destination. Most shopping is confined to La Quinta Avenida (Fifth Avenue), which is paved with brick and restricted to foot traffic.

Shops are interspersed with restaurants and bars, so taking a break to drink a cool beverage and people-watch is all part of the day's fun. Exclusive shops can be found at the Paseo del Carmen Mall near the town square and on Calle Corazon, which intersects Quinta between 14th and 16th Streets. The local market is located on Quinta at 26th Street. The price and quality of goods is varied, so it is important to shop around before buying. It is appropriate to haggle over prices in the market and in lower-end stores, as well as with street and beach vendors, but not in the shops or boutiques.

Products are as varied as the ethnicity of the tourists who shop here and are priced for every pocketbook. Jewelry shopping is always fun, and in Playa the discerning shopper can find silver, turquoise, opal, and amber. In this resort town, swimsuits, sarongs, and other beachwear abound and can be had for a bargain even in the more exclusive shops. Hats are available in almost every color, fabric, and style and are affordably priced, so treat yourself to a newly purchased one instead of packing your own. Shoes, especially sandals and flip-flops, are another item you needn't take with you. They are trendy, cheap, and available in styles you're not likely to find at home. For example, you can find Brazilian Havaianas sandals in several shops and pay the same price for them as you would in Rio de Janeiro.

Shops are generally open from 10 AM until 10 PM or later, but the street becomes more congested as the day progresses. If you're a true shopping aficionado, you'll likely want to shop early, before the beach crowd decides to break for some shade and bargain hunting. Even if you are a sun worshipper, be sure to take at least one afternoon to browse the varied merchandise along Quinta and bring home a few memories from your trip to Playa.

Sample prices: Havaianas sandals: $22   Fake silver bracelets: $1 each   Mexican blanket: $5 Maracas: $2 a pair   Sarong beach wrap: $4.50

SACBE
Quinta between 2nd and 4th Streets

This interesting store has Mayan-inspired artwork, mostly from local artisans. There are artifact re-creations, home decor items, leatherwork, jade carvings, and natural fiber apparel.

SEÑOR FROG'S GIFT SHOP
Quinta at 20th Street
Second location at the ferry dock

Nothing like a T-shirt to prove you were there—or to rub it in the face of someone who wasn't. The "world famoso" bar and restaurant chain's off-site gift shop has hats, shorts, T-shirts, jackets, bags, and other items emblazoned with the happy frog logo. Great for gifts.

Groceries, Liquor, Books, Music, Cigars & Conveniences

BONTAN BOOK STORE
Calle Corazon near Quinta

Bontan sells books, newspapers, and current-issue magazines in English and Spanish.

CAPTAIN TEQUILA
Quinta between 2nd and 4th Streets

This liquor store sells dozens of tequilas, ranging from barely slammable varieties to uber-smooth barrel-aged sipping tequilas suitable for serving on the rocks and enjoyed with a fine cigar.

CASA PARTAGAS
Quinta at 14th Street

This is a good spot to purchase real Cuban cigars. Ask the staff for an explanation of how to spot the fakes. T-shirts, smoking accessories, and gifts are also sold.

CASA TEQUILA–LA TEQUILARIA
984-873-0195
Quinta between 4th and 6th Streets
Quinta at 14th Street

This liquor store/sampling bar is a great spot to shop for tequila if you're looking for something specific. One-liter bottles range from $7 to $250. It has a few sidewalk tables, plus an upstairs balcony with a couple of tables overlooking Quinta. Souvenir bottles and flasks are also available. The bar serves many of the tequilas that it sells, plus some light snacks. (Salt and lime count as snacks, right?)

CASITA DE LA MUSICA
Quinta between Avenue Juárez and 2nd Street

They sell local and international music, including merengue, salsa, Cuban, Mayan, pop, mariachi, and lounge music. There's also a selection of nonmusical souvenirs available.

CHEDRAUI SUPERMARKET
Highway 307, adjacent to Playacar

This massive grocery superstore has fresh produce, meats, dairy, deli items, prepared foods, packaged goods, beer, liquor, cigars, clothing, electronics, furniture, and much more than you'd need on vacation. It has a great selection of domestic and imported goods and better prices than the convenience stores downtown.

DON ROBERTO
Quinta at 6th Street
www.tequiladonroberto.com

Tired of Sauza and Jose Cuervo and want to try a new brand of tequila? Cattle breeder, farmer, and rodeo promoter Don Roberto Orendain started a tequila distillery in the Mexican state of Jalisco and this Playa shop exclusively sells the Don Roberto brand. Popular varieties include La Arenita, a white tequila that makes great margaritas. The higher-end Belsanto tequila is 100 percent agave, making for smooth sipping. The shop also sells the company's Tequishot bottled tequila drink, pre-mixed with grapefruit soda, which is superb chilled very cold and served as a poolside refresher. It's kind of like a Salty Dog, but with more kick. Looking for something really different? It may not be traditionally Mexican, but the Green Fairy absinthe soda that the shop sells is sure to make for an interesting night.

Market & Deli

Cuban Cigars: Don't Get Ripped Off

For many travelers, the question of where to find authentic Cuban cigars comes up at least once during their trip to the Riviera Maya. A little information can go a long way toward losing your hard-earned pesos on fake Cohibas on Playa del Carmen's Quinta Aveninda.

Counterfeits Abound

First, be aware that the majority of so-called "Cuban" cigars you'll see in Playa are counterfeit, even those sold in cigar stores. If you see a Cohiba sitting in a jar next to a cash register it is almost certainly fake. The scam here is that the store owners know that visiting Americans will pay high prices for authentic Cubans, so they re-label secondhand cigars (factory rejects) or cheaper brands.

DON'T buy so called "Cuban" cigars from any shop or vendor unless the box has a holographic sticker of authenticity attached. The Cuban government now places a hologram on genuine boxes (or the three and five packs) of legitimate Cuban cigars. Even the Montecristos at the high-end resorts usually don't have these holograms, and most are just pretty good looking fakes.

Where to Find Authentic Cuban Cigars

What's a tourist to do? The best source for authentic Cuban cigars is, believe it or not, the Wal-Mart tobacco shop on the corner of 30th Avenue and 8th Street. You can be assured that not only are they authentic, they are likely the cheapest source in town (you can purchase budget-priced booze while you are there, as well).

La Casa del Habano on Quinta between 26th and 28th Streets, is also a reputable source for authentic Cubans cigars and offers a good local alternative if you are opposed to "big box" stores.

If you choose to stay at a resort, many of them carry a limited number of brands in their store. Some do have authentic Cubans, but be sure to look for the hologram label.

Bringing Cigars Home

It is illegal for U.S. citizens to bring Cuban cigars into the U.S. or even to purchase and consume them in Mexico. We do not condone the illegal importing of Cuban products to the U.S. and if you do choose to purchase Cuban cigars, it would be wise to smoke them while in Playa.

That said, many U.S. citizens carry cigars back with them in their luggage. Less than 10 percent of travelers arriving in the U.S. are randomly selected to have their luggage inspected, so the odds are in your favor. Some U.S. citizens have been known to ship unlabelled Cuban cigars back home via an international courier. Be aware that this will be very expensive and there is a good chance that if you ship labelled cigars they will be confiscated.

Content courtesy of SeePlaya.com, a great online source for insider's information on the Riviera Maya.

FLOWER SHOP
Avenue Juárez between 20th and 25th Streets

Surprise your travel companion with a bouquet of fresh tropical flowers. This local shop has a wide assortment of tropicals, roses, and other flowers, plus premade bouquets, plants, and arrangements. Prices are about half of what you'd expect to pay back home.

HABANA CIGARS
984-803-1047
Quinta between 10th and 12th Streets

Top 10 Books for Riviera Maya Travelers

Try these great reads in preparation for your trip, while you're there lying on the beach, or to help ease your transition back to the real world.

Don't Stop the Carnival by Herman Wouk. This meandering tale may change your mind about wanting to open a hotel in the Caribbean.

Incidents of Travel in Yucatán by John Lloyd Stephens and Frederick Catherwood. Originally published in the 1840s, it's an amazing account of the life and times of the Mayans.

Cinnamon Skin by John D. MacDonald. A boat-bum detective travels to Cancún and the Riviera Maya to solve a crime for a friend.

A Salty Piece of Land by Jimmy Buffett. A cowboy moves to Sian Ka'an to become a fishing guide. Plenty of Riviera Maya and Buffett-song-inspired references.

A Tourist in the Yucatán by James McNay Brumfield. An action-adventure mystery set among the Mayan ruins.

Where the Sky Is Born: Living in the Land of the Maya by Jeanine Lee Kitchel. Thinking of moving to the Riviera Maya or just want to know what it would be like? Learn from someone who's done it.

Chaos in Cancún by Susan Murray. A detective novel for teens that takes the main characters on a whirlwind tour through the Riviera Maya. Includes some fun references to local spots that kids will find entertaining.

Wicked Spanish by Howard Tomb. This tongue-in-cheek language guide will teach you some naughty phrases and fun sayings to try out on bartenders and fellow bus riders.

The Ruins by Scott Smith. A group of friends on holiday to Cancún and the Riviera Maya stumble across a mysterious secret in the Mayan jungle and struggle to get away. It may make you think twice about hiking in the jungle!

Captains Outrageous by Joe R. Lansdale. A comedic and bumbling tale of intrigue, with travels from east Texas to the land of the Mayans.

Habana Cigars specializes in Cohibas (Cuba), Partagas, and Trinidad cigars, and it also sells lighters, newspapers, and gifts, as well as empty cigar boxes for $4. Though officially Cuban cigar boxes are still illegal to import into the United States, it's doubtful that U.S. Customs would hassle you for it.

KODAK
Quinta between 2nd and 4th Streets

This authorized Kodak dealer carries medium-quality cameras, plus simple point-and-shoots for travelers. Film, batteries, and CD creation are also available.

MARKET & DELI
Quinta at 6th Street

A large store offering deli sandwiches, snack foods, some groceries, over-the-counter and prescription drugs, liquor, T-shirts, souvenirs, hot sauce, film, batteries, cold drinks, and many sundries

MARSAN MARKET
30th Avenue at South 1st Street

Six blocks straight back from the ferry dock, this local market has fresh meats and fish, fishing supplies, clothing, shoes, fresh fruits, and a wide variety of items found at a typical Mexican market. It's a good place for picking up a unique gift item or just strolling around to get a sample of the local color.

MORGAN'S TOBACCO SHOP
984-873-2166
Quinta at 6th Street

Morgan's offers cigars, cigarettes, T-shirts, smoking accessories, current magazines, and daily newspapers, including the *New York Times* and *USA Today*. Cigars are hand rolled in front of the shop each evening.

MUNDO BOOKSTORE
984-879-3004
1st Street between 20th and 25th Avenues

With more than 10,000 books in stock, Mundo is a great place to purchase a good beach novel, magazines, regional history books, Mayan literature, and other finds. The store also takes book donations to support local students. Open 9–9 daily.

PLAYA MART
Quinta at Avenue Juárez

The busiest convenience store in town offers cold drinks, snacks, magazines, T-shirts, sunglasses, souvenirs, liquor, and beer to go. It is convenient to the ferry dock.

SAM'S CLUB
Highway 307, adjacent to Playacar

Just like back home, Sam's has a massive selection of groceries and other items. A membership card is required, and your stateside card is valid.

SAN FRANCISCO DE ASIS
30th Avenue at 12th Street

This Mexican chain grocery store is not quite as well stocked as Chedraui on the freeway, but it's within easy walking distance of many Playa hotels. It has a good selection of beer and liquor, deli items, and snacks, and such basics as sandals, toiletries, batteries, and film.

SEÑOR HABANO
Quinta between 6th and 8th Streets

Here is one of several local stores offering regional and international cigars (including Cuban cigars), smoking accessories, lighters, T-shirts, and gifts.

SUPER DELI & DRUG STORE

Quinta between 2nd and 4th Streets

This big, modern store with several coolers and well-stocked shelves sells liquor, snacks, deli sandwiches, Gatorade, yogurt, cheese, cold cuts, tobacco, pharmacy items, personal hygiene products, and a fair range of souvenirs.

SUPER HO

Quinta at 22nd Street

Its name may be funny, but the selection of cold drinks, snacks, fruit, and deli foods at this mini grocery store is fairly serious. It also has batteries, film, and other sundries.

WAL-MART

8th Street at 30th Avenue

This full-size discount department store opened in early 2006 and quickly became a favorite of locals.

Well-stocked local pharmacy

WINERY & PLUS

8th Street at 30th Avenue, in front of Wal-Mart
10th Avenue at 28th Street

Locally owned liquor store has wines from around the world, plus a selection of tequilas, rums and more. The 10th Avenue location has a lounge area where shoppers can linger and try their selection.

Spas, Gyms & Body Work

AREA BODY ZONE

984-803-4048
www.areafitnesscenter.com.mx
Paseo del Carmen Mall

This modern gym is up the same stairs that lead to the Moon, next to Rolandi's Italian restaurant (see Dining). Visitors can participate in sculpting classes, yoga, Spinning, step, combat training, body zone, and Tai Chi. There are free weights, cardio equipment, workout stations, complimentary workout towels, and clean locker rooms. Some classes and personal trainers are extra. Daily use fee is $15, 5 days available for $60, 10 days for $100.

CABELLISIMO HAIR STYLE
20th Street between Quinta and 10th Avenue

This full-service hair salon offers tinting, cuts, and styling.

MUSCLE-BEACH GYM
984-803-0478
6th Street between 30th and 35th Avenues

They have a weight room and exercise machines, plus a climbing wall and steam room. Private instruction is available. Classes include Spinning, Pilates, aerobics, Tae Bo, and kickboxing. Open 8–1 and 4–8 Monday–Saturday.

PLAYA PIERCINGS
Quinta between 8th and 10th Streets, in front of Pygmee's

Playa uses sterile needles and modern equipment and has a large selection of studs, earrings, and belly rings.

SCREAMINK TATTOOS
10th Street at Quinta

This tattoo artist offers tribal tattoos, Mayan designs, and custom jobs. T-shirts and piercings are also available.

SPA HA
984-803-1564
www.spasmexico.com
10th Avenue between 38th and 40th Streets

On the northern end of Playa's tourist zone, this "spa" is not recommended for serious patrons in search of quality therapeutic treatments, as it seems to be more of a place to get rubbed by a pretty young woman than it is a serious spa. It offers massages, body treatments, steam baths, and a rooftop plunge pool. A 45-minute massage goes for $45. Additional "relaxation services" for men can be added for a $20 tip.

SPA ITZÁ
984-803-2588
www.spaitza.com
Calle Corazon/14th Street near Quinta, on the Calle Corazon pedestrian walk

Founded by veteran Californian holistic health practicioner Sharon Sedgwick, this modern spa takes a traditional approach to body treatments, accenting its services with ancient Mayan healing principles. Offerings include Mayan healing baths (aphrodisiac, milk, seaweed, tonic rescue, sunburn relief, anti-itch), body treatments (Mayan salt exfoliation, cellulite treatment, black mud, Mayan clay), flotation chamber, oxygen bar, body waxing, facials, and manicures. Package deals are available for bride and groom, jet lag recovery, a mom's escape, and other specialties. The in-house boutique carries spa products from OPI, Fridda Dorsch, CV Aromatherapy, and Rain Forest Remedies. There is also a Mayan-themed terrace and rooftop sundeck. Open 10–9 daily.

The terrace at Spa Itzá

TATUAJES LA SUERTE
Quinta between 2nd and 4th Streets

Here you can get artful tattoos and piercings, as well as T-shirts.

VERONICA'S MASSAGE
984-807-5023
1st Avenue between 24th and 26th Streets

This boutique massage center offers sports, stone, Swedish, and deep-tissue massage, plus reflexology. Walk-ins accepted, based on availability. Excellent prices.

YOGA BY THE SEA
984-873-0735
www.morethanyoga.com
8th Street at the beach

Operating out of the Alhambra Hotel (see Lodging), instructors Arielle Thomas Newman and Ellen de Jonge offer daily Hatha yoga classes, yoga retreats, specialized programs, and meditation and relaxation techniques. They also have special yoga programs for couples, divers, and golfers.

Shops at Paseo del Carmen Mall

Shopping Plazas

EL MERCADO LOS PORTALES
10th Avenue at 6th Street

With a pair of inexpensive restaurants (El Caguamo and Los Portales) serving typical local foods (such as *torta* sandwiches and tacos), plus a few T-shirt shops, souvenir stores, and junk shops, this is a good spot for budget travelers to get a quick bite or stock up on supplies. It is conveniently close to the youth hostel.

PASEO DEL CARMEN MALL
1st Street at Quinta

This modern outdoor shopping plaza has more than two dozen shops, restaurants, bars, and other attractions.

Street scene in the Riviera Maya   Courtesy of Philip Gammon

PLAZA MAYA
Highway 307, across from the southernmost entrance to Playacar

A massive shopping complex containing restaurants, bars, boutique stores, a movie theater, discount stores, department stores, and a pedestrian plaza.

PLAZA PELICANOS
10th Avenue between 8th and 10th Streets

This mall has a bank, Blockbuster, Papa John's, several clothing stores, a duty-free shop, and a three-screen movie theater, showing movies about two months after they are released in the United States.

3

THE RIVIERA MAYA—SOUTH OF PLAYA DEL CARMEN

Travelers venturing farther south of Playa del Carmen will find a striking variety of options for lodging and recreation, and the farther south you go, the more remote, unspoiled, and adventurous things become. Playacar is a stone's throw from Playa del Carmen and home to nearly a dozen all-inclusive mega-resorts, where travelers from around the world visit to play golf, lie on the beach, and be pampered in every way possible. The beachfront towns of Puerto Aventuras and Akumal beckon scuba divers and fishing enthusiasts with excellent conditions year-round, while the abundant cenotes, hidden beaches, eco-adventure parks, and Mayan ruins provide venturesome travelers with the kind of vacation experiences that turn postcards home into exotic tales of intrigue and exploration.

Many of the hotels and resorts south of Playa are all-inclusives, with vast campuses featuring luxurious accommodations, multiple dining options, on-site nightlife, spas, recreational activities, and everything else guests need to spend a week of fun in the sun without ever getting into a car. Other lodging options in this area include local inns; eco-conscious cabañas with an emphasis on nature, rather than luxury; and low-cost hutlike properties fashioned from native materials and devoted to students, traditionalists, and other budget-conscious travelers who want to experience the splendor of the Riviera Maya much as the locals have been doing for hundreds of years.

Playacar

Just south of Playa del Carmen, off Highway 307, at km 285, the large-scale, gated resort community of Playacar surrounds the ancient Mayan ruins of Xaman-Ha and is composed of resort hotels, condos, private residences, shopping plazas, restaurants, a golf course, activities centers, and one of the most pristine stretches of beach in the whole Riviera Maya.

The creation of Playacar was the single most important event in the development of large-scale tourism in the Riviera Maya. Before that, travelers were content with small, locally owned hotels, relatively few services, and European plan (no meals included) rates. Aside from a few standouts, accommodations were generally simple affairs, with basic amenities and very few luxuries but a strong feeling of tradition and harmony with the surroundings. Strict density restrictions in Playa del Carmen made the town less than ideal for large resort development, and had allowed the town to grow slowly and organically, unlike the rampant development seen in Cancún.

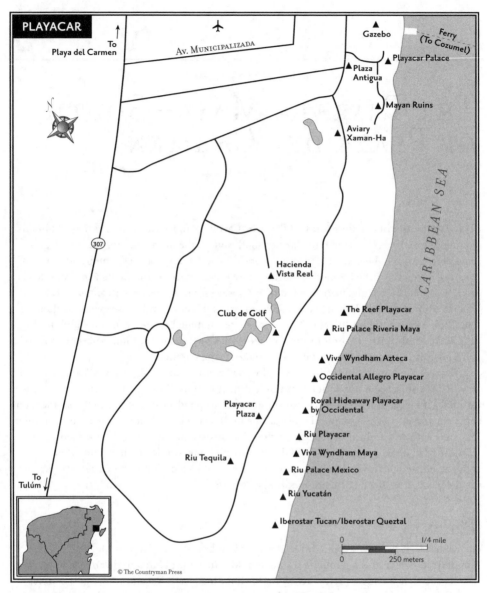

In the early 1990s, though, things started to change. Mexico's real estate conglomerate Grupo Situr purchased a huge plot of barren beachfront land just south of Avenida Juárez and christened it Playacar, a term deemed more marketable and English-friendly than the name of the town itself. Since it was out of the jurisdiction of the development restrictions, the Riviera Maya had its first opportunity to build international-class hotels, which needed a larger scale and higher volume of guests to turn a profit.

Today, there are more than a dozen large resorts owned by international corporations and averaging some 300 rooms each. Unlike the small inns and guest houses of a few years ago, these resorts offer a vast array of services and luxuries, including imported linens, efficient air-conditioning, abundant hot water, water-sports centers, on-site scuba train-

Beach wedding in front of Las Palapas Courtesy of Robyn Eden

ing, dry-cleaning service, Jacuzzi tubs, tennis courts, swimming pools, and kids' clubs. Most are operated as all-inclusives, where guests pay one price that includes accommodations plus all meals, drinks, and activities. Many hotels have on-site gourmet restaurants, multiple bars, and even amphitheaters and nightclubs.

The area has become a playground for tourists from the United States, Canada, and Europe. It is an extremely popular wedding and honeymoon destination, and the resorts are quite adept at catering to vacationing couples with welcome amenities (fruit baskets, chilled champagne, flowers), special dinner reservations, and couples' spa treatments. Other common Playacar visitors are families and budget travelers with flexible schedules, who compare prices weekly, waiting for a bargain. Frequently, these travelers will choose their resort based on what special offers are available and tend to be less loyal to the brands or specific hotel properties. Others have had a good experience at one of the resorts and become avid ambassadors for it, claiming that its services and amenities are unbeatable. These travelers wouldn't dream of staying anywhere else and pride themselves on returning year after year, sometimes bringing gifts for their favorite bartenders and waiters.

The main road through the complex, Xaman-Ha Avenue, is made of cobblestone and is lined with manicured tropical plants and an occasional actual Mayan ruin, lending a timeless quality to the otherwise modern resort community. The road parallels the beachfront and splits Playacar into two sides. Phase I, along the water, features a nearly solid line of hotels, though they are mostly low-rise buildings of two or three stories surrounded by tropical vegetation, so the area does not feel overdeveloped or crowded. Phase II, on the other side of the avenue, includes the golf course, hundreds of vacation villas and private homes, and several hotels that are not directly on the beach. These hotels shuttle guests to

The accommodations in Playacar are upscale and all-inclusive. Courtesy of Riviera Maya Tourism Authority

a beach club, so even though their rooms don't front the beach, their guests are still able to have a beach vacation. Craft stores, restaurants, bars, and tour agencies are housed in various shopping plazas along Xaman-Ha and at Plaza Marina, near the ferry dock. Most guests, however, either take their meals on-site at their all-inclusive resorts or venture into the neighboring town of Playa del Carmen to experience the abundant dining options offered along Quinta Avenida and throughout town. Shopping, nightlife, and other tourist attractions can be found in Playa as well.

During the day, the beach bustles with activity. Some guests stroll along the water, play volleyball, sail, kayak, windsurf, swim, Jet Ski, and enjoy the plethora of activities, while others seek respite in a lounge chair or hammock and read and snooze in the warm breezes. To the north of Playacar is the town of Playa del Carmen, reachable by bicycle (loaners available at most hotels) or a short taxi ride. To the south is a mile-long stretch of deserted beach decorated with massive boulders, which starts at the Gala Resort and ends at the Xcaret resort and ecopark.

Guests at Playacar resorts can spend an entire week without leaving the complex and have all their needs and whims catered to. Others, however, like to visit Playa del Carmen in the evening to go shopping, stroll the tourist plazas, try some local foods, and enjoy the nightlife.

LODGING

It can be a bit difficult to differentiate the all-inclusive resorts of Playacar. For the most part, the hotels share a common beach, which is just about perfect anywhere along the stretch. The hotels themselves are large-scale affairs, with comparable pools, gyms, restaurants, bars, and activities programs. Nearly all the rooms offer good air-conditioning, plenty of hot water, comfortable bedding, private balconies, minibars, and standard amenities. Most have bicycles for guest use, which makes the couple-mile trip into Playa del Carmen a breeze. The main considerations and differentiating factors are the size of the resort, whether or not the hotel is adults-only, whether it's on the beach or the golf course, and your budget. Rates range from $100 per person per night up to $250. As the price goes up, generally, the rooms are larger, the grounds are better maintained, the food and beverage quality is higher, and the vibe is more exclusive.

Lodging Prices

$ -	less than $75 per night
$$ -	$75 to $125 per night
$$$ -	$125 to $225 per night
$$$$ -	$226 to $350 per night
$$$$$ -	more than $350 per night

ALLEGRO OCCIDENTAL PLAYACAR RESORT

1-800-858-2258 (U.S.)
www.occidentalhotels.com
Paseo Xaman-Ha, Playacar

A family-friendly, beachfront, all-inclusive resort with 296 rooms housed in two-story villas scattered around the property, it was originally constructed in 1992 (it was the first all-inclusive in Playacar) and underwent $5 million worth of renovations in 2003, plus updates after Hurricanes Emily and Wilma in 2005. Rooms feature tropical colors, Mayan paintings, marble bathrooms, and private balconies. Casual and family-oriented, this moderately priced resort provides guests endless opportunities to have fun—and equal opportunities to be alone with the sun and the water. There is an activity pool, quiet pool, and children's pool, a kids' club, and an outdoor theater with live shows nightly. Rates: $$$$.

HACIENDA VISTA REAL

984-803-1585
www.vistareal.com.mx
Paseo Xaman-Ha, Villas Pakal

This luxurious villa-style property has 78 rooms and is surrounded by the Playacar golf course, straight back from the Reef Playacar hotel. The decor is a combination of Mexican hacienda, Roman, and Mayan, with dark woods, marble floors, columns and arches, granite accents, and warm colors. Rooms have air-conditioning, satellite TV, safes, glass showers, original artwork, and amazingly soft sheets and duvets. Suites have up to three bedrooms and feature Jacuzzis, terraces, and large living rooms. The resort has a grill restaurant and pool facing several water hazards, the fairway of the first hole, and the clubhouse beyond. There is a massive fitness center with more than 30 LifeFitness machines, a kids' club, a convenience store, a bakery, a VIP TV lounge, an Internet café, and a Thai restaurant and sushi bar. Guests have access to the resort's exclusive beach club, located on Xpu-Ha beach, 15 minutes south of the hotel. The attached day spa is housed inside a recreation of a Mayan temple that is a marvel just to look at. It is the most lavish facility of its kind in all of Playacar, featuring a 30-foot waterfall, climbing wall, Mayan murals and stonework, and the most modern medical, therapeutic, and relaxing facilities available. Popular treatments include coconut-milk body wraps, aroma facials, Turkish baths, hot stone massages, Shiatsu, hydrobaths, and full beauty salon services. There is even an indoor *temazcal*, with upgraded seating and amenities from the traditional Mayan sweat lodges. Rates: $$$$.

IBEROSTAR RESORTS

984-877-2000 or 1-888-923-2722 (U.S.)
www.iberostar.com
Paseo Xaman-Ha, Playacar

This complex near the southern end of Playacar includes the Tucan and Quetzal resorts, each with 350 rooms. Accommodations are all-inclusive, with unlimited food and drinks, nonmotorized water sports, nightly shows, and other activities. There is a great rock-free beach-front, multiple pools, outdoor Jacuzzis, restaurants, bars, scuba center, workout room, tennis courts, and nightly live shows. Water sports include windsurfing, kayak-ing, and snorkeling. Rates: average $$$$.

✪ OCCIDENTAL ROYAL HIDEAWAY

984-873-4500
www.royalhideaway.com
Paseo Xaman-Ha, Playacar

Luxury and all-inclusives don't always go together. At this adults-only, 13-acre, 200-room resort, though, the two go together like piña coladas and sunset—which, by the way, are included in the all-inclusive room rate. The lavish property has meandering rivers, waterfalls, tropical gardens, and six pools (three reserved for quiet relaxation). There are several restaurants and bars (men are required to wear long pants, closed-toe shoes, and collared shirts for dinner). There is a large fitness center, two tennis courts, a water-sports center, and a dinner theater with live nightly shows. The rooms are housed in two- and three-story villas, with a mix of Spanish and Colonial Mexican architecture. They have air-conditioning, ceiling fans, CD/DVD play-ers, and marble bathrooms with jetted tubs. Internet access is complimentary in the business center. Tours, scuba diving, and a

wide range of spa services (algae body wraps, massages, body scrubs) are available for an extra fee. Rates: $$$$ to $$$$$. Luxury room classes, upgraded amenities, and preplanned tours are available for an additional fee. Highly recommended for high-end travelers.

PLAYACAR BEACH PROPERTIES

984-873-0418 or 1-866-862-7164 (U.S.)
www.playacarbeachproperties.com

This company has an inventory of more than 50 condos and villas in Playacar, including locations on the beach, on the golf course, and around the development. Their Web site lists all of the properties and their amenities and helps you select one that may fit your needs. Rates: range from $650 a week for a basic one-bedroom condo up to $4,000 a month for an immac-ulate five-bedroom villa right on the ocean.

PLAYACAR PALACE

www.palaceresorts.com
North end of Paseo Xaman-Ha, Playacar

Previously the Continental Plaza Playacar, this was the first large hotel in the Playa del Carmen area and the flagship resort of Playacar. It was completely renovated and reopened in 2005 with 185 rooms, a chic lobby, and a beachfront pool. As it is adja-cent to the Cozumel ferry dock and the Playa del Carmen town plaza, it's a good spot for travelers who desire the luxury of Playacar but still want ready access to the town of Playa del Carmen. Rates: $$$$.

REEF CLUB PLAYACAR

984-873-4120
www.thereefplayacar.com
Paseo Xaman-Ha, Playacar

This boutique all-inclusive property, located on the beach in the middle of the Playacar development, is within walking distance of the town of Playa del Carmen.

With only 200 rooms, it has a more exclusive feeling than its larger neighbors. It is a family-friendly property, with a kids' pool, and Mayan and tropical design influences. Rooms have a private balcony or patio, air-conditioning, and ceiling fans. The rate includes meals at three restaurants (buffet, Italian, and snack bar), drinks at five bars (including a swim-up bar and beach bar), activities program (water aerobics, beach volleyball, water basketball), theme parties, kayaking, windsurfing, sailing, and snorkeling. There are two pools, an outdoor Jacuzzi, and a kids' club. Bicycles are available for guests who want to ride into Playa del Carmen. Rates: $$$ to $$$$ per person, all-inclusive.

RIU HOTELS AND RESORTS
1-888-666-8816
www.riu.com
Paseo Xaman-Ha, Playacar

Spanish-owned Riu Hotels has five all-inclusive properties on the southern end of Playacar: Riu Palace Mexico, Riu Tequila, Riu Yucatán, Riu Playacar, and Riu Lupita. The Mexican Street shopping plaza adjacent to the resort complex offers a gym, hair salon, crafts market, clinic, tour office, and other attractions. Guests staying at one hotel can enjoy the facilities at the others, including the nightclub, which is located at the Tequila (well, that makes sense!). The Palace Mexico is the most upscale and has 434 rooms and a wedding chapel. The

VIDAS—Helping Pets and People in the Riviera Maya

A group of volunteer animal lovers called International Veterinarians Dedicated to Animal Health (VIDAS) travels each year to the Riviera Maya, providing education and free veterinary care in an effort to fight pet overpopulation, which can cause starvation, disease, and other health problems. They work with the local communities to improve the lives of pets and the people who love them. Their first trip, in 2002, involved two vets and six students and resulted in the sterilization of 100 cats and dogs over five days in Playa del Carmen. Since then, more than 1,000 animals have been sterilized and vaccinated in Akumal, Bacalar, Cobá, Chemuyil, Playa del Carmen, Tulum, Puerto Morelos, and Puerto Aventuras.

If you'd like to help the group by sponsoring a pet, making a contribution, or participating in a program, log on to www.vidas.org.

Mayan sculptures adorn many resorts.
Courtesy of Philip Gammon

This relatively small property has 234 units, all within a short walk of the beach. The rooms have a bright and tropical vibe and are housed in low-rise Mexican Colonial–style villas on either side of a central pool and courtyard. There is a buffet restaurant, plus an Italian and an Asian restaurant, open for dinner only. At night, guests head to the theater for live entertainment, then on to the on-site nightclub, where drinks are included. Guests can also enjoy the restaurants, bars, and other facilities of the adjacent Wyndham Maya property. There's even an affiliated Viva Café restaurant in Playa del Carmen, where guests can have a full dinner with wine, beer, and soft drinks for a surcharge of only $10. Rates: $$$.

Tequila is the largest, with 664 rooms and an on-site nightclub; it appeals to the active crowd that's ready to party. The 507-room, hacienda-style Yucatán was renovated in mid-2005 and is just north of the Iberostar complex. The Playacar, which appeals to a young and budget-conscious crowd, has 396 rooms and 24-hour drink service. While the 300-room Lupita is in the middle of the golf course and not on the beach, guests receive complimentary transportation to the hotel's beach club, where food and drinks are included, just like at the resort. Rates: $$$$.

VIVA WYNDHAM AZTECA
984-877-4100 or 1-800-WYNDHAM (U.S.)
www.vivaresorts.com
Paseo Xaman-Ha, Playacar

VIVA WYNDHAM MAYA
984-874-4600 or 1-800-WYNDHAM (U.S.)
www.vivaresorts.com

The larger of the two Viva Wyndham properties has 13 acres of land and 400 rooms, with colonial and contemporary Mexican design. The rooms run on both sides of a central courtyard, where the pool, Jacuzzi, theater, and restaurants are located. Guests have their choice from three restaurants (international buffet, Mexican, and Mediterranean) and three bars, and can also visit the eateries and bars at the nearby Wyndham Azteca resort. For a real change of pace, visitors can head into the town of Playa del Carmen to dine at the Viva Café and pay only a $10 surcharge for a multicourse meal and drinks. Rates: $$$.

Xcaret to Paamul

South of Xcaret, visitors get their first glimpse of the wild side of the Riviera Maya. No longer will you see souvenir stands, gas stations, and convenience stores every few miles. In this part of the region, a thick jungle canopy has kept tourism development at bay, while palm trees, unexplored Mayan ruins, and tiny traditional villages dot the landscape. To visit this part of the Yucatán, travelers either take a shuttle bus from the airport or rent a car so they can go where they choose. Public bus service is spotty and will let travelers off only along the main road, while most of the hotels and attractions are located along the beach, a few miles away. Tourists either take their meals on-property at their resort or, if staying at an EP (European plan) hotel or condo, stop off at the supermarket in Playa del Carmen to stock up on foodstuffs and other essential supplies.

LODGING

✪ OCCIDENTAL GRAND XCARET

987-871-5400 or 1-800-858-2258 (U.S.)
www.occidentalhotels.com
Highway 307, km 282

Located adjacent to the Xcaret ecology park, this 769-room hotel is a wondrous all-inclusive playground that caters to families and travelers looking for a lot of activities on their trip. The massive resort is about an hour south of the Cancún airport and 10 minutes south of Playa del Carmen. The rooms are housed in low-rise buildings surrounded by five free-form swimming pools, winding rivers, and tropical gardens. There is a private man-made beach on a tranquil cove with easy water access and sheltered snorkeling. The hotel's laundry list of amenities includes 11 restaurants, 10 bars, 10 whirlpools, mini-golf, tennis courts, fitness center, spa, kids' club, and yoga studio. The rooms have contemporary Mexican decor and a mini-fridge stocked with beer, water, and soft drinks. Rates start at $$$$$, including admission for two to the park.

PAAMUL

984-876-2691
Highway 307, km 273

This RV haven is gaining in popularity with day-trippers who come by to see the sea turtles nest, go snorkeling or diving, or just lounge around the beach. The main road is lined with RV shelters, some of which have been there for years. Visitors can camp on the beach or stay at the small hotel. There are also a couple of super-casual beachside restaurants. ScubaMex has a water-sports center here and offers snorkeling and diving trips to the nearby reef. The beach along this shallow bay is rocky, so it's not the best for swimming. Rates: $$$.

ATTRACTIONS

CALICA

Highway 307, km 280

Formerly used only as a commercial port and dock for the Cozumel car ferry, the Calica facility is becoming a popular stop-off point for international cruise ships, as it is a lower-cost alternative to the busier ports at Cancún, Cozumel, and Playa del Carmen. A commercial plaza with shops, restaurants, and souvenir stands was recently added with the intention of attracting more and more cruise ships to the port. The Cozumel car ferry, operated by Transcaribe (987-872-7671), charges $25 per vehicle plus $1 per person for the 40-minute ride. It departs for Cozumel each day at 4 PM and 6 PM and returns at 6 AM, 10 AM, 4 PM, and 8 PM. See the "Practical Information" section for information on the pedestrian ferry.

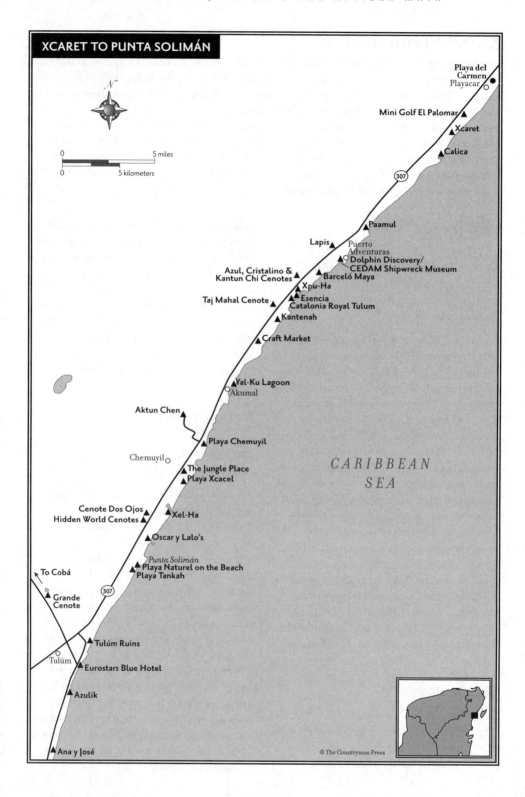

XCARET TO PUNTA SOLIMÁN

Playa del Carmen
Playacar

Mini Golf El Palomar
Xcaret
Calica

307

Paamul
Lapis
Puerto Adventuras
Dolphin Discovery/
CEDAM Shipwreck Museum
Azul, Cristalino &
Kantun Chi Cenotes
Barceló Maya
Xpu-Ha
Esencia
Taj Mahal Cenote
Catalonia Royal Tulum
Kantenah

Craft Market

Yal-Ku Lagoon
Akumal

Aktun Chen

Playa Chemuyil
Chemuyil

The Jungle Place
Playa Xcacel

Cenote Dos Ojos
Hidden World Cenotes
Xel-Ha

Oscar y Lalo's

CARIBBEAN
SEA

Punta Solimán
Playa Naturel on the Beach
Playa Tankah

To Cobá

307

Grande
Cenote

Tulúm Ruins
Tulúm
Eurostars Blue Hotel

Azulik

Ana y José

© The Countryman Press

N

0   5 miles
0   5 kilometers

Puerto Aventuras (Highway 307, km 269)

The exclusive resort town of Puerto Aventuras is the only true sheltered marina in the Riviera Maya. It was also the first major development south of Cancún, though it has not had the rapid growth that has been seen in Playa del Carmen. If you talk to the locals, they'll tell you that it's by design in order to retain the small-town feel and exclusive nature of the resort. Hurricane Emily passed directly over the marina in 2005, sinking boats, beaching others, and wreaking havoc across town, but thousands of palm trees have been replanted, and the area is quickly regaining its prestorm appeal. In fact, encouraged by the way the town survived the hurricane, condo sales have been booming, and the community's main challenge now is keeping its small-town luster. Visitors enter through a large security gate just off Highway 307. The road winds down to the beach and ends at the 250-slip marina, which is packed with fishing boats, dive boats, sailboats, and pleasure yachts. The marina channels wind through an open-air pedestrian plaza, which is lined with restaurants, shops, bars, pharmacies, Internet cafés (which are a little expensive at $1 for 10 minutes), and a few grocery/convenience stores. A Dolphin Discovery location is built into the marina, and visitors can stroll the plaza while watching the dolphins cavort, swim, and even jump out of the water. There are relatively few places to stay, given how pleasantly landscaped and maintained everything is. There is a nine-hole golf course, museum, crafts market, tennis courts, and a beautiful beach where the reef is close to shore, keeping the wave action to a minimum.

LODGING

✪ AVENTURA SPA PALACE

984-875-1100
www.palaceresorts.com
Highway 307, km 270

With a romantic design inspired by a traditional Mexican hacienda but with a more contemporary flair, the 1,266-room Aventura Spa Palace is an adults-only, all-inclusive resort occupying 85 tropical acres along the beach. The entrance is separate from the main marina entrance and is well marked. The resort is built around a natural ocean inlet, making it ideal for protected-water snorkeling, swimming, and sunbathing. Most guests are vacationing couples celebrating a honeymoon, anniversary, or other special occasion. From the stone fountain in the main plaza to the ornate archways, tile floors, and locally crafted furnishings, the hotel embraces its Mexican heritage while surrounding guests with plenty of modern amenities and luxuries. Facilities and activities include four pools, seven Jacuzzis, scuba training pool, two gyms, theater, nightclub, volleyball, billiards, bicycles, rollerblades, beauty salon, activities program, cooking lessons, tennis courts, water-sports center, yoga, climbing tower, and meditation pond. All rooms have ocean or garden views, private balcony with hammock, minibar, coffeemaker, and bathrobes. There are even liquor dispensers, so you don't have to go to the bar to mix yourself a drink. The hotel provides complimentary transportation to the town square in Playa del Carmen and to Cancún once each day. Guests at any Palace Resort have access to the facilities, restaurants, and bars of all of the others. Rates: $$$$ to $$$$$.

✪ CASA DEL AGUA

984-873-5184
www.casadelagua.com
Highway 307, km 268

On a beach south of the marina and 1 mile

Get a Job and Stay a While

Though it's not always easy to make the transition from tourist to local, it can be possible. With a bit of determination and luck, you can find a job and live in paradise. The Mexican government requires that all foreign workers have an FM3 visa, which your employer must obtain for you. Fluency in Spanish is required, though exceptions are sometimes made. And don't expect to make anything near what you could earn back home: Minimum wage in Mexico is about $10 per day, and most jobs available to foreigners generally pay around $1,000 per month. Depending on the job, sales commission, bonuses, room and board, and other perks can help sweeten the pot. The cost of living can be much less, but only if you plan on living like a local. If you're looking for a permanent vacation and expecting to work during the day and then party at tourist clubs every night, you'll probably need additional financial resources.

Top 10 Jobs for Foreigners

Bartender

English teacher

Hotel activities staff (all-inclusives)

Hotel front desk, guest services,
  or concierge

Real estate sales

Restaurant host/hostess

Scuba instructor

Time-share representative/sales

Tour guide

Waiter/waitress

from the main plaza in Puerto Aventuras, the very upscale Casa del Agua, formerly a private residence, has four rooms for rent, making it a good option for guests seeking simplicity, luxury, romance, and privacy. The house is contemporary Mexican, with handcrafted furniture, colorful Mexican textiles, and original artwork throughout. Rooms feature private garden bathrooms, minibars, and cold air-conditioning, and the rate includes a full breakfast served in a common dining room or in the privacy of your room. The El Arroyo room has a round bed, a large sunken bathtub, a double shower, and a stream of water that flows around the bed, cascades onto the floor, and then goes into the bathroom and behind the tub. The home is right on a perfect beach in a residential area with very little beach traffic. Rates: $$$$, including breakfast. Highly recommended.

CATALONIA RIVIERA MAYA

984-875-1020

www.cataloniarivieramaya.com

Avenue Xcacel, Lot 1 (off Highway 307, near km 271, just north of Puerto Aventuras)

An upscale and family-friendly all-inclusive, the 324-room Catalonia gives guests an authentic taste of the Mexican Caribbean while still providing the luxuries of a high-end resort. Hosting honeymooners, families, couples, and others in the mood for an active vacation, the hotel's location is great, with a calm-water beachfront surrounded by jungle. The property features several pools, a beach bar, a dance club, a kids' club, a tennis court, and a daily activity program that helps guests socialize and have fun all day long. There are also free scuba clinics, bicycles, and a gym. The hotel entry gate is located off the highway, separate from the marina entrance. Rates: $$$.

OMNI PUERTO AVENTURAS

984-873-5101 or 1-800-THE-OMNI (U.S.)

www.omnihotels.com

Highway 307, km 269; behind the village center and on the beach

With only 30 rooms, the Omni offers personal service and boutique hotel-style comfort, along with the amenities and high standards normally associated with the Omni chain. Each room has a coffeemaker as well as a private balcony or patio with a Jacuzzi. Each morning the staff delivers

Spinning through Life on Spiral Island

A unique chapter in Puerto Aventuras history ended when Hurricane Emily rumbled through the marina in July 2005.

The story began in 1998, when British ex-pat, artist, and musician Richy Sowa (or "Reishee," as the locals call him) moved to the Riviera Maya with a dream of living a life of relaxation and simplicity while stressing recycling and low-impact survival. To that end he started collecting empty water bottles (he had accumulated more than 250,000 of them when the storm hit) and loading them into fishing nets, which were arranged in a spiral pattern to create an artificial island, which he cast adrift in Puerto Aventuras. He planted mangroves and fruit trees, added some 10 tons of sand, and built a house from discarded wood, bamboo, and thatched palm.

The island, sometimes called Bottle Island, reached the size of half a basketball court and could be maneuvered around the marina with an outboard boat motor attached to one end. It had a solar cooker (with reflectors laid out in a spiral) and a self-composting toilet, and was home to several cats, dogs, and sometimes ducks. Richy's island was featured on Ripley's *Believe It or Not!* in 2000. His self-stated long-term goal for the project was to "use the waste from this world as a foundation to create a tranquil piece of paradise and sail around the earth on a floating island with the message of love and faith."

During the hurricane, Richy and his animal friends took shelter on the mainland. When morning dawned, his island lay in ruins, ripped apart and beached on the sand. He planned to transport the island by truck to nearby Soliman Bay and reconstruct it, thus keeping his island—and his dream—afloat.

coffee, juice, and Mexican pastries to a "magic box" built into the room. Since there's access from outside the room, you don't even have to get up to receive it. Just open your side of the box, and it's there waiting for you. The hotel features two restaurants, two bars, car rental, and a souvenir shop. Rates: $$$, all-inclusive available for more.

SUNSCAPE PUERTO AVENTURAS

984-875-3000
www.sunscaperesorts.com
Highway 307, km 269

With 305 rooms, the Sunscape resort is a medium-size all-inclusive on a pristine beach in the heart of Puerto Aventuras, within walking distance of the marina, museum, restaurants, and other attractions. Rooms have air-conditioning, satellite TV, and private balconies, most with a view of the marina or ocean. There are two pools, five à la carte restaurants, one buffet eatery, several bars, fitness center, day spa, and nightly live entertainment. The featured attraction here is a massive 30-person beachside Jacuzzi, which becomes the central meeting point for guests looking to meet other travelers. Rates: $$$ to $$$$. The resort is popular with families and offers an Explorer's Club with childcare and activities for kids during the day. Higher rates for oceanfront, suites, or other room upgrades.

DINING

Most restaurants in Puerto Aventuras are located around the central marina plaza, overlooking the Dolphin Discovery waterway, and most have small interior dining rooms and a patio with shaded tables. They are all in close proximity, so it's easy to walk from one to the next, checking to see what looks good. Prices are a bit higher than in other areas of the region due to the exclusive nature of the resort and the lower volume of visitors.

DOS CHILES
At the Puerto Aventuras marina

This casual outdoor eatery offers a view of the dolphin shows, shops, and entertainment plaza. The menu offers good Mexican food, shrimp, fajitas, and tacos. Check the chalkboard for drink specials and featured menu items. Moderate.

JONES' SPORTS BAR
At the Puerto Aventuras marina

This café has pleasant alfresco dining at umbrellaed tables bordering the marina, in front of the Dolphin Discovery area. You can watch the dolphins jump and play while dining on nachos, tacos, burgers, steaks, and even grilled shrimp. Moderate.

LA CARIBENA
At the Puerto Aventuras marina

This sidewalk café serves Caribbean and Mexican food. It has a view of the tree-lined marina and the many surrounding shops and attractions. The dining area is alfresco and overlooks the Dolphin Discovery area of the marina. Moderate.

✪ THE PUB
At the Puerto Aventuras marina

A popular spot all day long, the Pub is surrounded by shade trees and overlooks the marina, where diners can watch the dolphins cavort and play. The menu offers popularly priced breakfast, pizzas, fresh fish, tacos, enchiladas, and shepherd's pie. Inexpensive.

TIRAMISU
At the Puerto Aventuras marina

Open for lunch and dinner, Tiramisu, as its name suggests, specializes in Italian food. Featured menu items include beef lasagna, pizzas, a variety of pastas, and a good selection of ice cream and desserts. Expensive.

ATTRACTIONS AND ACTIVITIES

✪ CEDAM SHIPWRECK MUSEUM
At the Puerto Aventuras marina

This museum, operated by the Club de Exploraciones y Deportes Acuáticos de México (Water Sports & Exploration Club), which is responsible for locating and protecting the region's wrecks, is free to the public (donations accepted) and displays a variety of artifacts recovered from shipwrecks in Mexico and around the world. It was founded in 1959 by Pablo Bush Romero, who is also the founder of Akumal. There are several rooms, and it's surprisingly easy to get disoriented given its relatively small size. Displays show how wrecks are excavated and how the materials are recovered and restored. There's also an interesting explanation of how the main cenote at Chichén Itzá was partially drained in a search for relics.

DIVE AVENTURAS
984-873-5031
www.diveaventuras.com
In the Omni Puerto Aventuras (see Lodging)

This full-service dive shop offers all levels of instruction in multiple languages, including a 45-minute tune-up course for certified divers who have not been in the water for a while. It also offers complimentary lockers, equipment rental, camera rental, and gear sales. Dive boats depart for one- and two-tank dives at nearby reefs at 9 AM, 11 AM, 1 PM, and 2:30 PM, and the shop's shuttle can pick you up at any hotel in the region. There are also twice-daily dives at local freshwater cenotes. For nondivers there are 1 1/2- and 2 1/2- hour snorkeling tours, including sodas and a guide. One-tank ocean dives cost $38; two-tank trips are $74. Night dives are $65 and include a flashlight. Cenote dives are $65 for one tank and $110 for two.

DOLPHIN DISCOVERY
At the Puerto Aventuras marina

You can interact with the dolphins at Dolphin Discovery, and there are several different packages, starting every hour. About half of the time is spent in orientation, and the remainder is with the dolphins. In the least expensive package, the Dolphin Encounter ($64), you touch the dolphins, and in the Dolphin Swim ($99) you get in the water with them. For $125 you can play a little more and even be propelled through the water by two dolphins in a maneuver called the foot-push.

RIVIERA MAYA PARASAIL ADVENTURES
984-873-5683
www.rivieramayaparasail.com
At the Puerto Aventuras marina

This well-respected outfit offers a variety of activities for vacationers seeking a bit of adventure, including "dry parasailing," in which tandem and solo riders take off from the back of a boat and soar high above the water, while taking in the view of the marina and surrounding beaches along the Puerto Aventuras bay and beachfront. The shop offers Sea Trek diving, which allows swimmers to don a helmet and breathe normally while sitting on the ocean bottom. It also offers Snuba, which is a type of forced-air snorkeling where participants swim freely underwater and breathe from a snorkel-like tube that is supplied with air from the surface. No scuba certification is required for either activity. Parasailing costs $65 for a solo ride or $99 for tandem.

SHOPPING

ITZCOATL
At the Puerto Aventuras marina

This small crafts and jewelry boutique specializes in handmade crafts and amber jewelry.

LAPIS
984-803-2077
www.lapis.com.tr
Highway 307, km 270

Xpu-Ha beach at Esencia Hotel

On the highway near Puerto Aventuras is the Lapis jewelry factory, which offers handmade rugs, leather goods, silver, diamonds, gold, and precious stones from Turkey, Italy, Spain, and the Czech Republic.

Xpu-Ha (*Highway 307, km 264*)

Several different access roads lead from Highway 307 to Xpu-Ha beach, making for fun exploration of the various areas. The picturesque beach is very low-key, with a wide bay, coconut palms, and a shallow reef, making it a good spot for snorkeling. To find the best spots, walk to the north near the Xpu-Ha Palace Resort (see Lodging), where the water is calm and the access is easier. The beach to the south is not as sandy, with some rocks, vegetation, and seaweed. There are a few small family-run restaurants serving fresh fish and cold drinks on the beach. The main one, called La Playa, has snorkeling equipment for rent ($15), WaveRunners, and several tables in the shade or right on the beach. For overnight stays there are several major resorts, mostly of the large-scale variety. There are also a handful of cabañas and villas for rent, as well as a small RV park. On the west side of the highway, across from the Xpu-Ha turnoff, are a pair of small but swimmable cenotes.

LODGING

✪ AL CIELO HOTEL

984-840-9012
www.alcielohotel.com
Highway 307, km 264.5

More like a private guest house than a hotel, this property next to the luxury Esencia Hotel has four rooms (2 on the ground floor, two above) with private bathrooms, nice showers, and balconies or terraces. They are built right on the beach, with easy access to the water. There is a small beach club and a gourmet restaurant specializing in fresh seafood and meat. An on-site spa offers shiatsu, Reiki, reflexology, and face and skin treatments. Rates: $$$$.

Baby turtle release at Barcelo Maya resort
Courtesy of Philip Gammon

✪ BARCELO MAYA RESORT COMPLEX

987-875-1500
www.barcelo.com
Highway 307, km 265, Xpu-Ha Beach; direct entrance from the highway

The Barcelo complex offers more than 2,000 rooms in five different hotels (Tropical Beach, Maya Beach, Caribe Beach, Colonial Beach, Maya Palace), which opened one-by-one through the middle of this decade, with the most exclusive, the Barcelo Maya Palace, opening in early 2008. The resorts are very popular for group trips, corporate incentive travel, family reunions, weddings, honeymoons, and other special ocassions. Due to the scale of the development, it makes a great place for first-time Riviera Maya travelers who would feel most comfortable surrounded by similar vacationers, rather than immerse themselves in the local culture. Visitors unfamiliar with the large-scale all-inclusive concept will be blown away by the abundance and idyllic environment that the resorts create. It really is a tropical wonderland and you could literally spend a week within the walls of the resort and never get bored. That said, the complex's central location makes exploring area attractions close and convenient.

The hotels range from four-star to five-star plus and are operated independently, but share some common facilities. The area offers more than a mile of pristine beachfront, 600,000 square meters of tropical forest and thousands of tropical plants, coconut trees, and flowers. There is a spa with Turkish bath, a sauna, a Jacuzzi, dive shop, shopping center, chapel, beauty salon, tennis courts, a gym, kids' club, aerobics classes, pitch-and-putt, minigolf, table tennis, billiards, several pools, convention center, sauna, dance club, tour desk, and a daily activities program. All guest rooms in the properties have a private terrace or balcony, ocean views, high-powered air-conditioning, and stocked minibar. Restaurant choices include a beachside buffet, a Mexican specialty restaurant, sushi bars, a seafood restaurant, and a traditional Spanish eatery. Rates: $$$$.

CATALONIA ROYAL TULUM

984-875-1800
Highway 307, km 264, Xpu-Ha Beach; direct entrance from the highway

With 288 rooms and suites, the Catalonia Royal Tulum (formerly Copacabana Beach Resort) is a medium-size high-end beach-front hotel set amid jungle foliage, tropical plants, swimming pools, and other water features. It is in Xpu-Ha, about five minutes south of Puerto Aventuras. The rooms are laid out nicely, with plenty of open space between the buildings, giving the resort an exclusive feel throughout. Rooms have contemporary Mexican decor, premium bedding, and private terrace. There are also a dozen restaurants and bars, including a *palapa* bar right on the beach. An on-site tour office and car-rental desk helps guests get out and explore the region. Rates: $$$$.

✪ HOTEL ESENCIA

1-877-528-3490 (U.S.)
www.hotelesencia.com
Highway 307, km 264, Xpu-Ha Beach

A unique resort built on 50 secluded acres along the beach, Esencia is more like an opulent private residence than a hotel. The inn, once the home of an Italian duchess, has 29 luxurious rooms and ultra-cool Italian-Mexican decor. The property has large breezy terraces, an idyllic beachfront, high ceilings, an organic spa, a fitness center, and an on-site cenote. The Sal y Fuego restaurant specializes in seafood and is run by a chef from the Four Seasons, and many of its signature dishes use organic ingredients native to the area. The rooms have

premium bedding, liquor (which includes full-size bottles, rather than the small sizes typically offered in minibars), and iPods for guest use. Many celebrities, including Gwyneth Paltrow, have been guests here. Rates: $$$$ to $$$$$. Highly recommended for the exclusive atmosphere and incredible beach.

DINING

CAFÉ DEL MAR

984-873-2194
Highway 307, km 264; near the Catalonia Royal Mayan (see Lodging), on Xpu-Ha Beach

Great grilled fish and seafood await visitors at this no-frills beachside haven. Eat at one of the plastic tables under the shaded *palapa* or get your food to go and have an impromptu beach-towel picnic. This is a good place to park if you have your own car and want to visit the beach for a while. Inexpensive.

RESTAURANTE AL CIELO

984-840-9012
www.alcielohotel.com
Highway 307, km 264.5; between the Xpu-Ha Palace and the Catalonia Royal Mayan (see Lodging)

On the grounds of the Al Cielo hotel (see Lodging), this beachfront restaurant has a *palapa* roof and several tables right next to the sand. The internationally trained chef prepares shrimp, seafood paella, Angus beef, duck, quail, and lamb. The signature dish is a whole fish coated with salt and roasted. It takes 30 minutes to prepare and costs $25. Desserts include crème brûlée, chocolate mousse, and ice cream. No credit cards. Expensive.

Kantenah

A small sign on Highway 307 at km 262 points the way to Kantenah beach, which is a couple miles down a washboard road. There are many coconut trees and a quiet bay with a shallow reef for snorkeling. Near the beach, there is a large handicrafts market with much better prices than in Cancún or even Playa del Carmen, and there's another one on the highway, at km 259.5, with a large assortment of pots, rugs, and blankets.

LODGING

EL DORADO SEASIDE SUITES

984-875-1910
www.karismahotels.com
Highway 307, km 262

This adults-only, 133-room, all-inclusive resort is a popular destination for honeymooners, couples, and even families who want to experience the less populated areas of the Riviera Maya but don't want to do without the service, comfort, and convenience of a first-class resort hotel. The rooms are spread out along the ocean, which gives each room easy access to the beach. The buildings are all low-rise, lending a more relaxed, less urban feeling to the development. All rooms have private balconies with hammocks. Guests congregate on the hotel's wide white beach, which has calm water and a rock-free area for swimming and snorkeling. There are three restaurants, serving Asian, Mexican, and seafood specialties, and no buffets. There is a bar at the beach, one by the pool, and another one by the main restaurant, which is the main place to be at night, with live music, souvenir kiosks, and a bustling bar with seat swings. Guests of the El Dorado can pay a day-use fee to visit the clothing-optional Hidden Beach hotel next door. Rates: $$$$; including all food, drinks, activities program, and nonmotorized water sports.

GRAND PALLADIUM COLONIAL RESORT & SPA

984-877-2100
www.fiesta-hotels.com
Highway 307, km 260

Sister property to the adjacent Grand Palladium Kantenah, this massive 836-room resort paradise was built in a Spanish Colonial design by the architects behind the Iberostar and Paradisus chains. Though it is large and sprawling, special care has been taken to preserve the natural surroundings and allow guests to wander and explore without feeling crowded. There are four outdoor pools, including one meandering giant that seems more like a lagoon. Though the hotel welcomes families, there are designated areas for kids, allowing them to be themselves without disturbing the couples and honeymooners. There are seven restaurants, including Mexican, Asian, Mediterranean, and steak specialty à la carte restaurants, and the other three are buffets serving continental, regional, and Creole fare. There are 11 bars, including a *palapa* beach bar, swim-up pool bar, and dance club. There are also four tennis courts and a basketball court, water-sports center, scuba/snorkeling center, health club, and Turkish spa, which specializes in Mediterranean and local body treatments. The resort shares a huge stretch of beach with its sister property, with plenty of room for everyone.

The rate includes all meals, snacks, and nonalcoholic drinks (alcoholic drinks, including premium liquors, are included from 6 PM to midnight), as well as a workout room, a Jacuzzi, a sauna, and steam baths, plus nonmotorized water sports. Rates: $$$ to $$$$.

Hidden Beach Resort: clothing, optional; relaxation, mandatory.

GRAND PALLADIUM KANTENAH RESORT & SPA

984-877-2100
www.fiesta-hotels.com
Highway 307, km 260

With 414 rooms, the Grand Palladium Kantenah is about half the size of its sister property, located just next door. The all-inclusive, family-friendly resort features Mayan architecture, which blends harmoniously into the natural surroundings. In fact, there is a staff biologist who monitors the hotel's impact on the environment and makes recommendations on ways to preserve the native flora and fauna. As a result, there are many trees, tropical gardens, and native animals on the property. There is a .5-mile stretch of open beach, perfect for jogging, sunbathing, and sun worshipping. The rate includes all meals, snacks, and nonalcoholic drinks (alcoholic drinks, including premium liquors, are included from 6 PM to midnight), as well as a work-out room, a Jacuzzi, a sauna, and steam baths, plus nonmotorized water sports. Rates: $$$ to $$$$.

✪ HIDDEN BEACH RESORT

984-875-7000
www.hiddenbeachresort.com
Highway 307, km 262

A 42-room, all-inclusive, clothing-optional resort, Hidden Beach is next door to the El Dorado Seaside Suites, separated from it by a high stucco wall. Guests enter through a private lobby, where a security guard is on hand to ensure that no outsiders enter. The upscale resort is on the beach, with a pool, hot tub, and beach cabañas. All rooms are spacious suites, with ocean views, private balconies with hammocks, air-conditioning, CD/DVD players, and a stocked minibar (which includes full-size liquor bottles). The ground-floor suites offer swim-up access, allowing guests to enter the pool from their terrace and then swim to the restaurant or bar. Guests can enjoy nude dining, sunbathing, and ocean swimming (though it's mostly rocky). The hotel's gourmet restaurant serves three meals per day, either in the shaded dining room or alfresco, next to the pool. There is a swim-up bar, where bartenders (clothed, for the most part) are more than happy to mix up special drinks for guests to try. An activities coordinator keeps you busy during the day, or you can sneak off on your own and camp out on a daybed at the beach and nobody will bother you, unless it's an attendant checking in to see if you need fresh towels, a bite to eat, or a cold drink. At night, guests head to the on-site mini-discotheque for nude salsa lessons, dance music, and socializing. This is not a swingers resort, and it does not allow any public displays of anything that's not allowed at a clothed hotel. Singles are welcome. Guests can use the facilities and take meals at the El Dorado Seaside Suites, next door, though they must be clothed to do so. Guests of the El Dorado can pay a day-use fee to visit the Hidden Beach. Rates: $$$$, all-inclusive.

Akumal (Highway 307, km 255)

Five separate highway exits lead to this marina town, whose name translates into "Place of the Turtles." It is known as a family-friendly resort area with calm and shallow coves, dozens of nearby dive sites, superior sportfishing, pleasant pedestrian plazas, quality restaurants, lively bars, and a variety of accommodations options. The area consists of three separate bays: Half Moon, Akumal, and Aventuras. The late author John D. McDonald wrote several of the books in his famous Travis McGee series of boat bum/private detective novels while lounging on the beaches of Akumal.

The area is still a nesting ground for sea turtles, and they are now closely protected by the government and privately funded preservation organizations. Visitors can take guided tours to see the turtle nests and, if the timing is right, see the turtles lay their eggs or watch the hatchlings return to the water. An information center at the main entrance can book tours, provide directions, and reserve accommodations ranging from simple hotel rooms to large private villas. There are several grocery stores, an Internet café, a scuba diving center, a kiteboarding office, and handicrafts available near the main entrance. There is free parking if you're just visiting for the day. Turn into the lot on the right prior to entering the main gate. It's a safe area with lots of visibility, so you can feel fine leaving your car and walking through the gate and to the beach. The best beach within a short walking distance is just beyond the dive shop.

In 2005 Hurricanes Emily and Wilma passed through the region, uprooting hundreds of trees, tearing away roofs, and flooding the ground floor of many properties. Though it will take a while for all the vegetation to grow back, the town quickly rebuilt and is ready for an exciting future as one of the area's fastest-growing destinations.

Akumal aims to protect its beaches.

The author and friends in Akumal Courtesy of Andrea Loera

LODGING

AKUMAL BEACH RESORT

983-875-7500
www.akumalbeachresort.com
Highway 307, km 255

With 241 rooms and a broad white-sand beach, this all-inclusive resort is ideal for families and couples who are seeking casual and comfortable surroundings but can do without superfluous luxuries. The hotel operates as an all-inclusive, with all food, drinks, and nonmotorized water sports included in the rate. The beach is long, flat, and mostly private, and thanks to the off-shore reef, the water is calm, with tame waves. There are three eateries and a nice pool with a view of the beach. Like most all-inclusives, there is a theater where shows are performed nightly. Rates: $$$ to $$$$.

GRAN BAHÍA PRÍNCIPE AKUMAL

983-875-5000
www.bahia-principe.com
Highway 307, km 254

This 1,440-room, all-inclusive hotel is the largest property in the region and has two separate sections: Tulum and Akumal. There is a private entrance off the highway, just before you reach the main Akumal entrance, if you're coming from Playa del Carmen. The resort is decorated with stonework, Talavera handicrafts, marble, native hardwoods, and thatched-roof *palapas*. Even with its immense size, it has a friendly feeling since the buildings are low-rise and grouped like homes in a small village. Many rooms have an ocean view, even though many of them are set back from the water in a junglelike setting. The resort's nine restaurants serve international, Italian, seafood, Mediterranean,

Mexican, and Caribbean cuisine. There are also several bars, including a lounge bar, beach bar, and swim-up bar. The rate includes all food and drinks, shows, and a wide range of activities, including kayaking, sailing, windsurfing, biking, tennis, basketball, volleyball, aerobics, and even horseback riding. In addition, there is an on-site European-style spa, and the resort's tour desk can plan scuba diving, fishing, and other excursions. Rates: $$ to $$$.

GRAND SIRENIS RIVIERA MAYA & MAYAN BEACH

984-875-1700
www.sirenishotels.com
Highway 307, km 256, Akumal

This massive complex is planned to eventually have four resorts. The first two, the Riviera Maya and the Mayan Beach have a combined 950 rooms and opened in the fall of 2006. They are perched on a rocky cove called Playa Xaac (or sometimes, Chac), a frequent stop for pleasure cruises. It is very close to Yalku Lagoon, a major snorkeling site. The huge property has several actual Mayan ruins, great beaches, freshwater cenote lagoons, two sprawling pools, a meandering river, and kids' club. The hotels seem more stylish than many resorts in the area. The large rooms have stocked minibars, coffeemakers, and double Jacuzzis. The all-inclusive rate includes dining at nearly a dozen restaurants, frequent theme dinners, weekly lobster dinner, water sports, sports programs, fitness center, and nightly shows. Rates start at around $300 per person per night.

✪ VISTA DEL MAR CONDOS & HOTEL

984-875-9060 or 888-425-8625 (U.S.)
www.akumalinfo.com
Half Moon Bay

Accommodations at this sprawling beachfront complex range from a clean and basic hotel room to a three-room condo right at the water's edge that's darn near luxurious. The 16 hotel rooms and eight condos all have contemporary tropical decor, air-conditioning, ceiling fans, satellite TV, refrigerators, and coffeemakers. Condos also have full kitchens, separate living and dining areas, laptop-compatible safes, plus balconies or terraces. Ground-floor units are directly on the beach and just steps from Half Moon Bay, making them ideal for whiling away the day as can only be done in the Caribbean. The complex offers beach towels and lounge chairs, VCRs and videos for rent, kayak and bike rental ($6/day), a convenience store, swimming pool, and a dive shop (akumaldiveadventures.com). The same owners run the idyllic La Buena Vida Restaurant and Bar, just south of the hotel. Hotel rates start at $. Condos start at $$ for a one-bedroom studio to $$$ for a three bedroom condo. Rates increase about 50 percent in high season. Wedding planning service is also available (akumal weddings.com).

OASIS GRAND RIVIERA MAYA

984-875-7300 or 1-800-521-5200 (U.S.)
www.oasishotels.com
Highway 307, km 254

This 180-room, all-inclusive resort is one of Akumal's longtime favorites, with many repeat guests. There is a private entrance located just south of the main Akumal entry gate. The accommodations have contemporary Mexican-style decor, and the rate includes all meals, snacks, drinks, nightly shows, activities, and sports. (Things like scuba diving and spa services are extra, of course.) The powdery-sand beach is on a wide, shallow cove, with very calm water and little current, making it great for swimming and snorkeling, even for beginners. There are several restaurants, serving international, Mexican, and Italian cuisine, and several bars, including a beach bar and a swim-up pool bar. Rates: $$$$. There are also several suites available.

✪ GRAN BAHÍA PRÍNCIPE

984-875-5000
www.bahia-principe.es
Chetumal–Cancun Highway, km 250

Open since the early 1990s, the family-friendly all-inclusive Bahía Príncipe is a massive upscale complex (totaling more than 2,000 rooms) that also includes the Bahía Príncipe Tulum and the Bahía Príncipe Akumal & Coba, plus the Hacienda Doña Isabel central plaza, which houses the resort's shops, tour desk, and most popular nightlife attractions. The property is about 75 minutes south of Cancún and 20 minutes north of Tulum. The architecture is reminiscent of the grand Mayan temples, with bold construction, solid columns, and subtle earth tones. The buildings utilize such native materials as stone, clay, thatched palm, and rich hardwoods. There are several options at mealtimes and guests have dining privileges at all the restaurants in the complex, including specialty outlets serving Italian, Mediterranean, Japanese, and Asian cuisine. For drinks, guests can choose from the beach bar, lobby bar, sports bar, pool bar, and even three swim-up bars. At night, the theater at the Hacienda Doña Isabel is the place to be, with live musical performances and shows, followed by DJ music, dancing, and cocktails.

One of the main attractions is the Bahia Spa, a luxurious European-style spa offering massages, body wraps, manicures, facials, beauty services and other therapeutic treatments. Guests congregate at the lake-like swimming pool for games or retreat to the two quiet pools for a bit of relaxation. There is a massive outdoor hot tub, a bustling sundeck, five tennis courts, a health club, and a water sports center, with kayaks, windsurfers, catamarans, and snorkeling gear. The resort is also home to the 27-hole Bahía Príncipe golf course, designed by Robert Trent Jones II. More info available at bahiaprincipegolf.com.

DINING

✪ LA BUENA VIDA
On the beach of Half Moon Bay

The ultracasual and delightfully rustic beach bar has chair swings, a long happy hour, good music, and an upstairs indoor dining room with a nice view of the beach. Treehouse seating areas 20 feet in the air are accessible via ladders, and waiters will even climb up carrying traysful of drinks. The menu features fried fish, lobster, ceviche, pasta, cheeseburgers, steak, and tacos. The main bar area is adorned with pirate-style décor, including skulls, driftwood, and a Mexican shrine. Hurricane Dean walloped the restaurant in 2007, bringing ashore a massive chunk of reef and lots of interesting driftwood. The area was thoroughly cleaned and serves as a proud example of perseverance, making it one of the best spots to pass the day in the Caribbean sun.

LA LUNITA RESTAURANT
At La Tortuga Condos, Half Moon Bay

The road that winds around the marina leads back to the main road along the beachfront. Follow that about .5 mile to the south and you'll come to La Tortuga Condos. Open to the public, this casual restaurant serves breakfast and dinner next to the beach. At night, the staff set up a few candlelit tables right on the beach. The menu features international and Mexican dishes. Moderate.

Treehouse drink service at La Buena Vida in Akumal

LOL HA

On the beach next to the Akumal Dive Shop (see Diving, Fishing, and Boat Tours)

Lol Ha has a *palapa* beach bar with snacks and a good happy hour, and the kitchen serves pizza and pasta, plus Mexican dishes and seafood. Alfresco tables offer dining right on the beach. Moderate.

✪ QUE ONDA

North side of town, near Yalku Lagoon

A small and romantic restaurant surrounded by palm trees and tropical plants, Que Onda is cheerfully decorated and serves gourmet Italian food and fresh seafood for lunch and dinner.

✪ TURTLE BAY CAFÉ

984-875-9138
www.turtlebaycafe.com
Just inside the main entry gate to Akumal and near the back of a cluster of thatched-roof buildings on the left side of the road

Just inside the main entrance to the left, you'll find a cluster of restaurants and shops. The Turtle Bay Café is housed in a small, homey building with a large palapa out front, which has several ceiling fans and is often one of the cooler spots in town. It is frequented by local ex-pats and villa owners and is home to an annual Thanksgiving party. They serve breakfast and lunch daily, and dinner Tuesday through Saturday. The menu features a variety of specialty cocktails and smoothies, sandwiches, fresh salads, fish tacos, and more than 20 breakfast options, ranging from American classics to Mayan delicacies. Off-site catering is available, including food, flowers, wedding cakes, and more for groups up to 150. The owner is an animal lover and even sells doggie treats.

DIVING, FISHING & BOAT TOURS

AKUMAL DIVE SHOP

984-875-9032
www.akumal.com
On the right, just after entering the main gate at Akumal

The Akumal Dive Shop offers several diving and nondiving tours, including a one-tank boat dive ($45), a two-tank boat dive ($60), a night dive (one tank, boat; $55), and a cavern dive ($65). There's also gear rental ($15/day), open-water certification ($420), and a scuba resort course ($100), which includes instruction and a shallow open-water dive. Non-divers can enjoy kiteboarding ($50 for one hour of instruction); sportfishing ($100 for the whole boat, additional hours cost $45) for barracuda, dorado, mackerel, and sailfish, on a two-hour trip that includes all refreshments, equipment, and bait; the Robinson Crusoe Cruise ($65/person), which departs at 10 AM and returns to the beach at 3 PM and includes catamaran sailing, fishing, snorkeling, hiking, drinks, and a stop-off at Xaak, a minor Mayan ruin site that was once home to a primitive lighthouse; or the Sunset Cruise ($35/ person), a two-hour sailing cruise along the beach that includes drinks. (Remember, though, the ocean is to the east, so don't expect to see the sun fall into the Caribbean. Instead, it sets over Akumal's thick jungle canopy.)

Live Like a Celebrity for a Week

If hotels and condos aren't your thing and you want to experience the Riviera Maya with first-class lux-ury and privacy, consider renting a beach house for your visit. **Akumal Villas** (678-528-1775, www.akumal-villas.com) manages a collection of some of the finest private rental homes and villas in the area, with properties in Puerto Aventuras, Akumal, Jade Bay, South Akumal, Soliman Bay, and Tankah. These homes have one to six bedrooms and feature swimming pools, hammocks, full kitchens, purified water, safes, balconies, satellite TV, DVD players, and other amenities. Full-time maids, caretakers, and on-call chefs and massage therapists are also provided.

Need some wine or spirits to liven up your house party? **Akumal Wines** (984-875-9287, www.akumalwines.com) offers more than 100 wines and liquors from around the world for delivery in the Riviera Maya.

Chemuyil *(Highway 307, km 249)*

Not really a touristy town, the dusty beachfront village of Chemuyil hosts many of the serv-ice workers for nearby Akumal and other developments. It has a gated entry, and the guards are not necessarily welcoming of foreign adventure-seekers, but if you can't get enough of the Riviera Maya beaches and you won't be content until you see them all, you should be able to talk your way in and make your way to the beach for a look.

The beach itself is relatively clean, and the water is very calm and shallow since the reef comes all the way to the surface and acts as a breakwater to keep out the waves. There are a couple of private campsites and some basic hotels to accommodate the few backpackers, naturalists, and escape artists who find their way here, and there are also a handful of beachside restaurants and local bars.

LODGING

✪ THE JUNGLE PLACE

www.thejungleplace.com
East of Highway 307, km 248; just inland from Chemuyil

Known in the native Mayan language as *kuxi k'aax,* the Jungle Place offers two bungalows set on a 20-acre nature preserve, home to dozens of spider monkeys and royal toucans. The units are surprisingly upscale, with stone walls, hardwood furnishings, air-condition-ing, full kitchen, satellite TV, Internet access, and a nature-friendly but contemporary vibe. Guests can watch and sometimes even cavort with the monkeys, depending on the monkeys' mood. Rates: $$$.

Relaxing area at Xel-H Courtesy of Philip Gammon

Xcacel *(Highway 307, km 247; between Chemuyil and Xel-Ha)*

A popular nesting ground for loggerhead and green turtles, Xcacel has very few services and no electricity. The area is a nature preserve with skunks, snakes, and other protected animals, plus a combination of beaches, cenotes, mangroves, and jungle terrain. The turtles are most common in the warmer part of the year, from May to October. If visiting during this time, it is very important to avoid the nests and not bother any of the turtles. A cenote large enough to swim in is on the southern end of the beach (walk to the right, as you're facing the ocean). A small path leads from the beach to the cenote; look for a small wooden sign. To the north, the reef comes close to the beach, making it a good spot for snorkeling. A primitive camping facility offers a place to pitch a tent.

Punta Soliman *(Highway 307, km 240)*

A restful beach good for jogging, sunbathing, and shell collecting, Soliman is the kind of place where you feel compelled to arrange your Corona bottles and lime on the table and take a picture with the sundown in the background. In fact, this beach has become famous for being the site featured in a popular series of Corona beer commercials. The majority of the ads were taped in front of Oscar y Lalo's restaurant (see Dining), and the waiters are eager to point out the different areas used.

A small cenote is located behind Oscar y Lalo's. To find it, head away from the restaurant entrance, behind the kitchen, and it's slightly hidden in a grove of trees. It's a bit salty and murky, though it's still a nice spot to jump in and cool off. Just to the south is a much larger inlet from the ocean, which is full of fish even though the water isn't very clear. Alltournative Tours offers kayak trips to the area, but kayaks can also be rented on-site.

LODGING

✪ PLAYA NATUREL
984-871-2387
www.playanaturel.com
Highway 307, km 238, South end of Playa Soliman (just north of Tankah)

Turn right when the road from the highway meets the road paralleling the beach, and the inn is about .5 mile down. It's a simple four-room complex with nicely decorated rooms large enough for four. There are bright furnishings and tropical decorations, giving it a cheery feeling. It's right on the beach, though the sand is not raked like at the big resorts, so it has seaweed and a bit of trash, though it is still quite nice. As its name loosely suggests, guests are free to go au naturel anywhere on the property (remember that full nudity is generally illegal on the beach, though it is frequently tolerated in isolated areas). The central focus is a small swimming pool, where guests socialize and relax the day away. Rates: $$$ to $$$$. One and two bedroom units are available.

Oscar y Lalo's is a perfect spot for lunch.

DINING

⊘ OSCAR Y LALO'S
984-804-6973
Highway 307, km 240

Take the main road from Highway 307 to the beach, and then turn left and wind through the bumpy, sandy road. Oscar y Lalo's is just about the only thing along that stretch, so you can't miss it. The restaurant is the un-official home base for **Alltournative Tours**, which always seems to have its tents up and its kayaks at the ready. There are a dozen tables in a shaded *palapa* and a dozen or so more stretched out along the beach. The best thing on the menu is the fried whole fish, large enough for two, and there's also great ceviche and fish fillets. Though this was the site of the filming of a popular series of Corona beer commercials, the restaurant has since stopped carrying Corona, so order a Sol instead. Kayaks are available for $8 an hour. Moderate.

Tankah *(Highway 307, km 237; between Xel-Ha and Tulum)*

Tankah is a small bay that was once an important ceremonial site for the ancient Mayans, and there are minor ruins in the area, though they are still being explored and are not open to the public. The main road parallels the beach and is home to several guest houses and inns, and one of the largest is Casa Cenote, which is between the beach and a large freshwater lagoon called Manatee Cenote, rumored to have a manatee living in it. The cenote has a channel that leads underground, below the road and the hotel, and ends 100 feet offshore from the beach. Only experienced cave divers should do the swim, however. Visitors can also stay at the **Blue Sky Resort** (see Lodging), located on the beach just north of **Casa Cenote**.

LODGING

✪ BLUE SKY RESORT

984-801-4004
www.blueskymexico.com
Highway 307, km 237; on
the beach, just past the
cenote in Tankah

Less of a resort and more of
a small inn, Blue Sky has
six rooms, each with a
minibar, ocean view, and
direct access to a nearly
private beach. There is a
small pool in the courtyard,
right by the beach. The
decor is thoroughly con-
temporary, and the rooms
feel like modern condos
inside. An on-site restaurant serves a varied international menu and is open
to the public. Across the
street is Manatee Cenote,
rumored to have a family of
manatees living in it,
though not even the locals
have seen them in recent
years. An underground
tunnel connects the cenote
to the ocean, which is a
great dive for those with
cave diving certification. (It should in no
way be attempted by anyone else.) Rates: $
to $$$, depending on room choice and time
of year.

Blue Sky gives guests access to the ocean and a cenote.

✪ CASA CENOTE

998-874-5170

This collection of charming casitas sits on
the beach between the calm waters of
Tankah Bay and a large freshwater lagoon
called Manatee Cenote. The rooms are
along the beach and have terra-cotta tile
floors, local artwork, and ceiling fans; some
also have air-conditioning. Nearby four-
bedroom villas offer ocean views, outdoor
grills, air-conditioning, and chef service on
request. They rent for $2,300 to $3,300 per
week depending on the time of year. The
main hotel has a small restaurant with a
palapa roof and grill and several plastic
tables on the beach. Popular dishes include
cheeseburgers, nachos, fajitas, grilled
shrimp, fried fish, and fresh lobster. The
bar sells beer to go for day trips or lounging
on the beach. Rates: $150 to $200, double
occupancy; includes breakfast, snorkeling
gear for two, and kayak rental.

Tulum Avenue is lined with shops and restaurants.

Tulum & the Mayan Coast

The dusty but incredibly fast-growing town of Tulum, which marks the official end of the Riviera Maya, lies along Highway 307 at km 230, about 80 miles south of the Cancún airport. The Mayan Riviera officially ends where Highway 307 intersects the road to Cobá, and just north of there is the turnoff to the Tulum ruins. Turn west at the crossroads, and the town of Cobá, a picturesque lagoon, and the Mayan ruins of the same name are about an hour away. For a traditional Mayan meal, stop at the Restaurante Campestre Las Cabañas, about 10 minutes before you get to town. Go south and you'll be in the Mayan Coast, also called the Sun Coast, where the road bypasses Laguna Bacalar and the turnoff to the beach town of Xcalak, as it skirts the Sian Ka'an biosphere and heads toward Kohunlich and on to Chetumal, and eventually to the border with Belize.

Turn east at the crossroads, and where the road meets the beach, you'll find the large gated Mediterranean-style **Eurostars Blue Tulum** resort. Beyond that, there is a small hotel zone that is a backpacker's paradise and a real treasure for eco-conscious travelers who value privacy, serenity, and natural beauty over modern luxuries and pampering services. Many of the resorts do not have power-line electricity and rely on solar power or generators to keep the lights on and the beer cold. It is common for rooms not to have electric light and for hotel staff to light candles along the walkway, and even in the rooms. Guests at these hotels are encouraged to bring flashlights, mosquito repellent, and nature guides, and to leave their mobile phones, laptop computers, and urban mindset behind.

To the left (north) are a few vacation homes and a couple of hotels; to the right (south) is the notoriously bumpy road through Sian Ka'an to the fishing town of Punta Allen. In the town of Tulum (called "Tulum pueblo," to differentiate it from the Tulum Mayan ruins) there is a gas station (Pemex, just before the crossroads), an ATM machine (at the HSBC bank), and several smallish hotels, restaurants, bars, and tour offices. At the Cobá turnoff there is a large San Francisco de Asis grocery store, a Hertz car rental office, and an El Point Internet and phone-calling office. The section of Highway 307 from the Tulum crossroads to the end of town is called Tulum Avenue. Along this 12-block stretch, travelers will find laundry services (Lava Easy, at Osiris Street), a huge gift shop and market (Plaza Fiesta Maya Mexican Outlet, at Jupiter Street), an Internet café (Internet Tulum, at Alfa Street), and a clinic with an English-speaking doctor (at Osiris Street).

Taxi Fares from Downtown Tulum
Tulum ruins: $3
Azulik, Copal, Zamas, Zahra: $3.50
Ana y Jose: $6
Tita Tulum: $7.50
Akumal: $16
Kantenah: $18
Cobá: $21
Playa del Carmen: $30
Puerto Morelos: $47
Cancún downtown: $62
Cancún hotel zone: $67

Buses depart for Tulum from Playa del Carmen from the bus station near the town square every hour and cost $2. A *colectivo* shuttle van departs Playa from 2nd Street between 15th and 20th Avenues and will drop passengers off anywhere along the way between Playa and Tulum for $2, even if the drop-off is off the main road. The van fits eight people and departs as soon as it is full, from 7 AM–8 PM.

There are two bus stations on Tulum Avenue, across the street from each other on the southern edge of town, between Alfa and Jupiter Streets. Buses depart hourly for Playa del Carmen ($2, one hour), Cancún ($4.50, two hours), Mérida, Chetumal, Bacalar, and other towns in the region. From the Tulum bus station, taxi fare to the ruins or to the hotel zone is about $3 to $5.

The road from Tulum village hits the beach and runs north and south.

A beachfront cabaña at Azulik.

LODGING

✪ ANA Y JOSÉ CHARMING HOTEL & SPA

998-887-5470
www.anayjose.com
On the Tulum beachfront, 5 miles south of
Tulum pueblo on the Punta Allen road

This 14-room inn, only 10 minutes from
the town of Tulum, offers clean, comfortable, and well-designed rooms with ceiling
fans, hot water, towels, and linens, as well
as garden, pool, or oceanfront views—but
no telephones or TVs. It has been open
since 1985; its owners wanted to create a
place that had homey comforts but that was
still close to nature. There is a pool by the
ocean and a beachfront restaurant known
for its fresh seafood and lobster. The hotel's
beach club has developed a reputation as
being a bit of a party scene and frequently
has day-tripping revelers from Playa del
Carmen and beyond, which can add to the
excitement in an otherwise fairly remote
spot. The tour desk can arrange scuba,
snorkeling, and fishing trips, and there are
great beaches and swimmer-friendly
cenotes within walking distance. The elec-
tricity stays on 24 hours. Rates: $$$.

✪ AZULIK

551-084-2820 or 1-877-532-6737 (U.S.)
www.azulik.com
On the Tulum beachfront, .5 mile south of
Tulum pueblo on the Punta Allen road

An adults-only, clothing-optional resort
with 15 rooms, Azulik features beachside
huts that are made from local hardwoods
and have waterfront decks ideal for sun-
ning and catching the ocean breezes. Each

villa has a private bathroom with hot water and a wooden bathtub, but don't expect much privacy since it's in the middle of the room. There is no electricity in the rooms, but candles and matches are provided. The beach right behind the hotel is rocky and has many sea fans, which are washed in with the tide, and there are sandy access points good for swimming just a short walk away. The reef is only a couple hundred yards from shore, and there is good snorkeling and kayaking in front of the resort when the waves aren't too rough. The tour desk also plans jungle hikes, ruins visits, and cenote trips. Spa services at the adjacent Maya Spa include aromatherapy, massage, body scrubs, and Reiki. Though there is no restaurant, guests can eat at the neighboring hotels and can even order room service, which is prepared at the villa. Just raise the red flag on your deck to summon a waiter. Rates: $$$ to $$$$.

CABAÑAS COPAL

551-084-2820 or 1-877-532-6737 (U.S.)
www.cabanascopal.com
On the Tulum beachfront, .5 mile south of Tulum on the Punta Allen road

This 47-room, clothing-optional hotel is eco-conscious and rustic, yet romantic with candlelight. There is no electricity in the rooms, though the lobby and restaurant do have power. A beach bar serves cold drinks at the water's edge and has hammocks for guests to relax in while enjoying the day. Rooms are simple, with thatched roofs and heated water, but all water must be trucked in or pumped from an on-site well, so guests are encouraged to use it sparingly. The rooms are on a bluff above the beach (just like Tulum is) and are built to blend with the natural surroundings. The staff advises that geckos, hermit crabs, iguanas, and even nonpoisonous snakes are sometimes seen on the property, but that they are treated like guests and should not be feared. Guests are encouraged to embrace nature and to appreciate all of it, rather than work to shut it out, like in most hotels. The hotel is just steps from the ocean, and all rooms have direct beach access. Room classes include simple bungalows with shared bathrooms ($), garden-view rooms with private bath ($ to $$), ocean-view rooms with private bath ($$), and even a small casita ($$$).

CABAÑAS PAPAYA PLAYA

www.papayaplaya.com
On the Tulum beachfront, just south of the turnoff to Tulum pueblo

This ultracasual hotel has 45 rooms, restaurant, bar, and more than .3 mile of pristine beachfront. Rooms range from sand-floor huts like the Mayans used to live in and cabañas with cement floors to villas with sealed walls, private bathrooms, and a touch of elegance. Electricity runs from sunset until 11:30 PM, with power in the rooms, restaurant, and bar. An on-site tourist information center offers free maps, a book exchange, and a tour office. Popular trips include a snorkeling tour with reef and cenote visits ($35), a two-cenote snorkeling trip ($40), scuba diving in Akumal ($50 for one tank, $80 for two), and a cenote dive ($65 for one tank, $105 for two). Rates: rooms with sand floors and shared bathrooms cost $30, rooms with concrete floors and shared bathrooms cost $30 (extra beds are $10), and one-bedroom villas cost $100 per night and have private bathrooms.

✪ COQUI COQUI SPA HOTEL

www.coquicoquispa.com
998-112-5428
On the Tulum beachfront, 5 miles south of the turnoff to Tulum pueblo

Past the simple hotels and Mayan-style huts of the main Tulum hotel zone, where the road is encroached by palm trees and brush, this upscale day spa and seven-room hotel offers guests a way to get away from it all, without sacrificing comfort. The property, known as the Xtabay Estate, offers a simple lifestyle designed to enhance the harmony between body, mind, and soul. Guests can reserve a single room or the entire home, which is decorated with Mexican artifacts, handmade furnishings, tapestries, and a variety of European and Asian influences. The spacious master suites have ocean views. Highly recommended. Rates range from $$$ for a courtyard suite in low season to $$$$$ for a master suite during high season.

DREAMS TULUM RESORT & SPA

984-871-3333
www.dreamsresorts.com
Highway 307, km 234

This all-inclusive resort is just five minutes north of the village of Tulum, and you can even see the cliffside Mayan ruins of the same name from the hotel beach. It features 238 rooms with air-conditioning, ceiling fans, 27-inch TVs, stocked mini-bars, CD players, coffeemakers, and private balconies or terraces with hammocks. There are four specialty restaurants (Mexican, Italian, Asian/sushi, and continental), plus a casual buffet. There are also five bars, including a pool bar and a beach bar. Included in the rate are the beachfront pool, freshwater lagoon, movie theater, wedding chapel, and fitness center. There's also an on-site Internet café, as well as a European day spa (complete with *temazcal*), golf, scuba diving, and tours (additional fees apply). Kids can spend the day at the Explorer Kids' Club and enjoy sports, swimming, and meals. Rates: $150 per person, based on double occupancy. Rates vary through the year.

✪ EUROSTARS BLUE TULUM

984-871-1000 or 1-866-636-4882 (U.S.)

www.eurostarsbluetulum.com
On the beach at the Tulum crossroads

Billed as the world's "first stress-free hotel," the Blue Tulum was opened in 2006 and enjoys a privileged setting at the center of the Tulum beachfront hotel zone. As the only large-scale property in the area, it can appear a bit garish, but if you don't let the size and slightly corporate feel bother you, it's an amazing property that truly can indulge travelers looking for a complete getaway. There are 96 rooms housed in small villas, with features such as rain showers, iPods, plasma TVs, Italian linens, and butler service. The resort offers three gourmet restaurants, a full-service spa, and a tour desk that can plan outings across the Riviera Maya. The hotel has a lavish day spa featuring a Mayan *temazcal* sweat lodge, meditation classes, and a wide variety of relaxing and therapeutic treatments offered in the air-conditioned treatment rooms, next to the beach, or in the guest suites. Guests lounging by the pool or on the beach are serviced by butlers, who bring fresh towels, refreshments, suntan lotion, and cooling misters. Guests should note, though, that there is no ocean access, due to a rocky waterfront and moderate wave action. The hotel offers free transportation to a nearby beach club. Upgraded packages are available that include spa services and other exclusive amenities. All-inclusive rates: $$$$$.

HOTEL LATINO

984-871-2674
www.hotel-latino.com
In Tulum pueblo, Andromeda Street at Colonia Centro

Located 1 block off the main strip in Tulum pueblo, this small and stylish hotel has a facade that is vaguely reminiscent of **Hotel Deseo** in Playa del Carmen (see chapter 2). There is a small pool, and rates include free wireless Internet access and the use of a bicycle. Rates: $18 to $85, depending on whether you want air-conditioning and a larger room with more amenities.

LA VITA È BELLA
www.lavitaebella-tulum.com
On the Tulum beachfront, 1.5 miles north of the turnoff to Tulum pueblo

La Vita è Bella is composed of 10 villas strung along the beachfront, each with a terrace with hammock and ocean view, a *palapa* roof, hardwood furnishings, showers with panoramic views, and original decorations. They are quite luxurious given the casual atmosphere of the Tulum beach area. The hotel offers in-room massage service, and there is an on-site restaurant serving Italian and Mexican food, plus wood-oven pizza, smoothies, and fruit juice. The staff can even set up a private table on the beach for a romantic candlelight dinner. There is also a beach club that offers lounge chairs, drink service, and snorkel gear rental. Rates: $$ to $$$, including breakfast.

LA ZEBRA BEACHFRONT CABANAS & CANTINA
www.lazebra.com.mx
998-112-3260
In the Tulum hotel zone, 3.7 miles south of the road to town

OK, so Tulum wasn't really like this in the '80s and '90s, before it was "discovered," but it's fun to think that it was. La Zebra offers nine decently sized cabanas right on the beach, surrounded by coconut palm trees and tropical flowers. Though it's owned by the same Aussies who own the super slick Mezzanine Hotel up the beach, La Zebra is intentionally understated, with a "jungle-chic, organic vibe," according to the owners. That doesn't mean it's overly rustic or lacking in amenities. In fact, with its premium bed linens, ceiling fans, large beds, hole-free mosquito nets, wireless

Internet access, and local artwork, it would have been a luxury standout back in Tulum's hippie days. The cabañas are staffed by a group of sisters who delight guests with their hearty Mexican cooking and drinks (including ice-cold beer and fresh fruit margaritas) at the on-site cantina. Salsa dancing lessons in the afternoon sun are offered all weekend (which starts on Thursday, around these parts). Outdoor pit-roasts are featured on the giant charcoal grill each Sunday. Guests and visitors are invited. Rates range from $$ for a standard room in low season to nearly $$$$ for the master suite in high season.

LOS LIRIOS
998-850-6486
www.loslirioshotel.com
On the Tulum beachfront, 5.5 miles down the road from Tulum pueblo to Punta Allen

If you want to experience the Tulum beach hotel zone but you don't want to give up your air-conditioning, spa, and clean showers, Los Lirios is a good bet. The hotel's 32 rooms are housed in villa-style buildings built back from the sea. They have air-conditioning, private terraces with hammocks, canopy beds, bright tropical colors, private bathrooms, and phones. There is an on-site restaurant serving Mexican, vegetarian, seafood, and international dishes; a massage and yoga center; a tour desk, and laundry service. Rates: $$ to $$$, depending on the time of year; includes American breakfast.

✪ MEZZANINE
984-804-1452
www.mezzanine.com.mx
On the Tulum beachfront, 1 mile north of the crossroads from Tulum pueblo to the beach

Just a stone's throw from the Tulum ruins, this Thailand/Mediterranean-influenced beachfront hotel and lounge oozes with

A swanky room at Mezzanine

style. The owners are longtime friends and backpacking companions and traveled the world picking up ideas for how to build their dream resort. Whether you visit for an afternoon or a whole week, Mezzanine seems to seep into your soul, with its provocative decor and deep-rooted romantic appeal. It has four hotel rooms fronted by a smallish cenote-like plunge pool and a cozy bar and lounge. Hugging a cliff over the beach are a few lounge chairs, affording a great view of the ocean. The restaurant offers Thai food and fusion specialties, including shrimp satay, wraps, curries, Thai soup, pad thai noodles, and lobster, served at a handful of mod orange tables perched on the cliff or in the veranda dining room. At night, tiki torches and red and orange candles bathe the entire pool deck and dining room in a welcoming and sensual amber glow. The bar has developed into a trendy spot for traveling hipsters and locals alike. Every Friday, visiting DJs from Europe and around the world spin house- and chill-out music for crowds of up to 250 people. A hidden mezzanine level above the dining room houses the VIP area, with swanky lounge seating and a pool table. The rooms offer rich Caribbean colors, premium bedding, a loft with futon, in-room safes, ceiling fans, and great ocean views. Steps lead down from the pool deck to the one of the region's best powder-white beaches, which is practically devoid of people. A few minutes' jog to the north and you can see the ruins of Tulum looking like a fortress on the horizon. Snorkels, masks, and sea kayaks are available free for guest use and the reef is just a couple hundred yards offshore. Happy hour by the pool is 1 PM–4 PM daily. Rates: $$$ to $$$$.

NUEVA VIDA DE RAMIRO ECOLODGE

984-877-8512

www.nuevavida.com.mx

On the Tulum beachfront, 6.5 miles south of the Tulum crossroads, on the road to Punta Allen

Feeling like a secluded jungle hideaway, this casita complex has 18 one- and two-room "eco-bungalows," each of which is a stand-alone building, more like a private beach house than a hotel. Units are spread over 41 acres and use wind and solar generators to power the public areas, but there is no electricity in the guest rooms. There is a gadget charging station and area with wireless Internet access in the reception lounge. Rates: $$ to $$$.

✪ OM TULUM HOTEL CABANAS & LOUNGE

984-8794784

www.tulum-playa.com

On the Tulum beachfront, 6 miles south of the Tulum crossroads, on the road to Punta Allen

Operated by the same team that runs the uber-popular **Om Hotel & Lounge** in Playa del Carmen, the Om Tulum opened in early 2008 and offers the same trendy casual attitude, plus a picturesque beachfront location that makes it even more unique. The hotel is about 5 miles south of the Tulum crossroads and 7 miles from the ruins. It includes nine cabañas with an ocean or garden view, a restaurant, a lounge, and a beach club. The rooms feature ocean or garden views, private bathrooms, and comfy beds. The restaurant is open for breakfast, lunch, and dinner, and serves Caribbean seafood, including fresh fish delivered daily by local fishermen. They also serve wood-oven pizza, plus chicken and meat dishes.

The beach club fronts a picture-perfect white sand beach with smooth sand and lapping waves. It is open from 10 AM to 6 PM and offers lounge chairs and beachfront cabanas. The lounge is open nightly until 2 AM, offering guests and visitors the opportunity to listen to chill-out music, enjoy a cocktail, and make new friends while gazing at the stars and the waves. The facility is available for private parties, weddings, and other group events.

Room rates: $$ to $$$. There is electricity in the rooms until 1 AM. The hotel's tour desk offers kite surfing, snorkeling, scuba diving, yoga, massage, and other activities. Free Internet service is available to guests. Rooms can be reserved online, but all local charges are cash only.

✪ SHAMBALA PETIT HOTEL

984-125-6474

www.shambalapetithotel.com

On the Tulum beachfront, 5 miles south of Tulum pueblo, on the road to Punta Allen

Part of the funky, but hip Tulum beachfront hotel zone, this serene complex of 10 beachfront casitas serve as a haven for couples and close friends that truly want to disconnect with their regular lives and reconnect—with each other, with nature, and with themselves. The hotel offers traditional Mayan-style rooms with *palapa* roofs and mosquito nets, plus yoga classes, Thai massage, scuba trips, wedding planning, and a pristine beach to sit and contemplate the waves. A special Spanish lesson package ($1,500/1 week) includes airport transportation, casita accommodations, bicycle usage, breakfast and lunch, and six hours of instruction per day. $$ to $$$.

TITA TULUM

984-877-8513

www.titatulum.com

On the Tulum beachfront, 5 miles south of Tulum pueblo, on the road to Punta Allen

This small property has six cabins with *palapa* roofs, mosquito nets, solar power, and hot water, and each has a private patio with hammock overlooking the powdery white-sand beach. An on-site restaurant serves Mexican and Mayan dishes next to the beach. Rates: $.

THE WEARY TRAVELER
Tulum pueblo, Tulum Avenue between Jupiter and Acuario Streets

This hostel and travel center is the center of low-budget info and activity for Tulum pueblo. There is a nice shaded courtyard and snack bar, a common refrigerator, and acceptable rooms with bunk beds. The hostel offers discounted tours, bike rental, snorkeling gear rental, and plenty of traveler camaraderie. It's also known to be a good place to party with other backpackers. Rates: $10 single, $18 double, including breakfast.

✪ UNO ASTROLODGE TULUM
984-134-7180
www.unoastrolodge.com
On the Tulum beachfront, near Punta Piedra beach

The AstroLodge is all about spiritual healing, global positivity, and energy balance. Rooms have a New Age vibe, with thatched roofs, native stone, primitive woodwork, and big windows with ocean views. There's a little kitchen for guest use, and a complimentary organic breakfast is offered each morning. When not lounging on the perfect beach, guests can enjoy a variety of therapeutic treatments, including a full-body massage accompanied with Egyptian harp music, Reiki, yoga class, and a moonlight *temazcal* ceremony. Rates: $$ to $$$. Some rooms have extra beds.

✪ ZAHRA
984-806-4406 or 1-877-532-6737 (U.S.)
www.zahra.com.mx
On the Tulum beachfront, 1 mile south of Tulum pueblo on the Punta Allen road

The 22 rooms at Zahra have thatched roofs, but they are not completely rustic, with ceiling fans, electric lights, hot water, in-room spa services, and even room service and wireless Internet access. Some rooms face the gardens and others face the ocean, and there are beaches on two sides of the hotel and lots of palm trees. An on-site restaurant serves traditional Mayan and Mexican food and often has live music, and there is an on-site Internet café open when the power is on. Rates: range from $ for a small cabin without ocean view or private bathroom in low season to $$$ for a two-level family suite with room for five, private bathrooms, and an ocean view. Other room classes are available. A small convenience store is right across the street. Highly recommended.

✪ ZAMAS BEACH CABAÑAS
415-387-9806 (U.S.)
www.zamas.com
On the Punta Allen road 3 miles south of Tulum pueblo

Zamas, which means "sunrise" in Mayan, was the original name for Tulum, which is only five minutes away. This beachfront inn has 15 *palapa* bungalows built in the traditional Mayan manner. Wind- and solar-generated power stays on until late at night. The complex has a few interesting touches, such as Mexican tile work, private shaded porches, and handmade hammocks. An open-air restaurant features Mayan-inspired dishes, Mexican specialties, wood-oven pizza, and fresh seafood, including lobster. The hotel sits on a small and quiet beach, ideal for beachcombing, swimming, and snorkeling. The hotel can organize dive trips, expeditions to the ruins, fishing, and bird-watching. Rates: $$ to $$$.

DINING

BUENOS AIRES GRILL
984-871-2708
Tulum Avenue at Calle Beta

This restaurant claims that it's the only steakhouse south of Puerto Aventuras. It serves Angus beef, grilled lobster, shrimp, fish, and vegetarian food. Open 1:30–11:30 daily. Moderate.

✪ IL GIARDINO
984-806-3601
Satelite Avenue at Sagitario Street

Italian food served in a garden setting. The tables are surrounded by tropical plants and stone carvings. The menu features lasagna, pasta, and fresh fish. Open 1 PM–1 AM daily. Moderate.

LA PALAPA DEL CHINO
984-804-3647
Tulum Avenue between Osiris and Beta Sur

This casual spot, which serves Chinese and Mexican food, is open 7 AM–11 PM daily. There are a few plastic tables with a view of the street. The menu offers a variety of rice dishes, chicken tacos, and other budget fare. Inexpensive.

✪ TAQUERIA GRINGA
Tulum Avenue between Jupiter and Acuario Streets; across from the Weary Traveler hostel

A typical local restaurant serving very inexpensive food for breakfast, lunch, and dinner. The plastic tables are along the sidewalk and the menu offers tacos, chicken enchiladas, quesadillas, and other local fare.

DIVING

ACUATIC TULUM
984-100-7122
www.hotels tulum.com/acuatic_tulum. htm
At the beach-side Cabañas Don Armando hotel, .5-mile north of where the main Tulum crossroad intersects with the beach road; second location is on Highway 307 at the Tulum crossroads.

Tulum's first dive shop, in operation since 1993, offers snorkeling, ocean diving, and cenote diving trips each day. It also has gear and bike rental.

SPAS

✪ MAYA SPA
551-084-2820
www.maya-spa.com
Next to Cabañas Copal in the Tulum beach hotel zone (see Lodging)

At this beachfront retreat with open-air massage huts and a candle-lit indoor spa, there are daily yoga classes, lucid dreaming courses, and a *temazcal*, a Mayan-style sweat lodge ($29 per person). The spa serves fresh fruit and tropical meals. Local shamans perform traditional Mayan treatments, and local healers use native plants and herbs to perform various healing ceremonies. Other services include body wraps, Reiki, aesthetic treatments, Mayan massage, and flotation chamber therapy. Highly recommended.

Boca Paila, Sian Ka'an & Punta Allen

Very few travelers will ever have the chance to visit a place as remote—and as starkly beautiful —as the Sian Ka'an biosphere reserve in their entire lives. Meaning "gift from the sky" or "the sky's beginning" (depending on which translation you believe), Sian Ka'an was officially designated a nature reserve in 1986. It spans more than 1.25 million acres, which is 10 percent of the land in the state of Quintana Roo, and it is an official UNESCO World Heritage site. Don't expect to find picnic tables, public bathrooms, concession stands, or beach bars—this is not a nature park like Xcaret or Xel-Ha. This land is remote and does not have any of the facilities or services that one sometimes associates with a "park." Once Sian Ka'an became a federal reserve, all development was frozen, and all activities are strictly regulated, which is designed to protect the wild diversity of flora, fauna, and geography encompassed in the reserve. There are more than 300 species of birds (including herons, ibis, roseate spoonbills, and parrots), 100 types of mammals (such as wild cats, monkeys, coatimundis, and deer), and such land features as barrier reefs, mangrove swamps, lagoons, marshes, and tropical forests. There are also more than two dozen Mayan relics, small native villages, and ruins of abandoned ranches, hotels, restaurants, and homes.

The goal of the reserve is to provide a place where nature can thrive on its own, without the negative impacts that come with the presence of humans and the development that always seems to follow. A portion of the biosphere is completely restricted, but much of it is open to exploration, as long as visitors follow the reserve's strict rules of low- or no-impact adventuring. A rocky and sometimes sandy road passes through the area, and vehicles may not depart from the path. There is no inland fishing or scuba diving, though snorkeling is allowed since it has less impact on the reefs. A handful of fishing lodges and rustic hotels operate in the reserve, though they must provide their own water and electricity since there are no utilities in the area.

There is a $2-per-person fee to enter the park, and all travelers must stop at the visitors center to check in. Jeeps and four-wheel-drive vehicles are recommended as the road is heavily rutted, rocky, and sometimes muddy. Taking a regular rental sedan on the road makes for slow going and may violate your renter's agreement, nullifying any sort of insurance you have purchased, so it's best to check in advance. There are plenty of picturesque and totally deserted beaches where you can stop for a bit of beach-combing, picture-taking, and stretching. Unfortunately, since the beach is not tended to like at the resorts, years of washed-up trash remains piled at the high-tide mark, making a silent yet very compelling case for the need for more awareness of garbage-dumping in the world's oceans.

The twin bridges of Boca Paila

What I Like about the Riviera Maya

Contributed by Ellyn Hloben

Exquisite beaches; glorious sunsets; turquoise aqua-teal colors of the Caribbean Sea; exciting nightlife; enjoying an all-inclusive resort with all you can eat and drink; exploring Xcaret; diving in a coral reef; enjoying a relaxing massage on the beach under the soothing shade of a palm tree or a day at a soothing spa; exploring azure cenotes.

Drinking Dos Equis beer; taking the ferry to Cozumel; feeling a balmy breeze on my face; hanging out with friends at the lobby bar; swimming with dolphins; climbing to the top of the pyramid at Chichén Itzá; watching a folkloric performance; eating tacos al pastor; enjoying the sidewalk enter-tainers; visiting Mayan ruins.

Parasailing; visiting the Xaman-Ha Aviary; dancing all night in a resort disco and then going into Playa for more music; playing at a championship golf course in Playacar; exploring historic archaeolog-ical sites; enjoying a traditional strolling mariachi band; getting a green light at the airport; dining on spectacular international cuisine; visiting the Hekab Be Biblioteca (a charming one-room library/schoolhouse in Akumal) and meeting the students; dancing to soca music; buying from beach vendors with their brightly colored wares.

Strolling quaint Fifth Avenue in Playa del Carmen and stopping at every cantina; getting braids in your hair; eating guacamole; visiting Tres Rios; exploring jungle lagoons; getting a henna tattoo like a teenager; strolling through craft-filled open-air marketplaces, buying straw hats, silver jewelry, and serapes; being surrounded by bougainvillea; taking a side trip to the Ruinas El Rey; buying Cancún perfume at the airport; basking in an oversize hot tub; riding in a colectivo; exploring the Yucatán Peninsula; witnessing breathtaking sunrises; spending a day at the historic city of Tulum and standing on a cliff overlooking a beautiful beach; scuba diving; drinking frosty, cold, salt-rimmed margaritas; seeing Cozumel at night in the distance under the glow of a Mayan full moon.

Listening to Venga Boys tunes by the pool; white powdery sand; spending a day at beautiful Xel-Ha; snorkeling in sparkling, crystal-clear waters; dining in gourmet restaurants; taking a siesta in a thatched palapa; visiting Sian Ka'an; swinging in a hand-knotted hammock; driving south of Playa del Carmen and stopping at a new beach, cenote, or city; hearing the sweet swishing sound of swaying palm trees; exploring the ruins at Cobá; listening to salsa music; watching the WaveRunners dart by; visiting ecological reserves and natural aquariums; sipping a chilled Corona with lime; lolling in a Jacuzzi; taking a lobster cruise; making footprints in the sand; visiting Crococun Zoo.

Renting Jet Skis; catching a glimpse of a flamingo, peacock, or howler monkey on your resort grounds; shootin' tequila slammers; seeing lush red tropical hibiscus; peeking at iguanas sunning atop the ruins; smelling coconut and cocoa butter suntan-lotion scents wafting in the air; playing tequila volleyball; driving thunder boats; hearing a marimba band by the pool; eating warm tortillas; witness-ing the sea turtle release program; and, my favorite thing of all: reexperiencing my pleasures by writing in my journal at the end of a glorious day in paradise.

Ellyn is from St. Louis, Missouri, and is a frequent traveler to the Riviera Maya.
Her zest for the area is typical of travelers who are deeply touched by their travel experiences.

At the southern end of the road, you'll reach the tiny village of Punta Allen. And no, some gringo named Allen doesn't own the town. The name comes from the Mayan word *allin*, which means "crocodile." The village is home to 600 inhabitants, said to originate from 90 original families. Most work as fishing guides in the area lodges or at the nearby lobster farm (which covers some 300,000 acres). There are a handful of lodges, a couple of restaurants, a bar, and a general store called Tienda Socorro, where travelers can purchase basic supplies.

With mangrove swamps, shallow lagoons, and a barrier reef that comes quite close to the beach, this region is a favorite for birdwatchers, anglers, and shell collectors. Crocodiles and manatees also make their home here, which adds to the excitement and your chance for a once-in-a-lifetime natural encounter. Jimmy Buffett fans will recognize this area as the setting for the singer's novel *A Salty Piece of Land*, which chronicles an American expatriate cowboy who sails with his horse to the fictitious island of Punta Margarita (sound familiar?) in Ascension Bay and becomes a fishing guide.

Speaking of fishing, the shallow flats, coves, and tiny coastal islands of Sian Ka'an, Punta Allen, and Ascension Bay offer some of the best fly- and light-tackle fishing in the world. Popular catches include barracuda, bonefish, and the coveted permit, which range from 2 to 20 pounds. Many of the lodges host fly-tying sessions for anglers who want to tie their own flies. If you're not familiar with fly-fishing techniques, local guides can teach you how to do it. If that's not your thing, you can fish in many of the same spots using light tackle. Most fish are caught by sightcasting, where the guide or the angler stands on the boat and searches the water for signs of fish, and then makes pinpoint casts to land the fish. At other times, anglers will wade into the waist-deep water and cast into the schools.

GETTING THERE

Take Highway 307, the main highway along the Riviera Maya, south from Playa del Carmen to the town of Tulum, about 45 minutes away. At the main Cobá crossroads, one stoplight past the turnoff to the Tulum ruins, turn east and follow the paved road a couple of miles to the end, and then turn right, to the south, and parallel the beach. After passing the Tulum beach hotel zone (which includes Cabañas Copal, Azulik, Ana y José, etcetera), you'll cross a usually empty guard post marking the unofficial beginning of the Sian Ka'an biosphere reserve. Three miles later, you'll come to an arch across the road and the official, always-manned biosphere entrance. All vehicles must stop to be logged in and pay a $2-per-person fee to enter. Once inside the park, follow the road along the beach for another 10 miles (about 45 minutes' worth of bumping up and down), and you will reach Boca Paila, marked by twin bridges (one wooden, one concrete, built in 2005) over the lagoon. Twenty miles into the trip, you'll come across a small unmarked Mayan temple partially hidden in the scrub brush next to the road, on the west side of the road. Several miles later, the road ends at the town of Punta Allen. Once you've left Tulum, the next gas station is in Punta Allen, which is 40 miles and about 90 minutes away (in good conditions), so be sure to gas up before you leave.

Colectivo shuttle service is available from Tulum to Punta Allen departing from a garage on Highway 307, two blocks north of the Weary Traveler. It leaves daily at 2 PM.

LODGING

If you thought Playa del Carmen was the antidote to Cancún's consumer-driven frivolity, this area quickly reminds you that even Playa's relative calm is wildly more developed and bustling than the region was in yesteryear. Around here, you won't find the margarita-fueled party scene, boutique bikini shops, or European spas of the resorts farther north. There are no ATM machines, gas stations, or money exchange booths, and no convenience stores, public bathrooms, or taxi stands. There's not even much running water or electric utilities. What you will find are miles of virgin beaches, awe-inspiring tropical landscapes, spectacular bird-watching, world-class flats fishing, and a timeless and relaxed atmosphere that helps to rejuvenate the soul and clear the mind.

Accommodations are eco-friendly "lodges," which means simple, no air-conditioning, no bathtubs, no swimming pools, and few luxuries. Travelers in these parts tend to be nature enthusiasts, back-packing adventurers, serious anglers, and others who are comfortable in tents, wooden cabañas, and other no-frills accommodations. For the hearty few that are up to the task, staying the night in the biosphere can reveal wondrous parts of the jungle that are rarely seen by others. The hotels in the area offer shuttle service from Cancún or the Riviera Maya, with advance notice required.

✪ ASCENSION BAY BONEFISH CLUB
984-877-8532 or 1-800-819-0750 (U.S.)
www.ascensionbay.com
On the edge of Ascension Bay, in Punta Allen

This private lodge hosts only six anglers per week, in a small house built right on the beach. The rooms are spacious and have ceiling fans, 24-hour electricity, and private bathrooms with hot water. Accommodations packages include meals, drinks, and fishing. A Friday-to-Friday package goes for $2,600 per person and includes transfers from Cancún, lodging, meals, and six days of fishing with a private boat and guide. Credit cards accepted on advance reservations.

BONEFISH BUM LODGE
984-877-8532 or 1-888-584-1453 (U.S.)
www.bonefishbum.com
Northern edge of Ascension Bay

Clean rooms, Mayan-style meals, and world-class bonefishing make this one of the world's best places to spend a week on the water, watching for the telltale flash of a bonefish as it turns to take a fly. After a full day of fishing, guests are welcomed back to the lodge with appetizers and cold drinks. Sample rates: four nights with three days of fishing is $1,200 each for two anglers sharing a room and boat; seven nights $2,400. Day-fishing trips are available for nonguests for $390 per boat, for up to three anglers. Alcohol, ground transportation, and equipment are extra. An ecotour package consisting of four nights' lodging and three days of tours (including snorkeling, boat trips, and Mayan ruins) goes for $875 per person, based on two participants, including room, meals, boat, and guide. Credit cards accepted on advance reservations.

CASA CUZAN
983-834-0358
www.flyfishmx.com
On the southern edge of Punta Allen

Casa Cuzan is a rustic hotel that offers 12 fan-cooled, thatch-roofed cabañas; a restaurant (think lobster, fish, Mexican/Mayan cuisine); and great access to the area's best fishing spots. All rooms have hot water, decent beds, 24-hour electricity, and patios with hammocks. They are a short walk to the beach, and the boats leave from right in front of the hotel. Rates: $ to $$, with all-inclusive fishing packages going for $1,999 per week. No credit cards.

CASA SIRENA
984-877-8521
www.casasirena.com
Punta Allen

This simple inn offers cabaña-style rooms with hot water, thatched roofs, and walls that stop short of the ceiling to let in the breeze. It may not offer a lot in the way of luxury, but it's a friendly and relaxing spot to get away from the hustle. Rates: $ to $$. Rooms range from a simple hut to a small cottage to a room in the main house. The inn also offers snorkeling trips for $40 and fly-fishing trips for $65, based on two people booking together. No credit cards.

✪ CESIAK

984-871-2499
www.cesiak.org
Two miles north of the Boca Paila bridge on the road from Tulum to Punta Allen

This eco-friendly lodge is located on a 15-acre ranch that once housed an upscale resort until it was abandoned in 1982. Cesiak opened in 2000 with a more eco-conscious approach. It has a learning center, tour office, and central kitchen for guest use. The guests are housed in private tents on wooden platforms and have terraces, hardwood furniture, and great views. Rates: $$ to $$$.

✪ LET IT BE INN

984-877-8506
www.letitbeinn.com
Punta Allen

With a maximum of six anglers at a time, Let It Be is about as secluded and private as it gets. Hosts Rick and Rosie Montgomery run the tiny lodge, cook the meals, help plan the fishing trips, and take care of anything else that guests may need. The restaurant serves up delicious meals, and there is a beachfront bar and fly-tying station where guests can make their flies and sip cocktails. Standard rates include all meals and drinks, plus transportation to and from the Cancún airport. Rates: start at $1,495 for three nights' lodging for two and two days of fishing, based on double occupancy. No credit cards.

✪ PESCA MAYA

998-845-6501 or 1-800-894-5642 (U.S.)
www.pescamaya.com

Three miles north of Punta Allen

Just when you think you can't take the bumps of the road through Sian Ka'an anymore, you arrive at Pesca Maya. Due to its close proximity to Punta Allen, guests can go into town for supplies or a tiny taste of civilization if they need it. Most visitors don't see another car once they arrive, though, and that's part of the charm. The lodge is built on the land of the Chenchomac (Mayan for "land of the foxes") ranch, which formerly operated as a coconut plantation. It has a large, well-built *palapa* restaurant and bar, which also serves as the library, fly-tying station, and social center. Guests get up at the crack of dawn, have breakfast at 7 AM, and leave by 8 for a full day of fishing. Each angler is assigned to a boat and a guide, with no more than two guests per boat. The boats return between 2 and 4 PM, and then it's off to the beach to relax or to the restaurant to recount the day and swap stories. Dinner is served family style each evening, and the bar stays open until 10 PM, though by that time most guests have retired to their rooms, exhausted from the day and excited for the next one. Nonanglers also enjoy Pesca Maya, since the beach is absolutely pristine and perfect for sunbathing, beachcombing, and relaxing. It's also a great place to snorkel, with frequent sightings of barracuda and other large fish. There's an old rusted anchor, about 5 feet long, half buried in the sand. Jorge, the on-site manager, says it's from a 1950s-era Cuban shrimp boat. A day-fishing package for two anglers, which includes eight hours of guided fishing, tackle, water, sodas, beer, sandwiches, snacks, and round-trip transportation from hotels in the Riviera Maya, is $450. Pickup is at 6–6:30 AM, with a return at 7 PM. Half- and full-week fishing/lodging packages are also available.

Pesca Maya has cabins right on the beach.

RANCHO SOL CARIBE
Km 48 on the Punta Allen road, 5 miles north of Punta Allen

There are only four rooms available at this secluded and well-kept inn. Each has a private bathroom, hot-water shower, terrace with hammock, and 24-hour electricity. Given the simple nature of accommodations in this region, this inn's special touches give it a casually elegant feeling and a touch of romance not necessarily found at the average fishing lodge. Each evening, the staff lights dozens of candles around the property and the bartenders are always at the ready to mix drinks, give tips about the area, and make everyone feel at home. Rates: $135 per person, double occupancy; includes all meals and drinks (including alcohol). For $350 per day, the rate includes a full day of fishing (deep sea or flats). Room-only rates are available for just $95 per night per room.

ACTIVITIES & TOURS

CESIAK CENTRO ECOLOGICO
984-871-2499
www.cesiak.org

Housed at the Cesiak eco-lodge camp in Boca Paila (see Lodging), this tour operator offers two primary trips. The all-day Sian Ka'an tour ($68 per person) includes a boat trip through the biosphere, a visit to Mayan ruins, a float down a freshwater river, a glimpse of sea turtles, bird-watching, snacks, and refreshments. The sunset bird-watching tour ($60 per person) includes a boat trip through the biosphere, with swimming, snorkeling, bird-watching, and a stop at a Mayan ruin. Each tour includes round-trip transportation from Playa del Carmen.

FRIENDS OF SIAN KA'AN TOUR
998-884-9583

This tour includes a bilingual guide, a driving tour through the reserve, a boat trip through the mangroves, and a visit to a freshwater spring. It departs daily at 9:30 AM from Ana y José in Tulum's northern hotel zone (see Lodging) and returns at 3 PM. The tour costs $50, including drinks and snacks.

SIAN KA'AN ECOTOURISMO
984-871-2363
siankaan_tours@hotmail.com
Tulum Avenue between Beta and Osiris Streets, Tulum pueblo

This tour company's main offering is a biosphere tour, which includes a tropical forest walk, Mayan ruin visit, boat tour through the wetlands, bird-watching, and cenote swimming. The trip includes entrance fees, equipment, transportation from Riviera Maya hotels, and a boxed lunch. The company also offers kayak tours, fishing trips, and other expeditions.

VEA EXCURSIONS
984-875-5040 or 1-866-646-6202 (U.S.)
www.jeep-safari.com

If you have only one day to visit Sian Ka'an but want to fit in as much as possible, try the VEA Jeep Safari. It includes a Jeep ride to the biosphere entrance, a boat tour to see dolphins, swimming, snorkeling, beachside lobster paella lunch, bird-watching, beachcombing, and a chance to see crocodiles. The cost is $95 per person. The company also offers an all-terrain vehicle tour through the jungle roads of Tulum and the surrounding area. It includes a dip in a freshwater lagoon and a nature tour with tamed jungle animals. The trip lasts four hours and costs $62 per person sharing a bike or $77 for a solo rider.

THE MAYAN COAST—SOUTH OF THE RIVIERA MAYA

Laguna Bacalar
About 2¼ hours south of Playa del Carmen and 90 miles from Felipe Carillo Puerto is Laguna Bacalar, a freshwater lake just east of Highway 307 that feeds into Chetumal Bay. With crystal-clear water and gleaming white sands, it is a rare jewel in the jungle. The lake has a dramatic setting and varying depths, which causes the colors to change from spot to spot—hence its nickname, the "Lake of Seven Colors." It is a prime spot for snorkeling, bird-watching, swimming, and photography.

LODGING

HOTEL LAGUNA BACALAR
983-834-2206
www.bacalarmosaico.com
North of Chetumal 25 miles, just off Highway 307

A full-service hotel with air-conditioning, suites, and incomparable views of the laguna, Hotel Laguna Bacalar is a great spot if you want to spend a couple of days exploring the area. There is a terrace restaurant overlooking the lagoon and a sundeck with direct access to the laguna itself. Rates: $$.

Mahahual

When you arrive in Mahahual you'll immediately notice a laid-back atmosphere, but with a sense that things could be changing. More villas and small inns are being built all the time, and the town is developing a rustic yet upscale tone, similar to the early days of Playa del Carmen. There are a few sandy streets and several open-air restaurants, and the hotels and private homes are stretched out along the beach.

The shallow reefs of the Chinchorro Banks are known for being the healthiest in the area, with huge sea fans, sponges, anemones, sea cucumbers, arrow crabs, and seahorses. There are also hundreds of species of fish (including large barracuda), sea turtles, and even dolphins, which sometimes follow the dive boats and play in the wake.

In 2000 Mahahual completed construction of a cruise ship terminal, and each month there seem to be more arrivals, which is steadily changing the face of the town. The cruise dock is only 5 blocks from the town center, and the street is becoming lined with new restaurants, bars, and souvenir shops. When the boats are in town, the beach is full of day-trippers snorkeling, swimming, riding WaveRunners, and enjoying the day. The rest of the time the village is more mellow, with locals talking in the storefronts, tourists lingering in the beachside restaurants, and only a few people relaxing on the beach.

The "real" Mexico is still easy to find. Courtesy of Philip Gammon

GETTING THERE

To get to Mahahual by car from anywhere along the Riviera Maya, take Highway 307 south toward Chetumal. Fill up with gas when you go through the town of Carillo Puerto, as there are not many stations in this area. Once you pass the village of Limones (about 2½ hours south of Playa), you will go about 2 more miles, and then you should see a sign for Mahahual and the Cafetal exit. Turn left and start heading east to the beach. From this point, Mahahual is still about an hour away. About halfway down this road, you'll arrive at a military

Way South: The Explorean Kohunlich

The Explorean is a remote all-inclusive jungle retreat for guests truly looking to get away and connect with nature. The low-rise hotel utilizes stone, thatched roofs and native materials to blend with the jungle surroundings. It is located adjacent to the Kohunlich Mayan ruins, 30 miles from the Chetumal International Airport and approximately 200 miles from the Cancún International Airport. The emphasis is on adventurous activities, with one excursion per day included in the rate. Recreational options include jungle treks, hiking, tours of Mayan ruins, kayaking at a nearby lagoon, cycling, rappelling, and bird watching.

Meals are taken at the hotel restaurant, La Palapa, with a thatched-roof dining room and an open terrace, perched above the swimming pool and the jungle canopy. Meals are served à la carte from a limited menu, with both Mayan and international cuisine available at each meal. Drinks and three meals per day are also included in the rate. A self-service bar is set up poolside, with mixed drinks and beer on ice.

The hotel Jacuzzi and pool are popular resting spots in the afternoons, when guests congregate to talk about the day's adventures. For even more relaxation, the small Kohunlich Spa offers massages, body treatments, and a complimentary steam room. An al fresco living room is set up near the pool, where guests can discuss the day's activities with the on-staff tour guides.

The hotel has 40 guest rooms, featuring a modern take on jungle chic, with Mayan artifacts, handcrafted furnishings, and furnished terraces with sofas and hammocks where guests can sit and enjoy

checkpoint, so don't be alarmed if you see men in uniform carrying machine guns. They may search your car for drugs, but they are courteous and will not cause any problems—as long as you don't. The road is a fairly straight shot through the jungle, finally arriving at the small beach town of Mahahual. Most hotels, restaurants, dive shops, and other attractions are close to the area where the main road meets the beach.

To get to Mahahual by bus, from the Cancún bus station take a bus to Limones, either a direct or a bus to Chetumal that stops there. Be sure to ask, as not all buses to Chetumal stop in Limones. From there transfer to a Mahahual bus, which leaves every hour or so from Limones.

Lodging

BALAMKU INN
983-838-0083
www.balamku.com
Three miles south of the Mahahual town square

To get to Balamku, take the main beach road south of town for about five minutes, and the hotel will be on your left. It's surrounded by trees and flowering plants, making it a great escape for nature lovers and others who want to get away from the hustle and bustle for a few days. The beach is perfect for tanning and relaxing. The large rooms feature colorful designs, dark wood furniture, hot-water showers, and ceiling fans, and Internet access is available. Guests have access to several sea kayaks. Rates: $ to $$; breakfast and use of sea kayaks included.

FORTY CANNONS HOTEL
www.los40canones.com
On the beach in the center of Mahahual

Right in the center of town, this 10-room hotel may seem bustling for the area, but if you compare it to the more touristy destinations up the coast, it is still ultrarelaxed. All rooms have ceiling fans, 24-hour electricity, and hot-water showers. The other main attraction is the hotel restaurant,

the natural landscape. Rooms don't have TVs or telephones, but they do have air-conditioning, safes, and complimentary turn-down service. There are also two master suites with their own pools, terraces, and gardens.

The hotel is popular with sophisticated and adventurous adults, who generally stay for a few days while touring the local attractions, Mayan ruins, and eco-friendly tours. It has a gift shop, boutique, and tour desk. There is no nightlife in the area and most guests retire fairly early, following an evening of star-gazing and listening to the nighttime fauna. Guests seeking a more bustling atmosphere but who still want to enjoy nature tours may consider staying in or near Playa del Carmen and taking day trips, rather than staying so far from town. Properties with similar atmosphere include the Azulik and Zahra hotels in Tulum.

Guests are urged to use caution when walking along the dark paths at night, as jungle critters are common. Rates start at $225 per night in a standard room and $400 in a suite.

More information:

KM 5.65 Ctra Chetumal Escarcega, Ruinas Kohunlich

Othon P. Blanco

Quintana Roo, Mexico 77981

983-201-8350

www.explorean.com

which fronts the beach and serves pasta, seafood, and other international dishes. Rates: $ to $$ (higher prices are for suites with air-conditioning).

KAILUUMCITO

1-800-538-6802 (U.S.)

www.mexicoholiday.com/destinations/kailuumcito.html

Rìo Indio

From the military checkpoint on the main road into Mahahual, go east a couple of minutes until you see a sign for Tampalam. Turn left and travel for 6 miles. Turn left again at the sign for Rio Indio, and follow that road along the beach for 2 more miles. The last stretch is completely unpaved, but just when you feel like you can't go any farther, you'll arrive at the hotel. There are 10 canvas tents set up on wooden platforms and surrounded by palm trees and a deserted beach, which leads to a shallow and very calm cove. Even though the accommodations are not luxurious, the service is very personal, and the staff does a great job of making sure you feel cared for. Meals are set up on an open-air deck, and the food is great. Rates: $$ to $$$.

MAYAN BEACH GARDEN

El Placer, 15 miles north of Mahahual

On a remote beach up the coast from Mahahual center, this solar-powered inn offers suites and beach cabañas that feature ceiling fans and direct beach access. There are also kayaks available for guest use and a lounge area. An on-site restaurant offers three meals per day, and there's excellent beachcombing, snorkeling, and relaxing to be had at the hotel beach. Rates: $$ to $$$, including full breakfast. Ask about the suite with a king bed and two singles, plus a dining room and private *palapa* terrace.

4

Activities

These are the primary attractions in the Riviera Maya, and they are no more than an hour away from any hotel in the area. Nearly every hotel tour desk can sell you tickets that include round-trip transportation. They're also easy to get to by rental car or even bus, so they make for good self-guided outings as well. Note: Secondary and local attractions are discussed in other chapters in this book, based on the area where they're located.

Nature Parks, Amusement Parks & Zoos

✪ AKTUN CHEN
998-877-8550
www.aktunchen.com
Highway 307, km 107, between Akumal and Xel-Ha

Aktun Chen, whose name means "underground river cave" in Mayan, is a 1,000-acre nature park with a large cave and jungle tour. The main cave (600 yards long) is said to have been a natural bunker for the native Mayans, who sought its protection during serious storms. An hour-long guided walk through the park reveals badgers, iguanas, spider monkeys, tropical birds, and wild turkeys. There is also a motorized ATV tour, if you'd rather ride than walk. Along the way, you'll see many tropical flowers, coconut palms, and a gum tree called the *chicozapote*. The cave itself has amazing formations of stalactites and stalagmites, and an amazing underground cenote that is more than 35 feet deep. Though the cave winds its way several hundred yards through the ground, there are frequent openings and areas where fresh air and the sun shine through, so it's not as claustrophobic as it may sound. A restaurant at the cave exit serves fresh fruit drinks, traditional Mayan and Mexican dishes, and cold drinks. Open 9–5 daily. Adults $19, children $9.

CROCOCUN CROCODILE FARM & ZOO
998-850-3719
Highway 307, km 323, near Puerto Morelos.

If you're more into fauna than flora, you'll enjoy the Crococun zoo. Formed in 1985 as a commercial croc farm where the animals were raised for their skins and skulls, it has been transformed into a preserve, where visitors' admission fees go toward rescuing the crocs rather than killing them. The park now has dozens of other animals, including white-tailed deer, spider monkeys, snakes, spiders, and birds. Except for the zoo's 300

At Crococun you can see crocodiles, iguanas, birds, and more.

crocodiles, many of the animals are tame enough to pet, which is a real kick for the kids. There is a souvenir shop with T-shirts, maps, and videos, as well as a small snack bar. Open 9–5:30 Monday–Saturday. Adults $16, kids $10; admission includes a one-hour guided tour through the park. Tours leave continually.

KANTUN CHI

984-873-0021
www.kantunchi.com
Highway 307, km 266.5; 14 miles south of Playa, 1 mile south of Puerto Aventuras

The entrance to Kantun Chi ecology and adventure park is marked by a small replica Mayan temple, across from the Barcelo Maya Hotel. The park, whose name means "yellow stone mouth" in Mayan, has nature trails, swimming holes, caves, and an animal sanctuary. There are hundreds of plant species, including many rare mushrooms. For fauna there are raccoons, spider monkeys, and white-tailed deer, along with several endangered local species, which the park is helping to bring back.

There are four cenotes large enough for swimming and snorkeling, including one called Uchil Ha, or "ancient water," which is said to have been an ancient Mayan religious site. Visitors can go horseback riding, mountain biking, or hiking. A *palapa* restaurant serves Mayan and Mexican food. Open 9–dusk daily. Entry is $35 for adults and $30 for kids, including the grotto tour, snorkeling gear, guide, and cenote hike. Fees are $20 for adults and $10 for children without the grotto tour, gear, or guide.

PARQUE NIZUC

998-881-3000
www.parquenizuc.com
Boulevard Kukulcán, km 25, Cancún

Just across the highway from the Cancún airport, as you head to the Cancún hotel zone, you'll come across the 18-acre Parque Nizuc water park. You can't tell from the road, but it's actually on a huge stretch of perfect white-sand beach. There are wave pools, water slides, a lazy river, tube rides, and many other freshwater attractions. There are also three bars and a large restaurant serving burgers, pizza, nachos, sandwiches, and ice cream. Dolphin-swim programs are offered through Atlantida, which is located at the back end of the park. Open daily, 10–6 May–October and 10–5:30 November–April. Entry is $29; the dolphin program costs extra.

TRES RIOS

1-800-224-4231 (U.S)
www.tres-rios.com
Highway 307, km 300, 7 miles north of Playa del Carmen

A 326-acre private activity and nature park, Tres Rios, which underwent a major renovation in 2005 and is now open only to guests of the adjacent Tres Rios Resorts. There are mountain bikes for cruising through the jungle, canoe trips, jungle rivers, sea kayaks, snorkeling beaches, freshwater swimming holes, and beach hammocks. Hiking tours and horseback expeditions are offered that take participants through the dense jungle to see cenotes, tropical flora, wild animals, and deserted beaches; guided nature walks with a biologist and canopy tours via hanging bridges are also offered. If you're interested in scuba diving, you can take a resort course that includes an hour of instruction and then an actual open-water dive, with an instructor at your side. The areas of the park are left as untouched as possible, giving visitors the feeling that they are seeing the land much as the Mayans did hundreds of years ago. An on-site restaurant serves Mexican lunches and snacks, and lockers are available for rent. Open 9–6 daily. Entry is $22 for adults and includes biking, canoeing, and kayaking.

XAMAN HA AVIARY

984-873-0330
www.ariarioxamanha.com
Paseo Xaman Ha, behind Plaza Playacar, Playacar

Popular with families and other nature buffs, this privately run aviary exhibits more than 50 species of tropical birds, including flamingos, toucans, macaws, and other favorites native to the region. Some are caged, while others roam free in their natural habitat. There are also lots of iguanas, butterflies, turtles, brown squirrels, and freshwater fish. Entry is $15, with one child free with each paying adult. Open 9 AM–5 PM daily.

✪ XCARET

www.xcaret.com
Highway 307, km 287, 3 miles south of Playa del Carmen

Once a sacred Mayan site, the Xcaret Mayan-themed recreational park is far and away the

Caring for the Dolphins at Xcaret

The biologists of Xcaret and area veterinarians meet all the needs of the park's dolphins. They monitor their health, weight, and food, and in some facilities they conduct research on their behavior. At Xcaret dolphins are treated with care and respect, and their well-being is always the main priority. In fact, biologists claim that the life expectancy of a dolphin, which is about 40 years, increases when it is placed in captivity or semicaptivity (in extensive areas of its natural habitat). Dolphins have actually been born in captivity at Xcaret, and the way in which baby dolphins are brought into this world is quite an experience. They come out of their mother's womb tail first so as not to drown, and they emerge like torpedoes to the surface as they take in their first breath. Their first year is a delicate time, because dolphins are born without antibodies; however, their mothers feed them for one to two years, providing them with these defenses.

Qualified dolphin trainers, who are constantly learning new skills, spend long hours with the dolphins. At this time, the magic goes well beyond expectations: The relationship between trainers and dolphins is as close as that found in a family, where every single approach of the dolphin trainer receives an answer from the dolphin. A jump that soars more than 2 yards up in the air, a tail dance, a flipper greeting, a friendly sound, and underwater tricks are some of the ways in which dolphins show their fondness and approval. Due to their high cognitive ability, these animals understand every instruction their trainers give them. Dolphins have the ability to associate, and this allows them to translate signs and develop a series of perfectly synchronized movements. With a so-called target pole, which functions as an extension of their trainer's hand, dolphins learn to identify instructions until they develop a language that allows them to establish a sophisticated way to communicate with their trainer.

Ancient Mayans saw the dolphin as a sacred animal and a source of inspiration for the creation of myths and legends. Today, dolphins contribute to aquatic therapies and humanities disciplines, and experience has shown that all they lack is the ability to talk.

top attraction in the area. There are ads for it everywhere—on nearly every city bus in Cancún, at every hotel tour desk, on placards at the airport, in every tourist publication, in the newspaper, and on dozens of billboards along Highway 307. True to its roots, it has several native ruins on-site, and each evening native dancers put on an incredible show of Mayan dances and rituals. There is an interactive museum, miniature models of many Mayan sites, and a petting zoo.

Visitors can go tubing or snorkeling through an underground river, watch horsemanship exhibitions, see native fish in a saltwater aquarium, watch butterflies in their natural habitat, swim with dolphins, and even visit a

Hard-hat diving at Xcaret

Xcaret eco-adventure park Courtesy of Riviera Maya Tourism Authority

re-creation of a native Mayan village. Near the village, an ancient ball court is set up where games of *pok-ta-pok* are played, with rules similar to those that were used more than a thousand years ago. In the game, players try to bounce the ball through an overhead hoop without using their hands or feet. It is said that in ancient times the losers were sacrificed to the gods. *Xcaret* means "inlet" in Mayan, and the park is right on the beach, so snorkeling, scuba diving, swimming, and sunbathing are popular as well.

At dusk, the wooden Mayan drums called *tunkules* start to play, signifying the start of the nightly show, complete with fire dancers, native costumes, and regional music. The Mayans originally called this area *P'ole*, which means "merchandise," since it was a popular trading village. Today visitors can shop for Mexican blankets, leather goods, glassware, and other souvenirs. Tour buses from Cancún come in hourly, so it's best to arrive early to experience the park before it gets too crowded. This trip is offered by nearly every tour operator in the area, so if you can't get there on your own, that may be a good option. Open daily, 8:30 AM–9 PM in winter and 8:30 AM–10 PM in summer. Basic admission is $59 for adults and $29.50 for kids ages 5–12. Numerous other pricing packages are available.

Sights and Activities Included in Basic Admission to Xcaret		
Water activities:	Crocodile exhibit	Mayan village
Beach, snorkeling cove, tidal pools	Deer island	Museum of Culture and Archaeology
Coral reef aquarium	Ecology tour	Observation tower
Manatee lagoon	Jungle walk	San Francisco of Assisi chapel
Mayan river tube ride	Monkey island	Spectacular Nights folklore festival (at dark on Sundays)
Paradise river tube ride	Mushroom farm	
Sea turtle farm	Orchid greenhouse	
Underground river tube ride	Puma and jaguar island	**Equipment and facilities use:**
Flora and fauna:	Wild bird aviary	Beach chairs and umbrellas
Beekeeping exhibit	**Shows and cultural experiences:**	Hammocks
Butterfly pavilion	Archaeology sites	Inner tubes
	Flying Men of Papantla	Life vests
	Horseback-riding show	Lock bag
	Live theater performances	

Xel-Ha   Courtesy of Riviera Maya Tourism Authority

✪ XEL-HA

998-883-3143
www.xel-ha.com
Highway 307, km 245, 8 miles from Tulum

This nature park was once a Mayan seaport, and later it became a popular snorkeling cove, frequented by the adventurous few who cruised the coast looking for new spots. Today it is one of the largest attractions in the Riviera Maya. Xel-ha, whose name means "where the waters are born," features underground rivers where fresh and salt water come together, an animal nursery, cliff jumping, a tubing area, a dolphin discovery center, massage huts, ocean snorkeling, mountain bike trails, and a hiking area. An all-inclusive package is available, which includes unlimited food and drinks, plus most activities (no dolphins or massages). The park is open 9–6 daily; dolphin swim is 9–3. Get there early for the best experience. Adults $29 weekdays/$22 weekends, children 5–12 $15 weekdays/$11 weekends. All-inclusive: adults $56, children $28. Other activities include Snuba (surface-fed air snorkeling) and SeaTrek (helmet diving) for $45 each. The dolphin discovery program costs $115, which includes a one-hour swim.

✪ YAAX-CHE JARDÍN BOTÁNICO (BOTANICAL GARDEN)
Highway 307, km 37, just south of Puerto Morelos

A fun stop-off between Cancún and Playa del Carmen is the 150-acre Jardín Botánico. Set up like a museum, with everything clearly marked and explained, this nature preserve has hundreds of species of plants, trees, and flowers. A long path snakes its way through the jungle, with everything growing in a natural setting. There is a hilltop overlook where you

Do You Have Margarita Mind?

Margarita Mind is a dangerous disease and it afflicts American, Canadian, and European real estate buyers equally and without mercy. It happens when you arrive in Mexico, checkbook in hand, with visions of a life hanging in a hammock on a white sand beach in front of your little dream cottage.

When you start saying things like: "I met this guy in a bar; he has a cute house he wants to show me." Or: "My friends say there are ways around the Mexican real estate laws," you know that you've been afflicted.

There's an infamous story of a financially comfortable American who hired an English-speaking developer to build his dream home on the beach with its own desalination plant, satellite Internet systems and a to-die-for view. One small problem—the builder put the house on the wrong lot! The neighbor was very appreciative of the American for so beautifully improving his property. A proper survey using GPS points would have saved the day.

Real estate laws in Mexico are not very different from in the U.S., Canada, or Europe. However, real estate agents in Mexico are not licensed, and while the vast majority are honest ethical people, the few predators are the ones you need to be wary of.

Mexico wants and actively seeks the foreign investment dollar (or Euro) and the government has put practices and systems in place to help and protect the foreign real estate buyer. In the "restricted Zones of Mexico," 100 miles from a border or 50 miles from a coast, foreign buyers obtain their properties in a "*fideicomiso*," which closely resembles a living trust and gives the foreigner peace of mind, clean title, and the right to sell, bequeath, mortgage, and improve the property. And it has a 50-year life that can be renewed ad infinitum in 50-year chunks.

Closing costs and fees are significantly higher in Mexico than in the U.S. and Canada, lower than in France though. Many buyers, taking the advice of uninformed friends or misguided agents, make foolish decisions in order to save a few thousand dollars up front.

With the advent of American style long-term mortgages and the safety requirements built into the mortgage industry, it is safe and sensible for foreigners to use a mortgage. Not only are foreigners able to obtain significant financing needs for their Mexican dream home, but securing a mortgage, using a well-reputable cross-border mortgage lender, ensures that your close is legal and done properly.

Content provided by ConfiCasa Mortgage International, a pioneering provider of cross-border financing of Mexican properties for Americans and Canadian dreamers. The U.S.-based company has offices in Houston and Chicago and maintains close partnerships in Mexico resort areas. For more information, contact 281-598-7060 or www.conficasamortgageinternational.com.

can see the jungle canopy and the ocean beyond, and a small Mayan ruin called *el altar* that dates from the 1400s. There is also a mock-up of an ancient Mayan homestead, as well as a chicle camp, where farmers would work to process the rubber gum from the chicle tree.

Also worth seeing is a native tree called the ceiba, which the Mayans called *yaax chen*. For the natives, this tree was a spiritual icon and was said to grow from the core of the earth, connecting the three levels of the universe. Many spider monkeys and other animals make their home in the gardens and can often be spotted by visitors. Open 9–5 Monday–Saturday. Admission is $5.

CENOTES

Cenotes are relatively small and the water does not circulate, so it is important that all swimmers and divers rinse off any mosquito repellent or sunscreen before entering the water.

CAMINO DE CENOTES

Across from the main entrance to Puerto Morelos, a gravel road heads inland, under a tall archway etched with CAMINO DE CENOTES at the top, at approximately km 321 of Highway 307. This road is a fairly straight shot for 25 miles, passing through the blue-collar town of Central Vallarta, past several cenotes, and on into the interior of Quintana Roo. There are dozens of cenotes in the area, though most of them are still unaccessible. The largest is Selvatica, which has established an ecopark complete with bike rentals, zip lines, and canopy tours. On the way to Selvatica, the road passes other cenotes in various stages of tour-readiness. Check for signs as you travel the road, and you could be the first to visit one of the newly opened ones. A few of the most established ones are:

Boca del Puma, Ruta de Cenotes, km 14. A small sign marks the turnoff to this medium-size cenote, which has a camping area and room for snorkeling and swimming. Admission is $7; slightly more for overnight stays.

Cenote Verde Lucero, Ruta de Cenotes, km 16, has several different cenote openings, with undergound caverns connecting them. There's not much to see for snorkelers, but trained divers can traverse underground to the connected lagoons. The owner is happy to introduce you to his dogs and show you around. There are some nice birds, a big nopal cactus

Cenote diving: It's like being in outer space. Courtesy of Riviera Maya Tourism Authority

A Mayan Legend

Following the great flood, the world was dark and full of chaos. Nothing moved and nothing existed. The sea and the sky were empty. On the second day, the gods became tired of dancing over cold waters, so they created a thin layer of solid land where they could rest while they finished their work. "Let there be land," they said, and a beautiful layer of earth rose from the ocean. On the third day, the gods called upon Chaac, the god of rain, who poured rich water into the cracks of the land, giving life to the plants, flowers, and trees. As the rain continued on the fourth day, water filled all the cracks and basins, producing amazing lagoons and cenotes. On the fifth day, Kukulcán, the god of wind, flapped his wings, blowing warm breezes over the land, giving all living things a gentle dance. On the sixth day, Kukulcán turned his winds toward the sea, creating waves and forming Ixchel, the goddess of the moon and womanhood. Ixchel rose to heaven and gave birth to Itzámna, the lord of the skies, who created the day and the night and then painted the night with thousands of stars. "Let the trees have their own guardians," the gods ordered on the eighth day, and birds were created in astonishing varieties, including Mo, the scarlet macaw, who became the guardian angel of the skies. On the ninth day, Hunab-Ku buried a white knife in the land, and from it flowed all sorts of animals, including reptiles, jaguars, monkeys, and Huh, the iguana, who was the guardian of the land. Like a falling star, Ixchel descended from the night sky on the tenth day. She dove naked into a cenote, and the waters came alive with millions of fish, of all colors and sizes. The gods then picked the parrot fish, or Kay-Op, as the guardian of the waters. The gods rested on the eleventh day, but they were feeling cold, so they asked the sun god to help them. He came from the skies with his magic fire and heated the waters of the sea, the lagoons, and the cenotes, thus creating a warm and gentle climate. On the twelfth day the gods created humans, the most perfect of living creatures. With their intelligence, speech, sight, smell, taste, hearing, and touch, they were the ones gifted with the right to enjoy all the magic the gods had made for them. The gods danced and sang, full of joy for what they had created, and then they returned to the heavens. Pleased with what they saw and the world they had created, they decided to name it Xel-Ha, or the place where the waters are born.

plant, and other interesting sites. The cenote is about a quarter mile from the entrance. You can park and walk or, if you want to brave it, drive your car right up to the edge. Admission is $7.

Selvatica, (998-847-4581, www.selvatica.com.mx), Ruta de Cenotes, km 19, runs adventure tours from hotels in Playa del Carmen and the Riviera Maya. The trip includes a visit to a 247-acre preserve, with bike riding, zip-lining, canopy tours, and lunch. Impromptu visits can also be accommodated. The park boasts a zip-line circuit that has 24 platforms and is more than 2 miles long, making it the longest circuit in North America. There is also a 160-foot-wide cenote, perfect for cooling off and swimming. Adults $59, children $42, including transportation; adults $42, children $29, entry only. Admission includes the zip-line canopy tour, biking, cenote swimming, lunch, drinks, and lockers. This trip was named, "one of the 35 great adventures of the world" by *Travel & Leisure* magazine. Highly recommended.

Siete Bocas, Ruta de Cenotes, km 13. There isn't yet a road connecting the cenote to the main road, so visitors have to walk 25 minutes down a jungle path to reach it. As the name suggests, there are seven different lagoons, though only a couple of them are large enough for swimming. Admission is $7.

Cenote water is as clean as air. Courtesy of Ybran Aragon

Other Cenotes around the Riviera Maya

Aktún-Ha—The Carwash, just south of Akumal, off Highway 307. One of the better known cenotes in the region, frequented by scuba-diving groups from the United States and beyond, the Carwash is only 50 feet deep, but the caverns are wide and long (nearly 2 miles long), making it very popular for certified cave divers. During the summer the surface is covered with algae, but in the cooler months snorkeling is possible.

Cenote Azul, Highway 307, km 266. www.cenoteazultravel.com. This cenote, half the size of a basketball court, is on a small ranch that borders the highway, and the family who owns it operates it as a private park. Look for the hand-painted sign along the road and slow down fast to avoid slipping on the gravel entryway. The lagoon is a short walk from the parking area and has a rope swing and 10-foot-high cliff, perfect for jumping into the water. You can climb the face of the cliff or take the less treacherous path to the left, which leads up the hill to the jump-off point. You can bring a cooler, but remember to leave the sunscreen behind. The water is cool and clear, and it's only about 10 feet deep, so it's good for snorkeling but not diving. An adjacent cenote, El Jardín del Eden, offers a similar experience and is a frequent stop for tour groups.

Cenote Dos Ojos, Highway 307, km 242. Part of an immense nature preserve and ranchers' cooperative, this ecopark offers several cenotes for exploring, snorkeling, and scuba diving. It was first discovered in 1985 by dive maven Mike Madden and has been extensively explored and mapped. Most of the cenotes connect through underground caverns, which require advanced cave-diving certification to experience. If you have your own gear and are comfortable poking around on your own, you can enter for $8 per person. A snorkeling tour, complete with equipment and guide, costs $40, and scuba diving costs $65 for one tank or $95 for two tanks. Dive gear can be rented for $8. These cenotes are popular spots to spot a local bird known as the toh, which has two long tail feathers and sits on exposed rocks deep in the cenote, where the air is dark and cool, wagging its tail back and forth. Every minute or so it will let out a loud cry, almost like a howler monkey. Locals tell tales of people being lost in the jungle listening for the call of the toh, which they knew would help lead them to water. There are also bats found in some of the caves. An on-site photographer has some incredible pictures of the cenotes and tunnels and offers photography services during snorkel and dive trips. The photos are delivered on CD, along with some stock images of the area, plus general information on cenotes ($35).

Cenote Ponderosa, Highway 307, 3 miles south of Puerto Aventuras. This cenote and cavern dive is made up of two separate cenotes, connected through an underground channel. The depth ranges from 25 to 55 feet, and the visibility is more than 300 feet. The water is a mix of fresh and salt water and hovers around 77 to 79 degrees. The cenotes have mostly small fish, but they're very brightly colored. The wide caverns are easy to maneuver and swim around, which helps prevent any feelings of claustrophobia. The main feature is an underground air dome called the Chapel, where divers can submerge and breathe natural air, even though they are under the water level. Most dive shops in the region can take divers on expeditions through the cenote. The price is $50 per person per dive.

Chaak Tun Ts'ono'ot, Avenue Juárez at 120th Avenue, Playa del Carmen. From downtown Playa, take Avenue Juárez across Highway 307 and keep going for about 5 miles. You'll pass several housing communities and get a firsthand look at how the local workers live. This cenote, whose name translates from Mayan as "rain rock cenote," has multiple caverns and a stunning cave formation. It's a good spot for snorkeling and just lounging in the water while you gaze in awe at the geology. Admission is $5. Open 9–5.

Grand Cenote. Take Highway 307 to the main intersection in Tulum and turn right, away from the coast, on the road to Cobá. Just 2 miles down that road, you'll see the signs for Grand Cenote (or Gran Cenote) on your right. You'll pay an $8-per-person fee and then hike about 100 feet through the jungle to the palm-ringed cenote. Popular with snorkelers and divers, the Grand Cenote features amazing underwater stalactites, stalagmites, and other limestone formations. You can swim a ring around the middle island sundeck area. The water is cool (77 degrees) and clear (400 feet of visibility), with a maximum depth of less than 25 feet. It makes for a great stop-off after a trip to the beach or a long drive back to Playa from Cobá. There are benches and plenty of room for sunbathing. Open until 4 PM daily.

✪ HIDDEN WORLDS CENOTES

984-877-8535
www.hiddenworlds.com
Highway 307, 30 miles south of Playa, 2 miles south of Xel-Ha

This site covers nearly 24,700 acres of land, and the cave system runs for 42 miles, most of it underground. It was discovered in 1986, and the park has been in business since 1994. It was the site of the filming of the IMAX film *Journey into Amazing Caves* and operates as a private scuba and snorkeling park, affording visitors an incredible underwater experience that feels more like being in space than being underwater. Visitors choose from several

Frolic with the dolphins at Dolphin Discovery.

different cenotes and caves, depending on their experience, the amount of time they have available, and whether they want to scuba or snorkel.

The lobby area is located just off the highway, and from there participants are driven on the park's rugged and odd-looking homemade four-wheel-drive truck. The first site is called *Dos Ojos* (Two Eyes), and it's essentially two separate cenotes connected by a channel. This is the main site where most of the IMAX footage was shot, and it is the third largest underwater cave in the world. Basic dive certification is required, and there is natural light the whole way, which adds a nice feeling of security. The water stays a constant 75 degrees, the depth ranges from 25 to 150 feet, and there is more than 1,500 feet of navigable space. Small groups of divers follow the dive guide as the group enters one cenote and swims through the channel and then on to the enormous chamber of the other cenote before surfacing 45 minutes later. The water is unimaginably clear, and if not for the air bubbles, it really would seem like outer space, especially given the otherworldly scenery, unlike anything you would ever see on the land.

The next dive, the *Caverna de los Murcielagos* (the Bat Cave), has been known to bring divers to tears with its awesome beauty. The cave is as dramatic as it is exquisite, with a sublime combination of steep drop-offs, Disney-worthy stalactites, and elaborate features that have taken millions of years to develop. There are also hundreds of brightly colored tropical fish, elusive cave shrimp, and other critters. The depth is only 35 feet, making it an especially safe dive that even scuba newcomers will enjoy. Since the water is so clear and the aboveground portions of the cave are as amazing as the underwater ones, snorkelers can easily appreciate the cave's grandeur.

The closest cavern to the reception area is called Hilario's Well. Given its relatively small size and shallow depth, this cenote is the best one for snorkelers. During a one-hour guided tour, snorkelers encounter stalagmites, stalactites, and other formations that are truly awe-inspiring. If you have enough time and you're up for a real Mayan-style adventure, sign up for the *Tak Be Ha* (Cave of Hidden Waters) jungle expedition. On this half-day outing, participants travel deep into the Mayan jungle in the four-wheel-drive Jungle Mobile to see secret cenotes, nearly virgin caves, and an assortment of the area's plant and animal life, including tropical birds, orchids, and mosquitoes. Led by an expert and multilingual guide, the group will explore the area, learning about the history, geography, and ecology of the region. Next, it's on with the mask and fins and into the cenote to see for yourself the amazing gin-clear waters and incomprehensible cave formations.

Scuba tours depart at 9 AM, 11 AM, and 1 PM, and snorkeling trips depart at 9 AM, 11 AM, 1 PM, 2 PM, and 3 PM. Snorkeling tours are $25 for adults and $20 for kids (8–12 years) for Hilario's Well only, or $45 for a visit to three different cenotes. Diving is $50 for one tank or $90 for two tanks. All equipment is included for snorkelers, but divers need to either rent or bring their standard equipment, light, and wet suit. Rental is $15 for all gear. There is an on-site snack bar.

TAJ MAHAL
Highway 307, 3.5 miles south of Puerto Aventuras, just past Xpu-Ha

A group of four cenotes and caverns, the Taj Mahal averages around 50 feet in depth and the water is as clear as air, making it good for both snorkelers and scuba divers. Known for a cavern called the Beam of Light Room, this spot is less crowded than many of the others, making it a good place to linger over a picnic lunch. The connected Sugarbowl cenote has a large cavern open to the daylight, which creates mind-numbing rays of light under the water. Dive shops around the area lead trips to the cenote for $50 per person, per dive.

WATER SPORTS & ACTIVITIES

ATLANTIS SUBMARINES
987-872-5671
Carretera a Chankanaab, km 4, Cozumel

See the amazing reefs of Cozumel, including Santa Rosa and Palancar, while in the comfort of a chair. The air-conditioned sub goes up to 100 feet deep and passes by many of the same dive sites that scuba divers visit. Trips depart every hour from 9 to 2 Monday–Saturday. The fee is $40 per person.

DOLPHIN DISCOVERY
1-800-417-1736 (U.S.)
www.dolphindiscovery.com
Villa Pirata, Isla Mujeres (998-877-0207)
Avenue Juárez, downtown Cozumel (987-872-6605)
Puerto Aventuras, on the marina (998-849-4757)

At Dolphin Discovery, you can interact with live dolphins, and there are several packages

Learning to Kitesurf with Ikarus

Ikarus, named for Ik, the Mayan wind god, and Icarus, the Greek god who took to the sky, has successfully taught more than 700 people in the Riviera Maya, and they claim that the most important prequalification a student can have is experience flying a two-line stunt kite. That, they say, is even more important than having experience hang gliding, wakeboarding, snowboarding, windsurfing, or even aeronautical engineering.

The first 45 minutes are spent talking about weather patterns, safety, kite dynamics, and kite control. Next, there are hands-on lessons covering kite and line setup, launching and landing techniques, and safe flight patterns. After that, it's into the water, armed with a life jacket and radio helmet for a bit of body-dragging and self-rescue practice. The next step is to stand up and sail through the water. Most students get to this point after two days of three-hour classes.

Requirements for successful kitesurfers:

- Love of nature, comfort in the water, and desire to harness the power of the elements
- Time, patience, and respect for nature
- Equipment designed for stability, safety, and ease of use
- A qualified and experienced instructor
- A safe beach zone in the water
- WIND

from which you can choose. In the Dolphin Encounter, participants gather around a trainer, and the dolphins swim up to join the group. You are allowed to touch the dolphins while you learn about their habits and life in the wild. The dolphins perform stunts while you watch from close up. The experience lasts 45 minutes and costs $75.

For the Royal Swim package, the group receives an orientation from the trainer and then actually gets to enter the water and participate in the stunts, including being propelled through the water by a dolphin. The group is limited to eight people, so each person gets plenty of time with the dolphins. This activitiy lasts 45 minutes and costs $130.

In the Swim & Snorkel Adventure participants enter the water wearing masks and snorkels and swim around the dolphins. They will come up to you, and you can touch them and interact with them. You will even be able to do what they call a "belly ride," where you hold the dolphin by the fin, close to the body, and get pulled through the water. This activity lasts 45 minutes and costs $99.

For all the dolphin adventures, the minimum age is 8, and children ages 8 to 11 must be accompanied by a paying adult. No pregnant women or people with physical or mental limitations are permitted. Open 8–6 daily.

IKARUS KITEBOARDING

984-803-3490
www.ikaruskiteboarding.com
Quinta at 20th Street, Playa del Carmen
Quinta at 16th Street, Playa del Carmen

Ikarus, which is PASA and IKO certified, offers lessons, equipment rental, and sales of windsurfers, skateboards, and kiteboards, and it also has bathing suits, backpacks, T-shirts, and other beach games. Lessons are $55 an hour with two or three students, or $65 an hour for private sessions.

Kiteboarding with Ikarus Courtesy of Dr. Joseph Will and the Ikarus crew

Great snorkeling abounds. Courtesy of Riviera Maya Tourism Authority

SNORKELING TOURS
984-879-3427
www.tankha.com
Tank-Ha Dive Center, Quinta between 8th and 10th Streets, Playa del Carmen

This is a great trip for snorkelers of all levels who want to wet their fins in the Caribbean. The three-hour adventure departs on a 25-foot boat with a sun shade, which leaves daily at 9:30 AM and/or 1:30 PM, and includes all snorkeling and safety gear, refreshments, and dive master. Advance reservations are highly recommended and can be made by phone or by stopping in at the shop. The cost is $30 per person.

SUB SEE EXPLORER
988-848-8300
www.aquaworld.com.mx
Boulevard Kukulcán, km 15.2, Cancún

Take an underwater ride through the reefs and undersea channels off the coast of Cancún. You can see living coral reefs, sea sponges, sea fans, angelfish, parrot fish, grouper, rays, sea turtles, moray eels, and other marine life. The trip, which includes lunch and drinks, departs every hour 9–3 daily. The price is $45 per person.

✪ YALKU LAGOON
North end of Akumal Bay

One of the top snorkeling spots in the area, this ocean inlet has a mix of fresh and salt

Contemporary sculpture meets ancient lagoon at Yalku.   Courtesy of Riviera Maya Tourism Authority

water, which provides a habitat for a wide variety of fish, including triggerfish, wrasse, parrot fish, needlefish, and sometimes sea turtles. The shoreline has several metal sculptures imported from Mexico City, plus a few picnic tables and stairways to the water. The bottom and sides are more rocky than sandy, so walking can be treacherous, but a pair of water shoes and a careful eye make it worth the effort. Float along in the cool water, watch the colorful fish, and listen to the tropical birds singing from the trees.

To get there, head through the main Akumal entrance and then turn left, paralleling the beach after the artificial-grass tennis court. You'll cross an abandoned checkpoint, but there is no need to stop. Keep going for about 2 miles, turning to the left wherever it's unclear, and the road will end at the lagoon. The cove is ringed by private homes, unreachable beaches, and a private park. Unless you're friends with one of the local homeowners, you'll need to enter the private park. Adults $6, kids $3. The park is open 8–5:30 daily.

Equipment rental and snacks are available from a small hut near the water, though visitors are welcome to bring their own gear, including coolers, drinks, and picnic supplies. A table with *palapa* roof makes the perfect spot for lunch. Follow the lagoon shoreline to the left to find it. Visitors are encouraged to use only biodegradable sunscreen, which is available for sale at the park entrance.

HORSEBACK RIDING

RANCHO LOMA BONITA
988-887-1708
Highway 307, km 315,
Along Highway 307, at km 315

This huge private ranch houses more than 150 horses and is a popular spot for tour groups and cruise-ship passengers. Typical packages include round-trip transportation; soft drinks; a ranch-style buffet; two hours of horseback riding; and two hours of ATV riding. The horseback rides go through the ranch and to the beach, where you can even take the horse in the water for a swim in the waves. The price is $65 per person. Other events, such as donkey polo and soccer matches, can be custom designed.

RANCHO PUNTA VENADO
998-898-1331
www.puntavenado.com
Along Highway 307 in Paamul, 10 minutes south of Playa del Carmen

Once part of one of the largest and most prosperous commercial ranches along the Yucatán coast, Punta Venado is now open to visitors. Occupied by Mayan natives 1,500 years ago, the ranch still exhibits evidence of their existence through stone fences, small dwellings, and other minor structures. In the 1950s cattle baron Miguel Joaquin Ibarra purchased nearly 10,000 acres of land at this site and ran more than 600 head of cattle, in addition to farming coconuts, watermelons, limes, and cucumbers. In the 1970s blight struck the coconut crop, and Ibarra sold all but 2,000 acres. In 1988 Hurricane Gilbert hit, thinning the herd down to only 40 head. Some 10 years later the ranch opened as a tourist destination, turning the working cowboys into riding instructors and expedition guides. Better care was taken during Hurricane Emily in 2005, and the only losses were to the structure and were quickly repaired.

The ranch has 30 cenotes, caves, pristine beaches, and unexplored jungle, and three main expeditions are offered:

Horseback riding: This 90 minute tour takes riders on a guided trip through the jungle and to a long stretch of beach where you and your horse can roam around, loosely following the trip leader. You can even take the horse into the shallows for a quick swim in the ocean. Groups are limited to 20 people. Departs at 9 AM, noon, and 3 PM; includes soft drinks. The price is $35 per person.

Ride a horse along virgin beaches. Courtesy of Riviera Maya Tourism Authority

Horseback riding and snorkeling: For 2½ hours, you can enjoy all of the wonders of the ranch, both in and out of the water. The trip starts with a one-hour horseback ride through the jungle and down to the beach. Once there, you'll be given snorkeling gear and have 40 minutes to swim in the ocean and snorkel along the reef. After that, the group rides the horses back to the ranch. Groups are kept small, with a maximum of 20 people. Expeditions depart at 9 AM, noon, and 3 PM; they include snorkeling equipment, snacks, and soft drinks. The price is $50.

ATV adventure: If you're more into adrenaline than nature, you're probably best off choosing the ATV tour over the horses. On this expedition, participants ride four-wheel-drive ATVs and visit several of the park's diverse attractions. You will motor through the jungle, trounce through the woods, explore an underground cave with flashlights, hike over ancient rock formations, cruise around a cenote, ride along the beach, go sea kayaking, and snorkel around the reef. This trip is limited to 14 riders, either one or two per ATV. Departs at 9 AM, noon, and 3 PM; includes all required gear and equipment, plus snacks and soft drinks. The price is $40.

Parasailing gives riders a great view. Courtesy of Riviera Maya Tourism Authority

With any paid expedition, guests can stay at the ranch all day and enjoy the other facilities, including the beach club, hiking trails, and snack bar.

BIKE RIDING

Bike rental is available in all urban areas. Many all-inclusive resorts also provide complimentary bikes for guest use.

AKUMAL TRAVEL SERVICES
984-875-9030
www.akumaltravel.com
Akumal Marina

Take a 5-mile bike ride on a private ranch just west of Akumal. The tour stops at a cenote and an underground river, and there's beautiful scenery. Advance reservations are required and can be made at the Akumal Travel Services offices in the Akumal Marina. The tour, which lasts 3½ hours and costs $35, departs at 7 AM and 2 PM Monday–Saturday.

EUROBIKE RENTALS
984-803-4733
30th Avenue at 26th Street, Playa del Carmen

EuroBike offers a variety of motorbike rentals, from Vespa and Piaggio scooters to Gilera, KTM, and Ducati motorcycles. Hourly and daily rentals are available.

PLAYA DEL CARMEN BIKES

984-879-4992
www.playadelcarmenbikes.com
On 8th Street at 10th Avenue

Rental rates: $3/hour, $8/half-day, $16/24 hours, $70/week. Includes lock and helmet.

PARASAILING, SKYDIVING & PLANE TOURS

AEROSAAB

www.aerosaab.com

Services Playa del Carmen, Cozumel, Holbox, and Chichén Itzá and offers sightseeing tours, private transportation, and air-taxi service. Rental rates range from $280 to $350 per hour.

RIVIERA MAYA PARASAIL ADVENTURES

984-873-5683
Oasis Hotel, Puerto Aventuras

This well-respected outfit offers tandem and solo rides around the Puerto Aventuras bay and beachfront.

SKY DIVE PLAYA

984-873-0192
www.skydive.com.mx
Plaza Marina, Playa del Carmen

Tandem skydiving Courtesy of Riviera Maya Tourism Authority

The facility, which offers tandem and solo jumps, is certified by the U.S. Parachute Association. Its rectangular parachutes have ram-air canopies, which allow for a very stable and controlled decent. Dives include instruction and transportation to the airport near the town square. Each dive has about 45 seconds of freefall, plus a six- to seven-minute parachute descent. Landings are on the main beach of Playa del Carmen. The cost is $200, plus an additional $95 for photos.

ULTRALIGHT FLIGHTS—ALAS SKY TOUR
984-871-4020

Small lightweight airplanes take off from an open field near Xcaret park, head north along the coast to Playa del Carmen, and then circle out over the water and back to the landing strip. The trip takes about 20 minutes. Standard rate is $99 per person.

BEACH CLUBS

COCO MAYA BEACH CLUB
14th Street at the beach, Playa del Carmen

This exclusive beach club next to the Blue Parrot Hotel (see chapter 2) is the preferred daytime hangout for stylish beachgoers showing off their new bathing suits, new boobs, or new gym results. It's a great place to sunbathe, listen to lounge music, and feel cool. At night, a DJ spins popular music in front of a dancefloor and lounge area and a movie projector plays old Mexican classics.

DEEP BLUE BEACH CLUB
16th Street at the beach, Playa del Carmen

Located behind the Deep Blue Hotel (see chapter 2), this beach club has a waterfront bar and restaurant, beach beds, and plenty of beachy activities.

✪ MAMITA'S BEACH CLUB
984-803-2867
www.mamitasbeachclub.com
28th Street at the beach, Playa del Carmen

Just north of Playa Chiquita is Mamita's, which attracts a more trendy crowd that gathers every afternoon to soak up the sun and sip cold beers and frosty margaritas. There is a small pool and several cabaña-style beach beds, available on a first-come, first-served basis. A DJ spins lounge and pop music suitable for bar-top dancing, while other patrons join in a game of group soccer-ball juggling.

PLAYA CHIQUITA/KOOL BEACH CLUB
26th Street at the beach, Playa del Carmen

This family-friendly beach hangout, just north of the Royal Resort (see chapter 2), is popular with day-trippers, cruise passengers, and beachgoers staying in Playa's downtown hotels. There are lounge chairs and beach umbrellas for rent, plus a kids' pool, a restaurant

Mamita's Beach Club

serving seafood and Mexican food, and, of course, cold beer right on the beach. Active folks can play beach volleyball and soccer, ride WaveRunners, or go parasailing, banana-boat riding, kiteboarding, or body surfing. Massage service is provided on the beach or in a shady cabana.

ORGANIZED TOURS

There are only a few group tour and travel providers servicing the Riviera Maya, and they own the vehicles, employ the guides, set the itineraries, negotiate rates, and provide the actual tour services. Sometimes they sell directly to the public, but primarily they rely on tour resellers to represent their tours to the public and book the majority of the reservations. Nearly every hotel has a tour desk, and there are tour offices on nearly every block of Quinta in Playa del Carmen. There are also tour kiosks at the entrance of some restaurants, and tour representatives even walk the beaches carrying a notebook describing the trips they can sell. Authorized agencies and individuals have licenses and ID cards, and it is recommended that you verify tour representatives' credentials before giving them any money. Most sellers have the same catalog of 20 or so tours, though there can be some variation in the selection. Prices are generally fixed and do not vary much from one operator to another.

Most tours require advance reservations so that transportation and meals can be planned accordingly. If you're interested in a spur-of-the-moment trip, your choices may be limited, but there's usually something available. When a tour is reserved, a deposit or even full payment is normally required, and you'll receive a voucher that proves you have paid and tells you when and where to go for the trip. Most major tours include hotel pickup and drop-off, while others begin at a predetermined location. The balance of the fee is paid at the start of the tour if you have only put down a deposit.

Many tours and adventures can be purchased well in advance, through your local travel agent, through the Web site where you booked your flight, or directly with the tour operator. This can be a good way to guarantee availability and set your itinerary before your trip even begins, but prices are generally the same whether you book in advance or not.

Tour Operators

✪ ALDEBARAN TOURS
984-803-3880
www.aldebarantours.com
10th Street between Quinta and the beach
Quinta between 14th Street and Constituyentes Avenue

This company's tours are available through many tour desks throughout the city. They take small groups in vans to many of the key attractions around the region, including Tulum, Coba, Xel-Ha, Sian Ka'an, Xcaret, Chichen Itza, Ek Balam, and Rio Lagartos. They also run a trimaran tour to Isla Mujeres. All tours include hotel pick-up, transportation, multilingual guides, entry fees, and meals.

✪ ALLTOURNATIVE EXPEDITIONS
984-873-2036
www.alltournative.com
Various locations along Quinta, Playa del Carmen

Alltournative specializes in natural and cultural tours, eco-adventure, and alternative adrenaline-rush activities. Activities include bird-watching, canoeing, cave exploring, cenote swimming, four-wheeling, hiking, rappelling, scuba diving, sea kayaking, snorkeling, zip-line rides, Mayan ruins tours, and even overnight camping trips deep into the jungle. Custom-designed trips can be put together for large groups, incentive trips, or team-building outings. The company's buses or signature Mercedes Unimog all-terrain vehicles pick up guests near their hotels and transport them to the location of the tour. Groups are matched with a guide, based on their language and similarity with other travelers. Depending on the tour, there are stops at the company's crafts shop, where profits are shared with the indigenous communities who offer their land to be used for the adventure trip. The tours are adventurous and educational, and they are a great way to meet other travelers. Most of the activities require participants to be in relatively good physical shape. Many of the locations for the tours are on private land and cannot be visited any other way. Trips can be reserved online, on the phone, or in person at one of their outlets. Most local tour agencies can book these trips, also. Prices are $50 and up and include lunch, snacks, water, and all necessary equipment. Participants should bring comfortable clothes, sport shoes, a bathing suit, and extra money for souvenirs, tips, and photos.

CANCÚNVISTA TOURS
998- 898-4312 or 1-800-860-5917 (U.S.)
www.cancunvista.com
Avenue Cobá, #31, Cancún

Alltournative Expeditions offers eco-friendly tours. Courtesy of Riviera Maya Tourism Authority

This tour operator offers some great combination tours for travelers who want to see and do a bit of everything during their stay. It also represents many of the standard water sports, adventure, and Mayan ruins tours offered by other agencies. All tours can be reserved in advance through the company's toll-free number or their Web site.

ECOCOLORS
www.ecotravelmexico.com

Environmentally conscious travelers who want to experience and enjoy the Riviera Maya but don't want to alter it will find those with a similar philosophy at this eco-friendly tour operator. Adventures include boat trips through Sian Ka'an, bird-watching, biking, kayaking, cenote swimming, and jaguar discovery trips. The company also offers guided trips to Chichén Itzá, Cobá, and the lesser-known ruins of Muyil. Tours can be booked direct or through an agent.

SEAMONKEY BUSINESS TOURS
984-876-3306 or 954-323-8227 (U.S.)
www.seamonkeybusiness.com

This budget tour office offers many of the same tours as other agencies, but often at a discounted rate. The company's Web site has destination information, travel resources, and photos and descriptions of dozens of tours and activities.

YUCATAN EXPLORER
984-873-1626
www.yucatanexplorer.com.mx

This adventure tour operator just south of Playacar offers expeditions by land, sea, and air. Their trips tend to be a bit more extreme than with other operators, but in a good way. The ATV tours take about two hours and take participants deep into the Mayan jungle to swim and snorkel in a hidden cenote. They have 12-man powerboat tours along the Riviera Maya coastline to secret snorkeling spots, and also do ultralight plane tours that afford amazing views of the beachfront and jungle. The ATV tour is $50/person for a double-rider and $59/person for a single rider, departs 9 AM, 11 AM, 1 PM, and 3 PM. The boat tour is $136 and starts at 9:45 AM and ends at 2:15 PM. Flights run continuously and cost $99 for a 25-minute sky tour.

✪ YUCATREKS FAR OUT ADVENTURES
984-106-3686
www.yucatreks.com

Boasting a catalog of "tours for people who don't take tours," this company features intensive tours to some of the area's top historical Mayan sites as well as some lesser-known alternatives that most people have never even heard of. They also make sure each tour has a taste of recreation and exploration. Their Sea Cenote tour includes zip-lines, cenote swims, and cenote snorkeling. It runs Mondays, 7:30 AM to 5 PM, $95. Their Ek Balam Valladolid tour runs on Wednesdays and includes a visit to Mayan ruins, lunch in a Colonial town, and a swim in a hidden cenote. The tour departs Playa at 7:30 AM and returns about 12 hours later. Fees are $99. On Thursdays they offer the Cobá tour, with a visit to the ruins, a cenote swim at Cho-Ha, and a visit to an authentic Mayan Village. The tour runs from 7:30 AM to 5 PM, $92. Tuesdays and Saturdays feature the Tulum & Beyond tour, with a visit to the ruins, a beach swim, and cenote visits. The tour runs from 7:30 AM to 5 PM, $107. All trips include all fees, lunch, drinks, water, beers, and just about anything you'd need. Attendees should bring comfy clothes, bathing suits, hats, sunglasses, and camera. Groups are small, around 12 people max.

Popular Tours
Unless otherwise specified, these tours can be reserved through the above tour operators or through local agencies. Availability, times, and prices can vary.

ATV TOURS
984-873-1606
www.atvexplorer.com
Highway 307, between Playacar and Xcaret, Playa del Carmen

An active adventure tour, this outing includes a two-hour ATV ride through the jungle, stopping at a freshwater lagoon, caves, Mayan ruins, and other attractions. Participants should bring walking shoes, a bathing suit, and a towel. Departs at 9 AM, 11 AM, 1 PM, and 3 PM daily. Rates are $38.50 per person riding double or $48.50 per person riding single; refreshments included.

Catamaran cruising in Puerto Aventuras. Courtesy of Philip Gammon

CAPTAIN HOOK DINNER CRUISE

Though there's no pillaging and plundering, there is plenty of eating, drinking, and laughing on this swashbuckling dinner cruise. Board a 93-foot Spanish galleon replica and sail the waters of Cancún while enjoying a pirate-themed show and dinner. The boat leaves the dock at 6:30 PM nightly, returning at 10 PM. The price for adults is $63 for steak and $73 for lobster and steak, including open bar, and children 5–11 cost $31.50 for steak and $36.50 for lobster and steak. There is also an additional $4 port fee per person. Transportation from any hotel in the Riviera Maya is $12 extra.

CATAMARAN SAILING ADVENTURES

984-876-3316
www.fatcatsail.com

Live the dream of sailing through the Caribbean, playing in the water, sipping cocktails on the deck, taking pictures, snorkeling, fishing, and exploring hidden Mayan ruins. You'll enjoy all this and more aboard a 41-foot catamaran: the *Fat Cat*. The trip departs between 9 and 10 AM, depending on your hotel. The first stop is the hidden beach of Xaac, where you can go snorkeling, climb the Mayan ruins, play on the beach, and grab a bite to eat. Next, it's back on the water for some real sailing adventures and goofing around in the boom net. The boat returns to the dock in Puerto Aventuras at 3 PM. The trip is available Monday–Saturday and includes food, drinks, water, transportation to/from the dock, and all equipment. Adults $80, children $55.

CHICHÉN ITZÁ DELUXE

If you're looking for a first-class way to visit Chichén Itzá, this tour is a good bet. The trip includes transportation, bilingual guide, Continental breakfast on the bus, bottled water and soft drinks, a pass through the colonial city of Vallodolid, entrance to Ik-Kil nature park, entrance to the Chichén Itzá ruins, buffet lunch at a Mexican hacienda, and a traditional folkloric show. Departing from Plaza Antigua in Playa del Carmen, with stops at Plaza Playacar, Puerto Aventuras, and hotels along the Riviera Maya, the tour is available Tuesday, Thursday, and Sunday and runs from 9 to 7. Adults $77, children 5–12 $47.

COBÁ & CHIMUCH

For a mix of Mayan history and modern adventure, this trip is a good choice. It includes a two-hour visit to the Cobá ruins, an authentic Mayan lunch buffet, and a trip to two different eco-parks for kayaking, rappelling, and zip-lining. This trip operates daily. Adults $90, children under 12 $81.

✪ DOS PALMAS MAYAN CEREMONY NIGHT

984-803-2462
www.dospalmas.info

This unique educational and entertaining tour includes Mayan cultural lessons, a Mayan jungle ritual with bonfire and torches, a *temazcal* steam bath ceremony, and cenote swimming. This activity must be reserved as a group and can accommodate groups of 10 or more. Prices vary according to menu and bar options. The organization also offers native jungle tours, whale shark swims, and other experiences. Highly recommended.

ECO-TOUR NOHOCH

Your ride will pick you up at your hotel and take you to the jungle, where you will be met by a Mercedes Benz Unimog four-wheel-drive truck. The group is transported to Rancho San Felipe and the Nohoch Nah Chich cenote system. Includes snorkeling, hiking, and all transportation. Adults $98.

FLY-FISHING OR LIGHT-TACKLE FISHING IN ASCENSION BAY

You don't have to spend the night in a sweaty, un-air-conditioned lodge to experience the incredible fishing in Ascension Bay. This trip starts with a pickup from your hotel at 5 AM for the adventurous drive past Tulum and down the bumpy road through the Sian Ka'an biosphere. You'll arrive at around 8 AM and have breakfast before boarding the boat at 9. Spend the day fishing for bonefish, permit, tarpon, snook, barracuda, and other game fish, plus have lunch on the boat. You'll return to the dock at around 4 PM, and then it's back in the van for the ride back to your hotel, where you'll arrive by 8. The trip includes all necessary tackle, food, drinks, and transportation and costs $450 for one or two anglers.

MARINA MAROMA PARADISE

www.maromaparadise.com

Adventure seekers will find a variety of exciting tours at Marina Maroma, including an ATV/speedboat combo trip ($65), snorkeling at Paradise Reef ($50), deep-sea fishing ($105 for four hours), snorkeling/horseback riding/lunch ($105), and the Paradise Combo, which includes horseback riding, ATV excursion, Jet Skiing, and lunch ($130).

MAYAN CANOPY EXPEDITION

For an all-day trip combining water fun and jungle adventure, try the Mayan Canopy tour. The trip includes a bike ride through a Mayan farm, zip-lining, a visit to the Xtabay cenote, snorkeling in Chikin-Ha cenote, and a visit to Aluxes cenote for a purification ritual, plus snacks and drinks for the entire day. Runs daily, departing at 8 AM. Adults $67, children $58.

PAC-CHEN TOUR

This is an eco-friendly trip deep into the Yucatán jungle offered by Alltournative tours. The first stop is Cobá, where you will have a guided tour of one of the most dramatic of all the Mayan ruins. Next stop is the traditional village of Pac Chen, a lagoon-side town of 100 residents living much as their ancestors did hundreds of years ago. The trip costs $98.

✪ RIO LAGARTO AND EK BALAM TOUR

This tour lasts a full day and takes travelers to the traditional town of Tizimin and to the Ek Balam ruins in the northern part of Yucatán State. The highlight, though, is the visit to Rio Lagarto, a remote river where hundreds of flamingos make their home. You will also see pelicans, falcons, and crocodiles. The tour includes a glass-bottom boat ride through the river, lunch (fresh fish in a traditional village), guide service, and hotel pickup. Advance reservations are required. The tour departs at 7:30 AM and returns at around 7 PM, and costs $90 per person.

✪ TULUM & COBÁ

If you're interested in seeing a couple of Mayan sites but don't have much time, this is a good trip for you. The air-conditioned tour bus picks you up at your hotel and transports you to two of the best-known Mayan sites: Tulum and Cobá. The trip includes transportation, bilingual guide, entrance fees, and lunch. Pickups are available from Plaza Antigua in Playa del Carmen or at any hotel in the Riviera Maya. It departs Monday–Friday at 7:30 AM, returning at around 5:15 PM. Adults $62, children 5–12 $38.

TULUM & XEL-HA

For travelers who want to see the ruins but also want something a bit more active, this combo trip is a good compromise. Since both sites are relatively close to Playa del Carmen, it's also a good way to minimize the amount of time you'll spend on a bus. The first stop is Tulum, where visitors will have a chance to see the cliffside ruins and the ocean below. Next, the bus heads to the Xel-Ha water park, where you can play in the water, snorkel, or lie on the beach. The trip includes air-conditioned bus transportation, bilingual host, entrance fees, lunch, drinks, and snorkeling equipment, and pickups are available from Plaza Antigua in Playa del Carmen or at any hotel in the Riviera Maya. Departs daily at 8 AM and returns at around 5 PM. Adults $103, children 5–12 $62.

✪ WHALE SHARK TOUR

Swim and snorkel with the docile 50-foot-long whale sharks at Isla Holbox, north of Cancún. The tour includes transportation to a dock north of Cancún and then the boat ride to Isla Holbox, and it costs $120 per person. Please note that this tour is not available year-round, and it must be scheduled in advance, based on availability and presence of the sharks. For more information contact the Holbox Adventures tour office at 10th Street between 1st and 10th Avenues in Playa del Carmen. Other tour agencies in the region can also sell this tour.

You can see an actual bullfight in Cancún.

OTHER ACTIVITIES

✪ BULLFIGHTS
Plaza de Toros, Bonampak Avenue, downtown Cancún

Bullfights are every Wednesday at 3:30 PM and sometimes on Sunday. Depending on the day, there will either be a tourist-oriented show with folkloric dancing, Mexican rodeo, and a single bullfight, or a full bullfighting competition with two matadors and six bulls.

MINI GOLF EL PALOMAR
984-803-2606
www.minigolfelpalomar.com
Highway 307, km 285.5

Just south of Playa del Carmen, before you get to Xcaret, you'll find a "Mayan-style" mini golf course on the west side of the road. There are 18 holes surrounded by fruit trees, water fountains, bridges, and tropical flowers, and there are also video games, a shooting gallery, and a snack bar. Open 10–9 daily.

Dribbling in Paradise

Each year, in mid-December, the Playa del Carmen Municipal Gym hosts the Fun in the Sun Shootout men's and women's college basketball tournament, an early-season invitational that includes four teams for each division. It is televised in the United States on Fox College Sports Network. The players stay in the area and enjoy tours to Xcaret, Xel-Ha, and other attractions during their visit. The tournament is open to the public, and tickets are available at the door for $20. For more information, log on to www.funinthesunshootout.net.

MOVIE THEATER
Plaza Pelicano, 10th Avenue between 8th and 10th Streets

This three-screen, air-conditioned theater shows fairly new releases that are usually in English with Spanish subtitles. Some older films and kids' movies are dubbed in Spanish.

Mayan Ruins

If you could travel back in time and see the Riviera Maya as it was hundreds of years ago, you would see a thriving civilization with a complex social, political, and religious community. From the Cancún hotel zone to the Playa del Carmen shoreline to the beaches and jungles of the Riviera Maya, there were hundreds of structures, religious temples, dwellings, stone roads, and even recreational facilities. When the Mayans abandoned their cities, their buildings were reclaimed by the jungle, and many of them deteriorated. Some sites retained their spiritual significance and were occasionally used as ceremonial sites by the local population until not long ago.

Archaeologists began uncovering the sites in the early 1900s, and little by little, more sites were rediscovered, studied, and, in some cases, restored to their original splendor. Many of the sites have been declared federal property by the Mexican archaeological institution and have been turned into public parks where locals and tourists can visit to learn about the Mayan culture and history and to experience firsthand the places where the ancient Mayans lived, worked, prayed, and played. Many other sites remain buried, shrouded by jungle, sometimes just out of view, and some are too remote to be easily discovered, but new sites are being uncovered all the time.

If you can't make time to visit any of the major sites in the area, you can always peek through the fence on the east side of Quinta Avenida at 14th Street in Playa del Carmen to see an authentic, though quite unassuming, bit of Mayan history. Surrounded by a chain-link fence and official-looking signs declaring it a federal archaeological site is a small temple built at the base of a tree. It's not labeled, but it's rumored to be a small ceremonial site or even an ancient dwelling.

Chichén Itzá

Mexico's best-known Mayan ruin site is 128 miles southwest of Cancún, a 2¼- to 3-hour drive from either Cancún or Tulum. To get there, visitors can take the toll road, Highway 180D (cost is about $40 each way), out of Cancún or take the road from Tulum and head inland past Cobá and through Valladolid. The drive through the jungle is long and not especially interesting, with few places to stop along the way. The beautiful town square of the colonial city of Valladolid is worth a few minutes' diversion.

Chichén Itzá is the jewel of the Mayan sites that are easily reachable from the resorts of the Caribbean coast, and its grandeur makes it the obvious choice if you have time to visit only one of the ancient cities. The site is amazing, and for first-time visitors it can be a bit overwhelming. The structures are awe inspiring, and the restoration work makes it easy to

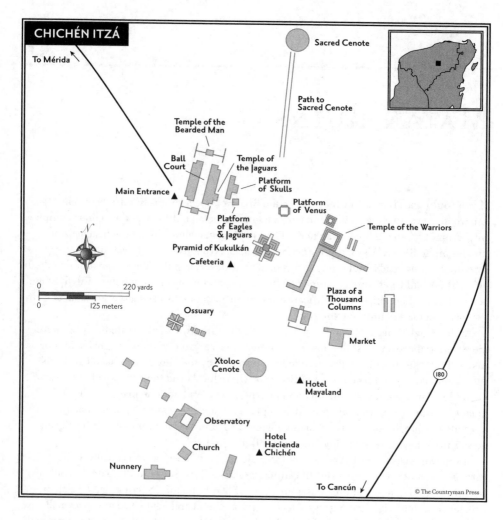

CHICHÉN ITZÁ

To Mérida

Sacred Cenote

Path to
Sacred Cenote

Temple of the
Bearded Man

Ball
Court

Temple of
the Jaguars

Platform
of Skulls

Main Entrance ▲

Platform
of Venus

Temple of the Warriors

Platform
of Eagles
& Jaguars

Pyramid of Kukulkán

Cafeteria ▲

Plaza of a
Thousand
Columns

0   220 yards

0   125 meters

Ossuary

Market

Xtoloc
Cenote

180

▲ Hotel
Mayaland

Observatory

Hotel
Hacienda
▲ Chichén

Church

Nunnery

To Cancún ↓

© The Countryman Press

picture what the city must have been like at the height of its splendor.

The area covers more than 6 square miles and is divided into two very distinct parts, and you can see classic Mayan as well as later Toltec-influenced structures. Be sure to get a glimpse of a map and see both—many tours cover only the later structures that are typically seen on postcards (the Pyramid of Kukulcán and the *pok-ta-pok* ball court, for example). These structures are the largest here, in particular the ball court (270 feet long and one of 22 on the entire site), which is the largest in Mesoamerica. However, the newer city is an area that is large enough that you could easily spend all your time in it if you were not aware of the older structures. These older structures also include examples of the softer *pu'uc* architecture (the church and its annex in particular) and display beautiful carvings not seen on later structures—they are not to be missed. A good plan is to head over to the older area and work your way back to where you started.

If you are investing the time to make the visit, it is also worth the trouble to read an article or two about the Mayans, or even check out the Mel Gibson movie *Apocalypto*. Many tour guides seem to want to stimulate the crowd with tales of human sacrifice (which did

Chichén Itzá's main pyramid has 365 steps. Courtesy of Mike Stone

indeed occur) at the expense of broader aspects of Mayan culture. The Pyramid of Kukulcán and the Nunnery (where an explosion was used in the 19th century to access one side of the structure) are the two places where you can really see that the Mayans built these structures in successive additions in their religious time cycle. The temple interior is interesting as long as you are not claustrophobic, but don't spend your time standing in line for it if you haven't seen the rest of the site, because the exterior features are more impressive.

There is a museum on the site that displays some of the small artifacts that were not taken to other museums around the world, which is interesting but not mentioned on many tours. If you are coming on your own, it is worth seeing, but if you are on an organized tour, your limited time is likely better spent outdoors.

There are night shows here with light and sound, but most of these are not practical for the traveler from the coast due to the long drive back after dark. Finally, make sure you bring some water and a hat when you visit these or any of the other ruins. The humidity and the sun will get to you more quickly than you think.

The entrance fee is $10 per person, and tours (including transportation, snacks, and drinks) can be arranged through any local travel agency or tour desk.

Keep in mind that this is one of the region's—indeed, the country's—top tourist attractions and it has become more "touristy" over time, with dozens of vendor stalls, packed tour buses, and all the other trappings of a major destination.

The pok-ta-pok *ball court Cobá.* Courtesy of Mike Stone

Tulum

Given its proximity to the hotels of the Riviera Maya, Tulum is one of the most frequently visited Mayan sites. It is located 2 miles east of Highway 307, 40 miles south of Playa del Carmen.

Tulum is unlike any of the other major Mayan ruins in Mexico in that it is right on the coast. Originally called *Zama*, which means "sunrise" in Mayan, it faces due east. The beauty of the Caribbean Sea enhances the structures, and many people say that this is what makes Tulum appeal to them. The site, known as the Walled City, rose to prominence during the post-Classic period (A.D. 1000–1500), and it is the polar opposite of Chichén Itzá in terms of the reasons behind its beauty.

While Chichén Itzá has a sense of isolation about it because of its distance and the thick jungle surrounding it, Tulum has a sense of openness and airiness brought on by the ocean itself, and the ocean views are amazing. At the same time, being next to the ocean leads to a great deal of erosion, and between this and the many hurricanes that hit the Caribbean, most of the detail of Tulum's structures has been lost. Some restoration work has been done, but the structures do not at all bear the crisp lines of those at Chichén Itzá. Instead, they are well-rounded, bleached limestone, and the few detailed carvings that remain are protected by woven structures to keep the rain off.

Since it is so close to the population centers, there are many more tourists for the size of the area than you would see elsewhere (this is also in part because it is a small area, and it is more difficult to find a place to retreat from large groups). The fact that it is easy to get to also means that many of the tourists are not particularly interested in the Mayans and come because it is close and worth looking into. This can make for a somewhat less sacred atmosphere than one sees at the other sites.

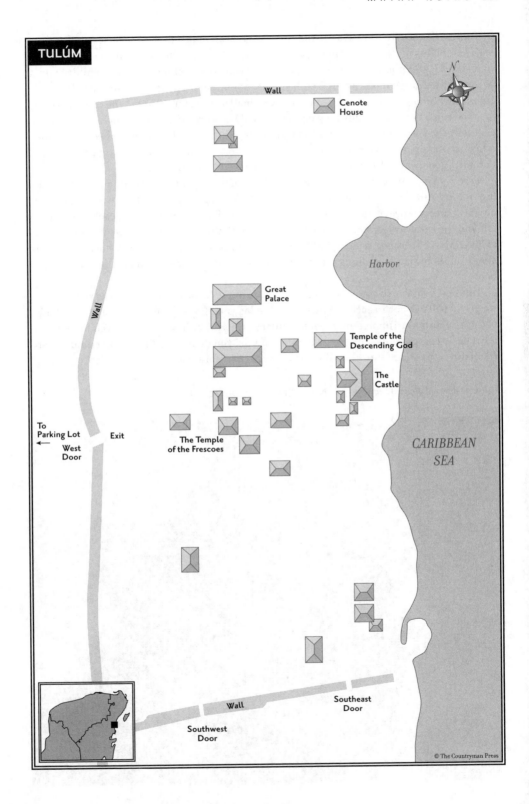

Tulum is a relatively small site, and there is no problem finding time to see all the major elements of the ruins. This makes it a good first ruins site to visit if you have time to visit several, and it is also a choice to consider if you are traveling with small children or anyone with limited mobility. In fact, if you have your own vehicle, you can start off at Tulum early and go to Cobá the same day. The small size also means that the time it takes to tour the ruins is not generally long enough to make it worthwhile for a commercial tour to visit only the ruins themselves, and so you will typically see this site combined with some other activity on a day tour. This may not interest you if your focus is purely on the Mayans, but it is a good way to fit other activities into a packed vacation schedule.

Free parking for Tulum is available at the back gate. To get there, head south of the main highway entrance to the ruins and turn east at the Tulum crossroads, by the San Francisco de Asis grocery store. After 2 miles, the road will dead-end at the Tulum beach road. Turn left and the ruins are straight ahead, 2 miles down the road, past a wonderful public beach at Playa Maya. This gate is used for bicycle and walking access by travelers staying at hotels along Tulum beach. Park along the side of the road and walk the .5 mile to the entrance booth.

Tulum is well worth your time because of its unique features, but since it is so time-worn you will not get an accurate picture of the Mayans if it is the only ruin you see. Many of the structures at Tulum tend to look similar because they have been reduced to their most basic components, and partly because of this, you do not see the architectural variety so readily apparent at the other sites. It is a very good contrast with Chichén Itzá and is a

Tulum is perched above a beautiful beach. Don't forget your bathing suit and towel!

Go to Tulum early to find some solitude.

good choice if you would like to combine an interest in the Mayans with a beautiful ocean view, but if you are interested in seeing less-restored ruins, Cobá has more to offer than Tulum.

Entrance is $5–$10, and bilingual guide service is available.

Cobá

In its heyday, Cobá city had 44 miles of urban sprawl, making it one of the largest cities in the Mayan civilization. It is located an hour inland from Tulum, on the road that starts at Tulum pueblo, and it passes several popular cenotes, such as Grand Cenote and the Carwash (see chapter 4), before yielding to the jungle.

The city of Cobá flourished during the Classic period (A.D. 300–1000) and was once home to more than 50,000 inhabitants. It is the least excavated of the major ruins on this side of the Yucatán. The site is surrounded by thick jungle, which lends an atmosphere of discovery to the site (Chichén Itzá is also surrounded by jungle, but the area around the structures themselves has been largely cleared). A number of the ruins at Cobá are partially reconstructed, but not in the finished way that one sees at Chichén Itzá, so the effect is that the ruins look like ancient unrestored buildings, as opposed to what one would see in Chichén Itzá or Tulum. Because of this, things appear more as they would have looked to the European explorers at the time of their arrival rather than a modern excavation.

The city of Cobá was very large, and the excavated ruins are in groups that are spread across the jungle. Bicycles come included with many commercial tours (or can be rented for $2.50; tricycle taxis for two go for $7.50) and are advisable. If you are on an organized tour you will have limited time here, and more of it can be spent exploring the ruins if you can move between the groups more quickly. That said, the jungle walk is also pleasant and relaxing if you can devote the time.

The highlight of Cobá is Nohoc Mul, the largest pyramid in southern Mexico (138 feet tall), and it is considerably larger than the Pyramid of Kukulcán at Chichén Itzá. The fact that it is surrounded by jungle rather than open space further exaggerates the size differ-ence. Like the Pyramid of Kukulcán, this structure can be climbed, but take great care: While the stone steps are stable, they are very irregular compared to the climb at Chichén Itzá. The view from the temple atop Nohoc Mul is beautiful, and you can see the tops of many other structures, the lake (rare in the Yucatán) on which Cobá sits, and also a vast canopy of surrounding jungle. The ball court here, one of the smallest in the Mayan world, is also an interesting comparison to the main court of Chichén Itzá.

There are also several other very significant structures, including Xaibe (the Crossroads Pyramid), which is a rounded, tiered structure that is very different from any of the struc-tures on this side of the Yucatán and is more reminiscent of Uxmal. There are also many stelae (standing stone markers) here that note important events in the history of the Mayans, and many are still detailed enough to see the forms carved onto them.

Tours to Cobá are still less common than to the other ruins, and so the area can be less crowded than the others. If you are looking for a place with fewer tourists, this is likely your best choice. A number of commercial tours combine a visit to Cobá with a tour of a local Mayan village, intending to both show the ancient architecture and give the visitor exposure to the Mayans in their modern lifestyle.

Entrance is $5, and guide service is available. Open 9–5 daily.

Chunyaxche/Muyil

The ruins of Chunyaxche/Muyil are located within the Sian Ka'an biosphere, 15 miles south of Tulum on Highway 307 and 7 miles from the coastline, and are significantly less visited than the better-known temples of the Caribbean coast. Some researchers believe, how-ever, that the site will one day rival Tulum in its scale and importance to the historical record. The site was inhabited from 300 B.C. until the Spanish conquest, and there are some 75 individual structures believed to still be hidden beneath the jungle vegetation. Excavation of the site is being led by the University of the Yucatán, though funds have been scarce, which has significantly delayed the project. Archaeologists have found evidence that the site was built to pay homage to Ixchel, the Mayan god of fertility.

The site is built on La Laguna freshwater lake and has narrow canals that lead to the ocean and once served as passageways for seafaring adventurers and traders.

Entrance fee is $5, and guide service is available.

6

DIVING & SNORKELING

The Riviera Maya is home to some of the most unequaled dive sites in the world. It's one of the few places where you can swim with a green moray eel on a 100-foot wall dive in the morning, go free-diving and snorkeling with dolphins after lunch, explore virgin caverns on a freshwater cave dive in the afternoon, and then pet sleeping sharks on a shallow-water dive that same night.

The Great Mayan Reef is the second longest living barrier reef in the world, and only Australia's Great Barrier Reef is larger. It starts in Cancún and extends just offshore along the eastern tip of the Yucatán Peninsula and all the way down to Honduras. From many towns the reef is only a short swim from the beach, making for excellent snorkeling without the need for a boat or special equipment. You can usually see the water breaking over the reef, which helps to pinpoint its location. The reef itself is razor sharp and extremely delicate, so touching it, bumping it with your equipment, or even kicking sand onto it can cause serious damage from which it takes years to recover. It is home to hundreds of species of live corals, fish, anemones, eels, rays, and other life forms, small and large.

The water itself is gin clear, with horizontal visibility up to 150 feet in some areas. The prevailing current is north to south, though it varies widely depending on the weather and local geographic conditions. Water temperature ranges from a low of 75 in the winter months up to the mid-80s in the height of the summer. Many divers choose to dive without a wet suit, which lessens the amount of weights they are required to carry, making for a less-encumbered dive and more bottom time. Other divers opt for a spring suit, shortie, or Farmer John–style wet suit, which provides a good layer of warmth while still allowing for freedom of movement.

There are a variety of open-water dives available. Divers in Cozumel and Akumal frequently go on shore dives, either in small independent groups or with a dive master. In these locations the reef comes within 100 yards of the shore, enabling divers to reach excellent dive spots with a short underwater or surface swim. Cozumel is also known for its wall dives and drift dives, where the dive boat will stop at one end of a reef and let the divers out, follow the divers' bubbles as they drift along with the current, and then be waiting to pick them up when they surface at the end of the dive. This type of diving can be very relaxing for the divers, who hardly need to swim as they are swiftly drawn along with the current, which travels up to 5 mph.

On other dives, when there isn't as much current, such as off the coast of Puerto Aventuras, Isla Mujeres, or Playa del Carmen, the boat will anchor, the dive master will lead the group on a dive, and then all divers will return to the entry point. Diving this way requires all divers to stay in sight of the others to ensure that nobody gets lost underwater. If you don't have a dive buddy, you will be assigned one on the boat before the dive begins.

A surprise to many first-time Riviera Maya divers is the presence of many freshwater dive spots that are just as close and accessible as the saltwater ones. Throughout the Yucatán Peninsula, there are caverns and spring-fed lagoons called cenotes that offer unique dive opportunities for both amateur and experienced divers. The word *cenote* comes from the Mayan word *dzonot*, which was used to describe the sinkholes that formed after the collapse of the thin limestone earth revealed a cave underneath, which then filled with freshwater from the water table (which is quite near the ground in the porous crust of the Riviera Maya). Once a major source of drinking water for the ancient Mayan villagers, these cenotes range from the size of a kiddie pool up to that of a large lagoon covering several acres of land. Some are on private ranches and have been recently opened to visitors, and others are commercially operated as recreational parks and have resident dive operations and on-site instructors and tour guides.

The water in the cenotes is crystal clear and remains a fairly constant temperature of around 72 degrees. Most cenotes are fairly shallow, making even snorkeling and freediving quite rewarding. Others have deeper holes, up to 50 feet deep, and are best explored with scuba gear. Since they are relatively small and the water does not circulate, it is important that all swimmers and divers rinse off any mosquito repellent or sunscreen before entering the water. The fish are colorful but fairly small, giving snorkelers and divers the feeling that they are diving inside an aquarium. The bottom is rocky and sometimes covered in algae, and the sides are craggy, making entry and exit a bit tricky, especially in areas that are less frequented by visitors. The major sites, though, have wooden docks and ladders and can be easily entered, even by divers in full gear. With their shallow depth, clear water, and easy accessibility, cenotes make for great dives for beginner divers. They are sometimes even used for training classes since there is no wave action and no current, and it's easy to keep track of where all the divers are.

Caves and caverns, on the other hand, offer a completely different scenario. Diving in these situations should be done only by experienced and certified cave divers since they often require the use of specialized equipment, including redundant air systems, lighting systems, and navigation aids. Cave and cavern diving requires the diver to leave the open-water realm and enter restricted areas where there is no easy escape and no way to surface without retracing your path to the entry point. Without the proper precautions, this type of diving can be extremely dangerous, though it can also be rewarding for divers who know how to do it properly.

The author descending into an underground cenote near Cobá.

The Riviera Maya and the Yucatán are home to some of the world's best spots for this type of diving, and it's an amazing feeling to be surrounded by water as clear as air and to see the incredible cave formations, the underwater stalactites and stalagmites, and the fish that call this realm their home. Some of the dives involve entering the cave at ground level and swimming through a series of caverns prior to entering the more enclosed caves, which twist and turn their way for several hundred yards, sometimes opening up into wide rooms where divers can congregate and rest before continuing the adventure. With the proper preparation, equipment, training, and guide, it's easy to see why this can be one of the most incomparable diving experiences you will ever have.

Each town has its own local dive shops, located around the town square, on the touristy streets, on the beach, or on-site at the larger hotels. Depending on the location, they offer NAUI and PADI training and certification, boat dives, shore dives, drift dives, reef dives, wall dives, night dives, cenote dives, and cavern/cave dives, as well as name-brand equipment and gear for sale or rent. All reputable dive shops and tour operators require divers to have a current certification, commonly called a C-card, prior to renting equipment or going on any guided trip.

Instruction and certification are offered at most shops, and many of the larger hotels offer free scuba introduction classes at their on-site pools. In this confined and safe environment, people new to the sport can practice using a mask and fins, snorkeling, and even breathing underwater from the scuba tank through the regulator. This can be a great way to experience the thrill of scuba diving for the first time, and it just may convince you to take a class and do it in the ocean.

Most dive operators offer a "resort course," which includes a bit of instruction on scuba theory and techniques, some time to practice in the pool, and then an actual scuba dive in open water with a certified dive master right by your side. Though the diver will not receive certification with this type of training, it is the best way to go from having no experience to going on an actual dive in only half a day. For safety reasons, the dive master will keep the dive above a depth of 30 feet and will monitor the diver throughout the adventure.

Many dive shops in the area offer full certification classes and even private certification classes. Though normal dive classes are spread out over a few weeks, a private instructor can take the student through a legal certification program in just a matter of days, including classroom lessons, pool practice sessions, and the open-water checkout dive. Some student divers take the classroom and swimming pool portions of the class at home and then just do their open-water certification dives while on vacation. If you plan on doing this, your home instructor will need to fill out a training referral form, and then your instructor in the Riviera Maya will complete the course with you and issue your C-card.

Experienced divers can go on self-guided dives right from the shore at many hotels, particularly in Cozumel and Akumal. You can bring your own gear or rent it at the hotel dive shop. Most shops have tanks available for less than $10, allowing you to custom-create the dive profile that you want and then go for it. On these dives, the maximum depth is usually around 50 feet, but divers can see just as much variety and just as much beautiful underwater scenery as on boat dives.

Organized boat trips are another way to go. These trips are normally booked at least one day in advance so that the boat captain can ensure that all the gear will be ready and that there will be enough assistants on the boat to handle the group. These trips offer either one or two dives and can be in the morning, afternoon, or even night. Most boat rides will be 30 minutes to an hour long, giving you plenty of time to prepare your gear, document the trip in your log book, socialize with other divers, and even do some sightseeing along the way. The boats range from 14-foot, open-hull "pangas" that carry just a couple of divers all the way up to 40-foot yachts that can accommodate more than a dozen divers and have air-conditioning, a galley, a shower, and other luxuries. Divers can choose to go on a private trip or can join a group trip with other divers. Nondivers can accompany divers on the boat trip for a nominal fee, though this must be arranged in advance so the captain can plan for the extra space and refreshments.

Most boats require divers to enter the water by performing a back roll or giant stride entry. The water is normally fairly calm, making either type of entry relatively simple for

A giant stride entry into a cenote. Courtesy of Riviera Maya Tourism Authority

experienced divers. If you have less experience and need additional assistance, just let the boat captain and the dive master know, and they will do everything they can to accommodate you. Depending on how strong the current is, the group will assemble either on the surface or at depth, and then the dive master will lead the group on the dive while the other divers, paired up with buddies, follow along. Oftentimes there is a safety diver who will stay behind the group to assist with any problems and to make sure everyone stays safe.

There are several types of open-water dives common in the area. One of the most common is a reef dive, where divers swim or drift along the top of the reef. Off many beaches there is a steep wall within a few miles of shore, where the depth drops from around 80 to 100 feet to more than 1,000 feet, almost straight down. On these dives either the divers swim along right at the edge of the drop-off, with the reef below them and the vast depths of the blue ocean just beyond, or they swim along the wall itself, with the reef to the side and the depths straight below them. When wall diving this way, it is important for divers to watch their depth gauges closely since it's deceptively easy to go deeper and deeper without even noticing it. For recreational scuba diving the maximum depth is usually considered to be 120 feet. Plus, the deeper you go, the shorter amount of time you can stay, so most divers prefer to keep their maximum depth to around 80 feet, which gives them 30 to 40 minutes of underwater time.

Most dive boats carry sodas, water, and juice, and many stop for lunch between dives. Lunch can be taken on the boat, or the boat will pull up to the beach, where buffet meals are served. This is most common in Cozumel, though it is being done in other areas as well.

Diving at night is a completely different experience than diving during the day, and it is a real thrill. All divers carry their own lights and backup lights and also wear glow sticks to

You'll see some breathtaking sights while scuba diving in the Riviera Maya. Courtesy of Riviera Maya Tourism Authority

make them visible, even if their lights should fail. Octopuses, sharks, rays, squid, and other marine life are more prevalent at night since this is the time they normally feed. The same dive site will look totally different at night, with different colors on the coral, different types of fish swimming around, and a different sense of depth for divers since they can see only where they point their lights. On a clear night with a big moon, the divers can also see light from above and can sometimes see large fish or the dive boat silhouetted against the moonlight.

Though some divers like to boast that the only reason to dive in freshwater is to rinse your gear off, others appreciate the difference between freshwater and open-water saltwater diving and consider them to be equally rewarding experiences. This is certainly true in the Riviera Maya, where the cenotes and underwater cave systems present unique diving opportunities that are unparalleled anywhere else in the world. Since most cenotes are fairly shallow, novice divers and even snorkelers find them great places to spend the day in the water. The Riviera Maya's underground river system is only 10 percent explored and holds many amazing and surprising sights. Even experienced cave divers revel in the number of possible dive spots and marvel at the variety of the dives, the clarity of the water, and the beauty of the natural formations.

In cave and cavern diving, divers carry extra air tanks and lights since they do not have the luxury of surfacing at any time should something go wrong. They also run lines of rope from their entry point so that they can always retrace their paths and will never get lost. Some caverns are quite narrow, requiring divers to actually remove their tanks from their backs and carry them in front of them so they can fit through. Others are wide enough to allow several divers through at a time and can even be enjoyed by relative newcomers to cave diving, as long as an expert guide is close at hand.

On group tours the depth and bottom time will be recorded by the dive master, and there will be time after each dive for participants to note the details in their log books.

Dive operators use the recreational dive tables to plan the dives, the maximum depth, the required surface interval, and the available bottom time. Divers using their own dive computers may plan alternate dive profiles as long as they communicate with the dive master and boat captain so they know what to expect. The crew performs a head count at the start and end of each dive to ensure the safe return of everyone in the group.

While ascending from a dive more than 30 feet in depth, it is customary to perform a safety stop at 15 feet for three minutes. This is a precaution to help eliminate any cases of decompression sickness. If anyone does experience symptoms of "the bends," the crew will take quick action to get the diver to a medical facility and even to a hyperbaric chamber, if necessary. There are several chambers in the Riviera Maya, usually within a 30-minute drive from shore. Most dive operators charge a $1 insurance fee for every dive, which ensures that divers will be covered if they need to enter the chamber. Divers should remember not to dive within 24 hours of flying on an airplane, since doctors say the risk of decompression sickness and other diving ailments increases if you do so.

For most dives, except for extensive cave and cavern diving, no special training or licenses are required beyond the basic open-water scuba diving certification. However you decide to dive, remember what you learned in dive training class: plan your dive, then dive your plan.

Cancún

Known across the world as a mecca for water sports, Cancún is at the far northern tip of the Great Mayan Reef and does not have as much coral growth as the areas farther south. The water is as clear as a shot of tequila blanco, though, and some 500 species have been documented. Most of the dives are fairly shallow and can be enjoyed by both snorkelers and scuba divers.

DIVE SITES

LA BANDERA
Accessible from either Cancún or Isla Mujeres, this reef stretches out for hundreds of feet at a depth of 40 to 50 feet. It is home to angelfish, parrot fish, barracuda, lobsters, moray eels, anemones, and living coral, including elkhorn and staghorn. The large Mexican flag (or bandera) that is on Cancún is due south of the dive spot.

PUNTA CANCÚN
This open-water dive is near the eastern tip of Cancún, offshore from the Hyatt Regency, Dreams, and Riu hotels. Divers see lots of colorful fish, sea urchins, sponges, and sometimes sharks. The average depth is 45 feet.

PUNTA NIZÚC
This shallow bay is offshore from the bridge that connects Cancún to the mainland near the airport, close to the Club Med Hotel. There is an artificial island here, where snorkeling tour groups make their home base.

Isla Mujeres

With an average underwater visibility of up to 100 feet and nearly 50 different dive sites within range of a 30-minute boat ride, Isla Mujeres, whose name translates to "island of the women," is also the island of the snorkelers and divers.

DIVE SITES

CAMARONERO

The site of a sunken shrimp boat that went down in a storm in the late 1990s, this dive spot ranges from 55 to 70 feet in depth and has become an artificial reef, home to brightly colored corals, Christmas tree worms, anemones, and tiny coral-dwelling fish.

CAVE OF THE SLEEPING SHARKS

Discovered by local lobster diver and fisherman Carlos Garcia Castilla in the 1950s, the site was visited by Jacques Cousteau in his survey of the area in the 1960s. An underwater cave at 65 to 70 feet is fed from a fresh spring and has a swift current carrying enriched water through the gills of the resident sharks, allowing them to temporarily halt the perpetual swimming normally required to oxygenate their bodies. The sharks fall into a type of stupor and appear to be sleeping, though their eyes remain open. In this state, the sharks seem not even to notice their human visitors, sometimes allowing themselves to be touched or petted. Most of the sharks are nurse sharks, but bulls, blacktips, and reef sharks have also been spotted.

GARRAFON NATIONAL MARINE PARK

A national marine sanctuary, Parque Garrafon is open to sunbathers, swimmers, snorkelers, and scuba divers. Two dive sites are just offshore of the park: the Arch and the Bridge. The average depth is 60 feet, and the dives feature healthy coral gardens in spur and groove formations, with several swim-throughs, which makes it an intermediate to advanced dive. Visitors can also try Snuba, a sort of combination of snorkeling and scuba diving where the diver breathes air from a tube into which air is pumped from the surface, without the need for heavy equipment.

HONDUREÑO

Popular with intermediate and advanced divers, this site's main attraction is a 120-foot shrimp boat that sunk in stormy waters during a direct hit by Hurricane Gilbert in 1988. The average depth is 75 feet, and the wreck is home to several large green moray eels, which sometimes leave their protective holes and swim freely above the boat's rusty hull.

LOS MANCHONES

Located close to shore in Mujeres Bay, on the Cancún side of Isla Mujeres, Manchones is about 35 feet deep, making it ideal for novice divers and for long bottom times. The reef is .5 mile long, with elkhorn, staghorn, and brain coral, plus many sea urchins, parrot fish, angelfish, trunkfish, and large schools of wrasses and grunts. In the mid-1990s a large bronze cross was attached to the reef to mark the founding of the island and as remembrance to sailors lost at sea, and each year, on Isla's founding day of August 17, an underwater mass is performed at this site.

LOS MARINOS
Lying at only 70 feet, a sunken Mexican Navy boat can be explored by intermediate and advanced divers. Divers can enter the hull and see the interior compartments of the ship, plus the gun mounts, railings, and exposed deck. Encrusted in coral and sea sponges in parts, the wreck is also home to many species of fish.

PUNTA NEGRA
Recognized as one of the northernmost sites along the Great Mayan Reef, Punta Negra is 60 to 70 feet deep and benefits from little to no current, making it a good spot to practice underwater navigation skills while observing the sea turtles, groupers, barracuda, and moray eels that call it home.

PUNTA SUR
This lively dive at the southern point of Isla Mujeres averages 40 feet and has strong currents, making it best for intermediate divers and above. Many visitors like to think of it as the meeting point of the Caribbean Sea and the Gulf of Mexico, though the exact spot is rather arbitrary. The dive features the coral-encrusted remnants of a shipwreck and a 400-year-old rusted anchor. Dolphins, sea turtles, groupers, and even sharks are known to swim by.

TAVOS REEF
A less visited site, Tavos is a shallow reef that features twisting and turning coral formations, huge sea sponges, swim-throughs, overhangs, and bridges. Common sightings include sea urchins, arrow crabs, groupers, rays, barracuda, lobsters, and sharks.

THE ULTRAFREEZE
Eight miles east of Isla, this dive is at the site of a 100-foot-long sunken cargo ship. The bottom is at 100 feet, which makes it an advanced dive. Groupers, sea turtles, manta rays, jewfish, moray eels, barracuda, and sometimes sharks call the wreck their home.

Isla Contoy

With white-sand beaches, shallow bays, and open-water drop-offs, this tiny island offers big variety for snorkelers and divers. Since Contoy is not sheltered by the mainland, the water can be rougher than in other areas along the Yucatán coast.

DIVE SITES

IXLACHE REEF
A very shallow reef, Ixlache is popular with snorkeling tours and beginner divers. The coral is in good condition, with large sea anemones, brain coral, and Christmas tree worms. An extension of the reef juts out into deeper water, up to 50 feet deep, so it is possible to start your dive at the deep end and then slowly work your way to the shallows.

LAS CALDERAS

This reef, whose name means "boiling pot" in Spanish, is so named for the wave action that occurs when the ocean swells crest on the exposed reef. The reef is virtually untouched and is home to many spider crabs, sea urchins, sponges, and anemones. Most dives are done at about 50 to 60 feet.

Costa Maya

The Costa Maya starts an hour south of Playa del Carmen and extends nearly to Mexico's border with Belize. The reef is especially healthy in this section because it sees fewer divers and cruise ships. The coral is healthier, the colors are brighter, and the fish are larger. Unfortunately, it is also harder to reach, so expect longer boat trips as well.

DIVE SITES

BANCO CHINCHORRO

A thriving and expansive coral reef that is just off the pristine beach, Chinchorro has various dive sites available. Popular sightings include hundreds of species of fish, playful arrow crabs, colorful coral, rays, lobsters, and anemones. Because parts of the reef are so shallow, this site was affected by Hurricane Wilma, which pulled water from this area and pushed it ashore near Cancún. The reef was left exposed in some areas and parts of it died. The deeper dives are still as vibrant as ever and it is still a great spot.

SIAN KA'AN

Part of the protected biosphere reserve, which was named a UNESCO World Heritage Site, this area has dozens of viable dive sites, many of which are so remote and seldom visited that they don't even have names. For divers who prefer untouched reefs and virgin dive sites, it is definitely worth the challenges of getting there.

Cozumel

One of the most popular dive destinations anywhere, Cozumel has enough world-class dive sites that you could stay there for a week, diving every day, and never go to the same spot twice. It is home to Palancar Reef, regularly ranked as one of the top five dive sites in the world. From shallow-water snorkeling spots to sheer walls that drop thousands of feet, Cozumel has superb dives for every skill level. The most popular type of diving is drift diving, which can take some getting used to but brings a whole new dimension to the diving experience. Most dive sites are on the island's southwest coast, facing the Riviera Maya mainland, where the reef runs parallel to the beach and the water is relatively calm since it is sheltered from the open ocean.

Dive Sites

CHANKANAAB
Chankanaab is a nationally preserved beach and underwater park whose name means "small sea" in the native Mayan language. There are several dive sites, both near the shore and several hundred yards from shore, where the water is deeper and the fish tend to be larger. The park also has a freshwater lagoon, botanical gardens, a dolphin show, restaurants, a museum, and a designated snorkeling area. This area was slammed hard by Hurricane Wilma in 2005 and the shoreline was heavily damaged. It has since been rebuilt and is once again one of Cozumel's favorite sites for snorkeling and diving.

PALANCAR
Cozumel's largest and most celebrated reef, plastered on T-shirts, sweatshirts, and hats sold across the island, is famous for good reason. The coral is healthy and brightly colored, and the marine life is incredibly diverse and abundant. Depths range from 20 to 120 feet, and there are several distinct sites, depending on the part of the reef you dive. The Gardens is a shallow reef bed, the Caves offer swim-throughs and steep overhangs, and Palancar Deep features huge coral formations, sheer drop-offs, and large fish.

PUNTA SUR
This dive at the southern tip of Cozumel Island is generally offered by special request only. It is deeper than most dives, averaging up to 120 feet, and often has swift currents, making it the exclusive realm of advanced divers. This is one of the most common dives to see gray sharks and reef sharks, in addition to nearly virgin reefs, large barracuda, manta rays, huge groupers, and massive coral heads.

SANTA ROSA WALL
A popular boat dive with an average depth of 90 to 100 feet, Santa Rosa is frequently the first dive visited on a two-dive tour. There are spur and groove formations and a steep drop-off where the depth increases dramatically. Divers should watch their gauges and be careful not to go too deep. Many large groupers, wrasses, rays, parrot fish, and angelfish can be seen here.

TORMENTOS
With the top of the reef at about 60 feet deep, this site is popular with intermediate divers and others who would gladly dive a little shallower in exchange for more bottom time. A resident green moray eel, more than 6 feet long, can usually be spotted, and it is known to eat fish right from the dive master's hand. While hiding in its hole in the reef, it slowly opens and closes its mouth as if anticipating its next meal. In actuality, it's just keeping a flow of oxygenated water through its gills. Sometimes this beautiful green monster leaves its lair and swims freely above the reef, occasionally swimming straight at divers who aren't sure whether they should swim away or stay and watch. There are also many rays, sea urchins, Christmas tree worms, and large groupers and barracuda.

Puerto Aventuras

Boats depart from the Puerto Aventuras Marina several times per day, shuttling divers to the nearby reefs. Though it's always best to book ahead, dives can sometimes be planned at the last minute if a boat has extra space available.

DIVE SITES

BRISA CARIBE

A steep drop-off in front of the Brisa Caribe condos between the public marina and the Oasis beach, this dive can be done as a shore dive or boat dive. The reef features deep crevices and overhangs, along with plentiful parrot fish, angelfish, and sea urchins.

LOS CANIONES

One of the deeper dives available in Puerto Aventuras, this reef lies at around 75 feet, making it best for intermediate and advanced divers. The visibility is more than 50 feet. Los Caniones features steep canyons and groove formations with elkhorn, staghorn, and brain coral. There are plenty of fish, including grunts, wrasses, barracuda, parrot fish, and angelfish.

MOOK-CHE

Just off the beach near Playa Xcalacoco, this dive site is accessible by boat from either Puerto Aventuras or Akumal. The average depth is 35 feet. The reef is colorful, and there are many small species of fish. An occasional barracuda lurks just above the reef.

Akumal

Akumal is a shallow bay with calm water, slow currents, and coral beaches. There are many good spots to dive in the 20- to 40-foot range, making it a good spot for beginning and intermediate divers who want the thrill of an ocean dive but aren't quite ready for deep walls and cave systems. More advanced divers will appreciate the deeper sites such as Gonzalo's Reef, which reaches 85 feet in some spots.

DIVE SITES

DICK'S REEF

Named for the retired owner of the Original Akumal Dive Shop, this bump dive ranges from 20 to 50 feet and features large coral heads and patches of white sand. There are also several swim-throughs and large overhangs.

GONZALO'S REEF

A fairly deep dive bottoming out at 85 feet, Gonzalo's Reef is famous for being one of the spots where divers can usually count on a close encounter with a sea turtle. There are several species native to the area, and they frequently make the rounds at the reef, looking for a bite to eat.

LAS REDES

This 50-foot dive, whose name means "the nets" in Spanish, features high concentrations of stingrays, lobsters, angelfish, sea urchins, Christmas tree worms, and anemones and an occasional barracuda or sea turtle.

MOTORCYCLE REEF

A sunken motorcycle lies in the sand at one end of this reef, which sits at 60 feet. There are abundant sponges, rays, grunts, and angelfish.

SHARK CAVE

Similar to the Isla Mujeres dive site with a similar name, this 30-foot dive features a healthy reef with large overhangs that funnel the current and shelter a group of resident nurse sharks. The current carries oxygen-rich seawater through the sharks' gills, allowing them to stay motionless in a sleeplike state.

TZIMIN-HA

Named for the remnants of a 20-foot fishing boat that sank here, this dive site is a good spot to see enormous blue jewfish, hungry groupers, and barracuda.

YAL-KU

A good spot for snorkelers and shallow-water divers, this spot is on the ocean side of Yal-Ku Lagoon, where the water from the lagoon mixes with the water from the open ocean. There are elkhorn and staghorn coral, sea urchins, sponges, and anemones, as well as lots of Caribbean lobsters.

Recommended Dive Shops

AKUMAL DIVE ADVENTURES

On the beach next to Buena Vista Restaurant
www.akumaldiveadventures.com
984-875-9157 or 1-888-4AKUMAL (U.S.)

Offers snorkeling, cave dives, cavern dives, cenote trips, and dives in Akumal and other nearby openwater sites, plus fishing trips.

AKUMAL DIVE SHOP

Near the main gate to the Akumal development
www.akumal.com
984-875-9032

Open since 1980, this Texan-owned dive shop was the first in the region. It offers individual and group dives in and around the Akumal area, plus certification classes, "bubble-maker" classes for kids, and sailing and fishing trips.

Paamul

This relaxing beach is home to some of the best diving in the area. With little in the way of tourism development, the reefs are still in pristine condition, and the sea life is prolific.

The shallow bay also offers excellent snorkeling since the reef is healthy and full of life, even in just a few feet of water.

DIVE SITES

HORST'S REEF
With a maximum depth of only 45 feet, this dive spot is good for all certified divers and even offers some small swim-throughs for an added bit of excitement. It's a popular site to see spotted drums, groupers, parrot fish, and an occasional sea turtle.

PAAMUL MINI WALL
With an average depth of more than 100 feet, this wall dive is for advanced divers only. Lobster, huge groupers, nurse sharks, green and spotted moray eels, and barracuda can usually be spotted.

PARAÍSO SHALLOW
Good for intermediate divers, Paraíso lies at about 60 feet and features large coral heads, sea sponges, Christmas tree worms, and abundant marine life.

XEL-HA
A government-regulated ecotourism park, Xel-Ha offers several shallow-water snorkeling sites where the coral reef comes nearly to the water's surface, so even novice snorkelers can see the amazing sea life.

XEL-HA REEF
Offshore from the park, the reef is open for exploration provided that divers follow the preservation rules of the park. Dive boats depart from the park itself and from nearby beaches. The depth ranges from 35 to 55 feet, depending on the part of the reef selected. Your dive master will choose a spot based on the experience of the divers, the prevailing currents, and the advice of the boat captain.

Tulum

Known for its Mayan ruins and relaxed atmosphere, the Tulum area also has some great snorkeling and diving sites.

DIVE SITES

LAS RUINAS
The beach right behind the ruins doesn't offer much in the way of reef life, but the water is clear and the waves are small, which makes it a popular swimming spot.

TULUM REEF
Offshore from the ruins, the barrier reef is in great condition, and many snorkelers and

divers enjoy the thrill of diving while in the shadow of the great Mayan temple. Dives range from 15 to 60 feet.

Playa del Carmen & Playacar

The unofficial capital of the Riviera Maya is also home to the greatest concentration of diving and dive-related activities and services. There are more than a dozen dive shops along Paseo del Carmen and in the water-sports centers of the larger hotels, particularly those in Playacar. Dive sites accessible by boat from Playa range from shallow reefs good for snorkeling to deep-water drop-offs best reserved for advanced divers. The Buceo Mexico hyperbaric chamber, the leading facility in the treatment of diving accidents, including cases of "the bends," is open every day and is well known by all major dive operators.

DIVE SITES

CHEN ZUBUL

This is a shallow-water dive averaging only 40 feet, and it is frequently visited by novice divers and for night dives.

LA TORTUGA

La Tortuga, whose name means "the turtle" in Spanish, is one of the more adventurous dive sites given the large schools of grunts and wrasses that let you swim with them, the friendly moray eels, the huge groupers, and, if you're lucky, a curious sea turtle or two. There is usually a fairly strong current, which can turn the dive into a drift dive. The reef depth is 60 to 70 feet.

LAS BARRACUDAS

A short boat trip from Playa del Carmen, this site is offshore from the Xcaret ecological park. The depth is 40 to 50 feet, and there are many tropical fish, including—of course— several large barracuda.

LOS CEREBROS

A middle-range dive averaging around 65 feet, this site is known for a large amount of brain (*cerebro* in Spanish) coral, towering coral heads, spider crabs, anemones, and plenty of angelfish and parrot fish, which can be seen hungrily chomping on the reef.

MOCHE DEEP

With an average depth of more than 100 feet, this is one of the more advanced dives in the area. The reef is in good shape, and there are lots of big fish.

PUNTA MAROMA

A few miles north of Playa del Carmen, this site offers several different dives within a close distance of each other. The reef isn't much, but there are lots of turtles, eels, lobsters, arrow crabs, and other sea life. Depths range from 60 to 120 feet.

Playa del Carmen Dive Shops & Hyperbaric Chambers

THE ABYSS
984-873-2164
Abyssdiveshop.com
Blue Parrot Hotel, 12th Street and the beach

They offer PADI and NAUI instruction, open-water dives, and cenote trips.

BUCEO MEXICO HYPERBARIC CHAMBER
987-873-1365
10th Avenue and 28th Street

Buceo Mexico offers diagnosis and treatment of the most common diving ailments, including decompression sickness and reef rash. The chamber is supported through a mandatory $1-per-dive donation, which is collected by dive operators. No other fees are charged for services, including x-rays and exams.

CYAN HA DIVERS
987-873-0978
buceocyanha@playadelcarmen.com
North of town, between Hotel Las Palapas and Hotel Shangri La

Open since 1983, Cyan Ha has several boats, an on-site training pool, and PADI instruction. The shop specializes in small groups, cenote dives, and reef dives.

EXPLORA DIVERS
Tukan Beach, 28th Street at the beach

Explora specializes in cenote and cave dives, but it also offers windsurfing instruction and board rental, sailing tours, and motorcycle tours.

Dive shop in Playa del Carmen

GO CENOTES

1st Avenue between 24th and 25th Streets

They offer cenote trips, open-water dives in Playa and Cozumel, snorkeling tours, and trips to Holbox Island.

SCUBA PLAYA DIVE SHOP

984-803-3123
www.scubaplaya.com
2nd Street between Quinta and the beach
10th Street between 1st Avenue and Quinta

This dive shop offers a variety of open-water and cenote dives, including a one-tank ocean dive for $35 (two tanks is $55), a two-tank trip to Cozumel for $95 (plus the price of the ferry), night dives or wreck dives for $45, a snorkel tour to reefs near Playa for $25, and a cenote dive package, including two cenote dives at two separate locations, transportation, lunch, and drinks, for $95. It also offers a three-day open-water certification course for $295 and a referral course for $190.

STUDIO BLUE

984-873-1088
1st Street between the beach and Quinta

On the north side of the town square, Studio Blue is a full-fledged dive shop with retail showroom, dive school, and snorkel and dive tours. It offers daily boat trips to local reefs, excursions to Cozumel, and cenote diving adventures.

TANK-HA DIVE SHOP

984-873-0302
www.tankha.com
dive@tankha.com
Quinta between 8th and 10th Streets

Tank-Ha has PADI and NAUI instruction and an on-site training pool and offers cenote dives, open-water dives, and reef dives, with hotel/dive combination rates available. Sample prices: two-tank dive, $60; one-tank dive, $40; two-tank cenote dive, $100; night dive, $55; open-water certification, $350; referral course, $220.

YUCATEK DIVERS

984-803-1363
www.yucatek-divers.com
15th Avenue between 2nd and 4th Streets
Quinta between 6th and 8th Streets

Yucatek offers a variety of dives, including one-tank dives for $40 and two-tank dives for $60, night dives for $55, and cavern and cave dives for $100, including transportation. It also offers scuba instruction, with discover diving courses ($80), refresher courses ($90), open-water certification (three days, $350), and open-water referrals ($220).

Courtesy of Cozumel Country Club

7

Golf

Though the Mayans never used the wheel, they did have the ball, and it is believed that they took great pleasure in playing various games. Their most famous ball game was called *pok-ta-pok*, and it was serious business. The ball was about the size of a kickball, and the game was played on a large field about the size of a basketball court. Similar to basketball, the game's object was to shoot the ball through a hoop mounted above the playing surface. Considering that players weren't allowed to use their hands, though, scoring was quite rare and was considered a tremendous feat. Large numbers of villagers turned out to watch the games, which had great religious and ceremonial importance. Fans sang songs, acted boisterously, and even bet on who would win. The winners of the game were given a hero's welcome, and a celebration was held in their honor. As legend has it, the losers were put to death.

Today, the open fields, beachfronts, and carved-away jungles of the Riviera Maya make a perfect backdrop for the more "civilized" ball game of golf. There are a dozen places to play within a short distance of the Riviera Maya, including courses in Cancún, Cozumel, and the town of Bacalar (south of the Riviera Maya). Some of the courses are par 3, but others are par 72 championship courses designed by some of the best golf architects in the business, including Jack Nicklaus, Robert Trent Jones Jr., and Robert Von Hagge.

Most of the courses have beautiful views of the ocean and the tropical jungle. Iguanas, colorful birds, and other animals are commonly sighted. Most have multiple water and sand features, and a couple even have actual Mayan ruins next to the fairways.

Most courses have clubs for rent, and unless you're a real pro or planning on playing multiple rounds, the loaners are normally sufficient. Balls can be expensive (and the loss ratio can be high), so it's usually best to bring some of your own since they're cheap back home and fairly easy to pack. The larger courses have full-service pro shops with name-brand equipment and apparel, club repair, and instruction.

Some of the courses operate with an all-inclusive concept, where the greens fee includes a cart, range balls, and all the food and drink you care to consume during your round. To keep the costs down, consider playing in the afternoon to take advantage of discounted twilight rates. Just make sure to bring a hat, sunscreen, and plenty of water.

The Riviera Maya is becoming more of a golf destination each year. More than 15 courses are currently under construction or are in the design/approval/development stages. For information on all area golf courses, log on to the Mexican Caribbean Golf Association's Web site, www.cancungolf.org.

GOLF COURSES

BAHÍA PRÍNCIPE GOLF CLUB
984-875-5085 or 866-347-1667
www.bahiaprincipegolf.com
Highway 307, km 250

Designed by Robert Trent Jones II, this 27-hole course is part of a massive real estate development with condos, private residences, and resorts. It's about an hour from the Cancun airport and 30 minutes south of Playa del Carmen. Construction on the complex began in the middle of 2007 and will continue for many years to come.

CANCÚN COUNTRY CLUB—POK-TA-POK
998-883-1230
www.cancungolfclub.com
Kukulcán Boulevard, km 7.5, Cancún hotel zone

Designed by Robert Trent Jones Jr., Cancún's original course (opened in 1976) is 6,636 yards long, with 18 holes and a par of 72. It has several holes along the beach and a few Mayan ruins scattered about. High-season (December 18–April 30) rates are $100 before 2 PM and $75 after. In the low season (May 1–December 17) it's $75 before 3 PM and $50 after. Rates include use of the practice tee and putting green and a shared cart. Club rentals are $40, shoes are $16, and nonplaying riders are $30. Reservations and discounts are available through the Fiesta Americana Coral Beach, Holiday Inn Express, and Marriott CasaMagna hotels. An on-site restaurant serves sandwiches, salads, and Mexican food. Open 6–6, with the last tee-off at 4.

CANCÚN OASIS GOLF CLUB
998-885-0867
www.oasishotels.com
Kukulcán Boulevard, km 16.5, Cancún hotel zone

This nine-hole par 3 course is between the Oasis Cancún hotel and the main road through the Cancún hotel zone. It covers nearly 900 yards and has a practice putting green. The greens fee is $40 per person.

COZUMEL COUNTRY CLUB
987-872-9570
www.cozumelcountryclub.com.mx
info@cozumelcountryclub.com.mx
Carretera Costera Norte, km 6.5 Interior, Cozumel

Designed by Nicklaus Design in 2001, this course has four sets of tees, with the longest being 6,734 yards. There are many sand and water features to contend with as the course skirts native mangroves and tropical swamps. Standard greens fees are $155.

GOLF CLUB AT MAYAKOBA
1-800-540-6088 (U.S.)
www.fairmont.com

Highway 307, km 297, north of Playa del Carmen

Managed by Fairmont Hotels, this is the first course in Mexico to be designed by Greg Norman. Dubbed the Camaleon course, it curls around the Fairmont Mayakoba hotel and along the beach of the 1,600-acre tourism development. Players enjoy unusual hazards such as cenotes, mangrove swamps, and other tropical features. The course spans more than 7,000 yards and has five sets of tees. While 15 holes have some sort of water hazard, 2 of the holes are right along the beach. There is a driving range and putting green, plus well-stocked pro shop and steakhouse overlooking the 18th hole. A novelty in Mexico, all carts have GPS navigation and yardage systems, allowing players to keep score, monitor other players' scores, and order refreshments while on the course. This course is the site of the yearly PGA Mayakoba Golf Classic pro tournament, first played in 2007 and won by Fred Funk, marking the first PGA event in Mexico. Greens fee is $198, including cart and water. Equipment rental is $60.

MOON PALACE SPA & GOLF CLUB
984-881-6000 or 1-800-525-5025 (U.S.)
www.palaceresorts.com
teetimes@palaceresorts.com
Highway 307, km 340, Cancún

This is the only Jack Nicklaus Signature golf course in Cancún and includes three separate courses (jungle, lake, and dune), totaling 27 holes and a par of 108. Total length is 10,798 yards. The layout requires golfers to navigate through native vegetation, wetlands, and a plethora of sandtraps. Each of the three courses offers a distinct environment. For non-golfers, there is a full-service European day spa. Fees include transportation from anywhere in Cancún and the Riviera Maya, plus food and beverages at the Club House, a shared cart and the snacks along the course. All carts have on-board GPS systems. Standard greens fee is $260, includes food, drinks and cart. Twilight fee is $150, after 2:30 PM.

HILTON CANCÚN BEACH & GOLF RESORT
998-881-8016
www.hiltoncancun.com
Kukulcán Boulevard, km 17.5, Cancún hotel zone

This course near Cancún's southern end has 18 holes, par 72, and 6,767 yards of play; it was designed by Isao Aoki and built in 1994. It features holes along Nichupté Lagoon, with peacocks, an occasional crocodile, and lots of iguanas. From the 15th and 16th holes, players have a great view of the Ruinas El Rey, Cancún's largest and most important Mayan ruins site. The standard rate for non-Hilton players is $175, with hotel guests paying $125. Twilight rates are $90. All rates include cart. Club rental is $25 (Mizuno and Precept) or $50 (Titleist and Calloway). There is a practice tee and practice green, plus a European day spa and the 19th Hole restaurant. No pull carts allowed.

IBEROSTAR PLAYA PARAÍSO GOLF CLUB
984-877-2847
www.iberostar.com
golfparaiso@iberostar.com.mx

Play golf around Mayan ruins at Playacar. Courtesy of Riviera Maya Tourism Authority

Highway 307, km 309, Playa Paraíso

Part of the massive Iberostar complex, this course, designed by P. B. Dye and opened in 2005, is convenient for guests staying anywhere in the Riviera Maya. It features 18 holes stretched across 6,800 yards, with wide fairways, deep sand traps, and undulating greens. Rental equipment from brands such as Titleist, Nike, and Mizuno is available. E-mail or call for pricing and tee-time reservations.

LAS VELAS GOLF CLUB
998-883-2222
Highway 307, km 350, Bacalar

A little-known course near the border of Belize, it has 18 holes and is par 72. It is part of the Club Las Velas Gold resort. The greens fee is $120 per person.

MELIA CANCÚN GOLF CLUB
998-883-1230
www.solmelia.com
Kukulcán Boulevard, km 16, Cancún hotel zone

Stretching more than 1,800 yards, this course, next to the Gran Melia Cancún hotel, has 18 par 3 holes and a nicely manicured putting green. It's a fun place to practice your chips and get in a round without spending all day. The greens fee is $40 per person.

PLAYA MUJERES
998-887-7322
www.playamujeres.com.mx
Bonampak Avenue, Punta Sam

Part of the newly developed Costa Mujeres region, just north of Cancún and across the channel from Isla Mujeres, this 18-hole course was designed by Greg Norman and snakes through tropical mangroves, the beachfront, and a saltwater lagoon. It has 18 holes, and covers 7,250 yards, with a par 72.

PLAYACAR CLUB DE GOLF

984-873-0624 or 1-800-635-1856 (U.S.)

www.palaceresorts.com

teetimes@palaceresorts.com

Paseo Xaman-há, 26 Fraccionamiento Playacar, Playa del Carmen

Opened in 1994, the Playacar golf course was designed by Robert Von Hagge and was acquired by Palace Resorts in 2005. The course runs 7,202 yards and has many jungle, sand, and water features to keep golfers challenged and entertained. There are even a few actual Mayan ruins along the fairways and greens. The standard greens fee is $190, including a shared cart and unlimited drinks and snacks while on the course. Twilight fees (after 2 PM) are $130. Clubs are available for rent for $30 (steel shaft) or $40 (graphite shaft), and transportation from Riviera Maya hotels is only $20. There is also a pro shop offering instruction, equipment, and apparel, plus a swimming pool, driving range, putting green, and on-site restaurant. E-mail or call to make reservations.

PUERTO AVENTURAS CLUB DE GOLF

984-873-5109

www.puertoaventuras.com.mx

Highway 307, km 269.5, Puerto Aventuras

This 9-hole, 3,236-yard, par 36 course, part of the Puerto Aventuras marina, tennis, and golf club, was designed by Thomas Lehman and built in 1990. Greens fees are $80 and include two rounds of golf, cart, and access to the practice green. The first tee time is 7:30 AM and reservations are not required. Astroturf tennis courts are available for $20 per hour. No credit cards.

PUERTO CANCÚN

998-884-7608

www.puertocancun.com

East of Bonampak Avenue, near where Kulkulcán Avenue meets downtown Cancún

Inaugurated in 2008 in a large-scale development just north of Cancún, the 808-acre Puerto Cancún resort features more than 2,000 condos, 435 private homes (including 40 fronting the golf course), a 350-slip marina, five hotels, and a large shopping plaza. The golf course, designed by Tom Wesikopf, features 185 acres of water features, sand traps, and manicured greens. An additional course, designed by Tom Fazio and Nice Price, is being contemplated. The course is 18 holes, par 72.

RIVIERA MAYA GOLF & TENNIS CLUB—MAYAN PALACE GOLF CLUB

984-206-4043

www.mayanresortsgolf.com

Highway 307, km 310, Playa Paraiso.

This rare Jack Nicklaus-designed par 3 course opened in 2003. It spans 2,823 yards and has lots of water and sand features. The signature 17th hole skirts a large lagoon and has an island sand trap, making your approach shot a crucial factor. The standard greens fee is $109, which includes use of a cart. Club rental is available for $25. The first tee time is at 6 AM.

8

FISHING

Fishing has been a way of life in the Riviera Maya since the indigenous inhabitants paddled their dugout canoes through the shallows, plunging their wooden spears into the water to snare their catch. They also fished with reed baskets or nets, woven with the same techniques that were used to make hammocks. In some areas fish were also caught with bows and arrows or with poisons that were thrown into the water, killing the fish, which then floated to the surface to be harvested. Later, the Mayans even used a pole and line, possibly even making a sport out of it.

With its variety of good fishing locations in such a relatively small geographic area, the Riviera Maya is one of the top spots for sportfishing and deep-sea fishing in the world. The waters off the northeastern coast of the Yucatán are prime for finding numerous fish species and a wide variety of fishing conditions. From deep channels to wide flats and shallow reefs to rocky points, there's always a spot that's producing, no matter the time of year and the weather conditions, unless a major storm keeps the boats in port.

Fishing options range from a do-it-yourself wade-fishing expedition to a full-day excursion trolling on a luxury yacht, complete with meals, drinks, guides, gear, and a video recording of all the action. From your hotel in Playa del Carmen or elsewhere in the Riviera Maya, several distinct fishing spots are within easy reach. From the deep waters off Cancún to the north, through the reefs of Puerto Morelos, to the shallows of Cozumel, to the drop-offs near Playa, to the bays of Akumal and Puerto Aventuras, and all the way down to the flats of Sian Ka'an, each area holds something unique and exciting for fishing. And whether you're a novice who just enjoys being out on the water and reeling one in, a regular enthusiast in search of your first marlin, or an old pro going for a coveted grand slam, you can find what you're looking for in the Riviera Maya.

There is great fishing year-round, but if you're looking for a specific type of fish, then you'll need to take note of the seasons to make sure the fish you're looking for is around when you plan to visit. Many visitors come to Playa seeking the majestic billfish, which produces a thrill like no other when it takes the bait and then jumps in the air for all to see. These beautiful creatures, weighing up to 500 pounds, are seen throughout the year, though the prime time is from March to July, when they ply the deep waters between Cozumel and the Yucatán mainland in abundant numbers. Each year, there are several billfish grand slams recorded, when a single group manages to boat a blue marlin, a white marlin, and a sailfish on the same trip. When fishing for these beauties, a strict catch-and-release policy is followed, so make sure to bring your video camera to capture the moments for bragging rights.

Fish	Jan	Feb	Mar	Apr	May	Jun	Jul	Aug	Sept	Oct	Nov	Dec
Amber jack	high season	high season	high season	high season	high season	high season	high season	high season	some catches	some catches	some catches	some catches
Barracuda	high season	high season	high season	high season	high season	high season	high season	high season	high season	high season	high season	high season
Blue martin	off season	off season	some catches	some catches	high season	high season	high season	high season	high season	some catches	off season	off season
Bonefish	some catches	some catches	high season	high season	high season	high season	high season	high season	some catches	some catches	some catches	some catches
Bonito	off season	high season	high season	high season	high season	high season	high season	high season	some catches	some catches	off season	off season
Bottom fish	high season	high season	high season	high season	high season	high season	high season	high season	high season	high season	high season	high season
Grouper	high season	high season	high season	high season	high season	high season	high season	high season	high season	high season	high season	high season
Kingfish	high season	high season	high season	high season	high season	high season	high season	high season	high season	high season	high season	high season
Mackerel	high season	high season	high season	high season	high season	high season	some catches	some catches	some catches	some catches	high season	high season
Mahimahi	off season	some catches	high season	high season	high season	high season	high season	high season	high season	off season	off season	off season
Permit	high season	high season	high season	high season	high season	high season	high season	high season	high season	high season	high season	high season
Sailfish	off season	some catches	high season	high season	high season	high season	high season	high season	off season	off season	off season	off season
Shark	high season	high season	high season	high season	high season	high season	high season	high season	high season	high season	high season	high season
Snapper	high season	high season	high season	high season	high season	high season	high season	high season	high season	high season	high season	high season
Tuna	off season	off season	some catches	high season	high season	high season	high season	some catches	off season	off season	off season	off season
Wahoo	off season	off season	high season	high season	high season	high season	high season	high season	off season	off season	off season	off season
White martin	off season	off season	some catches	high season	high season	high season	high season	high season	off season	off season	off season	off season

Tuna, mahimahi, bonito, bonefish, and wahoo prefer the warmer waters and generally are more active from March to August or September, though catches of each have been recorded in every month of the year. Due to the varied underwater terrain and the year-round temperate climate, however, many fish species can be caught all through the year, such as barracuda, grouper, kingfish, shark, skipjack, snapper, and other reef and bottom fish. They are so abundant, in fact, that many chartered boats promise to prepare a meal on the boat or on a hidden beach, and they rely exclusively on the day's catch to supply the main course. Though certainly it has happened that bad luck strikes and the group is left to dine on crackers, salsa, and sides, the trips almost always end with a bounteous feast of ultrafresh ceviche or fried fish.

A Mexican fishing license is required for boat fishing, and the fees go toward worthwhile conservation and regulation programs. Reputable tour operators, such as those listed in this guide, include all required licensing in the prices of their tours.

PRIZED CATCHES OF THE RIVIERA MAYA

Barracuda
Often seen while snorkeling, hovering nearly motionless next to the reef, seemingly watching every move you make, the barracuda is one of the most feared of all ocean creatures. Given its muscle-packed body, large eyes, gaping mouth, and razor-sharp teeth, it's easy to see why. Barracudas' fearless nature makes them great fighters, and they are commonly caught while drift fishing or bottom fishing, all across the shallows and deepwater cuts of the Mayan Riviera. Caught year-round.

Blue Marlin
The largest of the billfish, the blue marlin can reach up to 1,800 pounds in the deeper Atlantic waters, though they seldom grow to more than 500 pounds in the local region. Average catches are in the range of 80 to 120 pounds. Caught while trolling using artificial baits, the blue marlin will be landed only if the angler is strapped in tightly to the fighting chair and ready for an exhaustive struggle. Keeping tension on the line is the only way to keep the blues from spitting the hook while jumping into the air. Best months: May to September.

Bonefish
Noted for their exceptional fighting strength given their relatively small size, bonefish are taken with light tackle, generally fly-fishing, though spinning tackle can also be used. The angler normally casts when the fish breaks the surface or is swimming just below. The strike is hard and fast, requiring a high level of skill and making for a thoroughly entertaining day of fishing. One of the best spots in the world for finding bonefish is in Ascension Bay, at the southern end of the Sian Ka'an biosphere. Best months: March to August.

Grouper
A member of the sea bass family, groupers are strong fighting fish and are quite abundant in the warm Caribbean waters. They come in various colors, from dark gray to bright

orange. Scuba divers are fond of watching groupers eat, a process that involves a slow circling around the prey, followed by a quick kick of the tail fin and a hard swallow, which lets them suck in large pieces of food at one time. They are generally caught while bottom fishing. Caught year-round.

Mahimahi

One of the best-tasting fish in the Caribbean, the mahimahi (sometimes called dorado or dolphin fish) has a big face with a high, protruding forehead and beautiful blue dorsal fin running the length of its back. The body is thick and strong and seems to glow with every color of the rainbow. Can be caught trolling or bottom fishing, depending on the water depth. Best months: March to September.

Permit

Members of the jack family, permit are broad fish with silvery blue bodies that range in size from 3 to 30 pounds. Great fighters with fierce striking power, they can be taken with flies and light tackle. They are common in the shallow flats of Ascension Bay and near Isla Holbox, and since they stay in the warm, shallow water, fishing is good year-round.

Sailfish

One of the most exciting sport fish around, the sailfish is known for its long, protruding dorsal fin, which looks like a sail. It is also known to fly through the air once it's hooked, offering up superb picture-taking opportunities. Sailfish, mostly 30 to 50 pounds, are caught by trolling through the drop-offs and deeper channels, and they can be very hard to land since they twist and turn a lot while jumping and fighting. Best months: March to August.

Shark

The Mexico Department of Tourism's supercomputer that picked Cancún as the next tourism megadevelopment neglected to factor in the high number of sharks that live in the region's warm waters, feeding off the abundant baitfish. Though attacks are very infrequent, sightings are somewhat common, especially by local fishermen and others who spend a lot of time on the water. Long prized by natives for their liver oil, sharks are still commercially fished for their meat, teeth, and jaws. The English word *shark* is said to come from the Mayan *xoc*. A year-round catch, they can be caught while trolling, bottom fishing, or even wade fishing.

Tuna

The Riviera Maya is home to yellowfin, blackfin, and skipjack tuna, and each is quick and strong and can put up a great fight. Most often caught while trolling, tuna can be served grilled, in lime-marinated ceviche, or even raw. Can't beat that for fresh sushi! Best months: April to July.

Wahoo

Wahoo are long and thin, with a barracuda-like face and sleek body that can cut through the water at an incredible 45 mph. When a wahoo hits the bait, you better make sure the pole is fastened in the rod holder or securely in someone's arms, or you'll end up losing your whole rig to the depths. Most often caught while trolling, wahoo can be cut into large steaks and are great for frying. Best months: March to September.

White Marlin

White and blue, with a beautiful pointed "horn," the white marlin (50 to 80 pounds on average) is famous for long fights and high jumps, often twisting its body when it's out of the water. Found in the highest numbers in the Cozumel channel, between the island and the mainland. Best months: April to August.

TOP FISHING DESTINATIONS

Akumal

Akumal has been a sportfishing town for more than 30 years. One of the top guides in the area, Pillo, who has been a resident for 20 years, offers two-hour trips for up to four anglers (and up to four others) for $100, including tackle, bait, and drinks. Four-hour trips cost $200. Reservations can be made in person at Lot 40, near the Nah Kin Condos.

Ascension Bay

Recognized as the best place in the world for a permit, tarpon, and bonefish grand slam, Ascension Bay and Boca Paila are also prime spots for snook, barracuda, Spanish mackerel, and permit. The bay has various inlets, ensuring that your boat captain can find fishing no matter the wind direction. Anglers can visit on a day trip from the Riviera Maya or can stay overnight at one of the many lodges found between Boca Paila and Punta Allen.

Cancún

A 55-foot boat accommodating 18 anglers departs out of Cancún on night-fishing expeditions to the reefs not far from shore, between the coastline and Isla Mujeres. Common catches include grouper, hogfish, mackerel, and snapper.

The trip includes five hours of fishing, all equipment and bait, an open bar, and a buffet meal featuring the fresh fish that is caught during the first part of the trip, plus lasagna, white rice, and steamed vegetables. It operates on Monday, Wednesday, and Friday and departs at 7 PM, returning at midnight. Adults $50, children under 12 $25. For more information call Cancún Vista Tours at 998-898-4312 (in Mexico) or 1-800-860-5917 (in the United States).

Cozumel

The lagoons, jagged shorelines, and flats of Cozumel Island offer up excellent bonefishing, which is most often done using fly-fishing tackle or a lightweight spinning reel. There is good bottom fishing along the northern coast near Passion Island and on the island's east coast, where the coral reef is not part of the federal reserve. Farther from shore, in the Cozumel channel, anglers troll for marlin, sailfish, and other large game.

Puerto Aventuras

The fishing mecca of Puerto Aventuras is the southernmost deep-water marina in the Riviera Maya, with many sportfishing and deep-sea fishing charters available. A walk around the marina reveals the dozens of well-equipped boats waiting for their next expedition.

One tour operator is **Tours Cancún** (998-887-3414; www.tours-cancun.com; Calle Lima, #18, Sm. 2-A, Mz. 2, Cancún), which offers share-fishing trips and chartered boat trips departing out of the Puerto Aventuras Marina. Boats are 30 to 35 feet and accommodate up to eight anglers and observers. The trip includes tackle, bait, drinks, water, license, and port fees. A four-hour trip is $90 for each angler and $50 for each observer; eight-hour trips are $180 and $75; and full-boat charters are $375 for four hours and $650 for eight hours. The half-day trip departs at 9 AM and 1:30 PM; the full-day trip departs at 9 AM.

Another option is Captain Walter of the **Puerto Aventuras Fishing company** (984-873-5463; www.puertoaventurasfishing.com; Puerta del Mar 1, Depto. 14, Puerto Aventuras), featuring half- and full-day charters aboard the 34-foot *Tanya* fishing boat, which accommodates up to 10 people. Trips include snacks, drinks, fishing gear, and bait, and the full-day trip includes lunch (including fresh ceviche) and snorkeling equipment. Fishing starts as soon as the boat leaves the marina. The crew will pack your fish fillets so you can take them home. Half day is $350, full day is $600.

General Index

Lodging by Price

$	Less than $75 per night
$$	$75 to $125 per night
$$$	$126 to $225 per night
$$$$	$226 to $350 per night
$$$$$	More than $350 per night

Riviera Maya—North

Playa del Carmen

MAYAN COAST—SOUTH

Dining by Price

Inexpensive: $15 or less
Moderate: $15–30
Expensive: $30–40

Riviera Maya—North

Inexpensive
Caffetto (Puerto Morelos), 103
Casa Denis (Cozumel), 88
Chen Rio Restaurant (Cozumel), 88–8990
Chi-Chi & Charlie's (Playa Norte), 74
Chiles Locos (Isla Mujeres), 74–75
Cocina Economica (Puerto Morelos), 103
El Tio (Puerto Morelos), 104
Le Café d'Amancia (Puerto Morelos), 104
Los Gauchos (Puerto Morelos), 104
Mezcalitos (Cozumel), 89–90
Monchis (Puerto Morelos), 104
Ojo de Agua Restaurant & Bar (Puerto Morelos), 104
Plaza Leza (Cozumel), 90
Restaurante El Muelle (Puerto Morelos), 105
Viva Zapata (Isla Holbox), 70
Zazil Ha Restaurant (Playa Norte), 75

Moderate
The Old Fisherman (Puerto Morelos), 104
Café Finca (Puerto Morelos), 103
Casa O's (Palya Sur), 74
Edelyn (Isla Holbox), 70
El Picudo Azul (Puerto Morelos), 03–104
La Adelita (Isla Mujeres), 75
La Marina (Puerto Morelos), 104
Las Palmeras (Cozumel), 89
Pasta Prima (Cozumel), 90
Pelicanos Restaurant (Puerto Morelos), 104
Pericos (Cancún), 83
Pinocchio's (Isla Holbox), 70
Porto Bello (Puerto Morelos), 104–105

Expensive
The Plantation House (Cancún), 83
La Habichuela (Cancún), 82
Lorenzillos Los Lobster House (Cancún), 82–83
Pepe's Grill (Cozumel), 90
Rolandi's (Isla Mujeres), 75
Yax-Che Restauant (Puerto Morelos), 105

Playa del Carmen

Budget
Aca Los Tacos, 156
Bambu, 158
Bip Blp Pizzas, 158
Chicas Grill & Bar, 158
Coctelería El Paisano Veracruz, 158
Dr. Taco, 158
El Amendro, 158
El Faisán y El Venado, 158–159

El Fogon, 159
El Fogoncito, 159
El Tropical-ito, 159
Killer Taco, 159
La Loncheria de la Quinta, 159
Las Arracheras, 160
Pizza 16, 160
Pizza Banana, 160
Pizza Pazza, 160
Super Panaderia Aguilar, 160
Tango Taco, 160
Vagabunda, 160

Inexpensive
Café del Mar (Xpu-Ha), 230

Riviera Maya—South

Inexpensive
The Pub (Puerto Aventuras), 226
Café del Mar (Xpu-Ha), 230
La Buena Vida (Akumal), 236
La Palapa del Chino (Tulum & Mayan Coast), 253
Que Onda (Akumal), 238
Taqueria Gringa (Tulum & Mayan Coast), 253
Turtle Bay Café (Akumal), 238

Moderate
Buenos Aires Grill (Tulum & Mayan Coast), 253
Dos Chiles (Puerto Aventuras), 226
Il Giardino (Tulum & Mayan Coast), 253
Jones' Sports Bar (Puerto Aventuras), 226
La Caribena (Puerto Aventuras), 226
La Lunita Restaurant (Akumal), 236
Lol Ha (Akumal), 238
Oscar y Lalo's (Punta Soliman), 242

Expensive
Restaurante Al Cielo (Xpu-Ha), 230
Tiramisu (Puerto Aventuras), 226

Dining by Cuisine